lonely p

D0401244

Syria

MVFOL

Andrew Humphreys
Damien Simonis

LONELY PLANET PUBLICATIONS
Melbourne • Oakland • London • Paris

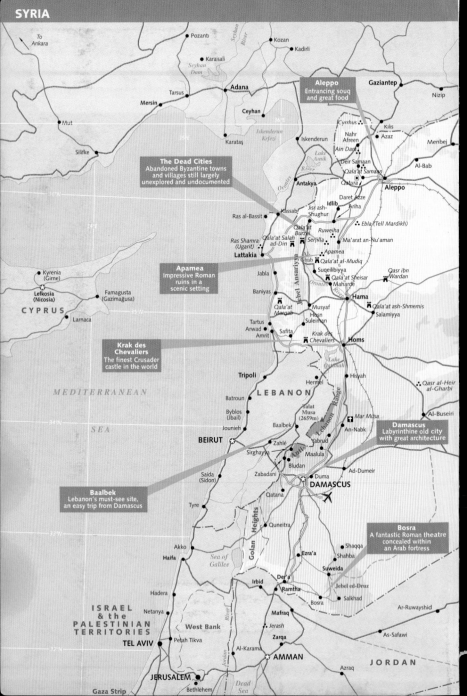

SYRIA

Aleppo
Entrancing souq
and great food

The Dead Cities
Abandoned Byzantine towns
and villages still largely
unexplored and undocumented

Apamea
Impressive Roman
ruins in a
scenic setting

**Krak des
Chevaliers**
The finest Crusader
castle in the world

Baalbek
Lebanon's must-see site,
an easy trip from Damascus

Damascus
Labyrinthine old city
with great architecture

Bosra
A fantastic Roman theatre
concealed within
an Arab fortress

To Ankara
Pozantı
Karaisali
Kozan
Kadirli
Qala'at Samaan
Gaziantep
Nizip
Menbej
Tarsus
Adana
Kilis
Azaz
Al-Bab
Mersin
Ceyhan
Karataş
İskenderun
Nahr
Afreen
Ain Dara
Deir Samaan
Cyrrhus
Mut
Silifke
Iskenderun Krfezi
Antakya
Daret Azze
Qala'at Samaan
Aleppo
Kyrenia
(Girne)
Lefkosia
(Nicosia)
Famagusta
(Gazimagusa)
Larnaca
CYPRUS
Kassab
Ras al-Bassit
Ras Shamra
(Ugarit)
Lattakia
Jabla
Baniyas
Tartus
Arwad
Amrit
Safita
Jisr ash-
Shughur
Idlib
Ariha
Ebla (Tell Mardikh)
Qala'at
Burzei
Ruweiha
Serjilla
Ma'arat an-Nu'aman
Qala'at Salah
ad-Din
Apamea
Qala'at al-Mudiq
Qasr ibn
Wardan
Suqeilibiyya
Qala'at Sheisar
Maharde
Hama
Musyaf
Hosn
Suleiman
Qala'at ash-Shmemis
Salamiyya
Qala'at
Marqab
Krak des
Chevaliers
Homs
Tripoli
Hermel
Hisyah
Qasr al-Heir
al-Gharbi
Batroun
LEBANON
Byblos
(Jbail)
Jounieh
Talat
Musa
(2659m)
Baalbek
Mar Musa
An-Nabk
Al-Buseiri
BEIRUT
Zahlé
Yabrud
Damascus
Sirghayya
Maalula
Bludan
Duma
Ad-Dumeir
Saida
(Sidon)
Zabadani
Qatana
DAMASCUS
Tyre
Golan
Heights
Quneitra
Bosra
Shaqqa
Akko
Ezra'a
Shahba
Haifa
Suweida
Sea of
Galilee
Der'a
Ramtha
Jebel ed-Druz
Salkhad
Ar-Ruwayshid
Hadera
Irbid
Netanya
Mafraq
Bosra
As-Safawi
ISRAEL
& the
PALESTINIAN
TERRITORIES
TEL AVIV
West Bank
Jerash
Al-Karama
Zarqa
Petah Tikva
JERUSALEM
AMMAN
Azraq
JORDAN
Gaza Strip
Bethlehem
Dead
Sea

MEDITERRANEAN
SEA

Seyhan River
Seyhan Dam
Orontes River
Lake Amik
Jebel Ansariyya
Lebanon Range
Anti-Lebanon Range
Lake Qattinah
Ebla

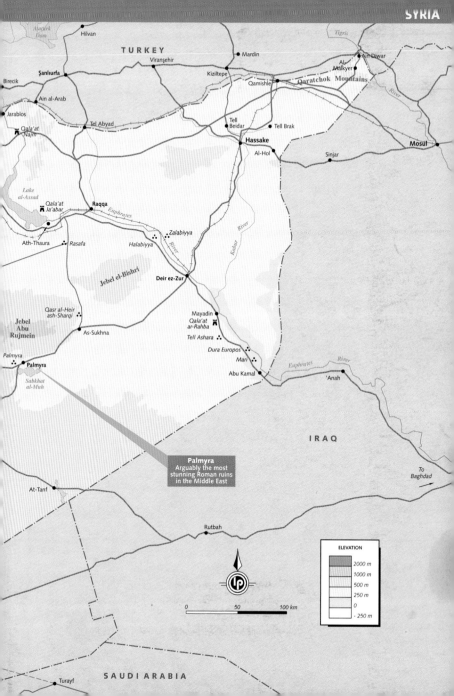

Majärk Daäi

Hilvan

Tigris

TURKEY

Mardin

Ain Diwar

Viranşehir

Al-
Malkyer

Kiziltepe

Şanlıurfa

Qamishle

Qaratchok Mountains

River

Birecik

Ain al-Arab

Tel Abyad

Tell
Beidar

Tell Brak

Jarablos

Qala'at
Najm

Hassake

Mosul

Al-Hol

Sinjar

Lake
al-Assad

Qala'at
Ja'abar

Raqqa

Euphrates

River

Zalabiyya

Ath-Thaura

Rasafa

Halabiyya

River

Kabur

Jebel el-Bishri

Deir ez-Zur

Qasr al-Heir
ash-Sharqi

Mayadin
Qala'at
ar-Rahba

Jebel
Abu
Rujmein

As-Sukhna

Tell Ashara

Dura Europos

Palmyra

Mari

Palmyra

Euphrates

River

Sabkhat
al-Muh

Abu Kamal

'Anah

IRAQ

Palmyra
Arguably the
most stunning Roman ruins
in the Middle East

To
Baghdad

At-Tanf

Rutbah

ELEVATION

2000 m
1000 m
500 m
250 m
0
- 250 m

0   50   100 km

SAUDI ARABIA

Turayf

Syria
1st edition – November 1999

Published by
Lonely Planet Publications Pty Ltd A.C.N. 005 607 983
192 Burwood Rd, Hawthorn, Victoria 3122, Australia

Lonely Planet Offices
Australia PO Box 617, Hawthorn, Victoria 3122
USA 150 Linden St, Oakland, CA 94607
UK 10a Spring Place, London NW5 3BH
France 1 rue du Dahomey, 75011 Paris

Photographs
Many of the images in this guide are available for licensing from
Lonely Planet Images.
email: lpi@lonelyplanet.com.au

Front cover photograph
Palmyra, Syria (Jean-Bernard Carillet)

ISBN 0 86442 747 6

Although the authors and Lonely Planet try to make the information as accurate as possible, we accept no responsibility for any loss, injury or inconvenience sustained by anyone using this book.

Contents – Text

Contents – Maps

MAPS

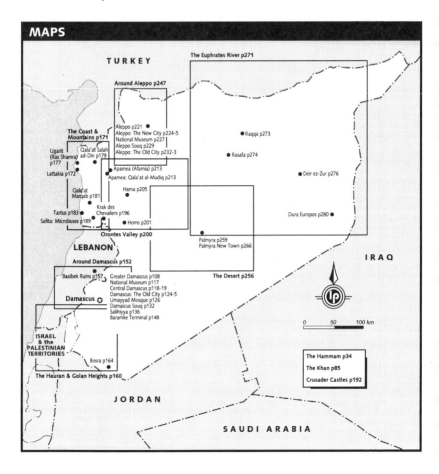

The Authors

Andrew Humphreys & Gadi Farfour

Andrew has been living, travelling and working in the Middle East on and off since 1988 when he arrived in Cairo on holiday and took three years to leave. Originally trained in London as an architect, he slid over into writing through a growing fascination with Islamic buildings. Following a spell in mainstream journalism when he was based for several years in the Baltic States, Andrew hooked up with Lonely Planet for a return to the Middle East and has since authored or co-authored guides to *Central Asia*, the *Middle East*, *Israel & the Palestinian Territories*, *Jerusalem*, *Egypt* and *Cairo*.

Gadi, courtesy of her mixed parentage, grew up spending summers in Tallinn, Estonia, and the rest of the year in Alexandria, Egypt. A designer by profession, she has accompanied Andrew on all his research trips, using her formidable language skills to reach the places he could never go. Gadi currently works as a designer and cartographer for Lonely Planet and produced most of the maps for this book.

Andrew and Gadi are two of the co-founders of the *Cairo Times*, an Egypt-based, English-language newspaper. They are currently based in London but wonder for how long.

Damien Simonis

With a degree in languages and several years' reporting and sub-editing on several Australian newspapers (including the *Australian* and the *Age*), Sydney-born Damien left the country in 1989. He has lived, worked and travelled extensively throughout Europe, the Middle East and North Africa. Since 1992, Lonely Planet has kept him busy with *Jordan & Syria*, *Egypt & the Sudan*, *Morocco*, *North Africa*, *Italy*, the *Canary Islands*, *Spain* and *Barcelona*. He has also written and snapped for other publications in Australia, the UK and North America. When not on the road, Damien resides in splendid Stoke Newington, deepest north London.

FROM ANDREW

In no particular order I would like to thank: Jim Watkins and Stasia for their championing of Deir ez-Zur; Jon Gore for dining leads in Damascus; Fares at the British Council for graciously sharing his contact book; Badr Tonbour for making Hama seem like the dining and drinking capital of the Middle East; Jeff Williams for sterling research into what time all the bars close; Brigid Keenan for her contribution on Damascus houses and for livening up some dull afternoons at the computer with her phone calls; William Dalrymple for permission to add sparkle to our text by quoting from his; Cathy Lanigan for the information on Baalbek; Pat Yale and Tony Wheeler for last minute updates; Jeremy Smith for being more readable on castles than TE Lawrence; and finally to Michelle Glynn whose enthusiasm for Syria and this project kept me churning out the text.

This Book

This book was based on the Syria chapters of the 3rd edition of Lonely Planet's *Jordan & Syria*, of which the 1st edition was written by Hugh Finlay; Damien Simonis researched and revised the 2nd and 3rd editions. This new guide to Syria was researched and written by Andrew Humphreys.

From the Publisher

This book was edited in Lonely Planet's Melbourne office by Julia Taylor, with assistance from Alan Murphy, Anne Mulvaney, Bethune Carmichael, Joanne Newell, Sarah Mathers, Shelley Muir and Susan Holtham. Gadi Farfour drew the maps in the UK office. Hunor Csutoros coordinated the design, with cartographic assistance from Anna Judd, Brett Moore and Katie Butterworth. Quentin Frayne organised the language section, Sarah Jolly drew the illustrations and Maria Vallianos designed the cover. Thanks to Mahmoud Alkhlawi for checking and correcting the gazetteer of Arabic place names. Thanks also to Peter Ward of Peter Ward Book Exports for his assistance with the bookshop information.

Acknowledgments

Many thanks to the following travellers who used *Jordan & Syria* and wrote to us with helpful hints, useful advice and interesting anecdotes about travelling in Syria.

Alex Retzleff, Alfred Heuperman, Andrzej Bielecki, Arne Klau, Barry Aitken, Bronwyn Hughes, Bryan & Alison Bluck, C Hoad, Charles Brown, Charles Stanford, Chris & Bev Bennett, Elien ten Broeke, Erica Sigmon, Fiona Dent, G Kennedy, J Keith Mercer, Jamie Doman, Jenny Wardall, Jo Kennedy, Joan Stokes, John & Jenny Mansbridge, Kristy Williams, Lara Cooke, Len Keating, Leone Marsdon, M Jackson, Marc Geara, Mark Conrod, Megan Sutton, Michael Bassett, Michael Ward, Nicky McLean, Pieter & Will Mastbergen, Rob Abbott, Sally Bothroyd, Tanya Campbell, Ted & Anne Last, Tommy Malmspren, Yasmina Volet and Yee Chun-hing

Foreword

ABOUT LONELY PLANET GUIDEBOOKS

The story begins with a classic travel adventure: Tony and Maureen Wheeler's 1972 journey across Europe and Asia to Australia. Useful information about the overland trail did not exist at that time, so Tony and Maureen published the first Lonely Planet guidebook to meet a growing need.

From a kitchen table, then from a tiny office in Melbourne (Australia), Lonely Planet has become the largest independent travel publisher in the world, an international company with offices in Melbourne, Oakland (USA), London (UK) and Paris (France).

Today Lonely Planet guidebooks cover the globe. There is an ever-growing list of books and there's information in a variety of forms and media. Some things haven't changed. The main aim is still to help make it possible for adventurous travellers to get out there – to explore and better understand the world.

At Lonely Planet we believe travellers can make a positive contribution to the countries they visit – if they respect their host communities and spend their money wisely. Since 1986 a percentage of the income from each book has been donated to aid projects and human rights campaigns.

Updates Lonely Planet thoroughly updates each guidebook as often as possible. This usually means there are around two years between editions, although for more unusual or more stable destinations the gap can be longer. Check the imprint page (following the colour map at the beginning of the book) for publication dates.

Between editions up-to-date information is available in two free newsletters – the paper *Planet Talk* and email *Comet* (to subscribe, contact any Lonely Planet office) – and on our Web site at www.lonelyplanet.com. The *Upgrades* section of the Web site covers a number of important and volatile destinations and is regularly updated by Lonely Planet authors. *Scoop* covers news and current affairs relevant to travellers. And, lastly, the *Thorn Tree* bulletin board and *Postcards* section of the site carry unverified, but fascinating, reports from travellers.

Correspondence The process of creating new editions begins with the letters, postcards and emails received from travellers. This correspondence often includes suggestions, criticisms and comments about the current editions. Interesting excerpts are immediately passed on via newsletters and the Web site, and everything goes to our authors to be verified when they're researching on the road. We're keen to get more feedback from organisations or individuals who represent communities visited by travellers.

Lonely Planet gathers information for everyone who's curious about the planet – and especially for those who explore it first-hand. Through guidebooks, phrasebooks, activity guides, maps, literature, newsletters, image library, TV series and Web site we act as an information exchange for a worldwide community of travellers.

Research Authors aim to gather sufficient practical information to enable travellers to make informed choices and to make the mechanics of a journey run smoothly. They also research historical and cultural background to help enrich the travel experience and allow travellers to understand and respond appropriately to cultural and environmental issues.

Authors don't stay in every hotel because that would mean spending a couple of months in each medium-sized city and, no, they don't eat at every restaurant because that would mean stretching belts beyond capacity. They do visit hotels and restaurants to check standards and prices, but feedback based on readers' direct experiences can be very helpful.

Many of our authors work undercover, others aren't so secretive. None of them accept freebies in exchange for positive write-ups. And none of our guidebooks contain any advertising.

Production Authors submit their raw manuscripts and maps to offices in Australia, USA, UK or France. Editors and cartographers – all experienced travellers themselves – then begin the process of assembling the pieces. When the book finally hits the shops, some things are already out of date, we start getting feedback from readers and the process begins again ...

WARNING & REQUEST

Things change – prices go up, schedules change, good places go bad and bad places go bankrupt – nothing stays the same. So, if you find things better or worse, recently opened or long since closed, please tell us and help make the next edition even more accurate and useful. We genuinely value all the feedback we receive. Julie Young coordinates a well travelled team that reads and acknowledges every letter, postcard and email and ensures that every morsel of information finds its way to the appropriate authors, editors and cartographers for verification.

Everyone who writes to us will find their name in the next edition of the appropriate guidebook. They will also receive the latest issue of *Planet Talk*, our quarterly printed newsletter, or *Comet*, our monthly email newsletter. Subscriptions to both newsletters are free. The very best contributions will be rewarded with a free guidebook.

Excerpts from your correspondence may appear in new editions of Lonely Planet guidebooks, the Lonely Planet Web site, *Planet Talk* or *Comet*, so please let us know if you *don't* want your letter published or your name acknowledged.

Send all correspondence to the Lonely Planet office closest to you:

Australia: PO Box 617, Hawthorn, Victoria 3122
USA: 150 Linden St, Oakland, CA 94607
UK: 10A Spring Place, London NW5 3BH
France: 1 rue du Dahomey, 75011 Paris

Or email us at: talk2us@lonelyplanet.com.au

For news, views and updates see our Web site: www.lonelyplanet.com

HOW TO USE A LONELY PLANET GUIDEBOOK

The best way to use a Lonely Planet guidebook is any way you choose. At Lonely Planet we believe the most memorable travel experiences are often those that are unexpected, and the finest discoveries are those you make yourself. Guidebooks are not intended to be used as if they provide a detailed set of infallible instructions!

Contents All Lonely Planet guidebooks follow roughly the same format. The Facts about the Destination chapters or sections give background information ranging from history to weather. Facts for the Visitor gives practical information on issues like visas and health. Getting There & Away gives a brief starting point for researching travel to and from the destination. Getting Around gives an overview of the transport options when you arrive.

The peculiar demands of each destination determine how subsequent chapters are broken up, but some things remain constant. We always start with background, then proceed to sights, places to stay, places to eat, entertainment, getting there and away, and getting around information – in that order.

Heading Hierarchy Lonely Planet headings are used in a strict hierarchical structure that can be visualised as a set of Russian dolls. Each heading (and its following text) is encompassed by any preceding heading that is higher on the hierarchical ladder.

Entry Points We do not assume guidebooks will be read from beginning to end, but that people will dip into them. The traditional entry points are the list of contents and the index. In addition, however, some books have a complete list of maps and an index map illustrating map coverage.

There may also be a colour map that shows highlights. These highlights are dealt with in greater detail in the Facts for the Visitor chapter, along with planning questions and suggested itineraries. Each chapter covering a geographical region usually begins with a locator map and another list of highlights. Once you find something of interest in a list of highlights, turn to the index.

Maps Maps play a crucial role in Lonely Planet guidebooks and include a huge amount of information. A legend is printed on the back page. We seek to have complete consistency between maps and text, and to have every important place in the text captured on a map. Map key numbers usually start in the top left corner.

Although inclusion in a guidebook usually implies a recommendation we cannot list every good place. Exclusion does not necessarily imply criticism. In fact there are a number of reasons why we might exclude a place – sometimes it is simply inappropriate to encourage an influx of travellers.

Introduction

As Syria starts to slowly come in from the cold, its profile as a travel destination is also beginning to rise. Participation on the US-led coalition side during the Gulf War in the early 1990s and, more recently, tentative moves towards peace with Israel, along with a relaxation in internal political and economic strictures, have softened the country's image. That's not to say that there's a tourist rush on; the most recent figures put the annual number of foreign visitors to Syria at 200,000. Compare that with 2.8 million a year for Egypt.

Yet Syria has never been afflicted with the sort of terrorist problems that tend to periodically drive tourists away from many other Middle Eastern destinations – no civil wars, no bombings and no kidnappings. There is even very little theft. Along with Jordan, it's probably the single most safe country for travellers in the whole of the region. The closest you'll come to being hijacked is to be dragged off by a friendly local to drink tea and chat.

Long run by a hardline and not entirely benevolent regime, what Syria does have is an image problem. Also, until very recently, Syria was backed by the then-Soviet Union and shared its host superpower's obsessions with secrecy and security.

Syria's President Assad still comes across as a mini-Stalin, but beyond this and the correspondingly unflattering western media profile, lies a country of immense historical wealth with a rich cultural tradition and a people who tend towards overwhelming hospitality.

Syria's location at a geographical crossroads where ancient civilisations met, clashed and traded has resulted in a history of permanent settlement going back some 11,000 years, from the Stone Age through the civilisations of the Phoenicians, Greeks, Romans and Byzantines, to the early Islamic

dynasties, Crusaders, Ottoman Turks, and even the British and the French. Add to this a few lesser known cultures such as the Palmyrenes, who had the audacity to threaten the might of Rome, and you start to get an idea of the diverse influences that have played a part in shaping this region.

The legacy of these great civilisations is an amazing collection of world-class sites. The Roman theatre in Bosra is one of the finest anywhere, and the desert ruins of Zenobia's oasis town of Palmyra rank with the Pyramids and Petra as one of the Middle East's must-see sights. The Umayyad Mosque in Damascus is the third most exalted site in Islam, while TE Lawrence rated Syria's Krak des Chevaliers as 'the finest castle in the world'.

TE Lawrence, or Lawrence of Arabia as he's more popularly known, is just one of the colourful characters whose past is entwined with Syria's. He stayed regularly at Aleppo's Baron Hotel, an establishment that remains little changed since Lawrence last checked out. Agatha Christie was a sometime guest here too, stopping off en-route when joining her archaeologist husband Sir Max Mallowan who was digging out along the Euphrates. Damascus was for a time the home of Sir Richard Burton, adventurer, diplomat, explorer and translator of *The Thousand and One Nights*, the spirit of which still lingers on in the coffeehouses and narrow alleyed souqs of the older quarters of the city.

Even today it is easy to imagine yourself in the era of Burton, when the west was first beginning to discover the ancient east. Many of Syria's amazing sites are visited by far more sheep than people, and there's a definite Indiana Jones quality to hitching a ride to some half-uncovered temple poking from the undergrowth on some far removed hillside. This is not going to last. It can't be too long before the lure of the tourist dollar has Syria opening up tourist offices abroad and welcoming charter flights that in previous years might have been bound for Turkey or Greece. And, to be honest, that will be no bad thing; Syria is a wonderful place and the more people who know it, the better.

Facts about Syria

HISTORY

Writing a history of the modern Syrian state is difficult because it only came into being little more than 50 years ago.

The name Syria is believed to have first been applied by the Greeks, and by Roman times, in the form of *Provincia Syria*, it had come to mean that part of the empire that lay between Egypt in the south and Anatolia in the north. Therefore, any history of Syria has also to deal with the regions now known as Lebanon and Jordan, both of which only came into being this century, and Palestine, which first appears as a name around the 13th century BC but has still not become a fully fledged political entity.

Early Empires & Alphabets

Although the modern state of Syria is a creation of the 20th century, the region it encompasses can lay claim to having one of the oldest civilisations in the world. Archaeological finds at Ras Shamra (Ugarit, circa 6600 BC) on the Mediterranean coast and at Tell Hariri (Mari, circa 4500 BC) on the Euphrates River, bear evidence of advanced settlements that would later become sophisticated city-states. Piecing together this early history is very much an on-going process and current archaeological digs at sites such as Tell Mardikh (Ebla, circa 2900 to 2300 BC), Ras Shamra and Tell Hariri continue to add to, revise and even rewrite the history books.

These emerging city-states were very much independent entities. They were first brought together under the imposed rule of the Akkadians, who marched out of Mesopotamia (modern-day Iraq) in search of conquest and natural resources. Under the rule of Sargon of Akkad (2334 to 2279 BC) the eastern Mediterranean area flourished, particularly ports like Byblos (now in Lebanon), which grew wealthy on trade with the Egyptians who needed plentiful supplies of the wood that was lacking in their own country.

The Egyptians were soon to become far more deeply embroiled in the affairs of the Akkadian provinces. Egypt had been itself under the occupation of Asiatic Hyksos invaders, who had fought for control of the country for just over a century. By about 1550 BC the Egyptians had routed the invaders and ended this challenge. To be sure that the threat did not return, the pharaohs pursued their former tormentors north, which led to a period of expansion of the Egyptian empire. By 1520 BC, the pharaoh Thutmose I claims to have reached the banks of the Euphrates River, although he was met by stubborn resistance from the local inhabitants and by no means controlled the entire area.

In 1480 BC, a revolt organised by more than 300 local rulers was easily crushed and Egypt was by this time firmly established in what is now Palestine and the southern Syrian region. In the north, however, the various principalities coalesced to form the Mitanni empire. They held off all Egyptian attempts at control, helped in part by their invention of the horse-drawn chariot.

In a relatively brief period of time, the Mitanni empire was subsumed by the encroachments of the Hittites (1365 BC) from a region that corresponds today with central Turkey. Despite some half-hearted attempts by the new pharaoh, Tutankhamun, to gain control, by 1330 BC all of Syria was firmly in the hands of the Hittites.

Bounded by the Mediterranean on one side and the desert to the east, the land-bridge between Egypt and the Hittite empire – the Syria, Lebanon, Israel & the Palestinian Territories of today – became a battle ground for these two great and ancient superpowers. They clashed at the bloody Battle of Kadesh on the Orontes River in Syria around 1300 BC.

Militarily it was an indecisive meeting, but it dealt the Egyptians a strategic blow and saw them retreat south. Finally, the two opposing forces signed a treaty of friendship in 1284 BC, which ended a long period of struggle for control of the coastal causeway. It left the Egyptians with the south and the Hittites with what corresponds to modern Syria and Lebanon.

Living in tandem with the Egyptians and Hittites were the Phoenicians, a Semitic people who had arrived in the region during the second millennium. The Phoenicians occupied a series of towns along the Mediterranean coast and successfully traded with Egypt to the south, Mesopotamia to the east and Anatolia to the north. Although the land was suited to the production of olives, grapes, barley and wheat, as well as the raising of livestock, the prosperity of the people of the coastal hinterland depended on the extent to which they controlled the mule and caravan routes. It was those routes that attracted foreign powers to vie for power in the area (see 'The Souq' special section in the Facts for the Visitor chapter).

One of the most important contributions to world history during this period was the development of written scripts. The ancient site of Ugarit in Syria has yielded the oldest alphabet yet known. Until then only Egyptian hieroglyphics and Mesopotamian cuneiform existed. Both required hundreds of symbols that were far too difficult for anyone but the scribes to use. By 1000 BC linear, rather than pictorial scripts, were in general use. It is from these alphabets that today's scripts are derived.

A Spoil of War

By about the 13th century BC the Egyptian empire was in decline. It had overextended itself and was under threat on several fronts. In the eastern Mediterranean this threat came in the form of the 'Peoples from the Sea', of whom we know little, except that one of the peoples were the Philistines who settled on the coastal plain in an area that came to be known as the Plain of Philistia. From this is derived the name Palestine, or

'Filasteen' in Arabic. These 'sea peoples' – possibly from the Aegean – overthrew the Hittites, destroying Ugarit in the process (although most of the Phoenician cities managed to survive). Much of their success in warfare was owed to their use of iron for weapons and armour, a material that neither the Egyptians nor the Hittites possessed.

Adding to the melange was a further influx of new people in the form of the Aramaeans, a seminomadic race from the deserts to the south. The Aramaeans settled particularly in the north where there was a series of small post-Hittite principalities including Halab (Aleppo) and Hamath (Hama). Although the Aramaeans managed to stand their ground against the expansionist ambitions of the kingdoms of Judea and Israel to the south, they were completely unable to repel the attentions of the powerful Assyrian empire (1000 to 612 BC) to the east and by 732 BC all of Syria was under the command of Sargon II.

For the next 400 years Syria was little more than a spoil of war, being ceded to the Babylonians after their king Nebuchadnezzar defeated the Assyrians, then to the Achaemenid Persians who captured Babylon in 539 BC.

Of all of these occupying empires – the Assyrians, Babylonians and Persians – little trace remains today in Syria, except for some spindly columns on the Mediterranean coast at Amrit that bear distinct Persian ancestry. And, of course, the name Syria itself which is probably a Greek corruption of 'Assyria' that stuck to what was once the Assyrian empire's western provinces.

The Greeks & Romans

It was the Greeks that wrested Syria from the Persians. Alexander the Great defeated the forces of King Darius III at Issus (333 BC) in what's now south-east Turkey, opening the way for his armies to storm through Syria and Palestine on his way to Egypt. On his death, his newly formed empire was parcelled up among his generals. Ptolemy I gained Egypt and southern Syria, while Seleucus I Nicator established a kingdom in

Babylonia that spread to include the north Syrian centres of Antioch, Apamea, Lattakia and Cyrrhus.

For the next century, the Seleucids disputed the Ptolemies' claim to Palestine and tried unsuccessfully to oust them, finally succeeding in 198 BC under the leadership of Antiochus III. This victory marked an aggressive campaign of expansion on the part of the Seleucids which brought them up against the new power of Rome. In the resulting clash, the Seleucids were defeated and in 188 BC Antiochus was forced to cede all his territories in Asia Minor. However, it wasn't until 64 BC that the Roman legate Pompey finally abolished the Seleucid kingdom making it a province of Rome *(Provincia Syria)* with its capital at Antioch.

In time Antioch became the third most important imperial city after Rome and Alexandria, and Syria grew rich on trade and agriculture. New trade routes were developed including the north-south *Via Maris* and east-west *Via Nova Traiana* which ran through the oasis settlement of Palmyra. Towns such as Palmyra, as well as Apamea, Bosra, Damascus and Lattakia, were replanned and expanded as Rome regarded Syria as a prime province.

In the 3rd century AD the Sassanian Persians (or Sassanids), the successors to the Parthians, invaded northern Syria but were repelled by the Syrian prince Odenathus of Palmyra. He was granted the title *dux orientalis* (commander of the east) by his Roman overlords for his efforts, but died shortly afterwards. Suspected of complicity in his death, his widow, the beautiful and ambitious Zenobia, assumed the title Augusta and, with her sights set on Rome, invaded western Syria, Palestine and Egypt. In 272, Aurelian destroyed Palmyra and carted Zenobia off to Rome as a prisoner (see the boxed text 'Zenobia' in The Desert chapter).

With the conversion, early on in the 4th century, of the emperor Constantine , Christianity became the dominant religion. Jerusalem became the site of holy pilgrimage and this did wonders for the prosperity of the area. During the reign of Justinian (527 to 565 AD), churches were built in many towns in Palestine and Syria.

This rosy state of affairs was abruptly shattered in the 7th century AD when the Persians once again descended from the north, taking Damascus and Jerusalem in 614 and eventually Egypt in 616, although Byzantine fortunes were revived when the emperor Heraclius invaded Persia and forced the Persians into a peace agreement. In the south, however, the borders of the empire were being attacked by Arab raiders – no new thing – but these Arabs were ambitious Muslims, followers of Mohammed.

The Advent of Islam

With the Byzantine empire severely weakened by the Persian invasion, the Muslims met with little resistance and in some cases were even welcomed.

In 636 the Muslim armies won a famous victory at Yarmouk, near the modern border between Jordan and Syria. At the same time Ctesiphon, the Persian capital on the Tigris, also fell. Within 15 years the Sassanian empire had disappeared and the Arab Muslims had reached the river Oxus on the northern frontier of modern Afghanistan.

In the west, the Byzantine forces never recovered from the Battle of Yarmouk and could do little but fall back towards Anatolia. Jerusalem fell in 638 and soon all of Syria was in Muslim hands.

Because of its position on the pilgrims' route to Mecca, Syria became the hub of the new Muslim empire which, by the early 8th century, stretched from Spain across northern Africa and the Middle East to Persia (modern Iran) and India. Mu'awiya, the governor of Damascus, had himself declared the fifth caliph, or successor to Mohammed, in 658 and founded a line, the Umayyads, which would last for nearly a hundred years. Damascus thus replaced Medina (in present-day Saudi Arabia) as the political capital of the Muslim world.

The Umayyad period was one of great achievement and saw the building of such monuments as the Umayyad Mosque in

Damascus and the Mosque of Omar and the Dome of the Rock in Jerusalem. The Umayyads' great love of the desert led to the construction of palaces where the caliphs could indulge their Bedouin past. Nevertheless, it was also a time of almost unremitting internal struggle, and Damascus found itself constrained to put down numerous revolts in Iraq and Arabia itself.

Umayyad rule was overthrown in 750, when the Abbasids seized power and transferred the caliphate to Baghdad. Syria and Palestine went into a rapid decline as a result; administratively, they were no more than a coastal strip stretching as far inland as Damascus and Jerusalem.

The Abbasids, too, had their share of problems, and by the 900s had lost their grip and been replaced by other families. Imperial control slipped increasingly out of Baghdad's hands and, by 980, all of Palestine and part of Syria (including Damascus) had fallen under Fatimid Cairo's rule. Aleppo and northern Syria and Iraq were controlled by the Hamdanids, a Shi'ite group.

The Crusades

It was into this vacuum of central power that the Crusaders arrived. A plea from Pope Urban II in November 1095 for the recapture of the Church of the Holy Sepulchre in Jerusalem resulted in the embarkation of hundreds of thousands of people on the road to the Holy Land. Knights and peasants, even entire families, set off, intending to carry the fight to the 'infidels' and to bring help to the Christians of the east. What followed was almost two centuries of destruction, massacre

Salah ad-Din (1138-93)

In contrast to the reputed barbarous antics and dishonourable reputation spaded out to the Crusaders, Salah ad-Din (known to the west as Saladin) tends to be portrayed as a true knight in the romanticised European tradition of chivalry. He was born in Tikrit (in modern Iraq) to Kurdish parents. At the age of 14 he joined other members of his family in the service of Nur ad-Din (Nureddin) of the ruling Zangi dynasty. Rising to the rank of general, by the time Nur ad-Din died in 1174, Salah ad-Din had already taken over de facto control of Egypt. He quickly took control of Syria and in the next 10 years extended his control into parts of Mesopotamia, careful not to infringe too closely on the territory of the by now largely powerless Abbasid caliphate in Baghdad.

In 1187 Salah ad-Din crushed the Crusaders in the Battle of Hittin and stormed Jerusalem. By the end of 1189, he had swept the Franks out of Lattakia and Jabla to the north and castles such as Kerak and Shobak (both in Jordan) inland. The blitzkrieg provoked Western Europe into action, precipitating the Third Crusade and bringing Salah ad-Din up against Richard III 'the Lionheart' of England. After countless clashes and sieges, the two rival warriors signed a peace treaty in November 1192, giving the Crusaders the coast and the interior to the Muslims. Salah ad-Din died three months later in Damascus.

and carnage in the name of Christ. All along the Crusaders' route, cities such as Antioch, Aleppo, Apamea, Damascus, Tripoli, Beirut and Jerusalem, weakened by their own rivalries and divisions, were exposed to the invaders' untempered violence.

The atrocities inflicted on the population of Ma'arat an-Nu'aman (see the Aleppo chapter) in December 1098 were perhaps the nadir of Crusading behaviour, but the taking of Jerusalem on 15 July 1099 was also marked by the same excesses of savagery, and only a handful of Jewish and Muslim inhabitants escaped alive.

Following the capture of the Holy City the Crusaders established four states and built or took over a string of castles, including the well preserved Krak des Chevaliers (see the 'Crusader Castles' special section in The Coast & Mountains chapter for more on this subject). Their hold was always tenuous as they were a minority and could only survive if the Muslim states remained weak and divided, which in fact they obligingly did until the 12th century.

Nur ad-Din, (Nureddin; literally 'light of the faith'), son of a Turkish tribal ruler, was able to unite all of Syria not held by the Franks and defeat the Crusaders in Egypt. His campaign was completed by his nephew Salah ad-Din (Saladin; literally 'righteousness of the faith'), who recaptured Palestine and most of the inland Crusader strongholds.

Prosperity returned to Syria with the rule of Salah ad-Din's dynasty known as the Ayyubids, who parcelled up the empire on his death. They were succeeded by the Mamluks, the freed slave class of Turkish origin that had taken power in Cairo in 1250, just in time to repel the onslaught from the invading Mongol tribes from Central Asia in 1260. The victorious Mamluk leader Beybars ruled over a reunited Syria and Egypt until his death in 1277. By the beginning of the 14th century, the Mamluks had finally managed to rid the Levant of the Crusaders by capturing their last strongholds – Acre in 1291 and the fortified island of Ruad (Arwad) in 1302.

Sultan Beybars

The fourth of the Mamluk sultans of Egypt, Beybars, who also controlled much of Syria, was the next great champion after Salah ad-Din to take to the field against the Crusaders. In 1263, within five years of beginning his campaigns, he had swept the Christians out of Jaffa (in modern-day Israel), Kerak (Jordan) and most importantly Antioch (Antakya). Not as chivalrous as Salah ad-Din, he torched Antioch, a devastation from which the city never recovered. But his brutality paid great dividends: where Salah ad-Din had shied away from attacking Krak des Chevaliers, Beybars breached its walls; where Salah ad-Din was forced to come to a compromise with the Assassins (see Musyaf in the Orontes Valley chapter), Beybars winkled them out of their mountain castles and put them to flight. He died in 1277 and is buried in Damascus.

However, more death and destruction was not far off and in 1401 the Mongol invader Tamerlane sacked Aleppo and Damascus, killing thousands and carting off many of the artisans to Central Asia. His new empire lasted for only a few years but the rout sent Mamluk Syria into a decline for the next century.

The Ottoman Turks

By 1516, Palestine and Syria had been occupied by the Ottoman Turks and would stay that way for the next four centuries. Most of the desert areas of modern Syria, however, remained the preserve of Bedouin tribes.

Up until the early 19th century, Syria prospered under Turkish rule. Damascus and Aleppo were important market towns for the surrounding desert as well as being stages on the various desert trade routes and stops on the pilgrimage route to Mecca. Aleppo also became an important trading centre with Europe, and Venetian, English and French merchants established themselves there (see 'The Souq' special section in the Facts for the Visitor chapter).

For almost the whole of the 1830s the Egyptians once again gained control, led by Ibrahim Pasha, son of the Egyptian ruler Mohammed Ali. The high taxation and the conscription imposed by Ibrahim were unpopular and the Europeans, fearful that the decline of Ottoman power might cause a crisis in Europe, intervened in 1840 and forced the Egyptians to withdraw.

The Muslim Arabs had accepted Turkish rule and the Ottoman empire as the political embodiment of Islam, but already in the 19th century groups of Arab intellectuals in Syria and Palestine (many of them influenced by their years of study in Europe) had set an Arab reawakening in train. With the Young Turk movement of 1909, imperial power was in the hands of a military group, the harsh policies of which encouraged opposition and the growth of Arab nationalism.

WWI & the Mandate

During WWI, the area of Syria was the scene of fierce fighting between the Turks, who had German backing, and the British based in Suez. The enigmatic British colonel TE Lawrence, better known as Lawrence of Arabia, and other British officers involved with the Arab Revolt, encouraged Arab forces to take control of Damascus and Emir Faisal, the leader of the revolt, to set up a government in 1918. (For more on Lawrence see The Hauran chapter.)

When Arab nationalists proclaimed Faisal king of Greater Syria (an area that included Palestine and Lebanon) and his Hashemite brother, Abdullah, king of Iraq in March 1920, the French, who the following month were formally awarded the mandate over Syria and Lebanon by the League of Nations, moved swiftly to force Faisal into exile.

Employing what amounted to a divide-and-rule policy, the French split their mandate up into Lebanon (including Beirut and Tripoli), where the Christians were amenable; a Syrian Republic, whose Muslim majority resented their presence; and the two districts, Lattakia and Jebel Druze. Hostility to the French led to uprisings 1925 and 1926 and France twice bombarded Damascus.

A Constituent Assembly set up in 1928 to hammer out a constitution for a partially independent Syria was dissolved because it proposed a single state, including Lebanon, as the successor to the Ottoman province. This was unacceptable to the French.

In 1932 the first parliamentary elections took place. Although the majority of moderates elected had been hand-picked by Paris, they rejected all French terms for a constitution. Finally, in 1936, a treaty was signed but never ratified; under the deal, a state of Syria would control Lattakia and Jebel Druze as well as the *sanjak* (subprovince) of Alexandretta, the present-day Turkish province of Hatay. After riots by Turks in the sanjak protesting against becoming part of Syria, the French encouraged Turkey to send in troops to help supervise elections. The outcome favoured the Turks and the sanjak became part of Turkey in 1939. Syria has never recognised the outcome, which further sharpened feeling against France. Syrian maps still show the area as theirs.

When France fell to the Germans in 1940, Syria and Lebanon came under the control of the puppet Vichy government until July 1941, when British and Free French forces took over. The Free French promised independence, but this did not come for another five years, after violent clashes in 1945 had compelled Britain to intervene. Syria took control of its own affairs when the last of the British troops pulled out in April 1946.

Meanwhile, what had been originally the mainly Christian Turkish province of Mt Lebanon became, with the annexation of some non-Christian (mainly Sunni, Druze and Shi'ite) territories, the state of Greater Lebanon.

The French governor was forced to bow to Lebanese demands for self-rule and, when the new constitution was adopted, Greater Lebanon became the Lebanese Republic. Full independence came in 1946, when France withdrew the last of its troops.

United Arab Republic

Civilian rule in Syria was short-lived, and was terminated in 1949 by a series of military coups that brought to power officers with nationalist and socialist leanings. By 1954, the Ba'athists in the army, who had won support among the Alawite and Druze minorities, had no real rival (see Islamic Minorities under Religion later in this chapter).

Founded in 1940 by a Christian teacher, Michel Aflaq, the Arab Ba'ath Socialist Party was committed to a particular form of pan-Arabism that led to Syria forfeiting its sovereignty. In a merger with Egypt under President Nasser in 1958, Syria became what amounted to the Northern Province of the United Arab Republic. In 1960, a united National Assembly came together, with 400 Egyptian and 200 Syrian deputies. Although this was at first a popular move with many Syrians, the Egyptians treated them as subordinates, and after yet another military coup in September 1961, Damascus resumed full sovereignty. Although outwardly civilian, the new regime was under military control and it made few concessions to Ba'ath and pro-Nasser pan-Arabists, resulting in yet another change of government in March 1963.

A month before the Ba'ath takeover in 1963, which first propelled an air force lieutenant-general, Hafez al-Assad, into a government headed by General Amin al-Hafez, the Iraqi branch of the party seized power in Baghdad. Attempts were made to unite Iraq, Egypt and Syria but the parties failed to agree on the tripartite federation. Syria and Iraq then tried to establish bilateral unity but these efforts also came to nothing when the Ba'ath Party in Iraq was overthrown in November 1963.

Syria was now on its own. The Ba'ath Party's economic policy of nationalisation was meeting with much dissatisfaction, expressed in a disastrous and bloodily repressed revolt in the city of Hama in 1964. Worse, the Ba'athists' pan-Arabism now posed an awkward dilemma. The existence of Ba'ath Party branches in other Arab countries implicitly gave non-Syrians a significant say in Syrian affairs, an issue that

Hafez al-Assad, Syria's president since 1971

led to a party split. In February 1966, the ninth coup saw Amin al-Hafez ousted and the self-proclaimed socialist radical wing of the party took control of the government. Hafez al-Assad, commander of the air force and the rising strongman, was instrumental in bringing about the fall of the party old guard and facilitating the arrival of the extreme left of the party to power.

War but no Peace

The socialist government was severely weakened by defeat in two conflicts. The first disaster came at the hands of the Israelis in the June 1967 war. Later known as the Six Day War, it was launched by Israel partly in retaliation for raids by Syrian guerillas on Israeli settlements and also because the Egyptians were massing troops near the Israeli border. The end result was a severe political and psychological reversal for the Arab states and saw vast areas of land fall into Israeli hands. Syria had been the target for a furious assault; the Golan Heights were taken and Damascus itself was threatened.

Next came the Black September hostilities in Jordan in 1970. In this clash, the Jordanian army smashed Syrian-supported Palestinian guerilla groups who were vying for power in Jordan. At this point Assad, who had opposed backing the Palestinians against the Jordanian army, seized power in November 1970 and ousted the civilian party leadership. He was sworn in as president for seven years on 14 March 1971.

On 6 October 1973, Egypt and Syria launched a surprise attack on Israel in an attempt to recover lost territories. After initial Arab gains, the Israelis managed to hold their ground and indeed in Syria came to within 35km of Damascus. Although Assad grudgingly accepted a UN cease-fire on October 22 (as Egypt had done), his troops kept up low-level harrying actions in the Golan area, enough to keep the front on the boil without pushing Israel into another full-scale fight. Egypt signed an armistice in January 1974 but it was not until the end of May that Syria did the same.

Assad's Success

Since 1971, Assad has managed to hold power longer than any other post-independence Syrian government with a mixture of ruthless suppression and guile. His success can be attributed to a number of factors: giving disadvantaged and minority groups a better deal; stacking the bureaucracy and internal security organisations with members of his own Alawite faith (which has led to widespread repression and silencing of opposition both at home and abroad); and an overall desire, no doubt shared by many Syrians, for political stability. In 1998, he was elected to a fifth seven-year term with a predictable mass vote of support. Assad rules through the so-called National Progressive Front, a Ba'ath-dominated body of allied parties.

In the 1980s, economic difficulties helped fuel growing discontent with Assad's regime. The main opposition came from the militant Muslim Brotherhood, who particularly object to Alawite-dominated rule, given that the Alawites account for only 11.5% of the population. Membership of the Brotherhood became a capital offence in 1981, but by 1985 the official attitude had

Relations with Lebanon

Since civil war erupted in Lebanon in 1975, Syria's involvement in its neighbour's affairs has waxed and waned. After several Arab summits, a 30,000-strong peace-keeping force, mostly Syrians, was sent in to quell fighting in Lebanon. At the same time, Soviet military support for Syria grew – by 1983 there were about 6000 Soviet military advisers in Syria.

Israel's invasion of Lebanon in 1982 and quick advance on Beirut heightened tensions, and for a while it seemed conflict between the two was inevitable. The invasion came shortly after Israel had formally annexed the Golan Heights. In the following years, Israel and Syria, with the PLO and various Lebanese factions, faced each other off. By the end of 1985, the Israelis had withdrawn from Lebanon, maintaining control over a buffer zone in the south, and Syria had also reduced its forces in the country.

Since then, Syria has attempted, with varying degrees of success, to gain control over the Lebanese mess, manoeuvring for leverage over the Palestinian, Lebanese and other factions at large in the country. Now that peace has returned to most of Lebanon, Syria seems to have won greater control over the country's affairs than ever. The cooperation pact signed between the two in 1991 has done nothing to diminish Damascus' role, and its troops remain stationed in eastern Lebanon. That neither country has diplomatic representation in the other's capital is seen as confirmation of a Syrian policy of 'two countries, one nation', and even a prelude to eventual moves for a 'Greater Syria'.

There's That Man Again

In Syria, there's one face that's plastered everywhere: that of the president, Hafez al-Assad. For the 6 October celebrations we saw him hung seven storeys high down the front of a building on a central Damascus square. The normally breakneck traffic seemed to slow down and crawl meekly along under his stern gaze. Every town and city across the country is filled with similar, albeit smaller, pictures in which *Ya Rais* (the 'boss') appears old or young, with or without glasses, looking sporty or dressed in military attire, grim-faced or warmed over with a paternal smile.

In addition to the hoardings and posters there are the statues. Every square, forecourt, plaza or traffic island has to have one. (The idea, it's said, came back with Assad after a trip to North Korea.) It seems as if the whole output of Syria's arts faculties must be directed into this hagiographic sculpting. It's fun to note the variations: outside the Mediterranean Games complex in Lattakia, Assad looks lithe and athletic; at Damascus University he wears a billowing academic robe; in Deir ez-Zur his jacket is open because it's warm out there. Elsewhere you see him variously beckoning, pointing and waving as if he's trying to flag a taxi. But, as Paul Theroux points out in *The Pillars of Hercules*, 'Any country which displays more than one statue of a living politician is a country which is headed for trouble'.

It would be wrong to call it a personality cult as that implies some sort of mass thrall. If Assad were to go tomorrow, scrap-metal merchants would find themselves with a sudden influx of bronzes, and posters would be coming down everywhere. This being the Middle East, however, Syrians will wisely refrain from rushing out to purchase replacement pictures of tranquil landscapes, fluffy kittens or pop stars of the moment, and instead they'll cautiously reserve the empty space for a new range of pin-ups of whichever leader comes next.

TONY WHEELER

softened and some 500 members were freed from jail. By the end of 1992, a further 2000 political prisoners had been freed. In 1995 another 1200 political prisoners were released and exiled leaders of the Brotherhood were allowed to return to Syria.

The Brotherhood's opposition has sometimes taken a violent course. In 1979, 32 Alawite cadets were killed in a raid in Aleppo. Anti-Ba'ath demonstrations were held in that city in 1980. In February 1982 as many as 25,000 people were killed in the town of Hama when the army, under Assad's brother Rifa'at, moved in to brutally quash a revolt led by Sunnis who ambushed Syrian security forces and staged a general insurrection. Since then, little has been heard of the opposition.

Syria Today

Syria joined the Allied anti-Iraq coalition in 1991's US-led Gulf War, no doubt spurred on by the collapse of the Soviet Union, its main superpower backer. Although no friend of Baghdad, having supported its enemy Iran throughout the first Gulf War, Assad saw in 1990 a chance to get into the good books with the west. In return for its modest contribution to the Allied effort, Syria hoped to be dropped from Washington's list of states supporting international terrorism, something it is still awaiting.

Assad has, by his moves, brought Syria out of the cold and his decision to join in the peace process begun in Madrid in 1991 was another step in the same direction.

Syria's main preoccupation in its relations with Israel remains the return of the Golan Heights, and while Jordan and Yasser Arafat's PLO have come to an accommodation with Israel, Syria remains cagey still about committing itself to a peace deal. Damascus has always maintained that no deal should have been signed with Israel in the absence of a comprehensive peace agreement, arguing, not without foundation, that separate deals weaken the Arabs' bargaining position.

In the longer term, Syria's foreign policy problems may come from a quite different direction. Turkey's plans to push ahead with new dam projects on the Euphrates River are cause for considerable alarm not only in Syria, but in Iraq too. Water is set to become the most vital issue in the Middle East and there is little doubt that Turkey is in a position to use its dams as a political weapon. Damascus has already accused Turkey of cutting the flow of the Euphrates on several occasions in retaliation for alleged Syrian backing of Kurdish guerillas operating in south-east Turkey. In 1998, as we were researching this book, friction between the two neighbours threatened to escalate into full-blown conflict and we witnessed armoured forces massed on the northern border before the situation was thankfully defused by the timely diplomatic intervention of Egyptian president Hosni Mubarak.

The biggest question mark hanging over the country is what happens after Assad finally goes? Back in 1984, when Assad was recovering from a heart attack, a vigorous internal power struggle ensued when his brother Rifa'at apparently attempted to seize power and was effectively exiled to France. In 1986 he was allowed to return but has since been forced to take a back seat.

For a time Assad's son Basel was being groomed for the top slot, but his death in a car accident (he liked fast cars) in January 1994 reopened succession worries. It's now likely that Bashar, the president's younger son, will ascend to power once the time comes (and that time may not be far off as the health of President Assad has long been a subject for speculation). But the question remains whether any successor will be able to take the baton cleanly, without violence, and once in power whether the successor regime will be able to recreate the conditions which have enabled the Assad government to remain so long in office.

GEOGRAPHY

Syria is not a large country – with an area of 185,180 sq km, it is a bit over half the size of Italy. It is very roughly a 500 x 500km square with Lebanon intruding in the south-west, Jordan and Iraq in the south and east, and Turkey to the north.

There are four broad geographical regions in Syria: the coastal strip, backed by the mountains, which then flatten out into the cultivated steppe, quickly giving way to the desert.

The coastline is not particularly extensive, stretching for just 180km between Turkey and Lebanon. In the north, the coast is almost fronted by the Jebel Ansariyya (also known as the Jebel an-Nusariyya), range of peaks with an average height of 1000m that forms a formidable and impenetrable north-south barrier dominating the whole coast. The mountains angle inland somewhat to give space to the Sahl Akkar (Akkar Plain) in the south. The western side of the range is marked by deep ravines, while to the east the mountains fall almost sheer to the fertile valley, the Al-Ghab, of the Orontes River (Nahr al-Assi), that flows north into Turkey.

The Anti-Lebanon Range (Jebel Lubnan ash-Sharqiyya) marks the border between Syria and Lebanon and averages 2000m in height. Syria's highest mountain, Jebel ash-Sheikh (Mt Hermon of the Bible), rises to 2814m. The main river flowing from this range is the Barada, which has enabled Damascus to survive in an otherwise arid region for over 2000 years.

Other smaller ranges include the Jebel Druze, which rise in the south near the Jordanian border, and the Jebel Abu Rujmayn in the centre of the country, north of Palmyra.

The fertile crescent is, as the name suggests, Syria's main agricultural region and forms an arc in which are cradled the major centres of Damascus, Homs, Hama, Aleppo and Qamishle. The Euphrates and Orontes rivers provide water for intensive farming, while away from the water sources, dryland wheat and cereal crops are grown. Irrigation is now stretching the area under cultivation, and another historically rich zone, the Jezira, is re-emerging. The name literally means 'island' and the area is bounded by the Euphrates and Tigris rivers in Syria and Iraq.

The Syrian desert, a land of endless and largely stony plains, occupies the whole south-east of the country. The oasis of Palmyra is on the northern edge of this arid zone and along with other oases used to be an important centre for the trade caravans plying the routes between the Mediterranean and Mesopotamia.

CLIMATE

Temperatures range widely from blistering summer peaks to snow-laden winter troughs. During summer daily highs average around 35°C (100°F) on the coast and inland in the fertile hinterland where most of the population lives. However, get out east into the desert and that rises to an average 40°C (110°F) and highs of 46°C (122°F) are not

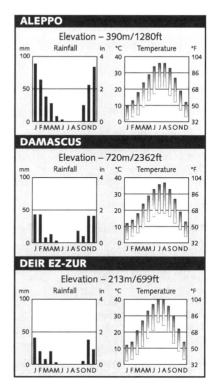

uncommon. In the winter an average daily temperature in Damascus might be 10°C (50°F), although it can get colder and snow is not uncommon. You certainly get snow on the higher peaks and it's even been known to fall as far east as Palmyra.

Annual rainfall is about 760mm in the coastal strip and mountain regions, dropping to about 215mm to 500mm in the steppe and less in the desert.

ECOLOGY & ENVIRONMENT

One of the worst things that could have happened to Syria is plastic, and certainly a 'sight' that leaps out at the eyes are grand sweeps of country whose sparse vegetation, scrappy fencing and any other obstacles are liberally draped with cheap plastic bags.

It is true there was a time when the nomadic Bedouin, as they moved on from one zone to another, would simply abandon whatever they could no longer use. This was OK when what little they could leave behind was generally biodegradable and easily absorbed into the environment. The habit has remained among their sedentary descendants, but what they discard, from plastic to scrap metal, has a more lasting and unpleasant effect.

Unfortunately, while Syrians have relatively recently embraced the technology of well-off western nations that has made plastic bags available to them, they have yet to develop waste management strategies, and appear not to have addressed the seriousness of this kind of pollution.

Tourism & the Environment

Tourism isn't sufficiently developed in Syria to pose the kind of problems faced in neighbouring Turkey, where irresponsible coastal development has resulted in enormous environmental degradation and pollution, or in Jordan where a site like Petra can no longer cope with the number of tourists it attracts. However, to help do your bit to preserve the present balance in Syria, we recommend that visitors observe a few loose rules. A British organisation called Tourism Concern (☎ 020-7753 333), Stapleton House, 177-281 Holloway Rd, London N7 8NN, has come up with some guidelines for travellers who wish to minimise negative impacts on the countries they visit. These include:

- Save precious natural resources. Try not to waste water. Switch off lights and air-conditioning when you go out. Avoid establishments that clearly consume limited resources such as water and electricity at the expense of local residents.
- Support local enterprise. Use locally owned hotels and restaurants and support trade and craft workers by buying locally made souvenirs.

To which we would add:

- Leave it as you found it: as long as outsiders have been stumbling over the ancient monuments of the Middle East, they have also been chipping bits off or leaving their own contributions engraved upon them. When visiting historical sites, consider how important it is for you to climb to the top of a pyramid or take home an unattached sample of carved masonry.
- Don't litter. Resist the local tendency to indifference and bin your rubbish or, in the case of there being no bins available, carry it with you until you can dispose of it properly.

FLORA & FAUNA

Heavy clearing has all but destroyed the once abundant forests of the mountain belt along the coast of Syria, although some small areas are still protected. Yew, lime and fir trees predominate in areas where vegetation has not been reduced to scrub. Elsewhere, agriculture dominates, with little or no plant life in the unforgiving stretches of the Syrian desert.

Your chances of coming across anything more interesting than donkeys, goats or the odd camel are next to nil. Officially, wolves, hyenas, foxes, badgers, wild boar, jackals, deer, bears, squirrels, and even polecats supposedly still roam some corners of the country, but don't hold your breath.

GOVERNMENT & POLITICS

Actual power resides in the president as leader of the Arab Ba'ath Socialist Party.

He can appoint ministers, declare war, issue laws and appoint civil servants and military personnel. Under the 1973 constitution, which was approved overwhelmingly by the Syrian electorate and defined the country as a 'Socialist popular democracy', legislative power supposedly lies with the people, and freedom of expression is guaranteed. Enforcement of these principles has been less than thorough, to say the least.

At the time of the promulgation of the constitution, which guarantees freedom of religious thought and expression, there was outrage that Islam was not declared the state religion. Bowing, but not all the way, to the pressure, Assad and his government amended it to say that the head of state must be Muslim.

All political parties are officially affiliated through the National Progressive Front, of which Assad is also the leader. Dominated by the Ba'ath Party, the Front is to all intents and purposes ineffective, serving as a tool by which Assad's regime can influence the non-Ba'ath parties. The 250 member People's Council has limited legislative powers, but, just as the Ba'ath Party is the dominant force in the Front, so the Front dominates the council.

The president has three vice presidents, possibly including his disgraced brother Rifa'at, although some reports suggest he resigned as long ago as 1988. That there is no clarity on that score is a measure of the lack in transparency of the Syrian political apparatus.

The country is divided into 14 governorates, or *muhafazat*, which in turn are further subdivided into smaller units of local government.

ECONOMY

After a particularly bad decade in the 1980s, the outlook for Syria's economy improved slowly throughout the 1990s. The country has been cautiously dropping its centralised economy in favour of a mixed economy, making space for the private sector. This process of reform has seen a loosening up in trade and finance laws and a breaking up of state monopolies, breathing some life into an economy otherwise stifled by regulations.

A ray of hope came from the development of petrol and gas finds in the Deir ez-Zur area along the Euphrates in the country's east. Production of the reasonably high quality light crude began in 1986. Most is produced by the Al-Furat Petroleum Company, a consortium of several foreign companies with a Syrian government component. Until then, only a small amount of poor, heavy crude was being extracted in the north-east of the country. Oil production appears to have peaked, but natural gas is also coming on line.

Agriculture accounts for about 25% of GDP and employs a quarter of the workforce, although a rural flight to the cities is slowly reducing this. Cereals and cotton are the main products of the fertile crescent and the Jezira, and improved irrigation in the first half of the 1990s led to a rapid increase in production. In the mountains and on the coast tobacco, various fruits, especially citrus, and olives are all intensively grown.

Industry accounts for 23% of GDP, including the production of phosphates and fertilisers at Palmyra and Homs, iron and steel in Hama, and cement in Tartus. Syrians are proud of their drive towards some degree of self-sufficiency. Textiles are the largest manufacturing industry; other products include rubber, glass, paper and food processing, along with the assembly of TVs, fridges and tractors.

Power generation remains a burning issue in Syria, although the blackouts that were a feature of daily life in Syria in the 1980s and early 1990s appear to be a thing of the past. The dam built on the Euphrates River at Lake Al-Assad was designed to solve the difficulties but has failed to meet expectations, partly because of Turkey's exploitation of Euphrates water upstream for its own dams in south-east Anatolia.

Severe strain is placed on the economy by defence, which still accounts for over 50% of total expenditure, more than five times that spent on education.

Syria's participation in the anti-Iraq coalition was partly calculated to win it lucrative new aid deals, not only with Gulf States, but also in the west. Some of the aid received went into weapons procurement, but much was also used to invest in a new telephone system, power stations and a sewerage system. Syria needs all the help it can get – national debt still stands at more than US$21 billion; three-quarters of it owed to the former Soviet Union and much may never be paid back.

Although business is benefiting from the slow process of reform, the reduction in control and subsidies has had its down side. Prices are rising – many items have doubled in price during the 1990s, including basic foodstuffs. True, wages have gone up too. The average government employee takes home from S£6000 to S£8000 a month, virtually double the pay at the beginning of the 1990s.

POPULATION & PEOPLE

Syria has a population of 17 million, and its annual growth rate of 3.4% (one of the highest in the world) is way out of proportion with its economic growth. The two biggest cities are Damascus and Aleppo, and rumoured figures from a census carried out in late 1995 put their respective populations at about six million and three million inhabitants.

Ethnic Syrians are of Semitic descent. About 90% of the population are Arabs, which includes some minorities such as the Bedouin – for more on these people see the boxed text 'The Bedouin' in The Desert chapter. The remainder is made up of smaller groupings of Kurds, Armenians, Circassians and Turks.

Of the estimated 20 million Kurds in the region, about one million are found in Syria and, along with their counterparts in Turkey, Iran and Iraq, would like to have an independent Kurdish state – a wish unlikely to be fulfilled in Syria. They have been blamed for some acts of terrorism in Syria, seen as part of their push for self-government, although the Kurds' main efforts have in past

years been concentrated on Turkey and Iraq. Since the late 1980s, Turkey has repeatedly accused Syria of sheltering Kurdish rebels making incursions into southern Turkey, an allegation Damascus flatly denies. Syria's Kurds will often say things are just fine, but many are quick to tell outsiders, discreetly, of their desires for greater autonomy.

The Armenians, much in evidence in Aleppo – where they inhabit whole quarters and their language abounds on street signs next to those in Arabic – are mostly descendants of those who fled the Armenian genocide in Turkey during WWI.

EDUCATION

In the 1970s, the literacy rate in Syria was estimated by some at about 50%. This has increased, perhaps to around 70%, but it is difficult to be sure of the figure. Officially at least, primary education from the age of six is free and compulsory. Secondary education is only free at state schools and there is fierce competition for places. Although there are private schools, they follow a common syllabus.

Jostling for places in the universities is also tough. Damascus and Aleppo have the two main universities, with two smaller ones in Lattakia and Homs, and another small higher education institute in Deir ez-Zur. About 170,000 students attend higher education institutions.

The United Nations Relief & Works Agency for Palestine Refugees (UNRWA) runs schools for Palestinian refugees living in Syria, who also have the right to free places in Syrian schools.

For a long time, French was the foreign language of choice. But that has all changed, and English is now the favourite of most young people. Compulsory instruction in English or French now takes place in school from the age of eight. The effects of the change have been dramatic over the past five years, with noticeably more people able to converse to some extent in English.

Something that most young Syrians have to contend with is 2½ years of military service.

ARTS

Political straitjacketing has very effectively stifled Syria's cultural scene. As one author we met said, 'We can only get published so long as we stay clear of politics, sex and religion. What's left to write about?' Similarly, film makers can't put anything into production without scripts first being scrutinised by the state's General Cinema Corporation – the result is that maybe one movie a year gets made. Syria's political isolation from the international scene means the only films they can get hold of are trashy Indian B-movies and Hong Kong martial arts flicks, which relegates cinema-going to the preserve of very bored young males. With no money in the business, cinemas are old, run-down and few and far between.

About the only bright spot on the arts scene is TV drama. At the end of the 1980s the government gave permission for independent companies to produce programming and since then there's been a boom in decent quality homegrown historical series and soaps, some of which are successfully sold abroad. Most actors and actresses coming out of the national high institute for drama therefore skip the moribund theatre and head straight for lucrative TV work.

Art & Architecture

There is little artistic tradition in the western sense of painting in Syria – which mirrors the situation throughout most of the Arab world. Islam's taboo on the depiction of living beings meant that the Arabs have traditionally limited their artistic endeavours to calligraphy and patterning (hence the term 'arabesque').

In the late 19th century a smattering of educated Syrians travelled abroad and returned to try and formulate a Syrian school of fine art. The styles were all imported and the painting was only 'Syrian' in subject matter. A regional identity has, however, begun to emerge in the latter half of the 20th century. The real works of art on show, though, are the great buildings left behind by the early Muslim caliphs and their successors, especially in the cities of Damascus and Aleppo.

Islamic Architecture The earliest construction efforts undertaken by Muslims – more often than not mosques – inherited much from Christian and Graeco-Roman models. The Umayyad Mosque in Damascus was built on the site of a Christian basilica, which itself had been the successor of a Roman temple. With the spread of the Muslim domain, various styles soon developed, each to some extent influenced by local artists' tastes, but increasingly independent of their architectural forebears.

The Umayyad Mosque is one of the earliest and grandest of Islam's places of worship. It conforms to a very simple plan (for an explanation of how a mosque works, see the boxed text 'The Mosque' under Religion later in this chapter) but from those beginnings, the vocabulary of Islamic architecture quickly became very sophisticated and expressive, reaching its apotheosis under the Mamluks (1250 to 1517).

The Mamluks extended the types of buildings to include not only mosques, walls and gates but also *madrassas* (theological schools), *khanqahs* (Sufi monasteries) and mausoleum complexes. Their buildings are typically characterised by the banding of different coloured stone (a technique known as *ablaq*) and by the *muqarnas*, the elaborate stalactite carvings and patterning around windows and in the recessed portals.

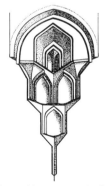

The stalactite-like stone carving known as *muqarnas*

The Mamluks were also responsible for the transformation of the minaret from the Umayyad's square tower into a slender cylindrical shape.

The Mamluks were defeated by the Ottoman Turks who ruled out of Istanbul. Damascus and Aleppo flourished during this era, growing rich on trade monopolies and many of the structures from this time reflect that. The most prevalent Ottoman building type is the *khan*, or merchants' inn, which is more fully described in 'The Souq' special section in the Facts for the Visitor chapter. Although purely practical in design and largely devoid of decoration, some of these khans (such as the Khan As'ad Pasha in Damascus) are structurally exquisite. The other great legacy of Ottoman trade is the domestic residence, in which decoration was paramount – see 'The Houses of Old Damascus' special section in the Damascus chapter.

Literature

Classical Writing The first great literature in Arabic has its source in the heartland of the Arab universe, the Arabian Peninsula itself (today made up of Saudi Arabia, Yemen, Oman and the Gulf States). The Quran itself is considered the finest example of classical Arabic writing. In fact, it underwent several transformations before a final version was settled upon, and this is what has come to us today.

Al-Mu'allaqaat, which predates the Quran and the advent of Islam, is a collection of some of the earliest Arab poetry and is widely celebrated. Prior to Islam, the poet was regarded as having knowledge forbidden to ordinary people and supposedly acquired from the demon. *Al-Mu'allaqaat* means 'the suspended', and refers to the tradition of hanging the poems for public view, possibly on the walls of the Qaaba in Mecca. Among the better-known later poets was Abu Nuwas, faithful companion to the 8th century Baghdad caliph Haroun ar-Rashid (who spent his summers at Raqqa on the Euphrates) and a somewhat debauched fellow. Apart from some humorous accounts

of court life, he left behind many odes to the wonders of wine (see the boxed text 'The Thousand and One Nights').

Towards the end of the 10th century, Syria became the focal point of one last great flash of classical Arabic poetry with the birth of three poets. Al-Mutanabi, born in Al-Kufah and thought of by some as the Shakespeare of the Arabs, spent his youth bragging to local Bedouin that he was a prophet.

A direct rival and contemporary was Abu Firas al-Hamdani, born in Aleppo, who wrote a good deal of his poetry while a prisoner in Byzantium.

The last representative of this flowering of poetic genius has come down to us known as the blind 'philosopher of poets and poet of philosophers', Abu al-'Ala al-Ma'ari. Born in Ma'arat an-Nu'aman (973-1057), he was something of a recluse, and his writings were marked by a heavy scepticism in the face of the decadent and fragmented society that surrounded him.

As the Middle Ages drew to a close and the fractious Arab world came to be dominated by other forces, most notably the Ottoman Turks, Arabic literature too faded, stagnating in a classicist rut until well into the 19th century, dominated by a complex and burdensome poetical inheritance.

Contemporary Literature Modern literary genres such as the novel are a relatively new area. Prose literature only began to emerge in the last century or so, largely due to increased contact with Europe and an awakening of Arab 'national' consciousness.

Egyptians (such as Nobel Prize-winning Naguib Mahfouz), Lebanese and, to a lesser extent, Palestinians have dominated the Middle Eastern scene. Repression in Syria has tended to hold literary production at a banal level. The exceptions generally turned first to more liberal Beirut and later to exile.

The self-taught Zakariya Tamir, perhaps Syria's most famous writer of short stories, has lived in exile in London since 1978. His work deals with everyday city life, marked by a frustration and despair born of a social oppression that probably explains why he

The Thousand and One Nights

Long before the advent of the novel, a deeply rooted tradition of Arabic literature existed in the form of oral storytelling. Without the benefit of print, tales and epics, fables and histories were all kept in circulation by professional storytellers – see the boxed text 'Keeping the Story Going' in the Damascus chapter. One of their standard entertainments was to entrance their audiences with tales attributed to the character of Sheherezade, part of the collection known as *The Thousand and One Nights*.

Also known as *The Arabian Nights*, this was a portmanteau title for a mixed bag of colourful and fantastic tales that were periodically committed to manuscript from the 12th century onwards, many of which have survived. Collectively they comprise many thousands of stories, sharing a core of exactly 271 common tales. They all, however, employ the same framing device – that of a succession of stories related nightly by the wily Sheherezade to save her neck from the misogynistic King Shahriyar.

In the earliest written versions available to modern historians, the adventures, enchantments and lowlife goings-on described in *The Nights* take place in the semi-fabled Baghdad of Haroun ar-Rashid who reigned from 786 to 809 AD, and in the Damascus and Cairo of the Mamluks (1250-1517). Regarding the last two cities in particular, *The Nights* provides a wealth of rich period detail, from shopping lists and prices of slaves, through to vivid descriptions of the types and practices of assorted conjurers, harlots, thieves and mystics.

The Thousand and One Nights enjoyed great popularity in Europe during the 19th century with the publication of several translations into French and English, including one 16-volume edition by Victorian adventurer Richard Burton (see the boxed text 'Richard Burton' in the Damascus chapter). However, during the 20th century its novelty declined and most people are only aware of the tales these days through garbled, westernised versions like the tales of Sinbad or Alaa ad-Din (Aladdin).

ended up in London. Initially his stories contained a strong realist tone, but from the late 1960s his writing turned increasingly to fantasy. For instance, in *Snow at the End of Night* (1961), Tamir deals in a slightly hallucinatory manner with the subject of family dishonour caused by a wayward daughter. By 1979, when *The Day on Which Genghis Khan was Angry* appeared, he had moved more clearly into fantastical political allegory.

Ghada al-Samman, born in Syria, now lives in Beirut. Much of her work is an angst-ridden ride through constraint and social alienation, with particular attention paid to the plight of women caught between love and traditional bourgeois values. Civil war in Lebanon has given her plenty of material; see, for example, *Beirut Nightmares* (1975).

Of those writers who have remained in Syria, the most celebrated is Ulfat Idilbi. Born in 1912, she lives, as she has always done, in Damascus, on the lower slopes of Jebel Qassioun. Although Idilbi's work has been translated into many languages, it is only relatively recently that it has started to become available in English (to date, *Sabriya: Damascus Bitter Sweet* and *Grandfather's Tale* have appeared). She writes about Syria during the late Ottoman empire and under the French Mandate, and the drive for liberation and independence, subjects which find favour with the state; accordingly many of her stories have been dramatised for television. But her work can be quite outspoken; *Sabriya* is quite scathing on the mistreatment of women by their families. Much of the anger in this, her first novel, stems from Idilbi's own personal experience of being married off at age 16 to a man nearly twice her age.

Despite the discovery of the novel in the 20th century, poetry remains the pre-eminent Syrian literary form. Until his death in 1998, the country's most famed living literary figure was poet Nizar Qabbani. He became popular in the 1950s both in Syria and throughout the Arab world for his love poems, which were made famous by being set to music by some of the Arab world's leading singers. After the defeats in the wars with Israel, Qabbani's poems took on political overtones, expressing Arab collective feelings of humiliation and outrage about their leaders. Newspapers and magazines that carried his writings were confiscated and banned in several Arab countries and Qabbani was forced to move to Beirut and eventually to London, which is where

Eastern Instrumentation

The traditions of Arabic music developed in the courts of the early Islamic empire from the 7th to the 13th centuries. The music is created using unharmonised melodies and rhythms. The structure is complex with the rhythmic cycles having up to 48 beats. In order to catch the rhythm, the listener must follow the long pattern. Set pieces are elaborated and improvised upon, in the style of Indian music and modern jazz.

Much of Arabic music is accompanied by singing. This can be long poetic recitations and even elaborate wordplay. The Arabic language lends itself to this kind of sophisticated, many-layered word game – the greatest singers are masters of this art.

Apart from the human voice, the most important instruments are the various lutes, both long and short-necked, such as the *oud*, the bowed lute or fiddle called the *rabab*, the oboe-style flute known as the *mijwiz* or *shawm* and the single-headed drum called the *tabla*. Various tambourines such as the *daff* (also called the *riqq* or *bandir*) are popular as is the double-headed drum and the *naker*, a small kettledrum.

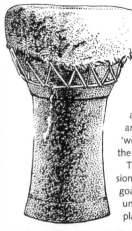

The **oud** has a deep and pear-shaped body, a fretless fingerboard, and between four and six strings. Body size, number of strings and tunings vary. The name oud, from the Arabic meaning 'wood', refers to the wood body of the instrument in contrast to the skin bellies of the earlier lutes.

The **tabla** is one of the most commonly played of the percussion instruments. It is usually made of clay, wood or metal with goat or fish skin stretched over its wide neck. It is held either under the arm, between the legs, or upright, upside down, and played by striking the edge or centre of the stretched skin.

he died. But on his death a plane was sent by Assad to London to bring the body home for burial in Damascus, where a street has been named in his honour. As far as we know, none of Qabbani's work is available in English translation.

Music

Arab music reflects a successful synthesis of indigenous harmony and taste, not to mention instruments, with some traits and instruments of the west. The popular music takes some time to get used to, and for many its attraction remains a mystery. Others, however, are eventually caught up in its particular magic – which is probably a good thing, because you'll hear it in one form or another wherever you go.

In the desert areas of eastern Syria, the Bedouin have long had their own simple but

---

Eastern Instrumentation

Corresponding to the European tambourine, the **daff** consists of a round frame with a goat or fish skin stretched to cover one side. Pairs of metal discs, set into the frame, make the tinkling sound which sets the rhythm of Arabic music. It is usually associated with belly dancing.

The **nay** is a single-reed, open-ended instrument which produces an extraordinary range of mellow sounds. It usually has six holes in the front for the fingers and one hole in the other side for the thumb. The sounds are produced by blowing from the pipe end and moving the fingers and thumbs over the holes.

The **qanun** is a trapezoid-shaped instrument with at least 81 strings stretched across its length. It is placed flat on the knees of the musician and the strings are plucked with the finger or two plectra attached to the forefingers of each hand. It has been an integral part of Arabic music since the 10th century.

Audiences applaud at the end of each section of the performance (as opposed to the western system of waiting until the end of all the movements of a piece before clapping). As well as clapping, audiences often exclaim out loud in appreciation of a performance and shouts of 'Allah!' can often be heard, which urge the performer on to the next section.

If you want to hear these instruments being put through their paces, look out for CDs by a group called the Al-Kindi Ensemble, a bunch of musicians based in Aleppo. Their latest release, *The Alleppian Music Room* (released by Le Chant du Monde CML5741108/9), has the ensemble performing a sort of Arabic chamber music accompanied by two octogenarian traditional singers with amazing vocal dexterity.

mesmerising musical traditions. The chanting of men, drifting across the desert from a distant wedding on a still night, is a haunting sound. Up close, the musical side of the evening's festivities is clearly rooted in ancient traditions. A row of men will, arm in arm, gently sway backwards and forwards engaged in what appears to be an almost trance-like chant. They are singing to and calling a lone woman who, veiled, dances before them with restrained but unmistakable sensuality. One is tempted to conclude that the belly dance, a largely Egyptian genre that has spread to nightclubs throughout the Arab world, is a considerably less demure offshoot of the purer desert art.

In recent years the 'Bedouin sound' has been updated to produce a unique semielectric, semi-traditional and totally hypnotic kind of music – see the introduction to Deir ez-Zur in The Euphrates chapter for more information.

The music that you hear in the streets of Damascus and Aleppo today, however, has precious little to do with timeless desert traditions. It has its roots in Egypt which, for much of this century, has been the undisputed music and film capital of the Arab world – Hollywood meets Memphis, Tennessee on the Nile. Even if the star artists weren't always Egyptian-born, it was necessary to be Egyptian bred, groomed and broadcast in order to make a name for oneself. Syria's most famed singing son, Farid al-Atrache, spent almost all his life in Cairo (see the boxed text).

The most common and popular style of music focuses on a star performer backed by anything from a small quartet to a fullblown orchestra. There appears to be a consensus that the all-time great remains Umm Kolthum, an Egyptian diva renowned in the Arab world as the Nightingale of the East ('Kawkab ash-Sharq' – a name you'll still find attached to hotels and restaurants). She died in 1975 and since then no one has really supplanted her in the affections of the Arabs. Perhaps the artist who has come closest is Fairouz, a Lebanese torch singer who has enjoyed star status throughout the Arab world

Farid al-Atrache

Although he lived most of his life in Cairo and was made a star in Egypt, Farid al-Atrache was born in Suweida in the Hauran region of Syria. He was a crooner, a singer of populist sentimental songs, who was made famous though his appearances in more than 30 films churned out mostly during the 1940s and 50s. But he was more than just an Arabic Sinatra; he was also a highly accomplished oud player and composer who succeeded in updating Arabic music by blending it with western scales and the rhythms and orchestration of the tango and waltz. He died in Beirut in 1974 and was buried in his adopted home of Egypt but he lives on in Syria today through continued mass sales of cheap cassettes, played on tinny taxi tape decks and in shops, restaurants and bars throughout the country.

since recording her first performances in Damascus in the 1950s. She later became an icon for Lebanon during the war (which she sat out in Paris) and her concert in downtown Beirut after the end of the fighting attracted 40,000 people and provided a potent symbol of reunification. Now in her late 60s, she rarely performs – her voice is no longer up to it.

The kind of orchestra that backs such a singer is a curious cross-fertilisation of east and west. Western-style instruments such as violins, the piano and many of the wind and percussion instruments predominate, next to such local species as the oud – see the boxed text 'Eastern Instrumentation' earlier. The sounds that emanate from them are anything but western. There is all the mellifluous seduction of Asia in the backing melodies, and the vaguely melancholic, languid tones you would expect from a sun-drenched and heat-exhausted Middle Eastern summer.

Contemporary Music Held in such esteem as they still are, singers like Farid al-Atrache, Umm Kolthum and Fairouz belong to a long past era. They have little appeal to more recent generations of Syrians, who have grown up on a diet again spooned out by Egypt where, in the 1970s, a blueprint for Arabic pop was developed. Characterised by a clattering, hand-clapping rhythm overlaid with synthesised twirlings and a catchy, repetitive vocal, the first Arab pop stars came out of Cairo. And while the Arab world's biggest selling song ever, Amr Diab's 'Nour al-Ain' (1998), was an Egyptian product, these days the Egyptians are being beaten at their own game. Many of the current biggest selling artists come from elsewhere, like Iraq (Kazem al-Saher), Lebanon (Majda ar-Rumi) or even Syria, in the form of George Wasouf, the country's biggest cultural export since Al-Atrache. But selling half a million albums in Damascus doesn't necessarily make his tapes listener-friendly to western ears – Arab pop is an acquired taste and one that few non-Arabs pick up.

SOCIETY & CONDUCT
Traditional Culture
Welcome! You could be forgiven for thinking that 'welcome' is about the first word of English learned by the people of Syria. At every turn you will hear it, and it seems to leave as many travellers perplexed

as enchanted. Behind this simple word and makeshift translation lies a whole series of social codes in the Arab world. It is worth giving a little thought to just what your average Syrian means by it.

One of the most common greetings in Arabic is *ahlan wa sahlan*. The root words mean people/family *(ahl)* and ease *(sahl)*, so you might say the expression loosely translates as 'be as one of the family and at your ease'. A nice thought, and one that ends up as simply 'welcome' in English. Among the Arabs it is used to mean anything from 'hello' to 'you're welcome' (after thanks). This at least explains a lot of the 'welcomes' you hear – people are just saying 'hi'.

There is, however, a lot more to it than that. Throughout the Arab world survives a deeply rooted sense of hospitality to strangers. There is little doubt that for many travellers this can be the most attractive aspect of travel in these countries. Equally true, westerners often have trouble in interpreting what is good form in these circumstances – and clearly each case will be different.

The Arab traditions of hospitality are not simply an expression of individual kindliness but are based in the harsh realities of life in the desert and have been virtually codified in social behaviour. As a rule, strangers were given shelter and food as a matter of course. Now there will be few times when the modern traveller will find themselves in the extreme desert conditions that first necessitated this life-supporting hospitality, but the code is deeply embedded and extends in some degree to the city as well as the country.

And so we come to another Arabic word that comes out more often than not as 'welcome'. In every daily exchange, people invite each other to drink or eat with them. It is part of the often complex exchange of social niceties. *Tafaddal* is the generic word for asking someone to come in (to the house, for instance), to invite someone to drink or to eat. It is usually rendered as 'welcome' in English.

How is one to respond to these invitations? Obviously, where possible, accepting an offer to join people in a meal or a cup of tea can be a wonderful way to learn more about the people and country you are travelling in. You really should take up the occasional offer, if possible. Some visitors voice the concern that they feel bad for accepting what is often very generous treatment and giving nothing in return. Small gifts or mementoes are a way around this. Some people travel armed with postcards or

The Hammam

A visit to a *hammam*, or bathhouse, is a wonderful experience that can leave you not just clean but feeling almost virginal. Their history in this part of the world goes back to the ancient Greeks and Romans, although with time the emphasis altered from the classical pursuit of leisure and sport to the Muslim concern with ritual and cleanliness. Everybody, rich and poor alike, went to the baths. 'Your town is only a perfect town when there is a bath in it', wrote Abu Sir, an early Arab historian.

Almost all Syrian towns still have hammams, usually located in the souq, although they have become scarcer as homes have acquired plumbed bathrooms. The custom of going to the hammam continues because the public facilities are so much grander than what is available at home, and because for Syrians it is still a social occasion. To steam clean, have a massage, relax, watch television, sip tea and chat with friends is looked upon as wonderful, affordable luxury.

Visiting a Hammam

What happens in a hammam? Well, you will be shown to a vacant area in the disrobing area *(maslakh)* where you undress, fold up and hang your clothes, lock up your valuables (it's a wise idea not to take any valuables with you, only the money you need) and wrap the provided cloth around you. Bath etiquette dictates that men (for women see Women & the Hammam) should keep this wrap on at all times, washing their own private parts without ever removing this modesty covering. You will also be provided with a pair of wooden clogs *(kabkabs)* which can make it perilously difficult to walk on the smooth, wet marble floors.

An attendant will lead you through to the hot room *(beit al-hara)* where you sit and sweat for a while. In some hammams there is a series of hot rooms, with the steam becoming hotter and thicker in each one.

After being steamed for as long as you can stand, you then move to the warm room and have to make a choice: wash yourself or be washed by an attendant *(musaubin)*. It's cheapest

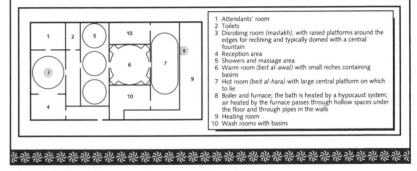

1 Attendants' room
2 Toilets
3 Disrobing room *(maslakh)*, with raised platforms around the edges for reclining and typically domed with a central fountain
4 Reception area
5 Showers and massage area
6 Warm room *(beit al-awal)* with small niches containing basins
7 Hot room *(beit al-hara)* with large central platform on which to lie
8 Boiler and furnace; the bath is heated by a hypocaust system; air heated by the furnace passes through hollow spaces under the floor and through pipes in the walls
9 Heating room
10 Wash rooms with basins

distinctive stickpins to distribute to people at appropriate moments.

At times you will find people truly insistent about you joining them, but nine times out of 10 this is not the case. Rather than curtly saying 'no', the way to deflect any kind of invitation that, for whatever reason, you feel disinclined to follow up, is to refuse politely with your right hand over your heart. You may have to do it several

The Hammam

to wash yourself with the soap *(sabun)* that you either brought with you or that was provided at the front desk. The warm room will be ringed with individual small rooms each with a basin that you fill from the taps above before sluicing the water over yourself with a plastic scoop. If you choose to have an attendant wash you, you'll be doused with warm water and then scrubbed with a coarse camel-haired mitten, loosening dirt you never suspected you had and stripping off several layers of skin in the process. Afterwards you'll be lathered with a sudsy swab, rinsed off and shampooed.

When all this is done you'll be offered the chance of a massage, an experience worth having at least once during your trip. Some massages are carried out on the floor but in other places there's a great slab-like table on which you lay yourself out like a corpse in a morgue. In touristy areas the massage is likely to be pretty cursory; elsewhere, however, it can be an unforgettable, if occasionally rough, even painful, experience.

The massage over, you'll be led back to the disrobing area, swathed and turbaned in towels, and usually offered tea, coffee or a soft drink.

The whole process can take as little as 15 minutes but most locals will stretch it out to an hour or more, languishing in the hot room and then later lounging in the cold room over several teas and lots of conversation.

Women & the Hammam

In the earliest days of Islam, women were forbidden from entering hammams. In light of the hygienic benefits of a good steaming, the ruling was later amended to allow women recovering from illness or who had recently given birth to attend. Eventually, the privilege of hammam-going was extended to all. An afternoon at the hammam became the way – almost the only way – for women to meet other women outside of the home. It was also a place where mothers could eye up prospective brides for their sons. Hammam-going became such an essential part of a woman's social life that at one time if a husband were to deny his wife her visits to the hammam, she had grounds for divorce.

But hammam-going these days is pretty much, once again, an all-male preserve. Hammams are expensive to operate and not enough women use them on a regular basis to make it worth having dedicated women's hours. That said, a few still do, although opening hours for women are almost invariably more restricted than for men.

In the women's section, the amount of modesty expected varies considerably: in some baths total nudity is fine, while in others it would be a blunder to remove your knickers. Play safe by keeping your underwear on under your wrap until inside the hot room when you can remove what looks appropriate. Women also wash their own private parts.

In touristy areas, a few hammams allow for foreign men and women to bathe together, usually for a premium price.

times. This is part of the ritual. Adding something noncommittal like 'perhaps another time, *in sha'allah* (if God wills it)' is a perfectly suitable, ambiguous and, most importantly, inoffensive way to turn down unwanted offers.

A way for men, at least, to mix with locals outside the home, is to visit a hammam. See the boxed text, 'The Hammam' earlier.

In the Home Many families, especially in smaller town and rural areas, remain very traditional in terms of divisions within the house. Should you be invited into one, it is worth bearing a few things in mind. As a rule various parts of the house are reserved for men and others for women. This becomes especially apparent when guests appear. Remember that on entering the home it is customary to take off your shoes, for simple reasons of cleanliness.

Given that the most likely reason for you ending up in someone's home is to eat, bear in mind that meals are generally eaten on the floor, everyone gathered around several trays of food shared by all.

Single men invited to eat or stay over at a house will be taken to a room reserved for men or perhaps a mixed dining area. You are a guest, so you will be served. Depending on how conservative your hosts are, you may be directly served by the women or simply observe them bringing food and drink to the men, who then deal with you, the guest. The foreign woman will in these circumstances more often than not be treated as an honorary male – not always for honorable reasons. The ambiguity of this situation is worth exploiting, however. In the case of a couple, the woman may be welcome to sneak off to hang around with the women and then come back to see how the men's world is getting on. In this sense, the foreign woman can find herself in the unique position of being able to get an impression of home life for both sexes.

Do's & Don'ts
- Do ask before taking close photographs of people.
- Don't worry if you don't speak the language – a smile and gesture will be understood and appreciated.
- Do have respect for local etiquette.
- Don't wear revealing clothing.
- Don't display affection in public.
- Do be patient, friendly and sensitive.

RELIGION
Islam
Islam is the predominant religion in Syria. Muslims are called to prayer five times a day and, no matter where you might be, there always seems to be a mosque within earshot. The midday prayer on Friday, when the imam of the mosque delivers his weekly sermon, is considered the most important.

Islam shares its roots with the great monotheistic faiths that sprang from the unforgiving and harsh soil of the Middle East – Judaism and Christianity – but is considerably younger than both.

The holy book of Islam is the Quran. Its pages carry many references to the earlier prophets of both the older religions – Adam, Abraham (Ibrahim), Noah, Moses and others – but there the similarities begin to end. Jesus is seen as one of a long line of prophets that ends definitively with Mohammed.

The Quran is said to be the word of God, communicated to Mohammed directly in a series of revelations in the early 7th century. For Muslims, Islam can only be the apogee of the monotheistic faiths from which it derives so much. Muslims traditionally attribute a place of great respect to Christians and Jews as *ahl al-kitab*, the People of the Book. However, the more strident will claim Christianity was a new and improved version of the teachings of the Torah and that Islam was the next logical step and therefore 'superior'. Don't be too surprised or concerned if you occasionally find yourself on the receiving end of attempts to convert you.

Mohammed, born into one of the trading families of the Arabian city of Mecca (in present-day Saudi Arabia) in 570 AD, began to receive the revelations in 610 AD, and after a time began imparting the content

The Mosque

Embodying the Islamic faith, and representing its most predominant architectural feature, is the mosque, or *masjid* or *jamaa*. The building was developed in the very early days of the Islam and takes its form from the simple, private houses where believers would customarily gather for worship.

The house belonging to the Prophet Mohammed is said to have provided the prototype for the plan of the mosque. The original setting was an enclosed oblong courtyard with huts (housing Mohammed's wives) along one wall and a rough portico providing shade. This plan developed with the courtyard becoming the *sahn*, the portico the arcaded *riwaqs* and the houses the *haram* or prayer hall.

The prayer hall is typically divided into a series of aisles; the centre aisle is wider than the rest and leads to a vaulted niche in the wall called the *mihrab* – this indicates the direction of Mecca, which Muslims must face when they pray.

Islam does not have priests as such. The closest equivalent is the mosque's imam, a man schooled in Islam and Islamic law. He often doubles as the *muezzin*, who calls the faithful to prayer from the tower of the minaret – except these days recorded cassettes and loudspeakers do away with the need for him to climb up there. At the main Friday noon prayers, the imam gives a *khutba* (sermon) from the *minbar*, a wooden pulpit that stands beside the mihrab. In older, grander mosques, these minbars are often beautifully decorated.

Before entering the prayer hall and participating in the communal worship, Muslims must perform a ritual washing of their

Mihrab: a niche in the wall indicating the direction of Mecca.

hands, forearms, face and neck. For this purpose, mosques have traditionally had a large ablutions fountain at the centre of the courtyard, often carved from marble and worn by centuries of use. These days, modern mosques just have rows of taps.

The mosque also serves as a kind of community centre, and often you'll find groups of children or adults receiving lessons (usually in the Quran), people in quiet prayer and others simply dozing – mosques provide wonderfully tranquil havens from the chaos of the street.

Visiting Mosques

With few exceptions, non-Muslims are quite welcome to visit mosques at any time other than during noon prayers on Friday. You must dress modestly. For men that means no shorts; for women that means no shorts, tight pants, shirts that aren't done up, or anything else that might be considered immodest. Some of the more frequently visited mosques provide wraparound cloaks for anyone improperly dressed. Shoes have to be removed or, again, some mosques will provide slip-on covers for a small fee.

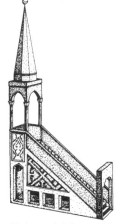

Minbar: pulpit from which the sermon is delivered.

of Allah's message to the Meccans. The essence of it was a call to submit to God's will ('islam' means submission), but not all Meccans were terribly taken with the idea.

Mohammed gathered quite a following in his campaign against Meccan idolaters and his movement especially appealed to the poorer levels of society. The powerful families became increasingly outraged and, by 622, had made life sufficiently unpleasant for Mohammed and his followers to convince them of the need to flee to Medina, an oasis town some 300km to the north and now Islam's second most holy city. This migration – the Hejira – marks the beginning of the Islamic calendar, year 1 AH or 622 AD.

In Medina, Mohammed continued to preach and increased his supporter base. Soon he and his followers began to clash with the Meccans, possibly over trade routes. By 630 they had gained a sufficient following to return and take Mecca. In the two years until Mohammed's death, many of the surrounding tribes swore allegiance to him and the new faith.

Upon Mohammed's death in 632, the Arab tribes exploded into the Syrian desert, quickly conquering all of what makes up modern Jordan, Syria, Iraq, Lebanon, Israel and the Palestinian territories. By 644 they had taken Egypt and spread into North Africa, and in the following decades they would cross into Spain and for a brief moment reach deep into France.

The initial conquests were carried out under the caliphs, or Companions of Mohammed, of whom there were four. They in turn were followed by the Umayyad dynasty (661-750) in Damascus and then the Abbasid line (749-1258) in the newly built city of Baghdad (in modern Iraq).

In order to live a devout life, the Muslim is expected to carry out at least the Five Pillars of Islam:

Shahada This is the profession of the faith, the basic tenet of Islam: 'There is no God but Allah and Mohammed is his prophet'. *'La il-laha illa Allah Mohammed rasul Allah.'* It is commonly heard as part of the call to prayer and at other events such as births and deaths.

Sala Sometimes written salat, this is the obligation of prayer, done ideally five or six times a day when the muezzins call upon the faithful to pray. Although Muslims can pray anywhere, a strong sense of community makes joining together in a mosque preferable to most.

Zakat Alm-giving to the poor was, from the start, an essential part of Islamic social teaching, and was later developed in some parts of the Muslim world into various forms of tax to redistribute funds to the needy. The moral obligation towards one's poorer neighbours continues to be emphasised at a personal level, and it is not unusual to find exhortations to give posted up outside some mosques.

Sawm Ramadan, the ninth month of the Muslim calendar, commemorates the revelation of the Quran to Mohammed. In a demonstration of the Muslims' renewal of faith, they are asked to abstain from sex and from letting anything pass their lips from dawn to dusk every day of the month. This includes smoking. For more on the fasting month, see Islamic Holidays in the Facts for the Visitor chapter.

Haj The pinnacle of a devout Muslim's life is the pilgrimage to the holy sites in and around Mecca. Ideally, the pilgrim should go to Mecca in the last month of the year. and join Muslims from all over the world in the pilgrimage and subsequent feast. The returned pilgrim can be addressed as Haj, and in simpler villages at least, it is not uncommon to see the word Al-Haj and simple scenes painted on the walls of houses showing that its inhabitants have made the pilgrimage.

Sunnis & Shi'ites In its early days, Islam suffered a major schism that divided the faith into two streams: the Sunnis and the Shi'ites.

The power struggle between Ali, the last of the four Companions of Mohammed – together with his son-in-law – and the Umayyad dynasty in Damascus, lay at the heart of the rift that tore apart the new faith's followers.

The succession to the caliphate had from the first been marked by intrigue and bloodshed. Ali, the father of Mohammed's sole male heirs, lost his struggle and was assassinated, paving the way to the caliphate for the Umayyad leader Mu'awiya. The latter was related to Ali's predecessor, Othman, in whose murder some believed Ali was implicated. Those who recognised Mu'awiya as caliph (the majority) came to be known as the Sunnis, who would become the orthodox bedrock of Islam. The Shi'ites, on the other hand, recognise only the successors of Ali. Most of them are known as Twelvers, because they believe in 12 *imams* (religious leaders), the last of whom has been lost from sight, but who will appear some day to create an empire of the true faith. The rest are called Seveners because they believe seven imams will succeed Ali. The Sunnis later divided into four schools of religious thought, each lending more or less importance to various aspects of doctrine.

Islamic Customs In everyday life, Muslims are prohibited from drinking alcohol and eating pork (as the animal is considered unclean), and must refrain from fraud, usury, slander and gambling.

Islamic Minorities

In Syria, the Shi'ites and other Muslim minorities, such as the Alawites and Druze, account for about 16% of the population.

Islam & the West

Unfortunately, Islam has been much maligned and misunderstood in the west in recent years. Any mention of it usually brings to mind one of two images: the 'barbarity' of some aspects of Islamic law such as flogging, stoning or the amputation of hands; or the so-called fanatics out to terrorise the west.

For many Muslims, however, and particularly for those in the Middle East, Islam is stability in a very unstable world. Many of them are keenly aware that Muslims are seen as a threat by the west and are divided in their own perceptions of western countries. Not without justification, they regard the west's policies, especially towards the Arab world, as aggressive and they often compare its attitudes to them with those of the medieval Crusaders. Despite this view that western culture is dangerous to Muslim values, and despite the growing influence of anti-western religious groups, many Muslims still admire the west. It is common to hear people say they like it, but that they are perplexed by its treatment of them.

If the west is offended by the anti-western rhetoric of the radical minority, the majority of Muslims see the west, and its support of Israel, as a direct challenge to their independence.

Although the violence and terrorism associated with the Middle East is often held up by the western media as evidence of blind, religiously inspired blood-thirstiness, the efficient oppression of the Palestinian Arabs by Israeli security forces has until fairly recently barely rated a mention. The sectarian madness of Northern Ireland is rarely portrayed as a symbol of Christian 'barbarism' in the way political violence in the Middle East is summed up as simple Muslim fanaticism. It is worth remembering that while the Christian west tends to view Islam with disdain, if not contempt, Muslims accord Christians great respect as believers in the same God.

Just as the west receives a distorted view of Muslim society, so too are western values misread in Islamic societies. The glamour of the west has lured those able to compete (usually the young, rich and well educated) but for others, it represents the bastion of moral decline.

These misunderstandings have long contributed to a general feeling of unease and distrust between nations of the west and the Muslim world, and often between individuals of those countries. As long as this situation persists, Islam will continue to be seen in the west as a backward and radical force bent on violent change, rather than as simply a code of religious and political behaviour that people choose to apply to their daily lives, and which makes an often difficult life tolerable for them.

Alawites The Alawites are an offshoot of the mainstream Shi'ite branch of Islam. Their origins are uncertain but it's believed the sect was founded on the Arabian Peninsula in the 9th century by a preacher named Mohammed ibn Nusayr. Their basic belief is that there is one God with a hierarchy of divine beings, the highest of whom is Ali (see Sunnis & Shi'ites earlier), hence the name Alawites, or 'followers of Ali'.

In Syria, the Alawites have traditionally occupied the mountainous ranges along the coast, which to this day are known as the Jebel Ansariyya, or Jebel an-Nusariyya, after the founder of the Alawite sect. Like the Ismailis, a similar sort of sect who also lived in the coastal mountains (see the boxed text 'The Assassins' in the Orontes Valley chapter), the Alawites have always suffered persecution at the hands of the ruling Sunni dynasties. Salah ad-Din and his Ayyubid dynasty, the Mamluks and the Ottoman Turks all either massacred Alawite communities, forced them to convert or imposed crippling taxes. Alawites traditionally always worked the poorest land or held down the least skilled jobs in the towns.

That situation was radically changed early in the 20th century when the French courted the Alawites as allies and granted them a self-ruled enclave in the mountains around Lattakia. From there the Alawites managed to insinuate themselves into national politics to the extent that, since Hafez al-Assad, himself an Alawite, took power in 1970, this minority sect of one million now holds complete power over the country's 16 million majority Sunni population.

Druze The Druze religion is an offshoot of Shi'ite Islam and was spread in the 11th century by Hamzah ibn Ali and other missionaries from Egypt who followed the Fatimid caliph Al-Hakim. The group derives its name from one of Hamzah's subordinates, Mohammed Darazi. Darazi had declared Al-Hakim to be the last imam and God in one, but most Egyptians found the bloody ruler to be anything but divine. When Al-Hakim died in mysterious circumstances, Darazi and his companions were forced to flee Egypt.

Most members of the Druze community now live in the mountains of Lebanon, although there are some small Druze towns in the Hauran, the area around the Syria-Jordan border. Their distinctive faith has survived intact mainly because of the secrecy that surrounds it. Not only is conversion to or from the faith prohibited, but only an elite, known as *'uqqal* (knowers), have full access to the religious doctrine, the *hikmeh*.

The hikmeh is contained in seven holy books that exist only in handwritten copies. One of the codes it preaches is *taqiyya* (caution), under which a believer living among Christians, for example, can outwardly conform to Christian belief while still being a Druze at heart. They believe that God is too sacred to be called by name, is amorphous and will reappear in other incarnations. Although the New Testament and the Quran are revered, they read their own scriptures at *khalwas* (meeting houses) on Thursdays.

Christianity

Statistics on the number of Christians in Syria are hard to come by but they are believed to account for about 10% to 13% of the population. What is more certain is that that number is in decline. The reasons are demographic. Over the centuries, Christians have moved from the country to the city and this urbanisation has led to a fall in their birth rates. Also, traditionally Christian church schools have provided a better education than state schools which, again, has had the effect of lowering the birth rate. The professional qualifications resulting from the better education and the subsequent wealth have also meant that Syria's Christians are far more prone to emigrate. Syrian churches are finding it impossible to staunch the flow as their parishioners trickle away to America and Australia.

Congregations may be small but there is still a bewildering array of churches representing the three major branches of Christianity – Eastern Orthodox, Catholic and Protestant.

Eastern Orthodox This branch of Christianity is represented by the Greek Orthodox, Armenian Orthodox and also the Syrian Orthodox churches. Greek Orthodox has its liturgy in Arabic and is the mother church of the Jacobites (Syrian Orthodox), who broke away in the 6th century, and the Greek Catholics, who split in the 16th century.

Armenian Orthodox (also known as the Armenian Apostolic Church) has its liturgy in classical Armenian and is seen by many to be the guardian of the Armenian national identity.

Syrian Orthodox uses Syriac, closely related to Aramaic. The patriarch lives in Damascus and the *see* (where the patriarch lives) has jurisdiction over foreign communities such as the Syrian Malankars in Kerala, India, and Syrian Orthodox in the USA.

Catholic These churches come under the jurisdiction of Rome and are listed here from largest to smallest.

Greek Catholics, or Melchites, come under the authority of the patriarch who resides in Damascus, but his jurisdiction includes the patriarchates of Jerusalem and Alexandria. The church observes the Byzantine tradition, where married clergy are in charge of rural parishes and the diocesan clergy are celibate.

Armenian Catholics form a tightly knit community. They fled from Turkish massacres in 1894-96 and 1915-21, and hold their liturgy in classical Armenian. The patriarch resides in Beirut, and more than half their members are from Aleppo.

Syrian Catholics have Syriac as the main liturgical language although some services are in Arabic. They are found mainly in the north-east of Syria and in Homs, Aleppo and Damascus.

The Maronites trace their origins to St Maron, a monk who lived near Aleppo and died around 410. Their liturgy is in ancient West Syrian, although the commonly used language is Arabic. They are found mainly in

Lebanon (about one million), where their patriarch is based, but there are sizable numbers in Aleppo. As with the other Christian groups of the Middle East, the majority live outside their countries of origin: there are estimated to be about three million living in Europe, North and South America, and Australia.

Roman Catholics live in western Syria and Aleppo. Rome recently restored the patriarchate of Jerusalem, and a patriarch was elected there in 1987.

Chaldean Catholics, who have preserved the ancient East Syrian liturgy, which they practise in Syriac, are found mainly in eastern Syria, Aleppo and Damascus. Their patriarch resides in Baghdad, the Iraqi capital.

Jews

The small Jewish population still left in Damascus at the beginning of the 1990s is now all but a memory.

In an attempt to curry favour with the USA, President Assad promised in early 1992 to ease restrictions and allow Jews to leave the country. This promise he made good on, and most of the few thousand Jews who for years had regularly been wheeled out in spontaneous demonstrations of affection for their president voted with their feet for the USA. It is estimated that only a few hundred remain.

LANGUAGE

Arabic is the mother tongue of the majority of Syrians – for a grammatical primer and basic vocabulary list see the Language chapter at the back of the book. Kurdish is spoken in the north, especially towards the east, Armenian in Aleppo and other major cities, and Turkish in some villages east of the Euphrates.

Aramaic, the language of the Bible, is still spoken in two or three villages. English is widely understood and increasingly popular as a second language, while French, although waning, is quite common, especially among the older generations.

Facts for the Visitor

PLANNING
When to Go

Spring (March to May) is the best time to visit as temperatures are mild and the winter rains have cleared the haze that obscures views for much of the year. Autumn (September to November) would be the next best choice. However, work or study schedules dictate that many people have no choice other than to visit in summer (June to August). The drawback is the heat.

While the coastal regions and the cities are bearable, travel in regions like the northeast and desert, and visits to the large exposed sites like Palmyra, Apamea and Bosra, can become real endurance tests. You need to always wear a hat and carry plenty of water. You'll also find that heading out early and returning to the hotel for a siesta mid-afternoon becomes a necessary strategy to prevent exhaustion.

Conversely, winter can be downright unpleasant on the coast and in the mountains with heavy rain and plummeting temperatures. In fact, from November to February be prepared for some nasty weather all over the country. Right up to the end of October the weather can be mild or even hot and the change, when it comes, can be quite dramatic. Bear in mind that most of the cheaper hotels (and quite a few of the more expensive ones) are not well equipped to deal with this kind of weather.

Religious Holidays & Festivals Most of Syria's religious and state holidays (for dates see Public Holidays & Special Events later this chapter) last only one or two days and should not seriously disrupt any travel plans. The exception is Ramadan, the Muslim month of fasting. During daylight hours many restaurants are closed, while bars cease business completely for the duration. Offices also operate reduced and very erratic hours.

The only special events that are worth bearing in mind when scheduling your trip are the biennial Bosra festival and, possibly, the Baalbek festival over the border in Lebanon – again, see Public Holidays & Special Events later in this chapter.

Maps

Lonely Planet's *Jordan, Syria & Lebanon travel atlas* is designed to complement this guide; it covers the country in 85 pages of detailed maps (scales 1:700,000 and 1:200,000) and it's fully indexed and light to carry. The best sheet map is one produced by Freytag & Berndt – distinguished by a red cover and selling for UK£6.95 in the UK. It covers the country at a scale of 1:800,000 and on the reverse carries very good city plans of Damascus and Aleppo. It's widely available in Syria where it's published under licence by the Avicenne bookshop and costs S£250 (roughly US$5). There's also another, far less good sheet map put out by GEOprojects, based in Beirut, on a scale of 1:1,000,000, also with city plans.

The tourist offices throughout Syria have free handout city and regional maps but they are generally way out of date and of very little use.

What to Bring

In Syria you will be able to find most things that you might need, but the choice will be severely limited. So: bring sunglasses, a flashlight (torch), a water bottle/canteen, sun screen, a hat, a flat drain stopper (not a plug), a pocketknife, a sleeping sheet, a small sewing kit and a moneybelt or pouch.

If you are visiting during winter, make sure you have plenty of warm clothes and a windproof and waterproof jacket. It gets surprisingly miserable at this time of year. Snow is not uncommon in Damascus and more likely still at higher altitudes. Bear in mind also that heating in most of the lower-end hotels is often inadequate or nonexistent.

Although most toiletries can be found in city pharmacies and supermarkets (and at

Highlights & Suggested Itineraries

From a sifting of the many hundreds of letters about Syria sent by readers to Lonely Planet, the most raved about sites are:

1. Palmyra
2. Krak des Chevaliers
3. Aleppo Souq
4. The Old City of Damascus
5. Bosra

See also the boxed text at the start of each regional chapter where we have added a few more of our own personal highlights.

Suggested Itineraries

Syria is not a particularly large place and most of the best things to see are concentrated in the west of the country. Using just the three cities of Damascus, Hama and Aleppo as bases you could get through an awful lot in just a week, although it would involve a very exhausting and hectic schedule. Two weeks would probably be the optimum amount of time to see most of what is truly worth seeing and to be able to take it at a reasonably relaxed pace. One month would give you the opportunity to spend much more time in the major cities, really soaking up the atmosphere and exploring some of the less-visited sites and regions, such as the extreme north-east.

One Week We'd divide the time equally, with two days each in Aleppo, Damascus and Hama, plus one overnight in Palmyra. In Damascus we'd spend our time exploring the Old City and visiting the National Museum and squeeze in a half-day excursion to Bosra; we'd use Hama as a base to visit Apamea and the Krak des Chevaliers on consecutive days; while from Aleppo we'd squeeze in a trip up to Qala'at Samaan.

Two Weeks A fortnight is really an ideal amount of time. We'd base ourselves in Damascus for at least five days, making repeated visits to the Old City, visiting the National Museum and the Salihiyya district and making several half-day trips out to Bosra, Seidnayya, Maalula and Mar Musa, maybe even spending a night at the latter. From Damascus we'd move to Palmyra, spending the night there before taking the whole of the next day to explore the wonderful ruins. We'd move on to Hama in the evening, spending three days there: one to visit Krak des Chevaliers; two to visit Apamea; three to visit Qasr ibn Wardan and the beehive villages. On to Aleppo, where during a further three days we'd use the city as a base for trips to Qala'at Samaan one day and the Dead Cities the next. If there is still some time left, we'd catch a bus and travel through the hills to Lattakia and visit Qala'at Salah ad-Din.

One Month Syria is not a particularly large country and with a month at your disposal you could cover it thoroughly. We'd do all of the things mentioned in the two week itinerary, but spend a day or two more in each of Aleppo and Damascus just getting to know the cities better and maybe making more trips to sites in the surrounding areas. We'd certainly make the overnight trip to the ruins at Baalbek in Lebanon.

In addition we'd take three or four days to make the loop out along the Euphrates to Deir ez-Zur, from where it's possible to visit some of the remote sites down towards the Iraqi border and up in the north-east of the country near the border with Turkey.

major hotels), certain items can be difficult to get, and expensive, so you may want to bring your own contact lens solution, tampons or sanitary pads and contraceptives.

TOURIST OFFICES

Syria is slowly waking to the potential bonnanza in tourism, but the desire to receive more visitors has yet to translate to any concrete measures for bringing this about. The country engages in no promotion at all and has no tourist offices abroad, anywhere.

For information on the country prior to your trip all you can do is contact any of the Syrian diplomatic missions overseas. However, during the course of researching this book we phoned one western Syrian embassy several times with simple requests for basic information and each time we drew a blank. The best they could do was give us a fax number for the tourism office in Damascus (fax 963-11-224 2636) and suggest we redirect our questions there.

Local Tourist Offices

There is a tourist office in every major town (addresses are given in the relevant sections) but don't expect too much in the way of information. Staff usually speak English and are often as helpful as they could possibly be but they have very little in the way of resources. All they generally have is a free map of often indifferent quality, although the Damascus one isn't bad and the newly published map covering the north-east and including town plans of Deir ez-Zur, Raqqa and Hassake is very good.

VISAS & DOCUMENTS
Passport

Make sure that your passport is valid well beyond the period of your intended stay. If it's just about to expire, Syrian immigration may not let you into the country. Also, make sure it has sufficient space for any new visa stamps that you're liable to pick up, such as extensions or a new visa if you're heading into Lebanon – if you are planning on a Lebanon side trip you need two blank pages to accommodate all the stamps it entails.

You should get into the habit of carrying your passport at all times while in Syria as you often need to present it to change money, cash travellers cheques, buy long-distance bus tickets and, in some places, even to make phone calls.

Visas

All foreigners entering Syria must obtain a visa. These are available at Syrian consulates outside the country. In all but a few cases you *cannot* get a visa at the border or on arrival at the airport. It's also difficult to get a Syrian visa while on the road. For more details on both of these issues see the separate sections following.

The easiest and safest way to get your visa is to apply for it in your home country, well before you intend travelling. Try to avoid applying in a country that is not your own or that you don't hold residency for as the Syrians don't like this. At best they will ask you for a letter of recommendation from your own embassy (which is often an expensive proposition), at worst they'll turn you down flat. In fact, US citizens must get their visas at home as US embassies abroad have a policy of not issuing letters of recommendation – the only place you can get around this is the Syrian embassy in Cairo which, at the time of writing, didn't ask for a letter. If your home country doesn't have a Syrian embassy or consulate, then there's no problem with you applying anywhere else.

At most embassies and consulates you can apply in person or by post and the visa takes from four days to two weeks to issue. There are rarely any problems with getting the visa; however, if there is any evidence of a visit to Israel in your passport, your application will be refused. That evidence includes not just an Israeli visa, but also entry and exit stamps for border crossings between Israel and Egypt or Jordan. There's also a question on some visa application forms that asks, 'Have you ever visited Occupied Palestine?' to which a yes response will see your application turned down flat. Should you plan on going to Israel after Syria, do not say so.

There are two types of visa issued: single entry and multiple entry but both are valid only for 15 days inside Syria and must be used within three months of the date of issue (six months for multiple-entry visas). Don't be misled by the words on the visa stating a validity of three months – this simply means the visa is valid for presentation for three months. Once in Syria it is no problem to get your visa extended.

On entry, you will fill out a yellow or white entry card (in English); keep this, as you'll need it to get visa extensions and on leaving Syria.

Visa Costs The cost of visas varies according to nationality and on where you get them, and it is not always cheaper the closer you get to Syria. There seems to be little rhyme or reason in deciding which nationalities pay what, except in the case of UK passport-holders, who always pay a lot.

In the UK, Britons must pay UK£32 for a single-entry visa or UK£49 for a multiple-entry visa, while Irish passport-holders are charged UK£33 and UK£61. Fees vary for other nationalities applying in the UK.

In Australia visas are currently A$35 for a single-entry visa and A$45 for a multiple-entry visa if applying at the Melbourne consular office; A$75/110 if applying at the Sydney consular office. New Zealanders will also need to apply to Melbourne or Sydney because there's no Syrian representation in New Zealand. The same costs apply.

In the USA visas cost US$61 for a single or 'double' entry. The latter allows you to enter twice – useful if you wish to enter Lebanon and return to Syria. Note that the cost includes a US$16 visa fee and a US$45 nonrefundable application fee. Canadian citizens pay US$56 for a single-entry visa and US$108 for a multiple-entry visa.

In France, a single-entry visa will cost 156FF. In Germany, a single-entry visa costs DM77, while a multiple-entry visa is DM126.

For addresses and phone numbers of Syrian diplomatic representations overseas see Embassies & Consulates later in this chapter.

Visas at the Border The official line is that if there is no Syrian representation in your country, you are entitled to be issued a visa on arrival at the border, airport or port. That said, there's no Syrian embassy or consulate in the Netherlands yet we've had letters from Dutch people who were turned back at the Turkish-Syrian border. Australian passport holders are sometimes an exception to this rule – we know of some who have arrived without a visa and simply paid a US$32 tax on arrival while others have gained entry but only after long delays. Our advice is that you most definitely should secure your visa in advance.

Getting Your Visa in the Middle East
The Syrian embassy in Amman issues visas only to nationals and residents of Jordan and to nationals of countries that have no Syrian representation. So, if you are from a country like the UK, the USA or France that has a Syrian embassy then you cannot get a Syrian visa in Jordan. Of course, there is always the odd Brit traveller who has proved the exception and has got a visa here but you cannot count on it. If you are in Jordan without a Syrian visa your best option is to go to Cairo where the Syrian embassy issues visas the same or next day depending on how early in the morning you get your application in (for the address see Embassies & Consulates later in this chapter). For Australians and Canadians the visa is free, Americans pay US$34, UK citizens pay US$60 and most other nationalities pay US$54. The embassy is open from 10 am to 12 noon, Saturday to Thursday.

In Turkey, you can get Syrian visas in both Ankara and Istanbul without too much of a problem. Australians and Canadians pay nothing, while New Zealanders pay about US$6. German, French and US citizens pay more, while Britons take all the prizes, paying about US$60. Nonresidents in Turkey need a letter of recommendation from their embassy, for which they may be charged. UK citizens, for example, have to pay UK £35 for this service. Visas in Turkey take one working day to issue. Note that the Syrian consulate in Istanbul is only open for applications from 9.30 to 11 am, and for pick-up from 2 to 2.30 pm the next working day.

Visa Extensions If your stay in Syria is going to be more than 15 days you have to get a visa extension while in the country. This is done at an immigration office, which you'll find in all main cities. You can get more than one extension and their length appears to depend on a combination of what you're willing to ask for and the mood of the official you deal with.

Extensions are usually only granted on the 14th or 15th day of your stay, so if you apply earlier expect to be knocked back. If, as occasionally happens, you are allowed to extend it earlier than this, check that the extension is from the last day of your visa or previous extension and not from the day of your application.

The specifics vary from place to place but there are always several forms to fill in, in French and/or English, usually containing questions repeated several times in slightly different ways. You need from three to five passport photos. The cost is never more than US$1. Processing time varies from on-the-spot (actually an hour or so) to 1 pm the following day. Damascus and Aleppo are about the most tedious places to extend your visa, while small towns like Deir ez-Zur or Tartus are the most straightforward.

Re-Entry Visas If you do not possess a multiple-entry visa and want to leave Syria and re-enter (to visit Lebanon or Jordan) it is possible to arrange this by visiting the immigration office in central Damascus; see the Lebanon section in the Around Damascus chapter for further details.

Visas for Egypt Applications for visas can be made at the Egyptian embassy in Damascus (see Embassies & Consulates in Syria later in this chapter) from 9 to 11 am Saturday to Thursday. Collect your passport and visa the same day at 2 pm. It will cost you S£750.

Visas for Jordan Applications for visas can be made at the Jordanian embassy in Damascus (see Embassies & Consulates in Syria later in this chapter) from 9 to 11 am Saturday to Thursday. Collect your passport and visa the same day at 1 pm. For UK citizens a visa costs S£900, for Australians it's free, Canadians pay S£1300 and US citizens pay S£1100.

Visas for Lebanon Lebanon has no diplomatic representation in Syria but you can get visas at the border – see the Lebanon section in the Around Damascus chapter.

Travel Permits
The only place for which you need a permit to visit is Quneitra in the Golan Heights – see the Passes entry under Quneitra in The Hauran chapter for more details.

Travel Insurance
However you're travelling, it's worth taking out travel insurance. Work out what you need and consult your travel agent for the most appropriate policy. You may not want to insure that grotty old army surplus backpack but everyone should be covered for the worst possible case: an accident, for example, that will require hospital treatment and a flight home. Check the details. In most cases you need to pay extra to cover yourself for 'dangerous sports' such as diving. Also, you often need to pay a surcharge for expensive camera equipment and the like.

It's a good idea to make a copy of your policy, in case the original is lost. If you are planning to travel for a long time, the insurance may seem very expensive but if you can't afford it, you certainly won't be able to afford to deal with a medical emergency overseas.

Driving Licence
An International Driving Permit is legally required if you intend to do any driving in Syria, although in practice most car rental companies seem satisfied with national licences. For more information on driving in Syria see the Getting Around chapter.

Student Cards

A student card will get you huge reductions in site fees which, after accommodation, are your major expense when travelling in Syria. The standard admission fee for museums and archaeological sites is S£300 but with a student card this drops to somewhere btween S£10 and S£30. That's a difference of more than US$5 a site and if you're visiting a couple of sites a day that sum mounts up. If you don't have a student card there are a few guys around Palmyra who sell International Student Identification Cards (ISIC) – they don't operate out of any particular place but they will probably find you. Obviously, they don't care if you're a real student or not – as long as you pay US$30, the card is yours. It's a worthwhile investment as standard admissions at Palmyra alone, taking in the museum, Temple of Bel and castle, come to S£1000 (roughly US$22); with a student card you pay less than one tenth, saving you more than half the value of the card in just one day.

EMBASSIES & CONSULATES
Syrian Embassies & Consulates

Following are addresses of Syrian embassies and consulates around the world:

Australia
    Consulate:
    (☎ 03-9347 8445, fax 9347 8447)
    57 Cardigan St, Carlton, Victoria 3053
    Consulate:
    (☎ 02-9597 7714, fax 9597 2226)
    10 Belmore St, Arncliffe, NSW 2205
Denmark
    No representation; closest option is Germany
Egypt
    Embassy:
    (☎ 02-377 7020, fax 335 8232)
    18 Abdel Rahim Sabry, Doqqi, Cairo
France
    Embassy:
    (☎ 01-45 51 82 35)
    20 rue Vaneau, 75007 Paris
Germany
    Embassy:
    (☎ 030-220 20 46)
    Otto Grotewohl Str 3, Berlin
    Consulate:
    (☎ 0228-81 99 20, fax 81 92 99)
    Andreas Hermes Str 5, D-53175 Bonn

    Consulate:
    (☎ 040-30 90 54 14, fax 30 90 52 33)
    Brooktor 11, 20457 Hamburg
Ireland
    No representation; closest option is UK
Jordan
    Embassy:
    (☎ 06-641 392)
    Sharia Afghani, Jebel Amman
Netherlands
    No representation; closest option is Germany
New Zealand
    No representation; closest option is Australia
Saudi Arabia
    Embassy:
    (☎ 01-463 3198)
    Cnr sharias Ath-Thamaneen and Ar-Riyadh, Riyadh
    Consulate:
    (☎ 02-660 5801)
    Cnr sharias Al-Andalus and Mahmoud Rasif, Jeddah
Turkey
    Embassy:
    (☎ 312-440 9657)
    Abdullah Cevdet Sokak No 7, Ankara
    Consulate:
    (☎ 212-248 2735)
    3 Silahhane Caddesi (aka Maçka Caddesi), Ralli Apt 59, Istanbul
UK
    Embassy:
    (☎ 020-7245 9012, visa line 0891-600 171, fax 7235 4621)
    8 Belgrave Square, London SW1 8PH
USA
    Embassy:
    (☎ 202-232 6313) 2215 Wyoming Ave NW, Washington DC 20008
    Consulate:
    (☎ 212-661 1313)
    820 Second Ave, New York 10017

Embassies & Consulates in Syria

Most embassies or consulates are open from 8 am to 2 pm and are closed Friday, Saturday and public holidays. The following are all in Damascus:

Australia
    (☎ 613 2626, fax 613 2478)
    128A Sharia al-Farabi, Al-Mezzeh, about 6km west of the city centre
Belgium
    (☎ 333 2821, fax 333 0426)
    Sharia al-Jala'a

Canada
   (☎ 611 6692, fax 611 4000)
   Block 12, Al-Mezzeh, 4km west of city centre
Egypt
   (☎ 333 3561, fax 333 7961)
   Sharia al-Jala'a
France
   (☎ 332 7992)
   Sharia Ata Ayyubi, Salihiyya
Germany
   (☎ 332 3800/1, fax 332 3812)
   53 Sharia Ibrahim Hanano
Iraq
   No representation in Syria
Ireland
   No representation in Syria; see UK embassy
Jordan
   (☎ 333 4642, fax 333 6741)
   Sharia al-Jala'a
Netherlands
   (☎ 333 6871, fax 333 9369)
   Sharia al-Jala'a
New Zealand
   No representation in Syria; see UK embassy
Saudi Arabia
   (☎ 333 4914)
   Sharia al-Jala'a, Abu Roumana
Turkey
   (☎ 333 1411)
   58 Sharia Ziad bin Abi Soufian
UK
   (☎ 371 2561, fax 373 1600)
   11 Sharia Mohammed Kurd Ali, Malki
USA
   (☎ 333 2315, fax 224 7938)
   2 Sharia al-Mansour, Abu Roumana

CUSTOMS

You can bring in up to US$5000 without declaring it. Officially, you can only export US$2000 without declaring it, or S£5000 to Jordan or Lebanon. If you have large sums, declare it on entering the country in order to be sure of avoiding problems upon leaving.

Customs officials seem really interested in hi-tech electronic gear. You'll be asked if you have a video camera and, if so, you may be hit with a heavy tax. Similarly, laptops and palm tops can attract taxes or result in an entry being written into your passport to make sure that you leave the country with these items and don't sell them while in Syria. To avoid complications it's best to keep this sort of stuff completely out of sight.

MONEY
Currency

The currency is the Syrian pound (S£), known locally as the *lira*. There are 100 piastres to a pound, but it's unlikely you'll ever need to know this, as few transactions nowadays involve the use of coins at all. Indeed only the ten pound coin is still around, and the main purpose for keeping it alive seems to be for use in public telephones. Notes are S£5, S£10, S£25, S£50, S£100 and S£500.

Exchange Rates

The official government exchange rates for a range of foreign currencies were as follows at the time of going to print:

Australia	A$1	=	S£30
Canada	C$1	=	S£23
Euro	€1	=	S£45
France	10FF	=	S£70
Germany	DM1	=	S£23
Japan	Y100	=	S£37
Jordan	JD1	=	S£63
New Zealand	NZ$1	=	S£23
UK	UK£1	=	S£70
USA	US$1	=	S£45

Black market rates are usually about 15% higher depending on what part of the country you are in and how good your bargaining skills are.

Exchanging Money

The banking system in Syria is entirely state-owned. Although there has been talk of creating openings for private and even foreign institutions, that still looks some way off, and initially would concern investment banks alone. The Commercial Bank of Syria (CBS) is the public face of the state system and there's at least one branch in every major town. The majority of branches of the bank will change cash and travellers cheques in most major currencies but each branch has its own quirks – some charge commission, some don't; some require the bank manager's signature to authorise transactions, some just hand over the cash without any form filling whatsoever. Generally speaking, the smaller the town, the less hassle there is.

There are also a small number of officially sanctioned private exchange offices. These change cash, and sometimes travellers cheques, at official bank rates but generally don't charge any commission. The other advantage is that whereas banks usually close for the day at 12.30 or 2 pm, the exchange offices are often open until 7 pm.

Travellers Cheques While cash is definitely king in Syria, travellers cheques are widely accepted and are obviously the safer alternative. Most major brands of cheque are accepted by the CBS, but you're much safer with widely known types like Thomas Cook, Eurocheque or American Express. Some branches of the CBS will charge a minimum one-off commission of S£25 per transaction, whether you change one or several cheques. Occasionally (most notably in Aleppo) you'll be asked to present sales receipts when changing travellers cheques, which of course you are not supposed to have together with the cheques.

More often than not, you'll find yourself being diddled for a pound or two, as bank employees (and others) tend to round everything off to the nearest five pounds.

Some store owners and hotels will accept travellers cheques but generally only those places that advertise their rates in dollars.

ATMs There are no ATMs at all in Syria.

Credit Cards Major credit cards such as American Express, Visa, MasterCard and Diners Club are increasingly being accepted by bigger hotels and stores for purchases. They are also handy for buying air tickets (as the only alternative is hard currency) and with some car rental companies (it will save you having to leave a large cash deposit).

Cash advances are officially not possible as the CBS has no links with any credit card companies. However, a few individual entrepreneurs carry out transactions via Jordanian or Lebanese banks. Bear in mind that

the rate they offer may not be too great and you may also have to pay a commission. For further details see the Money sections in Damascus and Hama.

Black Market The black market in currency is alive and well, in spite of a 1986 law providing for up to three years in prison for the unwarranted possession of hard currency or its illegal exchange. The thirst for hard currency is easily enough explained. It can be used to make many purchases, mainly of foreign goods, that otherwise remain inaccessible to Syrians.

Although it is increasingly common practice, and at its most alive in Damascus, do exercise caution if you decide to change money on the black market.

Cash is obviously the most welcome object of illicit exchange, and the US dollar the preferred currency. At the time of writing, the best rate you could hope for was S£50 to the dollar. Outside Damascus you will be looking at more like S£48. Treat the black market like any other transaction and bargain – often enough the initial offer will be for S£45. Sometimes you will find people willing to change travellers cheques in this way, although for a rate usually a couple of pounds lower than you would get with cash.

It's not difficult to find people willing to change money. In Damascus and Aleppo, in particular, you may well be approached in the street, or by hotel staff, while the *souqs* (markets) are major money-changing areas. If you want to change and have not been approached, jewellery stalls in the souqs are a logical place to start. Be discreet, as there is a degree of risk involved for all sides.

Costs
By international standards Syria is still fairly cheap. It is possible to get by on US$15 a day or maybe less if you are willing to stick to the cheapest hotels (you can get a bed for as little as S£150 – US$3), make felafel, shwarma and juice the mainstays of your diet, and carry a student card to offset site admission costs. If you stay in a modest hotel and have a room with a fan and private

bathroom, eat in regular restaurants, with the occasional splurge, and aim to see a couple of sites each day, you'll be looking at between US$20 and US$30 a day.

To give some indication of daily costs, a felafel costs about S£15 to S£25 (around US$0.30 to US$0.50) and shwarma S£25 to S£35 (US$0.50 to US$0.70), while a meal in an average restaurant will set you back around S£150 (US$3). If you prefer to go a little upmarket you can usually eat very well for S£250 (US$5) a head. A beer retails for around S£35 (US$0.70) in a liquor shop and about S£50 to S£65 (US$1 to US$1.30) in a restaurant or bar, while a bottle of mineral water should be S£35 (US$0.70) in a shop. A kilogram of apples costs S£30, while bananas sell for about S£50 a kilogram. Fruit juices can cost anything from S£20 to S£50, depending on the size of the glass (the latter is generally a pint glass of pure juice).

Getting around the country is cheap: the four hour bus ride between Damascus and Aleppo costs only S£150 (US$3) on a luxury air-con bus, while if you want to slum it on an old battered bus you can do it as cheaply as S£60 (US$1.20).

Entry Fees A major expense is the entry fees to tourist sites. Foreigners are seen as dollars on legs so places where they flock tend to be pricey. Many museums, castles and other sites now cost S£300, which at the official exchange rate is over US$7. While such a fee can possibly be justified at sites such as the Krak des Chevaliers, there will be plenty of times when you have to ask yourself whether any one site is worth paying such money. In the text we've tried to give some indication of whether we think a particular site is worth its entrance fee. One way around this is to get yourself a student card – see the Student Cards section earlier in this chapter.

Tipping
Baksheesh, the tip, is part of the oil that makes the Middle East run. Syrians are not particularly shrill about tips, which makes a nice change from some other countries in the

area. Waiters in better restaurants generally expect a tip, and some will even help themselves by short-changing you a little, but otherwise a standard 10% of the bill is a good benchmark. Other services are also carried out with a view to being tipped – everything from having your luggage taken to your room to having doors opened for you comes into this category. In most cases a tip of S£25 is considered fair.

Bargaining
Whatever you buy in the way of souvenirs, remember that bargaining is an integral part of the process and listed prices are always inflated to allow for it. When shopping in the souqs, bargain – even a minimum effort will see outrageous asking prices halved. Unlike in other countries, such as Egypt and Morocco, where the stream of tourists has been long and steady for many years, Syria is a pretty relaxed place to trawl the markets and have a dabble at the ancient game of haggling – for a few hints on how it's done see the boxed text 'The Art of Bargaining' under Shopping later in this chapter.

POST & COMMUNICATIONS
The Syrian postal service is slow but effective enough. Letters mailed from the main cities take about a week to Europe and anything up to a month to Australia or the USA. Mailing letters to the UK and Europe costs S£17, while to the USA and Australia it's S£18; stamps for postcards to the UK and Europe cost S£10, while to Australia and the USA they're S£13. In addition to post offices, you can also buy *tawaabi* (stamps) from most tobacconists.

To send a parcel from Damascus or Aleppo, take it (unwrapped) to the parcel post office for inspection. After it's been cleared it has to be wrapped and covered with cotton material. You have to buy the material from one guy, pay another to give you some cardboard tags for the address, and yet another to wrap it. It's basically the enforced baksheesh gravy train for unemployed Syrians, which will cost you about S£30. For all that, the process doesn't usually take more than about half an hour. A 10kg parcel to Australia costs S£3500, S£2850 to the USA and S£1670 to the UK.

The poste restante counter at the main post office in Damascus is more or less reliable. Take your passport as identification and be prepared to pay an S£8 pick-up fee.

Telephone

Things are improving all the time – Syria has been investing in satellite and optic fibre cable projects to modernise its long-disastrous phone system, and the card phone has arrived.

For police call ☎ 112
For an ambulance call ☎ 110
For the fire service call ☎ 113
For traffic police call ☎ 115

International Calls International calls can be made three ways: via the operator at a telephone office, by using a card phone or through any of the four or five-star hotels.

Booking an international call through the operator at the phone office is the traditional way of doing things and away from the big cities it's often the only option. There is a three minute minimum charge and you can wait up to two hours for a connection to be made. Bring your passport along, as the operator will want to see it. Most main phone offices are open from early morning until late at night and occasionally around the clock.

Thankfully, card phones are becoming more prevalent – they're all over central Damascus and you're also starting to find them at telephone offices in smaller towns like Palmyra and Hama. Note: there's more than one type of phonecard and one that's bought and works in Damascus will not necessarily work for the phones in Palmyra. The phonecards come in denominations of S£200 and S£500 and are sold either at the post office or, in the case of Damascus, also from outlets close by the card phones (details are given in the individual city chapters). With a card phone you dial direct and there is no minimum call period. The inter-

Dialling Codes

To call Syria from abroad the international dialling code is ☎ 963 followed by the national area code minus the initial zero, then the subscriber's number.

Some national area codes are as follows:

Aleppo	☎ 021
An-Nabk	☎ 012
Bosra	☎ 015
Damascus	☎ 011
Deir ez-Zur	☎ 051
Der'a	☎ 015
Hama	☎ 033
Hassake	☎ 052
Homs	☎ 031
Lattakia	☎ 041
Palmyra	☎ 031
Qamishle	☎ 053
Quneitra	☎ 014
Raqqa	☎ 022
Suweida	☎ 016
Tartus	☎ 043
Zabadani	☎ 013

national access code is 00, then dial the country code, city code and number.

Normal rate calls with card phones or through the operator cost S£100 per minute to most destinations in Europe, S£115 per minute to Australia and S£125 per minute to the USA. There is a cheap rate, but the hours differ wildly from one country to the next. For Australia, cheap rate calls cost S£58 per minute from 2 to 7 pm. The rate to the USA is S£63 and calls can be made from 3 to 8 am. Cheap calls to Europe cost S£50 and can be made from 1 to 7 am.

The third option is to place a call through a big hotel or one of the several private international phone offices that are beginning to spring up. This is the most expensive way of doing things, with calls to Australia being charged at S£290 a minute and to the UK at S£200 to S£250.

Reverse-charge calls cannot be made from Syria. If you need to call through an operator, the number is ☎ 143/144.

Local & National Calls Local calls have to be made with normal coin-operated telephones – if you can find one in working order. You can identify working local call booths by the queues that form around them. They accept S£10 coins. It's actually much easier to make such calls from your hotel and as long as it's only a local call most hotels don't charge.

The best bet with national calls is the phonecard.

Fax & Telex

It is possible to send telexes, telegrams and faxes from telephone offices or sometimes from main post offices but they are very expensive. For faxes normal phone call rates are charged, and what you pay depends on how long it takes for the fax to go through. For instance, from the main telephone office in Damascus to fax the UK costs S£180 for the first minute and S£90 for each further minute. As there's a two minute minimum charge that means that at the least your fax will cost S£270. To Australia it's S£220 for the first minute and S£110 per minute beyond that.

Email & Internet Access

The Syrian government forbids Internet service providers (ISPs) in Syria, effectively banning email and access to the Web. A small number of organisations get round this by subscribing to ISPs in Lebanon but telephone costs are prohibitively high. To our knowledge the only publicly accessible on-line terminal in Syria is at the Al-Assad National Library out in the west of Damascus on Saahat Umawiyeen. There's just the one terminal and users, we are told, are nervously scrutinised by a permanent 'cyber guardian'.

If you are lugging around your own laptop then you can get connected in some of the better hotels by using an RJ-11 standard telephone connector but this, apparently, is not entirely legal, so be discreet.

INTERNET RESOURCES

As is to be expected with a country that is unequivocally 'off line', there are very few Syria-related Web sites. Curiously, however, the Syrian Ministry of Tourism does have a site – presumably, government employees can be trusted to keep their Web browsers well away from any seditious and corrupting material.

Lonely Planet
www.lonelyplanet.com
(follow the links to the travellers' reports for the latest updates on Syria)
Ministry of Tourism
www.syriatourism.org
(some surprisingly good site descriptions but precious little else)
Syria Times
www.teshreen.com
(updated daily but there's next to nothing here beyond a few headlines)
syria.on.line
www.syria-online.com/index.htm
(wide-ranging but shallow coverage; includes examples of the work of modern Syrian artists)

You could also try searching some of the other Arab-oriented link sites such as Arab-Net (www.arab.net) and 1001 Sites (www.1001sites.com), both of which are heavy on culture and news, or Cafe Arabica (www.cafearabica.com).

BOOKS

Most books are published in different editions by different publishers in different countries. As a result a book might be a hardcover rarity in one country but readily available in paperback in another. Fortunately, bookshops and libraries search by title or author, so your local bookshop or library is the best place to get advice on the availability of the recommendations to be found in this section.

For information on literature by Syrian authors see the Arts section in the Facts about Syria chapter.

Bookshops in Syria

If you forget to bring some reading matter with you, then pickings are very slim in Syria. English-language literature is hard to find and extremely limited in range with the same small array of airport novels (Stephen King, Danielle Steele, Jeffrey Archer etc) hogging the shelves of the scant few outlets that stock foreign publications. The other thing you'll find is women's erotica – any shop that supplies English-language fiction has a selection of this stuff. Why? We've no idea.

If copper-tone bodies and tremulous clinches aren't your thing, English and French-language books about Syria are fairly abundant, although only those which concentrate on art and architecture; society, history and politics are all seemingly highly subjective areas in which wilful foreign writers tend to stray too far from the official line.

None of the books we list below are available in Syria, except where noted. No traveller, by the way, as far as we know, has ever had any books taken off them so don't worry about carrying these 'nonsanctioned' titles. In fact, the previous edition of this guide wasn't permitted to be sold in Syria (how this one will fare we don't yet know) but there was, thankfully, no hustling of LP travellers out of the country.

As to be expected, Damascus has the best bookshops. Elsewhere try five-star hotels; more information is given under individual city entries.

Lonely Planet

As well as this book, Lonely Planet also publishes books devoted to Syria's neighbours in the *Israel & the Palestinian Territories*, *Jordan*, *Lebanon* and *Turkey* guidebooks. Travellers contemplating a longer swing through several countries of the Middle East should check out other Lonely Planet titles to the area, particularly *Middle East* (which also takes in Libya, Egypt, Jordan, Lebanon, Israel & the Palestinian Territories, Turkey, Iran, Iraq, the Gulf States and Yemen) *Iran*, *Egypt* and *Istanbul to Cairo*.

Guidebooks

A ragbag of slim booklets to specific sites such as Palmyra, Bosra and Ebla can occasionally be turned up on the dusty shelves of museums or bookshops throughout Syria.

These are generally pretty old and appallingly translated but sometimes they contain some interesting information nonetheless. Otherwise there are two very good international guides to Syria's old stones:

Monuments of Syria: An Historical Guide, by Ross Burns. The best companion for touring the country, this is a wonderfully comprehensive and opinionated gazetteer of Syria's castles, Islamic monuments and archaeological sites – although again, save for how to find the places, it contains no practical information. It's widely available in Syria in a cheap locally published edition.

Syria – An Historical and Architectural Guide, by Warwick Ball. A bit academic and dry and devoid of any practical information.

Travel

There are precious few travel accounts that focus wholly on Syria, largely because up until this century an independent political entity called Syria didn't exist. Historically, Damascus and maybe Aleppo were often visited as part of a greater tour of the Holy Lands and they appear in this context in Mark Twain's *Innocents Abroad* and in Alexander Kingslake's *Eothen*, both classics of travel literature and both still in print. Even in the travel literature of today, though, Syria is still somewhere passed through enroute and it's rarely treated as a destination in its own right. Paul Theroux ticks off the major sites in Syria as part of his tour around the eastern Mediterranean recounted in *The Pillars of Hercules*, while historian Garrie Hutchinson spends time in Damascus as part of his pilgrimage to the places at which Aussie soldiers fought during the Middle Eastern campaigns of WWI and WWII, recounted in *An Australian Odyssey: From Giza to Gallipoli*.

Cleopatra's Wedding Present, by Robert Tewdwr Moss. Written by a foppish gay journalist ('Perfume is the one luxury I allow myself when travelling into the unknown.') this is a very individual take on Syria. His experiences (such as an affair with a Palestinian commando) are unlikely to be shared by many but they do make for entertaining reading.

Come Tell Me How You Live, by Agatha Christie. An autobiographical account of Christie's time in the Middle East with her husband Max Mallowan which conveys a fascinating picture of archaeology and life in the desert areas in the middle of the 20th century. Republished in 1999. (See the boxed text on the couple in The Euphrates River chapter.)

From the Holy Mountain, by William Dalrymple. Not strictly about Syria, this is a ramble through eastern Christendom revisiting, 1500 years on, places described in a 6th century record left by a wandering monk. The potentially heavy subject matter is handled with a light touch and the book is warm and frequently funny despite its pessimistic prognosis.

Mirror to Damascus, by Colin Thubron. One of the earliest books written by this now fêted travel writer and not one of his best.

Syria: The Desert & the Sown, by Gertrude Bell. A sympathetic and quirky account of the area known as Syria prior to WWI, then an ill-defined province of the crumbling Ottoman empire, written by a remarkable Victorian adventuress.

History & Politics

The Assassins, by Bernard Lewis. A slim but authoritative book that demolishes a few myths but strips away none of the interest.

Crusader Castles, by TE Lawrence. A personal account of Lawrence's travels around the castles of Syria in 1909, this also contains photographs and plans. Although he never intended this thesis to be published (it's written from a dilettante's perspective) it is a thoroughly readable tract.

The Crusades Through Arab Eyes, by Amin Maalouf. The title is self-explanatory but it belies what a fascinating read this is, heavily supported by contemporary eyewitness accounts.

A History of the Crusades, by Steven Runcimen. The classic work on the subject – at least as far as the west is concerned – although at three volumes it's hardly what you'd call concise.

Saladin, by Tariq Ali. A fictionalised account of the life of the Crusaders' nemesis, Salah ad-Din (Saladin), that intertwines the history with sex and scheming but still comes across as authentic and very enjoyable.

The Struggle for Syria, by Patrick Seale. A highly readable account by a British journalist of the political intrigues in Syria from independence in 1945 until the ultimately aborted attempts at pan-Arab union in 1958.

Syria: An Historical Appreciation, by Robin Fedden. Despite first being published almost 50 years ago now, this still remains the best book on Syria. It's an engaging travelogue, heavy on history but written in a very accessible style. And it's surprising to note just how little has changed in the intervening time. Out of print, but you may be able to pick it up second hand.

Culture & Society

The Gates of Damascus, by Lieve Joris. Through her friendship with a local woman and her family, Belgian author Joris paints an insightful portrait of contemporary Syria that goes far deeper than a traveller's tale. It's grim and claustrophobic and a million miles from the Syria most visitors will encounter, but that's perhaps all the more reason for reading it.

Wilder Shores of Love, by Lesley Blanch. The biographies of four 19th century European women whose lives became linked with the Middle East. Isabel Burton, wife of Sir Richard (see the boxed text in the Damascus chapter) is included, as is Lady Jane Digby, who married a Bedouin chief who controlled the route to Palmyra.

Art & Architecture

Arts & Crafts of Syria, by Johannes Kalter. A weighty, heavily illustrated coffee-table book that focuses mainly on clothing and jewellery, particularly of the Bedouin.

The Bazaar, by Walter M Weiss. This looks at bazaars and souqs all across the Middle East but, of course, those of Damascus and Aleppo are featured prominently. The text is a little lightweight but the photography is stunning – a real 'wish you were still here' book.

Damascus: Hidden Treasures of the Old City, by Brigid Keenan and Tim Beddow. The old houses of Damascus brought to life in engaging prose and beautiful photographs.

Syria in View, by Michael Jenner. Scholarly, but readable and informative, this book explores the successive civilisations in Syria while celebrating the work of archaeologists and historians. Widely available in Damascus.

NEWSPAPERS & MAGAZINES

Although censorship is undeniably a feature of Syrian life, the locals do have a broad range of Arabic-language papers and magazines to choose from, not only from Syria, but from Egypt, Jordan, Lebanon and some of the Gulf States.

For non-Arabic readers, the situation is quite a bit more dire. The country's English-language daily newspaper, the *Syria Times*, is published under direct government control and is predictably big on anti-Zionist, pro-Arab rhetoric and largely acts as a press puff for presidential goings-on. Of more interest is its 'What's on Today' section listing exhibitions, lectures and films as well as important telephone numbers and radio programs. The paper is also very difficult to find and we rarely saw a copy outside central Damascus.

Foreign newspapers and magazines such as the *The Middle East*, the *International Herald Tribune*, *Le Monde*, *Der Spiegel* and *Newsweek* are intermittently available at selected newsstands and bookshops, though largely confined to Damascus. Any articles on Syria or Lebanon are so lovingly removed you'd hardly notice there was something missing.

RADIO & TV

The Syrian Broadcasting Service used to have a foreign-language service with programs in French, English, Turkish, German and Russian. This seems to have bitten the dust – at least a determined dial-twiddling stint turned up nothing – and the broadcast times of this service no longer appear in the *Syria Times*. In any case, the best way to keep in touch with events both inside and outside the country is through the BBC World Service, which can be picked up from about 4 am to midnight GMT/UTC on at least some of the following frequencies: 6195 kHz; 7325 kHz; 9410 kHz; 12,095 kHz; 15,070 kHz; 15,575 kHz; 17,640 kHz; and 17,705 kHz. Some broadcasts are transmitted on medium wave too at 1323 kHz. It is also possible to pick up medium wave broadcasts on 9.41 MHz, 9.51 MHz, 21.7 MHz and 15.31 MHz. Anyone with access to satellite services can pick up broadcasts on AsiaSat. The BBC alters its programming every six months or so, and the British Council in Damascus will usually have the latest information.

The Voice of America (VOA) broadcasts to the Middle East from 4 am to 10 pm GMT/UTC on a wide range of frequencies, including: 792 kHz; 1197 kHz; 1260 kHz; 1548 kHz; 3985 kHz; 5995 kHz; 6010 kHz; 6040 kHz; 7170 kHz; 11,965 kHz; and 15,205 kHz. Some of these broadcasts can also be picked up on medium wave frequency 11.84 MHz.

The Syrian TV service reaches a large audience and programs range from news and sport to American soaps. There is news in English on Syria 2 at around 10 pm and in French at about 8 pm.

You can see Turkish TV as far south as Aleppo, Iraqi TV in the east of the country and, since jamming was stopped in 1994, Jordanian TV in the south.

Satellite TV is technically illegal but it's widely and openly available and all who can afford to, have it. Channels available are predominantly those broadcast from the Gulf like ArabSat and Orbit but Syrian receivers also pick up CNN, Sky or EuroNews. Ironically the most popular channels are those originating in Israel, because of their superior programming (largely US-produced soaps, comedy and films).

PHOTOGRAPHY & VIDEO

Syria is full of great photo opportunities. Early morning and late afternoon are the best times as during the rest of the day the sunlight can be too bright and the sky too hazy, resulting in washed-out photos. There are a few remedies for this: a polarisation filter will cut glare and reflection off sand and water; a lens hood will cut some of the glare; and Kodachrome film with an ASA of 64 or 25 and Fujichrome 50 and 100 are good slide films to use when the sun is bright.

Cameras and lenses collect dust quickly in Syria but lens paper and cleaner are difficult to find, so bring your own. A dust brush is also useful.

Film & Equipment

In Damascus and Aleppo there's a good choice of film available including Ektachrome, Elite, Kodak Gold and K-Max film, sold at specialist photo shops that seem to take pretty good care of their stock. Film generally costs as much as, if not more than, it does in the west.

Colour print processing costs vary depending where you go, but in Damascus we paid S£25 for processing plus S£10 per print and the quality was fine.

Restrictions

Be careful when taking photos of anything other than tourist sites. It is forbidden to photograph bridges, train stations, anything military, airports and any other public works. If anyone kicks up a fuss when you point your camera apologise and get the message across that you're just a 'dumb tourist' who doesn't know any better.

Syrians are also sensitive about the negative aspects of their country. It is not uncommon for someone to yell at you when you're trying to take photos of things like a crowded bus, a dilapidated building or a donkey cart full of garbage.

Photographing People

It can sometimes be tricky taking photos of people, so it's always better to ask first. Children will almost always say yes, but their parents or other adults might say no. Some Muslims believe that taking photos of children casts an 'evil eye' upon them. And similar attitudes sometimes apply to taking photographs of women, especially in the countryside.

TIME

Syria is two hours ahead of GMT/UTC in winter (October to March) and three hours ahead in summer (April to September).

One important thing to bear in mind regarding time is that Syrians always seem to have plenty of it – something that should take five minutes will invariably take an hour. Trying to speed things up will only lead to frustration. Take it philosophically and don't try to fight it – a bit of patience goes a long way here.

ELECTRICITY

The current in Syria is 220 volts, 50 AC. Sockets are the two-pronged variety.

A lot of Syria's electricity is generated using thermal power, but the single biggest source of electricity is the hydroelectric generating station at the Lake Al-Assad

dam on the Euphrates River. Daily power cuts seem largely a thing of the past, although they do occur occasionally.

WEIGHTS & MEASURES

Syria uses the metric system. There is a standard conversion table at the back of this book.

LAUNDRY

Syria's laundries are not always that easy to find, so if you want to use one ask at your hotel where the nearest is. It may organise things for you. Be aware though that the going rate is a pricey S£25 to S£35 an item. We're not talking about one hour laundromats either – expect anything from 24 hours to a three or four day turnaround time. Don't be surprised to find things scribbled in wash-resistant black felt pen inside your garments – that's just to remind them who they belong to. And if you don't like your jeans with sharp creases down the front emphasise that they are not, repeat not, to be pressed!

TOILETS

Toilets are generally the hole-in-the-floor variety and are, in fact, far more hygienic than sit-on toilets, as only your covered feet come into contact with anything. It takes a little while to master the squatting technique without losing everything from your pockets. Carry your own toilet paper or tissues, or adopt the local habit of using your left hand and water. There is always a tap at a convenient height for this purpose – whether any water comes out is something else again!

Remember, for the sake of those who come after you, that the little basket usually provided is for your toilet paper. Trying to flush it will soon clog the system.

HEALTH

Travel health depends on your predeparture preparations, your daily health care while travelling and how you handle any medical problem that does develop. While the potential dangers can seem quite frightening, in reality few travellers to Syria experience anything more than upset stomachs.

Predeparture Planning

Immunisations Plan ahead: some of your vaccinations will require more than one injection, while others should not be given together. Note that some vaccinations should not be given during pregnancy or to people with allergies – discuss this with your doctor.

It is recommended you seek medical advice at least six weeks before travel. Be aware that there is often a greater risk of disease with children and during pregnancy.

Discuss your requirements with your doctor, but vaccinations you should consider for this trip include the following (for more details about the diseases themselves, see the individual disease entries later in this section). Carry proof of your vaccinations with you, especially yellow fever, as this is sometimes needed to enter some countries.

Diphtheria & Tetanus Vaccinations for these two diseases are usually combined and are recommended for everyone. After an initial course of three injections (usually given in childhood), boosters are necessary every 10 years.

Polio Everyone should keep up to date with this vaccination, which is normally given in childhood. A booster every 10 years maintains immunity.

Hepatitis A This vaccine provides long-term immunity (possibly more than 10 years) after an initial injection and a booster at six to 12 months.

Alternatively, an injection of gamma globulin can provide short-term protection against hepatitis A – two to six months, depending on the dose given. It is not a vaccine, but ready-made antibodies collected from blood donations. It is reasonably effective and, unlike the vaccine, it is protective immediately, but because it is a blood product there are current concerns about its long-term safety.

Hepatitis A vaccine is also available in a combined form, Twinrix, with hepatitis B vaccine. Three injections over a six month period are required, the first two providing substantial protection against hepatitis A.

Medical Kit Check List

Following is a list of items you should consider including in your medical kit – consult your pharmacist for brands available in your country.

- ☐ **Aspirin** or **paracetamol** (acetaminophen in the USA) – for pain or fever
- ☐ **Antihistamine** – for allergies, eg hay fever; to ease the itch from insect bites or stings; and to prevent any motion sickness
- ☐ **Antibiotics** – consider including these if you're travelling well off the beaten track; see your doctor, as they must be prescribed, and carry the prescription with you
- ☐ **Loperamide** or **diphenoxylate** – 'blockers' for diarrhoea; **prochlorperazine** or **metaclopramide** for nausea and vomiting
- ☐ **Rehydration mixture** – to prevent dehydration, eg due to severe diarrhoea; particularly important when travelling with children
- ☐ **Insect repellent, sunscreen, lip balm** and **eye drops**
- ☐ **Calamine lotion, sting relief spray** or **aloe vera** – to ease irritation from sunburn and insect bites or stings
- ☐ **Antifungal cream** or **powder** – for fungal skin infections and thrush
- ☐ **Antiseptic** (such as povidone-iodine) – for cuts and grazes
- ☐ **Bandages, Band-Aids (plasters)** and other wound dressings
- ☐ **Water purification tablets** or **iodine**
- ☐ **Scissors, tweezers** and a **thermometer** (note that mercury thermometers are prohibited by airlines)
- ☐ **Syringes** and **needles** – in case you need injections in a country with medical hygiene problems. Ask your doctor for a note explaining why you have them.
- ☐ **Cold** and **flu tablets, throat lozenges** and **nasal decongestant**
- ☐ **Multivitamins** – consider for long trips, when dietary vitamin intake may be inadequate

Typhoid Vaccination against typhoid may be required if you are travelling for more than a couple of weeks in Syria and other parts of the world. It is available either as an injection or as capsules to be taken orally.

Cholera The current injectable vaccine is poorly protective and has many side effects, so it is not generally recommended for travellers. All countries and the WHO have dropped cholera immunisation as a health requirement for entry. However, in Syria the occasional outbreak does occur; a good sign is the absence of salad, especially parsley, being served in restaurants.

Hepatitis B Travellers who should consider vaccination against hepatitis B include those on a long trip, as well as those visiting countries where there are high levels of hepatitis B infection, where blood transfusions may not be adequately screened or where sexual contact or needle sharing is a possibility. Vaccination involves three injections, with a booster at 12 months. More rapid courses are available if necessary.

Rabies Vaccination should be considered by those who will spend a month or longer in a country like Syria where rabies is common, especially if they are cycling, handling animals, caving or travelling to remote areas, and for children (who may not report a bite). Pretravel rabies vaccination involves three injections over 21 to 28 days. If a vaccinated person is bitten or scratched by an animal, they will require two booster injections of vaccine; those not vaccinated require more.

Tuberculosis The risk of TB to travellers is usually very low, unless you will be living with or closely associated with local people in high risk areas such as Asia, Africa and some parts of the Americas and Pacific. Vaccination against TB (BCG) is recommended for children and young adults living in these areas for three months or more.

Malaria Medication Antimalarial drugs do not prevent you from being infected but kill the malaria parasites during a stage in their development and significantly reduce the risk of becoming very ill or dying. Expert advice on medication should be sought, as there are many factors to consider, including the area to be visited, the risk of exposure to malaria-carrying mosquitoes, the side effects of medication, your medical history and whether you are a child or an adult or pregnant. Travellers to isolated areas in high-risk areas such as the north of Syria may like to carry a treatment dose of medication for use if symptoms occur.

Health Insurance Make sure that you have adequate health insurance. See Travel Insurance under Visas & Documents earlier in this chapter.

Travel Health Guides If you are planning to be away or travelling in remote areas for a long period of time, you may like to consider taking a more detailed health guide.

CDC's Complete Guide to Healthy Travel, Open Road Publishing, 1997. The US Centers for Disease Control & Prevention recommendations for international travel.
Staying Healthy in Asia, Africa & Latin America, by Dirk Schroeder, Moon Publications, 1994. Probably the best all-round guide to carry; it's detailed and well organised.
Travellers' Health, by Dr Richard Dawood, Oxford University Press, 1995. Comprehensive, easy to read, authoritative and highly recommended, although rather large to lug around.
Where There Is No Doctor, by David Werner, Macmillan, 1994. A very detailed guide intended for someone, such as a Peace Corps worker, going to work in an underdeveloped country.
Travel with Children, by Maureen Wheeler, Lonely Planet Publications, 1995. Includes advice on travel health for younger children.

There are also a number of really excellent travel health sites on the Internet. From the Lonely Planet home page there are links at www.lonelyplanet.com/weblinks/wlprep.htm#heal to the World Health Organization and the US Centers for Disease Control & Prevention.

Other Preparations Make sure you're healthy before you start travelling. If you are going on a long trip make sure your teeth are OK. If you wear glasses take a spare pair and your prescription.

If you require a particular medication take an adequate supply, as it may not be available locally. Take part of the packaging showing the generic name rather than the brand, which will make getting replacements easier. To avoid any problems, it's a good idea to have a legible prescription or letter from your doctor to show that you legally use the medication.

Basic Rules

Food There is an old colonial adage which says: 'If you can cook it, boil it or peel it you can eat it ... otherwise forget it'. Vegetables and fruit should be washed with purified water or peeled where possible. If a place looks clean and well run and the vendor also looks clean and healthy, then the food is probably safe. In general, places that are packed with travellers or locals will be fine, while empty restaurants are questionable. The food in busy restaurants is cooked and eaten quite quickly with little standing around and is probably not reheated.

Water The number one rule is *be careful of the water* and especially ice. If you don't know for certain that the water is safe, assume the worst. Reputable brands of bottled water or soft drinks are generally fine, although in some places bottles may be refilled with tap water. Only use water from containers with a serrated seal – not tops or corks. Take care with fruit juice, particularly if water may have been added. Milk should be treated with suspicion as it is often unpasteurised, though boiled milk is fine if it is kept hygienically. Tea or coffee should also be OK, since the water should have been boiled.

Water Purification The simplest way of purifying water is to boil it. Vigorous boiling should be satisfactory; however, at high altitude water boils at a lower temperature, so germs are less likely to be killed. Boil it for longer in these environments.

Consider purchasing a water filter for a long trip. There are two main kinds of filter. Total filters take out all parasites, bacteria and viruses and make water safe to drink. They are often expensive, but they can be more cost effective than buying bottled water. Simple filters (which can even be a

Nutrition

If your diet is poor or limited in variety, if you're travelling hard and fast and therefore missing meals or if you simply lose your appetite, you can soon start to lose weight and place your health at risk.

Make sure your diet is well balanced. Cooked eggs, tofu, beans, lentils (dhal in India) and nuts are all safe ways to get protein. Fruit you can peel (bananas, oranges or mandarins for example) is usually safe (melons can harbour bacteria in their flesh and are best avoided) and a good source of vitamins. Try to eat plenty of grains (including rice) and bread. Remember that although food is generally safer if it is cooked well, overcooked food loses much of its nutritional value. If your diet isn't well balanced or if your food intake is insufficient, it's a good idea to take vitamin and iron pills.

In hot climates make sure you drink enough – don't rely on feeling thirsty to indicate when you should drink. Not needing to urinate or small amounts of very dark yellow urine is a danger sign. Always carry a water bottle with you on long trips. Excessive sweating can lead to loss of salt and therefore muscle cramping. Salt tablets are not a good idea as a preventative, but in places where salt is not used much, adding salt to food can help.

nylon mesh bag) take out dirt and larger foreign bodies from the water so that chemical solutions work much more effectively; if water is dirty, chemical solutions may not work at all. It's very important when buying a filter to read the specifications, so that you know exactly what it removes from the water and what it doesn't. Simple filtering will not remove all dangerous organisms, so if you cannot boil water it should be treated chemically. Chlorine tablets (many brand names) will kill many pathogens, but not some parasites like giardia and amoebic cysts. Iodine is more effective in purifying water and is available in tablet form. Follow the directions carefully and remember that too much iodine can be harmful.

Medical Problems & Treatment

Self-diagnosis and treatment can be risky, so you should always seek medical help. An embassy, consulate or five star hotel can usually recommend a local doctor or clinic. Although we do give drug dosages in this section, they are for emergency use only. Correct diagnosis is vital. In this section we have used generic names for drugs – check with a pharmacist for brands that are available locally.

Everyday Health

Normal body temperature is up to 37°C (98.6°F); more than 2°C (4°F) higher indicates a high fever. The normal adult pulse rate is 60 to 100 per minute (children 80 to 100, babies 100 to 140). As a general rule the pulse increases about 20 beats per minute for each 1°C (2°F) rise in fever.

Respiration (breathing) rate is also an indicator of illness. Count the number of breaths per minute: between 12 and 20 is normal for adults and older children (up to 30 for younger children, 40 for babies). People with a high fever or serious respiratory illness breathe more quickly than normal. More than 40 shallow breaths a minute may indicate pneumonia.

Antibiotics should be administered only under medical supervision. Take the recommended dose at the prescribed intervals and use the whole course, even if the illness seems to be cured earlier. Stop immediately if there are any serious reactions and don't use the antibiotic if you are unsure that you have the correct one. Some people are allergic to commonly prescribed antibiotics such as penicillin or sulpha drugs; make sure you carry this information when travelling.

Heat Exhaustion Dehydration and salt deficiency can cause heat exhaustion. Take time to acclimatise to high temperatures, drink sufficient liquids and do not do anything too physically demanding.

Salt deficiency is characterised by fatigue, lethargy, headaches, giddiness and muscle cramps; salt tablets may help, but adding extra salt to your food is better.

Anhidrotic heat exhaustion is a rare form of heat exhaustion that is caused by an inability to sweat. It tends to affect people who have been in a hot climate for some time, rather than newcomers. It can progress to heatstroke. Treatment involves removal to a cooler climate.

Heatstroke This serious, occasionally fatal, condition can occur if the body's heat-regulating mechanism breaks down and the body temperature rises to dangerous levels. Long, continuous periods of exposure to high temperatures and insufficient fluids can leave you vulnerable to heatstroke.

The symptoms are feeling unwell, not sweating very much (or at all) and a high body temperature (39°C to 41°C or 102°F to 106°F). Where sweating has ceased, the skin becomes flushed and red.

Severe, throbbing headaches and lack of coordination will also occur, and the sufferer may be confused or aggressive. Eventually the victim will become delirious or convulse. Hospitalisation is essential, but in the interim get victims out of the sun, remove their clothing, cover them with a wet sheet or towel and then fan continually. Give fluids if they are conscious.

Jet Lag Jet lag is experienced when a person travels by air across more than three time zones (each time zone usually represents a one hour time difference). It occurs because many of the functions of the human body (such as temperature, pulse rate and emptying of the bladder and bowels) are regulated by internal 24-hour cycles. When we travel long distances rapidly, our bodies take time to adjust to the 'new time' of our destination, and we may experience fatigue, disorientation, insomnia, anxiety, impaired concentration and loss of appetite. These effects will usually be gone within three days of arrival, but to minimise the impact of jet lag:

- Rest for a couple of days prior to departure.
- Try to select flight schedules that minimise sleep deprivation; arriving late in the day means you can go to sleep soon after you arrive. For very long flights, try to organise a stopover.
- Avoid excessive eating (which bloats the stomach) and alcohol (which causes dehydration) during the flight. Instead, drink plenty of noncarbonated, nonalcoholic drinks such as fruit juice or water.
- Avoid smoking.
- Make yourself comfortable by wearing loose-fitting clothes and perhaps bringing an eye mask and ear plugs to help you sleep.
- Try to sleep at the appropriate time for the time zone you are travelling to.

Motion Sickness Eating lightly before and during a trip will reduce the chances of motion sickness. If you are prone to motion sickness try to find a place that minimises movement – near the wing on aircraft, close to midships on boats, near the centre on buses. Fresh air usually helps; reading and cigarette smoke don't. Commercial motion-sickness preparations, which can cause drowsiness, have to be taken before the trip commences. Ginger (available in capsule form) and peppermint (including mint-flavoured sweets) are natural preventatives.

Prickly Heat Prickly heat is an itchy rash caused by excessive perspiration trapped under the skin. It usually strikes people who have just arrived in a hot climate. Keeping cool, bathing often, drying the skin and using a mild talcum or prickly heat powder or resorting to air-conditioning may help.

Sunburn In the desert you can get sunburnt surprisingly quickly, even through cloud. Use a sunscreen, a hat, and a barrier cream for your nose and lips. Calamine lotion or a sting relief spray are good for mild sunburn. Protect your eyes with good quality sunglasses, particularly if you will be near water, sand or snow.

Infectious Diseases

Diarrhoea Simple things like a change of water, food or climate can all cause a mild bout of diarrhoea, but a few rushed toilet trips with no other symptoms is not indicative of a major problem.

Dehydration is the main danger with any diarrhoea, particularly in children or the elderly as dehydration can occur quite quickly. Under all circumstances *fluid replacement* (at least equal to the volume being lost) is the most important thing to remember. Weak black tea with a little sugar, soda water, or soft drinks allowed to go flat and diluted 50% with clean water are all good. With severe diarrhoea a rehydrating solution is preferable to replace minerals and salts lost. Commercially available oral rehydration salts (ORS) are very useful; add them to boiled or bottled water. In an emergency you can make up a solution of six teaspoons of sugar and a half teaspoon of salt to a litre of boiled or bottled water.

You need to drink at least the same volume of fluid that you are losing in bowel movements and vomiting. Urine is the best guide to the adequacy of replacement – if you have small amounts of concentrated urine, you need to drink more. Keep drinking small amounts often. Stick to a bland diet as you recover.

Gut-paralysing drugs such as loperamide or diphenoxylate can be used to bring relief from the symptoms, although they do not actually cure the problem. Only use these drugs if you do not have access to toilets, eg if you *must* travel.

Note that these drugs are not recommended for children under 12 years.

In certain situations antibiotics may be required: diarrhoea with blood or mucus (dysentery), any diarrhoea with fever, profuse watery diarrhoea, persistent diarrhoea not improving after 48 hours and severe diarrhoea. These suggest a more serious cause of diarrhoea and in these situations gut-paralysing drugs should be avoided.

In these situations, a stool test may be necessary to diagnose what bug is causing your diarrhoea, so you should seek medical help urgently. Where this is not possible the recommended drugs for bacterial diarrhoea (the most likely cause of severe diarrhoea in travellers) are norfloxacin 400mg twice daily for three days or ciprofloxacin 500mg twice daily for five days. These are not recommended for children or pregnant women. The drug of choice for children would be co-trimoxazole with dosage dependent on weight. A five day course is given. Ampicillin or amoxycillin may be given in pregnancy, but medical care is necessary.

Two other causes of persistent diarrhoea in travellers are giardiasis and amoebic dysentery.

Giardiasis is caused by a common parasite, *Giardia lamblia*. Symptoms include stomach cramps, nausea, a bloated stomach, watery, foul-smelling diarrhoea and frequent gas. Giardiasis can appear several weeks after you have been exposed to the parasite. The symptoms may disappear for a few days and then return; this can go on for several weeks.

Amoebic dysentery, caused by the protozoan *Entamoeba histolytica*, is characterised by a gradual onset of low-grade diarrhoea, often with blood and mucus. Cramping abdominal pain and vomiting are less likely than in other types of diarrhoea, and fever may not be present. It will persist until treated and can recur and cause other health problems.

You should seek medical advice if you think you have giardiasis or amoebic dysentery, but where this is not possible, tinidazole or metronidazole are the recommended drugs. Treatment is a 2g single dose of

tinidazole or 250mg of metronidazole three times daily for five to 10 days.

Fungal Infections Fungal infections occur more commonly in hot weather and are usually found on the scalp, between the toes (athlete's foot) or fingers, in the groin and on the body (ringworm). You get ringworm (which is a fungal infection, not a worm) from infected animals or other people. Moisture encourages these infections.

To prevent fungal infections wear loose, comfortable clothes, avoid artificial fibres, wash frequently and dry yourself carefully. If you do get an infection, wash the infected area at least daily with a disinfectant or medicated soap and water, and rinse and dry well. Apply an antifungal cream or powder like tolnaftate. Try to expose the infected area to air or sunlight as much as possible and wash all towels and underwear in hot water, change them often and let them dry in the sun.

Hepatitis This is a general term for inflammation of the liver. It is a common disease worldwide. There are several different viruses that cause hepatitis, and they differ in the way that they are transmitted. The symptoms are similar in all forms of the illness, and include fever, chills, headache, fatigue, feelings of weakness and aches and pains, followed by loss of appetite, nausea, vomiting, abdominal pain, dark urine, light-coloured faeces, jaundiced (yellow) skin and yellowing of the whites of the eyes. People who have had hepatitis should avoid alcohol for some time after the illness, as the liver needs time to recover.

Hepatitis A is transmitted by contaminated food and drinking water. You should take medical advice for its treatment, but there is not much you can do apart from resting, drinking lots of fluids, eating lightly and avoiding fatty foods.

Hepatitis E is transmitted in the same way as hepatitis A; it can be particularly serious in pregnant women.

There are almost 300 million chronic carriers of **Hepatitis B** in the world. It is spread through contact with infected blood, blood products or body fluids, for example through sexual contact, unsterilised needles and blood transfusions, or contact with blood via small breaks in the skin. Other risk situations include having a shave, tattoo or body piercing with contaminated equipment. The symptoms of hepatitis B may be more severe than type A and the disease can lead to long-term problems such as chronic liver damage, liver cancer or a long-term carrier state.

Hepatitis C and **D** are spread in the same way as hepatitis B and can also lead to long term complications.

There are vaccines against hepatitis A and B, but there are currently no vaccines against the other types of hepatitis. Following the basic rules about food and water (hepatitis A and E) and avoiding risk situations (hepatitis B, C and D) are important preventative measures.

HIV & AIDS Infection with the human immunodeficiency virus (HIV) may lead to acquired immune deficiency syndrome (AIDS), which is a fatal disease. Any exposure to blood, blood products or body fluids may put the individual at risk. The disease is often transmitted through sexual contact or dirty needles – vaccinations, acupuncture, tattooing and body piercing can be potentially as dangerous as intravenous drug use. HIV/AIDS can also be spread through infected blood transfusions; some developing countries cannot afford to screen blood used for transfusions.

If you do need an injection, ask to see the syringe unwrapped in front of you, or take a needle and syringe pack with you. Fear of HIV infection should never preclude treatment for serious medical conditions.

Intestinal Worms These parasites are most common in rural, tropical areas. The different worms have different ways of infecting people. Some may be ingested in food such as undercooked meat (eg tapeworms) and some enter through your skin (eg hookworms). Infestations may not show up for some time, and although they are generally not serious, if left untreated some can cause severe health

problems later. Consider having a stool test when you return home to check for these and determine the appropriate treatment.

Schistosomiasis Also known as bilharzia, this disease is transmitted by minute worms. They infect certain varieties of freshwater snails found in rivers, streams, lakes and particularly behind dams. The worms multiply and are eventually discharged into the water.

The worm enters through the skin and attaches itself to your intestines or bladder. The first symptom may be a general feeling of being unwell, or a tingling and sometimes a light rash around the area where it entered. Weeks later a high fever may develop. Once the disease is established abdominal pain and blood in the urine are other signs. The infection often causes no symptoms until the disease is well established (several months to years after exposure) and damage to internal organs irreversible.

Avoiding swimming or bathing in fresh water where bilharzia is present is the main method of preventing the disease. Even deep water can be infected. If you do get wet, dry off quickly and dry your clothes as well.

A blood test is the most reliable way to diagnose the disease, but the test will not show positive until a number of weeks after exposure.

Sexually Transmitted Infections HIV/AIDS and hepatitis B can be transmitted through sex – see the relevant sections earlier for more details. Other STIs include gonorrhoea, herpes and syphilis; blisters or rashes around the genitals and discharges or pain when urinating are symptoms. In some STIs, such as wart virus or chlamydia, symptoms may not be observed at all, especially in women.

Chlamydia infection can cause infertility before any symptoms are noticed. Syphilis symptoms eventually disappear but the disease can cause problems later. While abstinence from sexual contact is the only 100% effective prevention, using condoms is also effective. The treatment of gonorrhoea and syphilis is with antibiotics. The different sexually transmitted infections each require specific antibiotics.

Typhoid Typhoid fever is a dangerous gut infection caused by contaminated water or food. Medical help must be sought.

In its early stages sufferers may feel they have a bad cold or flu on the way, as early symptoms are a headache, body aches and a fever which rises a little each day until it is around 40°C (104°F) or more. The victim's pulse is often slow relative to the degree of fever present – unlike a normal fever where the pulse increases. There may also be vomiting, abdominal pain, diarrhoea or constipation.

In the second week the high fever and slow pulse continue and a few pink spots may appear on the body; trembling, delirium, weakness, weight loss and dehydration may occur. Complications such as pneumonia, perforated bowel or meningitis may occur.

Insect-Borne Diseases

Leishmaniasis, Lyme disease and typhus are all insect-borne diseases, but they do not pose a great risk to travellers. For more information on them see Less Common Diseases at the end of this health section.

Malaria This serious and potentially fatal disease is spread by mosquito bites. If you are travelling in endemic areas it is extremely important to avoid mosquito bites and to take tablets to prevent this disease. Symptoms range from fever, chills and sweating, headache, diarrhoea and abdominal pains to a vague feeling of ill-health. Seek medical help immediately if malaria is suspected. Without treatment malaria can rapidly become more serious and can be fatal.

If medical care is not available, malaria tablets can be used for treatment. You need to use a malaria tablet which is different from the one you were taking when you contracted malaria. The standard treatment dose of mefloquine is two 250mg tablets and a further two six hours later. For Fansidar, it's a single dose of three tablets. If you were pre-

viously taking mefloquine and cannot obtain Fansidar, then other alternatives are Malarone (atovaquone-proguanil; four tablets once daily for three days), halofantrine (three doses of two 250mg tablets every six hours) or quinine sulphate (600mg every six hours). There is a greater risk of side effects with these dosages than in normal use if used with mefloquine, so medical advice is preferable. Be aware also that halofantrine is no longer recommended by the WHO as emergency standby treatment, because of side effects, and should only be used if no other drugs are available.

Travellers are advised to prevent mosquito bites at all times. The main messages are:

- wear light-coloured clothing
- wear long trousers and long-sleeved shirts use mosquito repellents containing the compound DEET on exposed areas (prolonged overuse of DEET may be harmful, especially to children, but its use is considered preferable to being bitten by disease-transmitting mosquitoes)
- avoid perfumes or aftershave
- use a mosquito net impregnated with mosquito repellent (permethrin) – it may be worth taking your own net
- impregnating clothes with permethrin effectively deters mosquitoes and other insects

Cuts, Bites & Stings

See Less Common Diseases for details of rabies, which is passed through animal bites.

Bedbugs & Lice Bedbugs live in various places, but particularly in dirty mattresses and bedding, evidenced by spots of blood on bedclothes or on the wall. Bedbugs leave itchy bites in neat rows. Calamine lotion or a sting relief spray may help.

All lice cause itching and discomfort. They make themselves at home in your hair (head lice), your clothing (body lice) or in your pubic hair (crabs). You catch lice through direct contact with infected people or by sharing combs, clothing and the like. Powder or shampoo treatment will kill the lice and infected clothing should then be washed in very hot, soapy water and left in the sun to dry.

Bites & Stings Bee and wasp stings are usually painful rather than dangerous and there are antivenins for most spider bites, although anyone who is allergic may suffer breathing difficulties, requiring urgent medical care. Scorpion stings are the cause of illness and occasional deaths in Syria. Scorpions often shelter in shoes or clothing. A sting usually produces redness and swelling of the skin, but there may be no visible reaction. Pain is common and tingling or numbness may occur. At this stage, cold compresses and paracetamol are called for. If the skin sensations starts to spread from the sting site, then immediate medical attention is required.

Cuts & Scratches Wash well and treat any cut with an antiseptic like povidone-iodine. Where possible avoid bandages and Band-Aids, which can keep wounds wet.

Snakes To minimise your chances of being bitten always wear boots, socks and long trousers when walking through undergrowth where snakes may be present. Don't put your hands into holes and crevices, and be careful when collecting firewood.

Snake bites do not cause instantaneous death and antivenins are usually available. Immediately wrap the bitten limb tightly, as you would for a sprained ankle, and then attach a splint to immobilise it. Keep the victim still and seek medical help, if possible with the dead snake for identification. Don't attempt to catch the snake if there is a possibility of being bitten again. Tourniquets and sucking out the poison are now comprehensively discredited.

Less Common Diseases

The following diseases pose a small risk to travellers, and so are only mentioned in passing. Seek medical advice if you think you may have any of these diseases.

Cholera This is the worst of the watery diarrhoeas and medical help should be sought. Outbreaks of cholera are generally widely reported, so you can avoid such problem areas. *Fluid replacement is the most vital treatment* – the risk of dehydration is severe as you may lose up to 20L a day. If there is a delay in getting to hospital, then begin taking tetracycline. The adult dose is 250mg four times daily. It is not recommended for children under nine years nor for pregnant women. Tetracycline may help shorten the illness, but adequate fluids are required to save lives.

Leishmaniasis This is a group of parasitic diseases transmitted by sandflies, which are found in many parts of the Middle East, including Syria.

Cutaneous leishmaniasis affects the skin tissue causing ulceration and disfigurement, and visceral leishmaniasis affects the internal organs. Seek medical advice, as laboratory testing is required for diagnosis and correct treatment. Avoiding sandfly bites is the best precaution. Bites are usually painless, itchy and yet another reason to cover up and apply repellent.

Lyme Disease This is a tick-transmitted infection which may be acquired in Syria as well as other parts of the world. The illness usually begins with a spreading rash at the site of the tick bite and is accompanied by fever, headache, extreme fatigue, aching joints and muscles and mild neck stiffness. If untreated, these symptoms usually resolve over several weeks but over subsequent weeks or months disorders of the nervous system, heart and joints may develop. Treatment works best early in the illness. Medical help should be sought.

Rabies This fatal viral infection is found in many countries. Many animals can be infected (such as dogs, cats, bats and monkeys) and it is their saliva which is infectious.Any bite, scratch or even lick from an animal should be cleaned immediately and thoroughly. Scrub with soap and running water, and then apply alcohol or iodine solution. Medical help should be sought promptly to receive a course of injections to prevent the onset of symptoms and death.

Tetanus This disease is caused by a germ which lives in soil and in the faeces of animals. It enters the body via breaks in the skin. The first symptom may be discomfort in swallowing, or stiffening of the jaw and neck; this is followed by painful convulsions of the jaw and whole body. The disease can be fatal. It can be prevented by vaccination.

Tuberculosis (TB) This is a bacterial infection usually transmitted from person to person by coughing but which may be transmitted through consumption of unpasteurised milk. Milk that has been boiled is safe to drink, and the souring of milk to make yoghurt or cheese also kills the bacilli. Travellers are usually not at great risk as close household contact with the infected person is usually required before the disease is passed on. You may need to have a TB test before you travel as this can help diagnose the disease later if you become ill.

Typhus This disease is spread by ticks, mites or lice. It begins with fever, chills, headache and muscle pains followed a few days later by a body rash. There is often a large painful sore at the site of the bite and nearby lymph nodes are swollen and painful. Typhus can be treated under medical supervision. Seek local advice in areas where ticks pose a danger. An insect repellent can help, and walkers in tick-infested areas should consider having their boots and trousers impregnated with benzyl benzoate and dibutylphthalate.

Women's Health
Gynaecological Problems Antibiotic use, synthetic underwear, sweating and contraceptive pills can lead to fungal vaginal infections, especially when travelling in hot climates. Fungal infections are characterised by a rash, itch and discharge and can be treated with a vinegar or lemon-juice douche, or with yoghurt. Nystatin, miconazole or clotrimazole pessaries or vaginal cream are the usual treatment. Maintaining good personal hygiene and wearing loose-fitting clothes and cotton underwear may help prevent these infections.

Sexually transmitted infections are a major cause of vaginal problems. Symptoms include a smelly discharge, painful intercourse and sometimes a burning sensation when urinating. Medical attention should be sought and male sexual partners must also be treated. Remember that in addition to these diseases HIV or hepatitis B may also be acquired during unprotected sex. Besides abstinence, the best thing is to practise safe sex using condoms.

Pregnancy It is not advisable to travel to some places while pregnant as some vaccinations normally used to prevent serious diseases are not advisable during pregnancy (eg yellow fever). In addition, some diseases are much more serious for the mother (and may increase the risk of a stillborn child) in pregnancy (eg malaria).

Most miscarriages occur during the first three months of pregnancy. Miscarriage is not uncommon and can occasionally lead to severe bleeding. The last three months should also be spent within reasonable distance of good medical care. A baby born as early as 24 weeks stands a chance of survival, but only in a good modern hospital. Pregnant women should avoid all unnecessary medication and vaccinations. Malarial prophylactics should still be taken where needed. Additional care should be taken to prevent illness and particular attention should be paid to diet and nutrition. Alcohol and nicotine, for example, should be avoided.

WOMEN TRAVELLERS
Attitudes to Women
Some of the biggest misunderstandings between locals and visitors occur over the issue of women. Half-truths and stereotypes exist on both sides: many westerners assume all Syrian women are veiled, repressed victims, while a large number of Syrians see western women as sex-obsessed and immoral.

For many Syrians, both men and women, the role of a woman is specifically defined: she is mother and matron of the household. The man is the provider. However, as with any society, generalisations can mislead and the reality is far more nuanced. There are thousands of middle and upper middle class professional women in Syria who, like their counterparts in the west, juggle work and family responsibilities. Among the working classes, where adherence to tradition is strongest, the ideal may be for women to concentrate on home and family, but economic reality means that millions of women are forced to work (but are generally still responsible for all domestic chores).

The issue of sex is where the differences between western and Syrian women are most apparent. Premarital sex (or, indeed, any sex outside marriage) is taboo in Syria, although, as with anything forbidden, it still happens. Nevertheless, it is the exception rather than the rule – and that goes for men as well as women. However, for women the issue is potentially far more serious. With the possible exception of the upper classes, women are expected to be virgins when they get married and a family's reputation can rest upon this point. In such a context, the restrictions placed on a young girl – no matter how onerous they may seem to a westerner – are intended to protect her and her reputation from the potentially disastrous attentions of men.

The problem is exacerbated by the fact that a man has to gather a respectable sum of money to become an attractive prospect to eligible women – and their families – with the result that many Syrian men are unable to get married until they are well into their late 20s or even 30s.

The presence of foreign women presents, in the eyes of some Syrian men, a chance to get around these norms with ease and without consequences. That this is even possible is heavily reinforced by distorted impressions gained from western media and, it has to be said, by the behaviour of some foreign women in the country, not least the influx of prostitutes into Aleppo and Damascus from the former Soviet Union. For some Syrian males all fair-skinned women are fair game, regardless of where they come from.

So, as a woman traveller you can expect some verbal harassment – though nothing like on the scale you would experience in

Tips for Women Travellers

- Wear a wedding band. Generally, local men seem to have more respect for a married woman.
- If you are travelling with a man, it is better to say you're married rather than 'just friends'.
- Avoid direct eye contact with a local man unless you know him well; dark sunglasses could help.
- Try not to respond to an obnoxious comment from a man – act as if you didn't hear it.
- On public transport, sit next to a woman, if possible.
- If you're in the countryside be extra conservative in what you wear.
- Be very careful about behaving in a flirtatious or suggestive manner – it could create unimaginable problems.
- If you need help for any reason (directions etc), ask a woman first.
- You may find it handy to learn the Arabic for 'don't touch me' (aa tilmasni).
- Being befriended by a local woman is a great way to learn more about life in Syria and, at the same time, have someone totally nonthreatening to guide you around. It's not always easy to engineer such an encounter but female travellers have frequently been invited home by local women they have met on public transport.
- Don't stay in any places that make you uncomfortable. In a few places we do repeat warnings about specific hotels and hostels that were forwarded to us. On the flipside, the following establishments have been recommended by readers as comfortable and secure places to stay for women travelling alone:

Sultan Hotel, Damascus
Al-Jawaher, Aleppo
Ishtar Hotel, Palmyra
Daniel Hotel, Tartus
Cairo, Riad and Noria hotels, Hama

somewhere like Egypt or Israel. This usually goes no further than irritating banter, proposals of marriage or even declarations of undying love, but harassment can also take the form of leering, sometimes by being followed and occasionally by groping.

You cannot make this problem go away and where possible, you should try to ignore this pubescent idiocy or you will end up allowing a few sad individuals to spoil your whole trip. But on the positive side, plenty of women travel through Syria, often alone, and never encounter serious problems. Just use your common sense.

What to Wear

The majority of Syrians are, to a greater or lesser degree, quite conservative about dress. The woman wearing short pants and a tight T-shirt on the street is, in some people's eyes, confirmation of the worst views held of western women.

Generally, if you're alone or with other women, the amount of harassment you get will be directly related to how you dress and how much skin is exposed. As hot as it gets in Syria you'll have fewer hassles if you don't dress for hot weather in the same way you might at home. Baggy T-shirts and loose cotton trousers or long skirts won't make you sweat as much as you think and will protect your skin from the sun as well as from unwanted comments.

As with anywhere, take your cues from those around you: if you're in a rural area and all the women are in long, concealing dresses, you should be conservatively dressed. If you're going out to an upmarket Damascus restaurant, you're likely to see some middle and upper class Syrian girls in slinky designer outfits and you can dress accordingly – just don't walk there.

Unfortunately, although dressing conservatively should reduce the incidence of any such harassment, it by no means guarantees you'll be left alone.

Restaurants, Cafes & Hotels

Some activities, such as sitting in coffeehouses, are usually seen as a male preserve and although it's quite OK for western women to enter, in some places the stares may make you feel uncomfortable. Quite a few restaurants have a so-called family area set aside for women and if you are travelling without male company you might feel more comfortable in these sections. As a rule, mixed foreign groups have no trouble wherever they sit, including in coffeehouses and bars. In some of the local bars and cafes there is only one toilet – since generally only men frequent these places. This does not necessarily mean women can't use them but you should be aware of this unwitting unisex situation before settling in for a long tea or beer session.

Staying in budget hotels can sometimes be problematic if you're alone. You may have to take a room for yourself if there are no other travellers to share with, and it's not a bad idea to look around for cracks: a wad of spare tissue paper or the like can come in handy for plugging up key and other holes if you're worried about Peeping Toms.

GAY & LESBIAN TRAVELLERS

Homosexuality is prohibited in Syria and conviction can result in imprisonment. In fact, the public position is that homosexuality doesn't exist in Syria, but of course it's no less or more prevalent than anywhere else in the world. However, this is not the place to flaunt it.

That said, in his travelogue *Cleopatra's Wedding Present* writer Robert Tewdwr Moss describes a few months in Syria during which time he was anything but discreet about his homosexuality – one reviewer suggested the book should have been subtitled 'Camping in Syria'. Neither were many Syrians he met backward about coming forward – he makes Syria seem like one great gay cruising ground with columns and castles for diversions.

And then Paul Theroux spent no more than a few days in Syria researching his book *The Pillars of Hercules* and, as he recounts, a couple of young Syrian men attempted to pick him up in Aleppo. So maybe Syria isn't so closeted after all. We would still, however, definitely advise discretion – public displays of affection by heterosexuals are frowned upon, so the same rules apply to gays and lesbians.

DISABLED TRAVELLERS

Scant regard is paid to the needs of disabled travellers in Syria. Every now and then in the big cities you might come across a wheelchair ramp when crossing the road, but that's about the extent of it.

Before setting off for Syria, UK-based disabled travellers might wish to get in touch with the Royal Association for Disability & Rehabilitation (RADAR, ☎ 020-7250 3222) at 250 City Rd, London EC1V 8AS.

TRAVEL WITH CHILDREN

Taking the kids adds another dimension to a trip in Syria but it also imposes a few strictures. Firstly, it is a good idea to avoid travel at the height of summer or in the middle of winter, as the extremes of heat and cold could make your family journey unpleasant.

With very young children in particular, you will find yourself having to moderate the pace. Keeping the ankle-biters happy, well fed and clean is the challenge.

Always take along a bag of small gadgets and a favourite teddy bear or the like to keep junior amused, especially while on buses. Luckily, you will rarely have to embark on really long journeys in Syria, so this should not pose too great a problem.

Powdered milk is available in Syria but otherwise stick to bottled mineral water.

Kids already eating solids shouldn't have many problems. Cooked meat dishes, the various dips (such as humous), rice and the occasional more or less western-style burger or pizza, along with fruit (washed and peeled) should all be OK as a nutritional basis. Nuts are also a good, safe source of protein and very cheap.

With infants, the next problem is cleanliness. It is impractical to carry more than about a half-dozen washable nappies around with you, but disposable ones are not so easy to come by. As for accommodation, you are going to want a private bathroom and hot

water. On occasion this will mean paying for something beyond the budget range.

Another potential worry is the high incidence of diarrhoea and stomach problems that hit travellers in the Middle East. If your kids get sick, keep in mind that children dehydrate far more quickly than adults and given the dry climate it is crucial to keep giving them liquids even if they just throw them up again. It's worth having some rehydration salts on hand just in case (they do double duty as effective hangover cures). These are available at all pharmacies (ask for 'rehydran') and they can prevent a bad case of the runs from turning into something more serious. Just stir a packet into 200ml of water (the size of a small coke bottle) and keep giving it until the diarrhoea has passed.

The good news is that children are as loved in Syria as anywhere else in the Middle East. Few people bring their young ones to this part of the world, so you'll find that your kids are quite a hit. In that way they can help break the ice and open the doors to closer contact with local people you might otherwise never have exchanged glances with.

For more comprehensive advice on the dos and don'ts of taking the kids away with you, take a look at Lonely Planet's *Travel with Children* by Maureen Wheeler.

DANGERS & ANNOYANCES

Despite being depicted in the western media as a land full of terrorists and similar nasties (many Syrians are aware of and hurt by this reputation), Syria is an extremely safe country in which to travel. You can walk around at any time of the day or night without any problem, although the area around the bars in central Aleppo and the quasi red-light zone in Damascus should be treated with a little caution. This aside, most Syrians are very friendly and hospitable and if someone invites you to their village or home you shouldn't hesitate about taking them up on it.

Tourists are becoming more common currency in Syria, and in some cases this means *your* currency. Independent travellers who have found their feet and at least look as though they know what they are doing will usually pay the standard price for transport, food and the like, but in the end, few completely avoid the odd petty rip-off. Attempts at ridiculous overcharging do seem to be a growing phenomenon – a sad and perhaps inevitable by-product of increasing tourist traffic. In all, the problem is a minor one. The courtesy, generosity and sometimes simple curiosity that are all hallmarks of Syrians remain unaltered.

Theft

The general absence of theft has got to be one of the most refreshing things about travelling in Syria. This is no excuse for inviting trouble through carelessness, but at least you don't have to keep a hawk-like watch over your stuff as you do in other parts of the world.

LEGAL MATTERS

The modern Syrian legal system has inherited elements from the Ottoman system and its French successor. The hierarchy of courts culminates in the Court of Cassation – the ultimate appeal court for cases not connected with the constitution.

The law is not necessarily a paragon of equal treatment. The country is full of political prisoners and the law can be arbitrary in the hands of the government. That said, tourists should have few opportunities to get to know the system personally. Drug-smuggling, long a problem in Lebanon, has been heavily clamped down on and carrying any kind of narcotics (including marijuana/hash) is a foolish undertaking. If you are caught in possession, you could well wind up doing a heavy jail sentence or even being sentenced to death. If you do cross the law in any way, remember that your embassy can do little to help other than contacting your relatives and recommending local lawyers.

BUSINESS HOURS

Government offices, such as immigration and tourism, are generally open from 8 am to 2 pm daily except Friday and holidays, but the hours can swing either way by an hour or

so. Other offices and shops keep similar hours in the morning and often open again from 4 to 6 or 7 pm. Most restaurants but only a few small traders will stay open on Friday.

Banks generally follow the government office hours, but there are quite a few exceptions to the rule. Some branches keep their doors open for three hours from 9 am, while some exchange booths are open as late as 7 pm.

In smaller places, the post office closes at 2 pm. In bigger cities it stays open longer; until 8 pm in Damascus and Aleppo, where it is open on Friday too. As a rule, telephone offices are open much longer hours; in Damascus, for example, around the clock.

Principal museums and monuments are open from 9 am until 6 pm in summer (4 pm from October to the end of March), while others are generally open from 8 am to 2 pm. Most are closed on Tuesday.

PUBLIC HOLIDAYS & SPECIAL EVENTS

Most holidays are either religious (Islamic and Christian) or celebrations of important dates in the formation of the modern Syrian state. Most Christian holidays fall according to the Julian calendar, which can be as much as a month behind the Gregorian (western) calendar.

The following are public holidays in Syria:

New Year's Day
　　1 January – official national holiday but many businesses stay open.
Christmas
　　7 January – Orthodox Christmas is a fairly low-key affair and only Orthodox businesses are closed for the day.
Commemoration of the Revolution
　　8 March – celebrates the coming to power of the Arab Ba'ath Socialist Party.
Commemoration of the Evacuation
　　17 April – celebrates the end of French occupation in Syria.
Easter
　　Different dates each year. The most important date on the Christian calendar.
May Day
　　1 May – official national holiday.

Martyrs' Day
  6 May – celebrates all political martyrs who died for Syria.

Islamic Religious Holidays

Because the Islamic, or Hejira (meaning 'flight', as in the flight of Mohammed from Mecca to Medina in 622 AD), calendar is 11 days shorter than the Gregorian calendar, Islamic holidays fall 11 days earlier each year. The 11 day rule is not entirely strict – the holidays can fall from 10 to 12 days earlier. The precise dates are known only shortly before they fall as they're dependent upon the sighting of the moon. See the 'Islamic Holidays' table for the approximate dates for the next few years.

Eid al-Adha Also known as Eid al-Kebir, the 'great feast', this marks the time of the *haj*, the pilgrimage to Mecca. Those who can afford to buy a sheep to slaughter on the day of the feast, which lasts for three days (although many businesses reopen on the second day). Many families also head out of town, so if you intend travelling at this time secure your tickets well in advance.

Ras as-Sana Islamic New Year's Day. The whole country has the day off but celebrations are low-key.

Moulid an-Nabi Birthday of the Prophet Mohammed. One of the major holidays of the year – the streets are a feast of lights.

Ramadan Ramadan is the ninth month of the Muslim calendar, when all believers fast during the day. Pious Muslims do not allow anything to pass their lips in daylight hours. Although many Muslims do not follow the injunctions to the letter, most conform to some extent. However, the impact of the fasting is often lessened by a shift in waking hours – many only get up in the afternoon when there are just a few hours of fasting left to observe. They then feast through the night.

The combination of abstinence and lack of sleep means that tempers are often short during Ramadan. Although there are no public holidays until Eid al-Fitr (see next entry), it is difficult to get anything done because of erratic hours. Almost everything closes in the afternoon or has shorter daytime hours; this does not apply to businesses that cater to foreign tourists, but some restaurants and hotels may be closed for the entire month.

Although non-Muslims are not expected to fast it is considered impolite to eat or drink in public during fasting hours.

The evening meal during Ramadan, called *iftar* (breaking the fast), is always a bit of a celebration. In some parts of town, tables are laid out in the street as charitable acts by the wealthy to provide food for the less fortunate. Evenings are imbued with a party atmosphere and there's plenty of street entertainment which often goes throughout the night until sunrise.

Eid al-Fitr A three day feast that marks the end of Ramadan fasting – see the comments for Eid al-Adha.

Special Events

Probably the only event really worth looking out for is the Bosra festival, which is held

Islamic Holidays

Hejira Year	New Year	Prophet's Birthday	Ramadan Begins	Eid al-Fitr	Eid al-Adha
1420	17.04.99	25.06.99	08.12.99	07.01.00	17.03.00
1421	06.04.00	14.06.00	27.11.00	27.12.00	06.03.01
1422	26.03.01	03.06.01	16.11.01	16.12.01	23.02.02
1423	15.03.02	23.05.02	05.11.02	05.12.02	12.02.03
1424	04.03.03	12.05.03	25.10.03	24.11.03	01.02.04

every odd-numbered year in September. It's a festival of music and theatre that in itself isn't necessarily too much to get excited about, but it offers a chance to watch a performance in the town's Roman theatre-cum-citadel – who cares what's showing, the venue's the thing.

Since 1993, a folk festival mainly aimed at tourists has been staged annually in Palmyra around the end of April. It lasts three or four days and appears to be a successful idea. Bedouin music performances are the main drawcard, and indeed the Bedouins themselves form most of the audience.

Every year, in September, Damascus holds a two week trade fair, of virtually no interest to the traveller, but usually accompanied by various cultural events, while every other year in October/November, the capital also hosts a so-called film festival. This is a chance for locals to see all sorts of foreign cinema, and not overly censored either. It is not quite a film festival in the commonly accepted meaning of the words, however. Rather than a celebration of current cinema and recent prizewinners, it seems more of an historical lucky dip.

For more details on these events all we can suggest is that you check the Syrian official tourism Web site (see Internet Resources earlier in this chapter) or fax the tourism office (see Tourist Offices).

Over the border in Lebanon, Baalbek hosts an international music festival in July and August each year which features orchestras, theatre groups and performers from all over the world. The concerts set in the floodlit temple ruins usually have a fabulous ambience. For more information contact the Web site: www.baalbeck.org.lb.

ACTIVITIES

The heat and predominantly desert landscape greatly limit the types of activities available in Syria but following is a brief index of some of the possibilities.

Archaeology

Most archaeological work in Syria is conducted by university teams. During the drier months of the year there are always teams working in Syria, on sites that range from the earliest settlements (Neolithic) right through the Bronze and Iron ages, and up until more modern times.

Many university expeditions only use student volunteers, but in some cases members of the public can also be accommodated. The best way to find out if any fieldwork opportunities exist is to get in touch with various universities and see if they are involved in archaeological work. Easier still, just do an Internet search on archaeology departments at various universities, or look up general archaeological sites on the Web.

Volunteers should be aware that excavation work is not all beer and skittles. The Syrian climate is often extreme, and volunteers and students are expected to work hard. Some indoor work is available cataloguing or drawing artefacts – illustrative skills can help to get a volunteer a place on a project. Additionally, many archaeological sites are located a long way from the cities, often in remote desert areas. Facilities for accommodation can be limited – some sites operate without running water and electricity.

Nevertheless archaeological work can be a rewarding and exciting experience. Syria is certainly a country where fabulous discoveries continue to be made every year.

Cycling

High temperatures, a limited road network and some fairly dull landscape mean that Syria is not the ideal place for cycle touring. See the Getting Around chapter for making the best of what there is.

Hammams

If you've never experienced a *hammam* (bathhouse), Syria is a great place to try one. Most towns have at least a couple, although the best are in Damascus and Aleppo. For more information see the boxed text 'The Hammam' in the Facts about Syria chapter.

Hiking

There are no organised facilities for hikers in Syria, but one or two possibilities suggest themselves. The desert is not really wonderful hiking territory, but the mountainous strip between Lebanon and Turkey (around the Kassab border crossing) might well appeal to some. See The Coast & Mountains chapter.

You could, for instance, set out to walk between some of the Crusader castles and similar sites. The Krak des Chevaliers, Safita and Hosn Suleiman are all linked by road. Pushing on, you could strike out north-east from Hosn Suleiman towards the Assassin's castle of Musyaf (see the Orontes Valley chapter) and swing more or less westwards towards Qala'at Marqab.

The problem with all this is that you are virtually obliged to follow roads as there are simply no maps available to guide you off the asphalt track. That detracts from the experience, but at least it means a microbus might come your way if you do get sick of the walk. Also worth bearing in mind is that in many small villages there are no hotels or banks. Weather is another important consideration. In summer it is really too hot for this sort of caper, and winter can be miserably wet and bitterly cold.

LANGUAGE COURSES

If you develop a more than passing interest in the Arabic language, there are several options in Damascus. The Arabic Teaching Institute for Foreigners (☎ 222 1538), PO Box 9340, Jadet ash-Shafei No 3, Mezzeh-Villat Sharqiyya, Damascus, has two courses a year: from June to September and October to May. Tuition is in classical Arabic only and costs US$450 a term. Classes are held from 9 am to noon daily, and the institute makes no distinction in fees between the two terms, even though the winter term is patently longer. The quality of tuition appears to be quite variable. AIDS tests are compulsory for students.

Those wishing to stay long-term in Syria should note that enrolling in a language course is one of the few ways of acquiring residence, saving you the hassle of continually applying for small visa extensions, which tend not to be granted beyond the second or third time anyway. A few people

enrol in the course to gain residence and then go off and do something else.

The Goethe Institut and the Centre Culturel Français (see Cultural Centres in the Damascus chapter) run courses in colloquial Arabic, and there is an expensive school used mostly by embassies and foreign companies working in Syria, MATC (☎ 224 3997). Enrolment in these will not allow you to get residence.

WORK
Language Teaching

Just as Syria is not top of the pops as a tourist destination, so it is few people's dream location for work, which means teachers do have limited possibilities. The American Language Center (ALC; ☎ 332 7236) is probably the best place to try your luck, followed by the British Council (☎ 333 8436); both are in Damascus. These are the only institutions that can secure residence for their employees.

Because the British Council is smaller and tends to recruit directly from the UK rather than locally, the ALC should be your first port of call. The school, if it needs anyone, prefers people with a Bachelor's degree and some form of teaching experience. Pay is calculated on a points system, so the better your qualifications, the better your chances of getting a job and the higher the dosh. A TEFL certificate or second language qualification, knowledge of Arabic, postgraduate studies and length of experience in teaching all affect your chances.

The ALC no longer pays in US currency. The bottom rate is S£420 per teaching hour, but bear in mind that new employees rarely get more than about 10 hours of work a week initially. The ALC also likes a commitment to at least six months. The best time to try is shortly before the beginning of a new term. This roughly means: late February, late May, early September and early December. The only people ALC hires directly from the USA are highly qualified MAs.

The local schools, including the language faculty of the Damascus University, all tend to pay around S£100 an hour (around US$2).

Tutoring is another possibility, but that requires time to build up a clientele – tutors generally charge S£400 to S£600 an hour. For tutoring, the best thing to do is contact the ALC for tips and possible contacts.

German and French travellers could try their luck at the Goethe Institut and the Centre Culturel Français (see Cultural Centres in the Damascus chapter for contact details).

ACCOMMODATION

There is only one so-called youth hostel in Syria, at Bosra, and the camping options are very limited. For the most part, it's hotels. You'll find every level of hotel accommodation in Syria, from the five-star, characterless, could-be-anywhere hotels down to the noisy, filthy hellholes that you can also find in virtually any city in the world, all with prices to match.

In the low season (December to March) you should be able to get significant discounts at all hotels including those at the top end – we were told that even the hotels in the Cham chain will drop a double room rate by as much as US$50. In Palmyra, low-season rates can be as little as 20% of rates in the high season. Conversely, during the high-season months from May to September it can be extremely difficult to get a room at any price in Damascus, Hama or Lattakia as these towns are flooded with Saudis fleeing the summer heat of the Gulf. Even as early as April you'll have trouble getting the hotel of your choice if you just turn up on spec – at such times you need to book in advance.

Camping

Officially, camping is allowed at only a few places around Syria such as at Harasta Camping near Damascus. Facilities at these places tend to be rudimentary. A few private hotels around the country also allow campers to set up in their backyard, such as the Zenobia at Palmyra. Facilities in most of these places are also pretty basic.

Budget Hotels

Rooms in many of the cheap hotels are let on a share basis and will have two to four beds. If you want the room to yourself you may have to pay for all the beds, or just as likely an intermediate sum. For solo male travellers these shared rooms are quite OK and your gear is generally safe when left unattended (lock it up, though). Where there are no other travellers about and no single rooms available, solo females will generally have to take a room with more than one bed to themselves. In practice, this generally isn't a problem.

The biggest drawback with cheap hotels is that more often than not they are noisy affairs. Rooms often open onto common TV lounges, or overlook busy, chaotic streets. A pair of earplugs can mean the difference between a good night's sleep and being kept awake by loud chatter, music and the TV. Rooms at the back, away from the street, are usually quieter and sometimes cheaper.

Most hotels will want to keep your passport overnight, usually in a drawer at the reception desk. Initially this is so that they can fill in a standard police registration slip (which sounds more sinister than it is), but the principal motivation is to have a security for payment of your bill. If you tell the receptionist you need the passport to change money or buy a bus ticket then they are generally fine about allowing you to keep it. Most hotels now have hot water at least in the evening or early morning but this is not always the case, so you should always ask.

With a handful of truly notable exceptions throughout the country, the bottom level hotels are fairly simple affairs. Beds come with one sheet (two if you're lucky) and, in winter, a blanket or two, and most rooms have a ceiling fan. Sheets often haven't been changed from the previous guest (sometimes from the previous year) but if you ask you'll generally be provided with a fresh set. Many rooms have a washbasin, but showers and toilets are generally outside. It is always worth looking around a bit, as the difference between basic and bloody awful is sometimes decisive.

You won't often get a bed for less than S£150, and for a single room the bottom rate is about S£250 and for a double S£400. A couple of the better cheapies charge up to about S£350/700 for singles/doubles, but in a few particular cases the difference is well worth it.

Mid-Range & Top-End Hotels

Hotels officially rated two star and up generally require payment in US dollars or the equivalent in another hard currency. In some it is also possible to change travellers cheques for the appropriate amounts. Prices in Syria's mid-range hotels are often overblown – the places are frequently old with antiquated fittings and poor facilities and you may well find yourself aggrieved at the amount you're being asked to pay.

Word on Syria's national five star chain of Cham (pronounced 'sham') hotels is not good either. We didn't stay in any but we talked to numerous people who had and common complaints were of poor service, inadequate facilities and gloomy, Soviet-style interiors. One notable exception was the Cham Palace in Damascus, which is reportedly significantly better than its sister hotels. Unfortunately, there are few alternatives to the Chams, with just one Sheraton (Damascus) and two Meridiens (Damascus and Lattakia) to represent the international chains. There are also two Safirs, which are both good, but they're in places that not many visitors would choose to stay: Homs and Maalula. Hope comes in the form of a new breed of private boutique hotels, of which there are currently two in Aleppo and at least one opening soon in Damascus; all of these are in converted historical residences and they are wonderful places, providing uniquely Syrian, but at the same time world-class, accommodation. Credit cards are accepted at all top-end hotels.

FOOD

The food of its neighbours is well known through the worldwide proliferation of Lebanese and Turkish restaurants, but very little is ever heard of Syrian cuisine – which makes it such a pleasant surprise to discover just how good dining can be here. Syrian cuisine is, in fact, very similar to Lebanese,

which shouldn't come as any surprise considering that the two countries only went their separate ways earlier this century.

Dining Out

In the traditional Lebanese manner, meals in Syria usually consist of great numbers of plates of varied *mezze*, or starters. These fill the table and everybody rips off pieces of bread and dips in. Meals are long drawn-out affairs and it's quite usual to linger over the mezze, chatting and drinking *araq* (alcoholic drink), for a couple of hours or more. The meat is often only ordered towards the end of the meal and, as with the mezze, it's ordered to share. Once the meat is finished – which is often quite quickly – the dining is at an end. In a restaurant, this is the cue to order coffee and *narjilehs* (water pipes).

The whole dining experience can quite easily fill an evening, especially as Syrians don't tend to dine until at least 8 or 9 pm.

Note that in some restaurants there is no menu. Syrians often know what they like and like what they know – a menu really isn't necessary. If you encounter this, simply restrict yourself to the standard choices (shish tawouk: yes; suckling pig: no), most of which are described in the following Mezze and Main Dishes sections.

Vegetarians

Although vegetarianism isn't a concept widely recognised in Syria and there are certainly no dedicated vegetarian restaurants as such, nonmeat-eaters will have no problems dining out. While at first glance menus may all look very meat heavy, the vast majority of mezze are vegetarian. At most better restaurants, the choice of mezze can run to 20 or 30 dishes, meaning that you shouldn't be restricted to just endless evenings of humous, felafel and baba ghanoug – see the mezze descriptions in the Mezze section.

Vegetable stews are also a Syrian speciality and they feature on quite a few restaurant menus – however, double check the ingredients as 'vegetable stew' doesn't necessarily mean the absence of meat, just that there's less of it than normal.

Food & Drinks Glossary

Some helpful vocabulary for shopping and ordering in restaurants.

Basics

butter	zibda
cheese	jibna
eggs	beid
fish	samak
milk	haleeb
mineral water	maia at-ta'abiyya
olives	zeitoun
pepper	filfil
rice	ruz
salt	milh
soup	shurbat
sugar	sukar
yoghurt	laban

Vegetables

cabbage	kharoum
carrot	jazar
cauliflower	arnabeet
cucumber	khiyaar
corn	dura
eggplant	badinjan
garlic	thom
lentils	ads
lettuce	khass
okra	bamya
onions	basal
peas	bisela
potatoes	batatas
tomato	banadura
vegetables	khadrawat
zucchini (courgette)	kousa

Meat

brain	mohk
chicken	farooj
kidney	kelawi
lamb	lahma dahnee
liver	kibda
meat	lahma

Fruit

apple	tufah
apricot	mishmish
banana	moz
grape	einab
lemon	limoon
nuts	goz
orange	burtuqaal
pineapple	ananas
strawberry	farowla
watermelon	bateekh

Common Foods

bread	khobz or a'aish
chicken skewered and spiced	shish tawouk
deep-fried chickpeas	felafel
chickpea and sesame-seed paste	humous
fava beans mashed	fuul
lamb or chicken in bread	shwarma
mixed starters	mezze

Drinks

araq	araq
beer	bira
coffee	qahwa
fruit juice	aseer
tea	shai
water	maia
wine	khamr

Street Food

If you are travelling on a very strict budget then unfortunately your experience of Syrian food is going to be less than inspiring. There are a few bright spots, such as roaming sweet potato sellers and hot boiled corn vendors who push their carts around some of the country's souqs. Also look out for the *tamarimoz* man, who sells pancakes spread with black honey, sprinkled with sugar and wrapped around a banana. But in the main, choices are limited to the traditional Middle Eastern staples of felafel and shwarma.

Felafel Felafel is mashed chickpeas and spices balled up and deep-fried. You usually buy felafel in the form of a sandwich, with several balls stuffed inside a pocket of pita-type bread along with salad and perhaps humous. A sandwich like this costs from S£15 to S£25 and, depending on the size, just one can make a substantial snack in itself.

Shwarma This is the Middle Eastern equivalent of the Greek *gyros* sandwich or the Turkish *doner kebab*. Strips of lamb or chicken are sliced from a spit, sizzled on a hot plate with chopped tomatoes and garnish, and then stuffed in a pocket of pita-type bread. Shwarma sells for S£25 to S£35.

Bread

Known as *khobz* or *a'aish* (which literally translates to 'life'), bread is eaten in copious quantities with every single meal. It's unleavened and comes in flat disks about the size of a dinner plate. It's used in lieu of knives and forks to scoop up dips and ripped into pieces that are used to pick up the meat.

Mezze

If there are, say, two of you dining then a spread of maybe six mezze plus bread will usually make for a totally satisfying meal – although some restaurants add a 30% surcharge for orders of mezze only. A more accepted way is to order a selection of maybe four mezze and one meat dish between two. This still works out to be a very cheap and satisfying way of eating out.

The following is a selection of mezze that might be found on a typical restaurant menu; note that because of the imprecise nature of transliterating Arabic into English, spellings will vary (for example, what we give as kibbeh may appear variously as kibba, kibby or even gibeh).

baba ghanoug A lumpy paste of mashed eggplant (aubergine) mixed with tomato and onion and

sometimes, in season, pomegranate. Done well, it has a delicious smoky taste.

borek Triangles of light pastry stuffed with usually either salty white cheese or spinach.

daqqeh Crushed thyme and sesame seeds, a dish of olive oil and bread – dip the bread in the oil then in the spices. Often served as a breakfast dish and said to be wonderfully effective against hangovers.

fattoush Very similar to tabouleh but with the addition of pieces of crunchy, deep-fried bread.

fuul Mashed fava beans with garlic and lemon.

humous Cooked chickpeas ground into a paste and mixed with *tahina* (a sesame-seed paste), garlic and lemon.

kibbeh Minced lamb, bulgur wheat and pine seeds shaped into a patty and deep-fried.

kibbeh nayeh Minced lamb and bulgur wheat served raw like steak tartare.

kibda Liver, often chickens' liver, and usually sauteed in lemon or garlic. Done correctly it should have an almost paté-like consistency.

labneh A cheesy, yoghurt paste which is often heavily flavoured with garlic or with mint.

loubieh French bean salad with tomatoes, onions and garlic.

mashi Various vegetables, such as zucchini (courgettes), vine leaves, peppers, or white and black eggplant stuffed with minced meat, rice, onions, parsley and herbs and then baked. Good when just cooked and hot but less so when served up cold.

muttabel Similar to baba ghanoug but the blended eggplant is mixed with tahina, yoghurt and olive oil to achieve a creamier consistency.

shinklish A salad of small pieces of crumbled tangy, eye-wateringly strong cheese mixed with chopped onion and tomato.

tabouleh A bulgur wheat, parsley and tomato based salad, with a sprinkling of sesame seeds, lemon and garlic.

yalenjeh Turkish-style stuffed vine leaves.

Main Dishes

In restaurants at the cheaper end of the scale, you'll have the choice of eating chicken, kebabs or other grilled meats, or vegetable stews.

Meat Chicken *(farooj)* is usually roasted on spits in large ovens out the front of the restaurant. The usual serving is half a chicken *(nous farooj)* and it will come with bread and a side dish of raw onion, chillies and sometimes olives. Eaten with the optional extras of salad *(salata)* and humous, you have a good meal.

Kebabs are the other standard, available absolutely everywhere. These are spicy lamb pieces pressed onto skewers and grilled over charcoal. They are usually sold by weight and are also served with bread and a side plate. There are a few kebab variants common to most menus:

kebab halebi Aleppine kebab: standard kebab but served in a heavy, chopped tomato sauce.
kofta Ground minced lamb, spiced (often with parsley), then pressed into sausage shapes, skewered and barbecued.
shish tawouk Like a kebab but with pieces of marinated, spiced chicken instead of lamb.

Stews Stews are usually meat or vegetable or both and, although not available everywhere, make a pleasant change from chicken and kebabs. *Fasoolyeh* is a green bean stew, *bisela* is made of peas, *batatas* of potato, *bamya* is okra and *molokheyya* is a spinach-like stew with chicken or meat pieces. Stews are usually served on rice *(ruz)* or, more rarely, macaroni *(makarone)*.

Syrian Specialities Other Syrian specialities that you may encounter in the better restaurants (it's always worth asking) include:

batorsh A base of baba ghanoug on top of which is lamb in a tomato sauce sprinkled with pistachios and peanuts.
cherry kebab An Aleppine speciality served only in season and hard to find but extremely delicious: balls of minced lamb served in a rich, thick cherry sauce.
makhlouba Similar to the Bedouin mensaf (see following), this is rice mixed with chopped eggplant, diced lamb or chicken, and almonds and walnuts. We also had it made with truffles, which was glorious.

Bedouin Cuisine

The Bedouin speciality is *mensaf*. It is traditionally served on special occasions and consists of lamb on a bed of rice and pine nuts, topped with the gaping head of the lamb. The fat from the cooking is poured into the

rice and is considered by some to be the best part. The Bedouin men sit on the floor around the big dishes and dig in (with the right hand only), while the women eat elsewhere in the town or camp. Traditionally, the delicacy is the eyes, which are presented to honoured guests! Don't worry if you miss out – there are other choice bits, like the tongue.

Once all have had their fill, usually well before it has all been eaten, you move off to wash your hands while young boys take away the leftovers and tuck in. The meal is eventually followed by endless rounds of coffee and tea and plenty of talk. If you stay with the Bedouin you may be lucky enough to eat mensaf this way, but you can also find it in some restaurants (minus the lamb's head) in places like Palmyra and the Euphrates region.

Desserts

Pastries Syrians love sugar and their desserts are assembled accordingly; the basic formula is lightweight pastry heavily drenched in honey, syrup and/or rose water. When buying from a pastry shop you order by weight – a quarter kilo *(roba kilo)*, which is generally the smallest amount they are prepared to weigh out, is more than enough for one person.

Many of the pastry shops are sit-down places. You walk in, make a selection and take a seat. They serve your order, some water to swig between each sweet and sometimes a coffee or tea as well. You pay on the way out. They are often good places for solo women travellers to relax. The most common pastry types are:

baklava A generic term for any kind of layered flaky pastry with nuts, drenched in honey.
isfinjiyya Coconut slice.
kunafeh Shredded wheat over a creamy sweet cheese base baked in syrup.
mushabbak Lace-work shaped pastry drenched in syrup.
zalabiyya Pastries dipped in rose water.

Other Desserts Away from pastries, you are unlikely to ever see much in the way of desserts on a menu (Syrians typically finish a meal with fruit). The exceptions are crème caramel, which has been adopted throughout the Middle East as an honorary staple, and *mahalabiyya*, which is a little like a blancmange made with rose water instead of milk. It's often sprinkled with pistachios and, occasionally, coconut.

The Syrians do their own version of ice cream which is made with semolina powder *(sahleb)*, milk, sugar, vanilla and rose water and is very different from the milky stuff we know in the west. It's usually also sprinkled with pistachios. By far the best place to sample this is Bekdach in Damascus – see that chapter.

There are also other, regional specialities such as Hama's *halawat al-jibn*, a cheese-based soft doughy delicacy that is served drenched in honey or syrup and often topped with ice cream.

DRINKS
Tea & Coffee

Tea *(shai)* and coffee *(qahwa)* are drunk in copious quantities. They are also extremely strong and when your body is not used to them, drinking either in the evening is usually a recipe for a sleepless night.

Tea is served in small glasses and is incredibly sweet unless you ask for only a little sugar *(shwaiyya sukar)*. If you want no sugar at all, ask for it *bidoon sukar*, but this is bitter and has a strong tannin aftertaste. In some places you can get the local version of a light chamomile tea, called *zuhurat* (known to some waiters as 'zuzu') and it makes a pleasant alternative to shai.

Coffee, usually Turkish, is served in small cups and is also sweet. It is thick and muddy so let it settle a bit before drinking. Don't try to drink the last mouthful (which in the small cups is about the second mouthful) because it's like drinking silt.

Traditional Arabic or Bedouin coffee is heavily laced with cardamom and drunk in cups without handles that hold only a mouthful. It is poured from a silver pot and your cup will be refilled until you make the proper gesture that you have had enough – hold the

cup out and roll your wrist from side to side a couple of times. It is good etiquette at private occasions to have at least three cups, although you are unlikely to offend if you have less. Coffee is then followed by tea *ad infinitum*. In some restaurants, a coffee-bearer wanders around at meal times offering Arabic coffee. Here the question of refusal is also somewhat related to good form. The man is doing it for a tip, and better-heeled patrons tend to take two or three cups as a matter of course, as part of the ritual of the meal.

Juice

All over the place, you will find juice stalls selling delicious freshly squeezed fruit juices *(aseer)*. These stalls are instantly recognisable by the string bags of fruit hanging out the front. Popular juices include lemon, orange, banana, pomegranate and watermelon, and you can have combinations of any or all of these (for the Arabic names of these fruits see the Food & Drinks Glossary in this chapter). Some stalls put milk in their drinks but you'd be well advised to stay away from this if you have a dodgy stomach.

Soft Drinks

Syrian soft drinks *(gazoza)* are cheap (starting as low as 10 cents) and not too sweet. The orange drinks are called Crush and the coke seems to go by several names. A range of more expensive canned drinks, mostly

Stalls selling freshly squeezed fruit juices abound in Syria.

produced under licence from Canada Dry or simply imported, is also widely available. They include 7-Up and others called Oranta or Double Cola.

Alcohol
Despite the fact that Islam prohibits the use of alcohol, it is widely drunk and readily available.

Beer Syria produces its own beers *(bira)*; the choice is between Al-Chark in Aleppo and the north and east of the country, and Barada in Damascus and around. Both are quite drinkable, although of the two, Barada is definitely preferable. (One local connoisseur reckons Al-Chark is greatly improved by a slight sprinkling of salt – it gives it some fizz and takes away some of the acidity.) The beer is cheap, at around S£35 a bottle from a liquor store or anywhere from S£36 to S£65 in restaurants. Imported beers are usually available in better restaurants and hotels (typically Heineken or Carlsberg) but these tend to be pricey.

Liquor *Araq* is the indigenous firewater and should be treated with care. It is similar to Greek *ouzo* or Turkish *raqi* and is available in shops, bars and restaurants throughout Syria. It is usually mixed with water and ice and drunk in accompaniment to meals. The best araq comes from Lebanon but Syria has a few prized brands, notably Al-Rayan, Al-Mimis and Nadim. Anything else may well bear a closer relationship to aircraft fuel than the aniseed-based drop it is supposed to be.

Various other forms of hard liquor are available in liquor stores, including several whiskies and local concoctions.

Wine This part of the world has an ideal climate for wine *(khamr)* production, so it is really a little surprising there isn't more about. The main wine-producing areas are to be found around Suweida. The output is hardly majestic but it is drinkable. Bought in a liquor store, it is hard to beat for price, with lower-quality bottles costing about S£50 to S£65 and something slightly more acceptable closer to the S£100 mark. Among the latter is Doumani, a decent, slightly sweet red; Muscatel, a rosé; and Faysal, a dry white.

ENTERTAINMENT
There is not a huge range of night-time entertainment to choose from anywhere in Syria. The arts and culture scene is incredibly underdeveloped (see Arts in the Facts about Syria chapter), while bars and nightclubs are few and far between and invariably sleazy. Instead, Syrians tend to rely on their own resources for entertainment and the main social pastime is visiting relatives and friends. Dining out is largely restricted to the wealthier classes. One common resort of males is the coffeehouse, which provides a cheap setting for an evening gathering over tea and narjilehs.

The Coffeehouse
The coffeehouse or *qahwa* (in Arabic the word means both coffee and the place in which it's drunk) is one of the great Arabic social institutions. Typically just a collection of cheap tin plate-topped tables and wooden chairs in a sawdust-strewn room open to the street, the coffeehouse is a relaxed and unfussy place where the locals hang out for part of each day reading the papers, meeting friends, sipping tea and whiling away the time. The hubbub of conversation is usually accompanied by the incessant clacking of *domina* (dominoes) and *towla* (backgammon) pieces, and the burbling of smokers drawing heavily on their narjilehs.

Coffeehouse-going is something of an all-male preserve. With few exceptions Syrian women do not frequent these places. That said, there is no reason why a foreign women shouldn't do so – although if you are unaccompanied by a male choose a large busy coffeehouse in which you aren't going to stand out too much.

In the hot summer months many coffeehouse-goers forgo the tea and coffee for cooler drinks like iced *karkadey*, a beautiful drink made from boiled hibiscus leaves,

The *jalabiyya* is the name of the full-length gown commonly worn by Syrian men of all ages, whether studying the Quran in a mosque, picking up mail or playing in the street.

PAUL DOYLE

TIM BEDDOW

DAMIEN SIMONIS

DAMIEN SIMONIS

RUSSELL MOUNTFORD

An elaborate device for serving cold drinks

RUSSELL MOUNTFORD

A man and his falcon on the streets of Damascus

TONY WHEELER

Smoking *narjilehs* (water pipes) in the cafes is a popular pastime for Syrian men.

CHRISTOPHER WOOD

ANDREW HUMPHREYS

ANDREW HUMPHREYS

PAUL DOYLE

In Syria's souqs you will find everything you could possibly want, from antique coffeepots and *ouds* (short-necked lutes) to baskets of chillies and every type of olive you care to mention.

RUSSELL MOUNTFORD

RUSSELL MOUNTFORD

Top: Gathering sweet-smelling rose petals in Aleppo's souq
Bottom: Make sure you sample some of the brightly coloured, sugar-coated sweets sold in the Damascus souq.

limoon (home-made lemon squash), or *zabady*, yoghurt-type drink. In winter many prefer *sahleb*, a warm drink made with semolina powder, milk and chopped nuts, or *yansoon*, a medicinal-tasting aniseed drink.

With the narjileh there's usually a choice of two types of tobacco: the standard *m'aasil*, which is soaked in molasses, or *tofah*, which is soaked in apple juice and has a sweet aroma but a slightly sickly taste. Filtered by the water in the glass bowl, the smoke is quite mild but the effort required to draw it can leave you quite light-headed. A good narjileh can last anything up to half an hour. When the tobacco is burnt out or the coals have cooled the *rais* (the waiter) will change the little clay pot of tobacco (the *hagar* or 'stone') for a fresh one.

Bars

Although many Syrians drink alcohol, there are few bars. This is because drinking is rarely done without the accompaniment of food. Even if it's only a few plates of mezze, drinking is an adjunct of dining. Therefore, almost all drinking goes on at restaurants. Locals will occupy a table for the whole evening, spending an hour or two over plates of mezze, and maybe ordering meat later, at the same time going through a bottle or more of araq (see the Drinks section), which is generally far preferred to beer. Almost the only dedicated bars that you'll find will be hotels.

Note that all bars except those in hotels are closed and no alcohol is served in restaurants for the duration of Ramadan (see Public Holidays & Special Events earlier in this chapter).

Nightclubs

Other than the belly-dances and cabaret-style performances that the big hotels and touristy restaurants often stage, the only other real possibility is the sleazy nightclubs, of which there is no shortage in Aleppo and Damascus.

Cinema

Most of the cinemas run heavily censored martial arts movies or Turkish titillation, and are only interesting for the (largely all-male) crowds that have no alternative. Of course, the names change, but Steven Seagal and Jean-Claude Van Damme seem to be perennial favourites. The only places you'll get to see anything different are the film screenings organised by the various cultural centres, and at the one upmarket cinema in Damascus.

SHOPPING

While Syria doesn't have much in the way of high street shopping, it more than compensates with its souqs. Every town and village has a small souq of some sort, although by far the best are in Aleppo and Damascus. If you want information on what to buy and where to find it, see the boxed text 'Shopping the Souq' in both the Aleppo and Damascus chapters. The range of goods on sale is phenomenal and the following section is intended to give some idea of what you might look out for. Prices are generally quite cheap by western standards, although you will have to be prepared to bargain hard (see the boxed text 'The Art of Bargaining' over the page).

Carpets, Rugs & Kilims

The markets of Damascus and Aleppo have large numbers of carpet dealers. The disappointing news is that the products, however decent they may be, do not represent the good value they once did. While it is still possible to stumble across a very good and aged handmade rug from Iran, the chances are that what you're looking at was sewn in an attic above you. This is not to say that the carpets are lousy, but it is worth taking a close look at quality. Inspect both sides of the carpet to get an idea of how close and strong the hand-sewing is. If you understand any Arabic, watch the locals haggle with salespeople and try to get an idea of what *they* think the merchandise is worth (bearing in mind that they are looking to use them as part of the household furnishing, not merely as a souvenir).

Designs generally tend to consist of geometric patterns, although increasingly the tourist market is being catered to with depictions of monuments, animals and such

The Art of Bargaining

All prices are negotiable in the souq and bargaining is expected. Prices of souvenirs are always inflated to allow for it. For those not used to it, bargaining can be a hassle, but keep your cool and remember it's a game, not a fight.

The first rule is never to show too much interest in the item you want to buy. Secondly, don't buy the first item that takes your fancy. Wander around and price things, but don't make it obvious otherwise when you return to the first shop the vendor knows it's because he or she is the cheapest.

Decide how much you would be happy paying and then express a casual interest in buying. The vendor will state their price and you state a figure somewhat less than that you have fixed in your mind. So the bargaining begins. The shopkeeper will inevitably huff about how absurd that is and then tell you the 'lowest' price. If it is still not low enough, then be insistent and keep smiling. Tea or coffee might be served as part of the bargaining ritual; accepting it doesn't place you under any obligation to buy. If you still can't get your price, walk away. This often has the effect of closing the sale in your favour. If not, there are thousands more shops in the souq.

If you do get your price or lower, never feel guilty – no vendor, no matter what they may tell you, ever sells below cost.

weight, and all pieces should have a hallmark guaranteeing quality. A hallmark normally indicates where a piece was assayed and a date. Verifying all this is difficult, and the best advice is to buy items you would be happy with even if you found on returning home that the gold content was not as high as you had been led to believe.

The same goes for silver, although of course its monetary value is in any case somewhat lower. For that reason, it is the most common material used by Bedouin women to make up their often striking jewellery. All sorts of things can be had, from crude earrings to complex necklaces and pendants laden with semiprecious stones. It is, by the way, wise to check on the nature of such stone, for example amber, with a lighted match. Black smoke, a mild stench and that melting feeling will reveal the plastic reality of some of the material. Depending on your tastes, a plethora of original and reasonably priced items can be purchased. Take most of the talk about antique jewellery with a shaker-full of salt. It is easy to make silver look very old.

Metalwork

For centuries Damascus was, along with Toledo in Spain, one of the greatest centres for the production of quality swords. Tamerlane forcefully transferred the Damascene sword-makers to Samarkand in the 15th century, but something of the tradition stuck. There is little use for such things these days, but several shops in Damascus still produce them for sale as souvenirs. Production seems rather half-hearted compared with the efforts of the city's Spanish counterparts.

Copper & Brassware From Morocco to Baghdad you will find much the same sorts of brass and chased copper objects for sale. The good thing about this stuff is that it is fairly hard to cheat on quality. Most common are the very large decorative trays and tabletops, but other items typical of the

things – rather kitsch and a poor reflection of Middle Eastern artistic tradition.

Unlike in Morocco, where the distinction is instantly clear, the difference between what salespeople call carpets and kilims seems to be a little blurred here.

Gold, Silver & Jewellery

You can find gold shops scattered about the bigger cities of Syria, but they are at their most concentrated in parts of the Damascus and Aleppo souqs. As a rule, gold is sold by

continued on page 88

THE SOUQ

TONY WHEELER

More than any other aspect of Syria, the souq panders to preconceptions of the 'orient'. It envelops the visitor in smells of spices, coffee and perfumes, seduces the eye with colour and glitter, and assaults the hearing with the sales cries of traders and warning shouts of porters.

But while primarily a place for selling goods, it would be wrong to view the souq simply as a market. That would be like calling the Quran simply a book. The term 'market' doesn't begin to address the central role that the souq has always played in Islamic society. Next to the mosque, the souq is a second cornerstone. According to historians, early Islamic settlements would first build a mosque and then set aside an adjoining area as a marketplace.

Not that the souq is an Islamic invention. Straddling the region where the three continents of the Old World meet, the eastern Mediterranean has always been an area of cultural and commercial exchange. When silk, previously unknown, became the fashion in Rome, a regular caravan route was established to bring bales of the precious fabric from the Chinese Han capital of Chang'an (now Xian) around the Takla Makan Desert to Samarkand and Bukhara. The route then travelled south via Baghdad and Palmyra to the Roman cities of Antioch, Damascus and Gaza. As trade increased, along with silk were brought medicines, porcelain and paper and the art of printing while, in return, gold and precious stones were sent east. Myrrh and incense, essential in early religious rites, were brought from southern Arabia (now Yemen) through the Hejaz to the rapidly developing markets on the eastern Mediterranean.

Such was the volume of trade focused on the ancient Middle East that some Arab peoples, such as the Nabataeans, existed solely on trade. From their rock-cut capital at Petra, this nation of 'middlemen' had their state and economy geared to providing camel caravans and safe passage through the desert and to getting other people's goods from A to B.

Box: Sandals are just one of many items available at the souq.

Right: The Aladdin's cave-like interior of the stone vaulted Souq al-Attarine in Aleppo.

Trade and souqs, therefore, were the established business of the region well before the advent of Islam. Mohammed himself

TONY WHEELER

was a merchant's agent who made the trip from Mecca to Damascus before, late in life, receiving the word of God and setting it down as the Quran. With the rapid spread of the new code of behaviour that was born of a trading desert society, the souq came into its own.

If the mosque catered to spiritual needs, then the souq took care of physical needs. Not only was the souq the place to buy food and provisions but it was also where you would find the barber, the hammam, the coffeehouse and the brothel. In the absence of banking (not introduced into Syria until the mid-20th century) souqs were also the country's financial centres with their merchants effectively controlling the economy. As such, they enjoyed great political clout, vestiges of which remain today. A politician upsets the souq traders at his peril – in nearby Iran, it was the disaffection of the *bazaris* (souq merchants) with the Shah that paved the way for the 1979 revolution.

Cubbyholes and Khans: Make-Up of the Souq

As distinctive as a mosque, the souq has its own immediately recognisable physical presence. Cross the threshold of the souq and the street suddenly narrows and presses in. The sky is cut out and the light dims.

TIM BEDDOW

Left: Copper working is one of the traditional trades that manages to survive in the souq.

Progress becomes difficult as sellers try to distract, buyers get in the way, and the crush of bodies ebbs and flows carrying you in directions you don't necessarily want to go.

Shops in the souq are traditionally no more than cubbyholes that at night can be closed up like cupboards and locked. Since last century, remodelling has created larger spaces with steel shutters that come rattling down at sunset. Some of the stone vaulted streets have great wooden gates and, even today, there are still entire lanes in Aleppo's souq that are shut up and locked from Thursday evening to Saturday morning. A lot of these big wooden gates, however, seal *khans*, not streets.

Medieval motel, warehouse and shopping centre rolled into one, the khans provided for the needs of the merchant caravans rolling into Syria from India, China and Central Asia. Big rectangular or square buildings, their outwardly blank walls had one main entrance – wide and tall enough to admit heavily laden camels and horses – that led through to a central courtyard, usually open to the sky and surrounded on four sides by two storeys of small rooms. On the ground floor these would serve as storage bays, stabling, shops and maybe even a coffeehouse, while the upper floor provided accommodation for the merchants.

Khan building reached its apogee in Egypt during the reign of the Mamluks, who ruled out of Cairo and had a virtual monopoly on east-west trade. Some of the splendid khans they built (there called *wikalas* or *caravanserais*) were up to four or five storeys high. Most of Syria's khans date from the later Ottoman period, when the importance of Cairo as a trading centre was in decline and the Syrian cities were favoured. There are plenty of them – virtually every second building in the old souq areas of Damascus and Aleppo is a khan. Less ostentatious than their Cairene counterparts, Damascene khans are unique in that many of them were roofed over by domes. Often these domes have long-since collapsed but you can still see the remains of where they used to be.

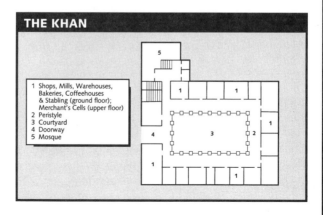

THE KHAN

1 Shops, Mills, Warehouses, Bakeries, Coffeehouses & Stabling (ground floor); Merchant's Cells (upper floor)
2 Peristyle
3 Courtyard
4 Doorway
5 Mosque

Although they no longer provide for travelling caravans, most of Syria's remaining khans are still busy centres of commerce and they continue to provide warehousing, sales or workshop space for modern day merchants.

From Silk to Souvenirs: Wares of the Souq

Silk drove the earliest caravans 14,000km from Asia to the markets of the Middle East, while in the 12th century traders from Amalfi, Genoa and Venice were drawn particularly by pepper and other spices that helped make the Europeans' staple of salted meat more palatable. In the 17th century came coffee, first discovered in Yemen, which spread into Europe through the Turks' occupation of Austria, and was sold via the souqs of Damascus and Aleppo. But what of today? What are the contemporary commodities that predominate?

Spices are still present, as is coffee, but all in much reduced quantities – just a few shops are devoted to each where once there would have been whole areas. (The central and busiest parts of the souq in both Aleppo and Damascus are the 'Souq al-Attarine', the 'Spice Souq', indicating just how big a fixture in the souq this business once was.) Instead, the larger part of the modern souq is given over to clothing and textiles, which, in the case of the latter, has been a backbone of the Syrian mercantile trade since Ottoman times. Damascus, in particular, has long been famous for its fine silks and cloths, hence the term 'damask', meaning a woven fabric with the pattern visible on both sides.

Although the tide of cheap, mass-produced goods has infiltrated the souq – imports from the east these days include cheap synthetic garments from India and plastic household goods from China – a lot of the

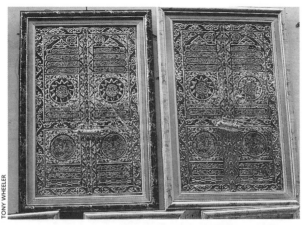

TONY WHEELER

Left: Syrian craftsmanship on display in these works of art for sale in the Damascus souq.

old trades and crafts survive. Fashioning and selling gold and silver jewellery is still important, and still largely carried out by Christians as Muslims consider that the business corrupts the soul. Copper and metal-working maintains a strong presence, as do carpentry, carving and furniture making. You'll still find perfume sellers and herbalists, soap makers and rug weavers and, in Damascus, there are even one or two sword makers.

And that is heartening. The fringes of Damascus' souqs might be taken over by tourist tat, but how wonderful to know that beyond that, buried away in a workshop in some back lane, a man labours over a bench indulging in work that elsewhere in the world died out two or three hundred years ago.

A lavishly produced coffee-table book on this subject exists called *The Bazaar: Markets & Merchants of the Islamic World* written by Walter M Weiss with some beautiful photographs by Kurt-Michael Westermann. In addition to chapters on Aleppo and Damascus the book also features souqs from Fez in Morocco to Samarkand in Uzbekistan.

Right: Trade in spices has greatly diminished but Syrian souqs still have several shops and stalls selling nothing else.

JEAN-BERNARD CARILLET

'There is a street of metal-workers, a street of leather-workers, of dyers, of cloth and silk merchants, and a street of spices, where the most remarkable selection I have ever seen lies piled in sacks, stored in trays, drums and jars. I saw sacks of cinnamon, clove, corriander, sumach, aniseed, aloes, nutmeg, saffron, tamarind, henna, camomile, and many spices whose names I did not know.'

Travel writer HV Morton in the Aleppo souq, 1936

continued from page 82

Middle East include Arabic coffeepots and even complete coffee sets with small cups (the little traditional cups without handles should preferably be ceramic, however). Incense-burners and teapots are among other possible buys.

Musical Instruments

Quite a few souq stalls sell either *ouds* (Arabic lutes) or *darbukkas*, the standard Middle Eastern-style drums. The latter can go quite cheaply, and even the lutes are hardly expensive at around US$40 for a typical model. Such an item's musical value must be considered unlikely to be high – it's the kind of thing you'd buy more for display than to play.

Cassettes

Locally produced cassettes sell for S£60. Quality, needless to say, is bad. As well as cassettes by Arab artists (see Arts in the Facts about Syria chapter for some recommended listening) most places have a limited selection of pirate copies of western artists.

Leatherware

Syria is not particularly good for leatherware. In Damascus you can find wallets, belts, pistol holsters and the like, but none of it is very exciting. There is nothing similar to the quality found in Cairo or Morocco.

Silk, Brocades & Textiles

Damascus, in particular, is known for its textiles, and has been since antiquity. This has to be one of the best places in the world to look for tablecloths and the like. They are generally made of fine cotton and handsomely adorned with silk.

Tablecloths In our opinion, about the most beautiful things to buy in Syria are the heavy Damascene tablecloths. Made from fine lustrous cotton they come in deep reds, burgundies, azure blues and emerald greens, patterned with geometric or paisley-style designs. The best have traditionally been made in Damascus but these are becoming much more difficult to find as far fewer are produced these days. Instead, what you'll often encounter are Aleppine tablecloths, which are virtually identical and equally as beautiful but they're made from a thinner, lighter cloth and are, presumably, not as long-lasting.

Brocade Brocade is another speciality, and the Bedouin-style vests on sale in some of the more reputable shops in the Damascus souqs are very popular. Good ones will go for around US$10. Along the same line are *jalabiyyas*, the long and loose robes that you'll see many men and women getting around in. The men's version tends to be fairly sober in colouring, while this kind of women's clothing can be almost blindingly gawdy.

Souvenirs

A popular buy with foreigners are the woodwork items. They range from simple jewellery boxes to elaborate chess sets and backgammon boards. The better-quality stuff tends to be of walnut and inlaid with mother-of-pearl. If the mother-of-pearl gives off a strong rainbow-colour effect, you can be almost sure it is the real McCoy. Otherwise it is more likely to be cheap plastic. The actual woodwork on many of these items tends to be a little shoddy, even on the better-quality items, so inspect the joints and inlay carefully.

The ubiquitous narjilehs are about as vivid a reminder of a visit to the Middle East as one can imagine. Some of the smaller, simpler ones can start from as low as US$2 or US$3, but ornate ones will cost considerably more. Remember to buy a supply of charcoal to get you going if you intend to use the thing when you return home. Of all the souvenirs you could buy, this has to be about the most awkward to cart around with you – and its chances of surviving the post are not good.

Another simple idea, and much easier to carry around, is the traditional Arab headcloth, or *kufeyya*, and '*iqal* (the black cord used to keep it on your head) so characteristic of the region. Be aware that the quality of kufeyyas varies considerably, with some being very bare strips of white cotton and others densely sewn in red or black patterns. Compare before you buy. Even the quality of the 'iqal can vary. A good set should not cost more than about US$4 to US$5 (S£200) at the most.

Herbs & Spices
Every conceivable herb and spice, and many you will never have heard of or seen, can be bought in most markets throughout the country. Generally they are fresher and better quality than the packaged stuff you'll find in the west, and four to five times cheaper. Exactly how much cheaper will, of course, depend on your bargaining skills.

Getting There & Away

If you're heading to Syria from Europe, you have the choice of either flying direct or, if you've plenty of time, going overland. If you're coming from any other continent, it may be cheaper to fly first to Europe, and then make your way to Syria. Whichever route you take there is always the inescapable search for the cheapest ticket and the certainty that no matter how great a deal you find, there will be someone out there with a better one.

AIR
Airports & Airlines
Syria has two international airports, one in Damascus and the other in Aleppo. Both have regular connections to Europe, Africa, Asia and other cities in the Middle East.

Warning

The information in this chapter is particularly vulnerable to change: prices for international travel are volatile, routes are introduced and cancelled, schedules alter, special deals come and go and rules and visa requirements are amended.

Airlines and governments seem to take a perverse pleasure in making price structures and regulations as complicated as possible. You should check directly with the airline or a travel agent to make sure you understand how a fare (and ticket you may buy) works. In addition, the travel industry is highly competitive and there are many lurks and perks.

The upshot of this is that you should get opinions, quotes and advice from as many airlines and travel agents as possible before you part with your hard-earned cash. The details given in this chapter should be regarded as pointers and are not a substitute for your own careful and up-to-date research.

Most air travellers arrive in Damascus; in fact, it may be difficult to find a flight that travels directly to Aleppo.

For destinations in Africa and the Middle East, there is generally only a choice between Syrianair and the national carrier of the country concerned. Most agents quote the Syrianair fares as the cheapest, although the difference is not always breathtaking.

You must pay for tickets purchased in Syria in hard currency or with a credit card. However, not all airlines or agents accept the main international cards. Syrianair, at the time of writing, accepted only American Express, though other agents selling Syrianair tickets often accepted Visa and MasterCard. With these three cards you should be able to pay for a ticket – you just have to find an agent accepting them. Only residents of Syria can pay for tickets with Syrian pounds.

fares from Syria	airline	one way (US$)
Cairo	EgyptAir	175
Frankfurt	Lufthansa	412
Istanbul	Turkish Airlines	200
London	British Mediterranean	400
Paris	Air France	507
Tehran	Iran Air	272

Damascus Airport Damascus international airport is about 25km south-east of the city. It has a branch of the Commercial Bank of Syria and a next-to-useless tourist office. Note, the bank will not change Syrian pounds back into dollars or any other hard currency – neither are there any shops or restaurants in which to spend leftover cash.

For information on how to get to and from the airport, see the Getting Around section of the Damascus chapter.

Buying Tickets
The plane ticket will probably be the single most expensive item in your budget, and

buying it can be an intimidating business. There is likely to be a multitude of airlines and travel agents hoping to separate you from your money, and it is always worth putting aside a few hours to research the current state of the market. Start early: some of the cheapest tickets have to be bought months in advance, and some popular flights sell out early. Talk to other recent travellers, look at ads in newspapers and magazines (not forgetting the press of the ethnic group whose country you plan to visit) and watch for special offers. Then phone a few travel agents and inquire about bargains. There is little point ringing the airlines direct as they rarely supply the cheapest tickets.

Find out the fare, the route, the duration of the journey and flexibility of the ticket (see Restrictions in the Air Travel Glossary in this chapter for some information). You may in fact discover that those impossibly cheap flights are 'fully booked', but you will be offered another that costs 'a bit more'. Or the flight may be on an airline notorious for its poor safety standards, leaving you in the world's least favourite airport mid-journey for 14 hours. Or the agent may claim to have the last two seats available for the whole of July, which it will hold for a maximum of two hours. Don't panic – keep ringing around.

Use the fares quoted in this book as a guide only. They are approximate and based on the rates advertised by travel agents at the time of going to press. Quoted air fares do not necessarily constitute a recommendation for the carrier.

If you are travelling from the UK or the USA, you will probably find that the cheapest flights are being advertised by obscure bucket shops. Many such firms are honest and solvent, but there are a few rogues who will take your money and disappear, to reopen elsewhere a month or two later under a new name. If you feel suspicious about a firm, don't hand over all the money at once – leave a deposit of 20% or so and pay the balance when you get the ticket. If the agent insists on cash in advance, go somewhere else. And once you have the ticket, ring the airline to confirm that you are actually booked onto the flight.

You may decide to pay more than the rock-bottom fare by opting for the safety of a better-known travel agent. Firms such as STA Travel, which has offices worldwide, Council Travel in the USA or Travel CUTS in Canada are not going to disappear overnight, leaving you clutching a receipt for a nonexistent ticket, and they offer good prices to most destinations.

Once you have your ticket, write its number down, together with the flight number and other details, and keep the information separate from the ticket itself. If the ticket is lost or stolen, this will help you get a replacement.

It's sensible to buy travel insurance as early as possible. If you buy it the week before you fly, you may find, for example, that you're not covered for delays to your flight caused by industrial action.

Travellers with Special Needs

If you have special needs of any sort – you've broken a leg, you're vegetarian, travelling in a wheelchair, taking the baby, terrified of flying – you should let the airline know as soon as possible so it can make arrangements. You should remind the airline when you reconfirm your booking (at least 72 hours before departure) and again when you check in at the airport. It may also be worth ringing various airlines before you make your booking to find out how each can handle your particular needs.

Airports and airlines can be surprisingly helpful, but they do need advance warning. Most international airports will provide escorts from the check-in desk to the plane where needed, and there should be ramps, lifts, accessible toilets and reachable phones. Aircraft toilets, on the other hand, are likely to present a problem; travellers should discuss this with the airline at an early stage and, if necessary, with their doctor.

Guide dogs for the blind will often have to travel in a specially pressurised baggage compartment with other animals, away from their owner, though smaller guide dogs may

Air Travel Glossary

Baggage Allowance This will be written on your ticket and usually will include one 20kg item to go in the hold, plus one piece of hand luggage.

Bucket Shops These are unbonded travel agencies specialising in discounted airline tickets.

Bumped Just because you have a confirmed seat doesn't mean you're going to get on the plane (see Overbooking).

Cancellation Penalties If you have to cancel or change a discounted ticket, there are often heavy penalties involved; insurance can sometimes be taken out against these penalties. Some airlines impose penalties on regular tickets as well, particularly against 'no-show' passengers.

Check-In Airlines ask you to check in a certain time ahead of the flight departure (usually one to two hours on international flights). If you fail to check in on time and the flight is overbooked, the airline can cancel your booking and give your seat to somebody else.

Confirmation Having a ticket written out with the flight and date you want doesn't mean you have a seat until the agent has checked with the airline that your status is 'OK' or confirmed. Meanwhile you could just be 'on request'.

Courier Fares Businesses often need to send urgent documents or freight securely and quickly. Courier companies hire people to accompany the package through customs and, in return, offer a discount ticket which is sometimes a phenomenal bargain. In effect, what the companies do is ship their freight as your luggage on regular commercial flights. This is a legitimate operation, but there are two shortcomings – the short turnaround time of the ticket (usually not longer than a month) and the limitation on your luggage allowance. You may have to surrender all your allowance and take only carry-on luggage.

Full Fares Airlines traditionally offer 1st class (coded F), business class (coded J) and economy class (coded Y) tickets. These days there are so many promotional and discounted fares available that few passengers pay full economy fare.

ITX An ITX, or 'independent inclusive tour excursion', is often available on tickets to popular holiday destinations. Officially it's a package deal combined with hotel accommodation, but many agents will sell you one of these for the flight only and give you phoney hotel vouchers in the unlikely event that you're challenged at the airport.

Lost Tickets If you lose your airline ticket an airline will usually treat it like a travellers cheque and, after inquiries, issue you with another one. Legally, however, an airline is entitled to treat it like cash and if you lose it then it's gone forever. Take good care of your tickets.

MCO An MCO, or 'miscellaneous charge order', is a voucher that looks like an airline ticket but carries no destination or date. It can be exchanged through any International Association of Travel Agents (IATA) airline for a ticket on a specific flight. It's a useful alternative to an onward ticket in those countries that demand one, and is more flexible than an ordinary ticket if you're unsure of your route.

No-Shows No-shows are passengers who fail to show up for their flight. Full-fare passengers who fail to turn up are sometimes entitled to travel on a later flight. The rest are penalised (see Cancellation Penalties).

On Request This is an unconfirmed booking for a flight.

Air Travel Glossary

Onward Tickets An entry requirement for many countries is that you have a ticket out of the country. If you're unsure of your next move, the easiest solution is to buy the cheapest onward ticket to a neighbouring country or a ticket from a reliable airline which can later be refunded if you do not use it.

Open Jaw Tickets These are return tickets where you fly out to one place but return from another. If available, this can save you backtracking to your arrival point.

Overbooking Airlines hate to fly empty seats and since every flight has some passengers who fail to show up, airlines often book more passengers than they have seats. Usually excess passengers make up for the no-shows, but occasionally somebody gets 'bumped' onto the next available flight. Guess who it is most likely to be? The passengers who check in late.

Point-to-Point Tickets These are discount tickets that can be bought on some routes in return for passengers waiving their rights to a stopover.

Promotional Fares These are officially discounted fares, available from travel agencies or direct from the airline.

Reconfirmation If you don't reconfirm your flight at least 72 hours prior to departure, the airline may delete your name from the passenger list. Ring to find out if your airline requires reconfirmation.

Restrictions Discounted tickets often have various restrictions on them – such as needing to be paid for in advance and incurring a penalty to be altered. Others are restrictions on the minimum and maximum period you must be away, such as a minimum of 14 days or a maximum of one year.

Round-the-World Tickets RTW tickets give you a limited period (usually a year) in which to circumnavigate the globe. You can go anywhere the carrying airlines go, as long as you don't backtrack. The number of stopovers or total number of separate flights is decided before you set off and they usually cost a bit more than a basic return flight.

Stand-by This is a discounted ticket where you only fly if there is a seat free at the last moment. Stand-by fares are usually available only on domestic routes.

Transferred Tickets Airline tickets cannot be transferred from one person to another. Travellers sometimes try to sell the return half of their ticket, but officials can ask you to prove that you are the person named on the ticket. This is less likely to happen on domestic flights, but on an international flight tickets are compared with passports.

Travel Agencies Travel agencies vary widely and you should choose one that suits your needs. Some simply handle tours, while full-service agencies handle everything from tours and tickets to car rental and hotel bookings. If all you want is a ticket at the lowest possible price, then go to an agency specialising in discounted fares.

Travel Periods Ticket prices vary with the time of year. There is a low (off-peak) season and a high (peak) season, and often a low-shoulder season and a high-shoulder season as well. Usually the fare depends on your outward flight – if you depart in the high season and return in the low season, you pay the high-season fare.

be admitted to the cabin. All guide dogs will be subject to the same quarantine laws (six months in isolation etc) as any other animal when entering or returning to countries currently free of rabies, such as Britain and Australia.

Deaf travellers can ask for airport and in-flight announcements to be written down for them.

Children under two travel for 10% of the standard fare (or free on some airlines), as long as they don't occupy a seat. They don't get a baggage allowance. 'Skycots' should be provided by the airline if requested in advance; these will take a child weighing up to about 10kg. Children between two and 12 can usually occupy a seat for half to two-thirds of the full fare, and do get a baggage allowance. Pushchairs can often be taken as hand luggage.

The USA & Canada

You are probably better off taking a cheap flight to London and searching around for the best bucket shop deals there. Syrianair has no direct flights from North America, and there are no North American airlines flying this route. If you want to fly direct with another airline, you're looking at about C$1250 return from Montreal in the high season and around US$1200 (with Gulf Air) from New York. Another possibility is to fly to Jordan or Turkey and travel overland from there. Flying to Israel is not an option as evidence in your passport of a visit to the Jewish state will bar you from entering Syria (see Visas in the Facts for the Visitor chapter).

The UK

You won't find much discounting on fares to Syria because it's not a popular destination. Syrianair (☎ 020-7493 2851) has its UK office at 27 Albemarle St, London W1X 3HF. It flies to Damascus on Tuesday, Thursday and Sunday – the Tuesday flight is direct; the other two involve an hour or so stopover in Budapest or Munich. Return fares for stays of two months or less were on special offer at the time of writing at UK£300; normally they are about UK£340.

It is worth shopping around for competition flights. At the time of writing, the cheap flight specialist chains Trailfinders and STA could offer return fares of UK£285 with Air France or Turkish Airlines, both of which involved a change of plane at Paris/Istanbul. Alitalia via Milan was UK£291 and KLM via Amsterdam UK£336. Other than Syrianair, British Mediterranean is the only airline with direct flights: Monday, Tuesday, Thursday and Saturday. The cheapest seats are UK£390 but they must be booked well in advance. All of these quoted fares are exclusive of taxes, which will add about another UK£33 to UK£45 (depending on the route) to the fare.

If you're planning to tour both Jordan and Syria, you should consider flying to Amman in Jordan, as a greater range of airlines serve that city with a wider spread of fares. Another option is taking a charter plane to Adana in southern Turkey and a local bus from there (see the Land section later in this chapter).

Continental Europe

You can fly to Damascus from most European cities with the major airlines including Air France, Alitalia, KLM-Royal Dutch Airlines (KLM), Lufthansa Airlines and Swissair. Syria's national airline, SyrianAir offers direct flights from Paris (twice weekly; return fares from around 3000FF) and from Frankfurt (twice weekly; return fares from around DM1000) as well as frequent indirect flights, often via Aleppo. From Amsterdam, KLM flies direct to Damascus four times a week with return fares starting at f1000. Alitalia flies direct from Milan to Damascus three times a week with return fares from L900,000. Air France also flies directly to Damascus from Paris with return fares from around 3500FF and offers cheaper indirect flights via Budapest, Frankfurt and London. Lufthansa has three direct flights a week from Frankfurt to Damascus, with return fares starting at DM1000. Athens and Istanbul can be good departure points for Syria. SyrianAir have return flights leaving from Athens starting at 130,000dr while Turkish Airlines also has deals with direct return flights from Istanbul to Damascus for 1,000,000TL.

Australia & New Zealand

With the increase in Middle Eastern carriers flying into Australia, fares to Damascus are now pretty cheap, starting at about A$950/1600 one way/return with Malaysian/Royal Jordanian. Gulf Air, Emirates and Egypt Air also offer reasonably good fare deals.

Lauda Airlines and Alitalia also fly from Australia to Damascus. Fares are a bit more expensive on these airlines so expect to pay around A$1100/1760 one way/return in the low season.

From Auckland, Gulf Air flies to Damascus via Singapore. Return fares start at around NZ$2129. Air New Zealand and Emirates also fly to Damascus via Melbourne and Dubai or Singapore. The return fare starts at NZ$2349.

It may be worth looking around for better deals on more popular destinations like Turkey, Egypt or even Greece and then going overland.

Middle East & North Africa

Syrianair has regular connections to Abu Dhabi, Algiers, Bahrain, Beirut, Cairo, Dhahran, Doha, Dubai, Istanbul, Jeddah, Khartoum, Kuwait, Muscat, San'a, Sharjah, Riyadh, Tehran and Tunis. The national carriers of these cities all have offices in Damascus. However, unless you have to fly it is certainly cheaper and more interesting to go overland.

LAND
Turkey

Bus There are at least four border crossings between Syria and Turkey. The busiest and most convenient is that linking Antakya in Turkey with Aleppo via the Bab al-Hawa border station. This is the route all cross-border buses take and traffic can get fairly congested here with waits of up to a couple of hours.

In Turkey you can buy tickets direct from Istanbul to Aleppo (approximately 24 hours)

or Damascus (30 hours), costing US$24 to US$30, depending on which company you travel with and regardless of whether you are going to Aleppo or Damascus. Buses leave daily, usually with five or six departures between about 11 am and early evening.

You will almost certainly have to change buses in Antakya (and again in Aleppo for Damascus), so you could buy a ticket for Antakya and another there for Aleppo, though there's little money saved. If you are looking for a ticket to Aleppo in Antakya, take the cheapest offer, as everyone ends up on the same bus anyway.

If you are really determined to save money you could take a local bus from Antakya to Reyhanli from where you can catch a *dolmus*, a Turkish minibus, to the border; after crossing on foot (a long and sweaty 2km in summer) you can try to pick up a lift on the Syrian side. This can greatly lengthen an already tiresomely slow procedure and the money saved is minimal.

From Antakya you also have the option of catching a dolmus south to Yayladag (these go from beside the Etibank, opposite the entrance to the bus station), from where you pick up a taxi or hitch the few kilometres further to the border. Once across (crossing takes just 15 minutes), you're only 2km from the Syrian mountain village of Kassab, from where regular microbuses make the 45 minute run to Lattakia (S£25) on the Mediterranean coast. To get to Kassab from the border, walk about 10 minutes to the main road at the point where it curves sharply to your right, and then flag down any northbound microbus. (Southbound microbuses will be heading from Kassab to Lattakia, but they'll probably be already full and won't pick you up here.)

From Damascus and Aleppo, there are direct buses to Istanbul and several other Turkish destinations, including Ankara. Fares are considerably cheaper from Aleppo: S£950 to Istanbul as opposed to S£1500 from Damascus. You could make the trip independently by taking a minibus from Aleppo to Bab al-Hawa, crossing the border by foot and then hitching a lift to Reyhanli to catch a dolmus on to Antakya, though the savings in terms of both time and money would be minimal. It's also possible to cross into Turkey from Lattakia, and at Qamishle in the north-east – see The Coast & Mountains and The Euphrates River chapters.

Train Here's one for trivia fans: what was the eastern terminus for the famed *Orient Express*? Istanbul is the wrong answer. It was in fact Aleppo. And at Aleppo travellers could then change trains and catch a service that went via Lattakia down through Beirut, Haifa, Jerusalem and Gaza in Palestine, and on across Sinai and all the way to Cairo. Sadly, that sort of rail travel came to an end in the Middle East soon after WWII when poor relations between the newly emerging states of the region meant minimal cooperation and locked down borders. However, a limited form of train travel between Turkey and Syria has persisted. Traditionally, a train has left Istanbul's Haydarpasa train station every Thursday for the 36 to 40 hour trip to Aleppo, returning on the Tuesday. At the time of writing this service was suspended but it was supposed to resume sometime in 1999.

Jordan

The only border crossing between Syria and Jordan is at Der'a/Ramtha, and it can become extremely congested. That said, it's easy to tackle on your own. You can cross by direct bus, service taxi or by using a combination of local transport and walking. For details see the 'Crossing Into Jordan' boxed text in The Hauran chapter. For details on getting a Jordanian visa in Syria see the Visa section in the Facts for the Visitor chapter.

Bus There is one air-con Karnak bus and one JETT bus daily in each direction between Amman and Damascus. You need to book in advance as demand for seats is high. For details of departure times and prices see the Getting There & Away section in the Damascus chapter.

Train The Hejaz Railway, a narrow-gauge line that was meant to link Damascus to

The Hejaz Railway

Begun in 1907, the Hejaz Railway was a great Ottoman project meant to connect Damascus to Medina in Saudi Arabia by rail. Ostensibly, this was to facilitate the Muslim's annual pilgrimage to Mecca but more importantly, it was a way of consolidating the Turks' hold on the region – the trains were as useful for troops as pilgrims.

This underlying military significance very quickly proved the undoing of the line. When war broke out in 1914 the Hejaz became a strategic target and it was this railway that was repeatedly blown up by Lawrence of Arabia in 1917.

The line had never, in fact, reached Medina and with the dissolution of the Ottoman empire that followed Allied victory, there was never any need for it to be completed. In recent times desultory talks on the possibility of resurrecting the Hejaz Railway in its full glory have concluded that such a project would only be viable if the line were reconnected to the European rail network – a long-term goal of more visionary thinkers in the Middle East, but some way from becoming reality.

Medina for the annual pilgrimage (see the boxed text), is alive and kicking feebly between Damascus and Amman. Train-watchers and nostalgics should be warned that the locomotive is generally a Romanian diesel-run machine, not a romantic, sooty steam job (but some travellers have had the luck to get the sooty version on the Syria leg).

Given the length of the trip, it may as well be a steam train, though. The 10 hour plus excursion starts in Damascus at 7 am on Sunday (or possibly Monday – see the Damascus Getting There & Away section for a note on a new revised schedule) and returns the following day at 8 am. Tickets cost S£157. Be warned, there are no comforts on board like a buffet or working toilets and carriages are battered and dust-filled as half of the windows are jammed open.

Service Taxi Service taxis are faster than the buses and depart much more frequently. Damascus to Amman costs JD5.500 (S£385) either way. Service taxis run between Damascus and Irbid for JD4 (S£300).

Lebanon

The stream of independent travellers heading for what was once known as the Switzerland of the Middle East is gradually increasing. For details on transport options see the Lebanon section in the Around Damascus chapter.

Saudi Arabia & Kuwait

It is possible to go direct from Syria to Saudi Arabia by bus, via Jordan. There are also irregular services all the way to Kuwait. For details inquire at the Karnak office at the Baramke terminal in Damascus.

Bringing Your Own Vehicle

It's no problem to bring your own vehicle to Syria, although you should get a *carnet de passage en douane* and your own insurance. The UK Automobile Association requires a financial guarantee (possibly a deposit well in excess of US$1000, about S£46,000) for the carnet, which effectively acts as an import duty waiver, as it could be liable for customs and other taxes if the vehicle's exit is not registered within a year. It is essential to ensure that the carnet is filled out properly at each border crossing or you could be up for a lot of money. The carnet may also need to list any expensive spares that you're planning to carry with you, eg a gearbox.

Despite this, drivers have brought their vehicles into Syria without a carnet. In such a case, you have to buy what amounts to a temporary customs waiver on arrival. In Syria this costs about US$50, plus possible bribes to grumpy customs officials. Third party insurance must also be bought at the border, costing US$36 a month. This supposedly also covers you for Lebanon, but double-check. The real value of these compulsory insurance deals is questionable, so make sure your own insurance company will cover you for Syria.

Obviously, you will need to bring your vehicle's registration and your ownership papers, but you do not, strictly speaking, require an International Driving Permit – your own national licence should generally be sufficient.

Finally, bring a good set of spare parts and some mechanical knowledge, as you will not always be able to get the help you may need. This is especially the case for motorcycles; there are precious few decent bike mechanics in Syria.

SEA

There are no longer passenger ferry sailings from Lattakia, so you cannot enter or depart Syria by sea.

LEAVING SYRIA

On leaving Syria, have your yellow entry card, or the equivalent you received on getting a visa extension, ready to hand in. There may be a small fine if you don't have it – which could be awkward if you have spent all your Syrian pounds before leaving the country.

Departure Tax

The airport departure tax is S£200. There is no tax for those leaving by land.

ORGANISED TOURS
Australia
Adventure World
   (☎ 1-800-133 322 or 02-9956 7766, fax 9956 7707)
   73 Walker St, North Sydney, NSW 2060. Agents for Explore Worldwide and Exodus in the UK. Also in Adelaide, Brisbane, Melbourne and Perth.
Passport Travel
   (☎ 03-9867 3888, fax 9867 1055, email passport@werple.net.au, Web site www.travelcentre.com.au)
   Suite 11a, 401 St Kilda Rd, Melbourne, Vic 3004. No packages, no brochures; instead Passport assists in arranging itineraries for individuals or groups. It specialises in the Middle East, Syria included.
Peregrine
   (☎ 03-9663 8611, fax 9663 8618)
   258 Lonsdale St, Melbourne, Vic 3000. Agents

for Dragoman and The Imaginative Traveller in the UK. Also in Adelaide, Brisbane, Perth and Sydney.

Ya'lla
(☎ 03-9510 2844, fax 9510 8425, email yallamel@yallatours.com.au)
West Tower, 608 St Kilda Rd, Melbourne, Vic 3000. A wide variety of pick 'n' mix packages and privately arranged tours, including Syrian itineraries.

UK

Bales Tours
(☎ 01306-885 991, fax 740 048)
Bales House, Junction Rd, Dorking, Surrey RH4 3HL. Pricey upmarket tours utilising five star accommodation.

Caravanserai Tours
(☎ 020-8691 2513, fax 8469 3091, email caravanserai@musicfarm.demon.co.uk)
225A Lewisham Way, London SE4 1UY. Specialises in Syria, Iran and Libya, and offers tailor-made arrangements and group travel.

Exodus
(☎ 020-8675 5550, fax 8673 0779, Web site www.exodustravels.co.uk)
9 Weir Rd, London SW12 OLT. Has a very good package covering most of the major sites of Jordan and Syria.

Explore Worldwide
(☎ 01252-319 448, fax 343 170)
1 Fredrick St, Aldershot, Hampshire GU11 1LQ. Small group exploratory holidays with titles like 'Lawrence's Arabia', 'Crusader Castles & Desert Cities'.

The Imaginative Traveller
(☎ 020-8742 8612, fax 8742 3045)
14 Barley Mow Passage, Chiswick, London W4 4PH. Small group tours to a single country with a few linkages (Jordan and Syria, Syria and Lebanon).

Voyages Jules Vernes
(☎ 020-7723 5066, reservations ☎ 020-7616 1000, fax 7723 8629, email sales@vjv.co.uk)
21 Dorset Square, London NW1 6QG. Topclass (and top price) tour operator offering seductively packaged itineraries.

USA & Canada

Abercrombie & Kent
(☎ 1-800-323 7308, fax 630-954 3324, Web site www.abercrombiekent.com)
1520 Kensington Rd, Suite 212, Oak Brook, IL 60523-2141. Classy packages using top-end hotels and domestic flights, and Jordan and Syria package feature on its itinerary.

Adventure Center
(☎ 1-800-227 8747, fax 510-654 4200, email tripinfo@adventure-center.com)
1311 63rd St, Suite 200, Emeryville, CA 94608. Agents for Dragoman, Encounter Overland and Explore Worldwide in the UK.

Archaeological Institute of America
(☎ 617-353 9361, fax 353 6550)
Boston University, 656 Beacon St, Boston, MA 02215-2010. Ancient civilisation tours led by prominent scholars. Itineraries include visits to archaeological sites, ongoing digs and museums.

Archaeological Tours
(☎ 212-986 3054)
271 Madison Ave, Suite 904AB, New York, NY 10016. Specialised tours led by distinguished scholars. Upmarket and pricey.

Bestway Tours & Safaris
(☎ 604-264 7378, fax 264 7774, email bestway@bestway.com)
103-3540 West 41st Ave, Vancouver, BC V6N 3E6. Small group tours to Syria.

Geographic Expeditions
(☎ 415-922 0448, fax 346 5535, email info@geoex.com)
2627 Lombard St, San Francisco, CA 94123. Has a 22 day tour that takes in Cairo, Upper Egypt, Petra, Damascus, Aleppo and Palmyra (US$5290).

Adventure & Overland Safaris

A popular mode of travel through Africa and Asia is by overland truck. This is not everyone's cup of tea, as you spend a lot of time with the same group of people, plus a lot of time travelling, camping and cooking. Organisers of these tours do take over much of the bureaucratic footwork, eg helping out with visas and dodging cross-border hassles. Syria features as a leg on trips run by the following outfits (all UK-based; see also Exodus under UK earlier in the Organised Tours section):

African Trails
(☎ 020-8742 7724, fax 8960 1414)
3 Flanders Rd, Chiswick, London W4 1NQ. Egypt to Turkey in six weeks for UK£600.

Dragoman
(☎ 01728-861 133, fax 861 127, Web site www.dragoman.co.uk)
99 Camp Green, Debenham, Suffolk IP14 6LA. Overland specialists with numerous itineraries through North Africa and the Middle East.

Economic Expeditions
(☎ 020-8995 7707, fax 8742 7707, email eco exped@mcmail.com)
29 Cunnington St, Chiswick, London W4 5ER. Istanbul to Cairo (five weeks) for UK£380.

Encounter Overland
(☎ 020-7370 6845, fax 244 9737, email adventure@encounter.co.uk)
267 Old Brompton Rd, London SW5 9JA. Range of overland tours.

Kumuka
(☎ 020-7937 8855, fax 7937 6664, email sales@kumuka.co.uk)
40 Earl's Court Rd, London W8 6EJ. Istanbul to Cairo over four/six weeks for UK£695/990.

Oasis Overland
(☎ 020-8759 5597, fax 8897 2713)
33 Travellers Way, Hounslow, London TW4 7QB. Five week Turkey-Syria-Jordan-Egypt trip for UK£590.

Getting Around

AIR

The national carrier, Syrianair, operates a reasonable internal air service and flights are cheap by international standards, though out of reach for most Syrians. Bear in mind that, given the time needed to get to and from airports, check in and so on, you're unlikely to save much time over the bus; the Damascus-Qamishle run is the only exception to this.

Sample one-way fares are as follows (return fares are exactly double):

Damascus to Aleppo	S£600
Damascus to Deir ez-Zur	S£600
Damascus to Qamishle	S£900
Damascus to Lattakia	S£500

For contact details for Syrianair see the Getting There & Away sections under individual cities and towns.

BUS, MINIBUS & MICROBUS

Syria has a well developed road network and, partly because private car ownership is comparatively rare, public transport is frequent and very cheap. Distances are short, so journeys are rarely more than four hours. About the longest single bus ride you can take is the nine hour trip from Damascus to Qamishle in the north-east.

In the past few years, a plethora of private bus companies has sprung up in Syria, in many cases offering very comfortable and modern services much like those of the better bus companies in neighbouring Turkey. There are several general categories of bus, although the distinctions are not always clear-cut.

Whatever type of transport you use, carry your passport with you, as the occasional ID check en route is still a remote possibility.

Luxury Bus

The new independent bus companies are designed to supplement the services run by the state company Karnak (see the following entry). The buses operated by these new companies – which throughout this book we refer to as 'luxury' buses – are considerably more comfortable than the older Karnak buses: they are all air-con, have a rigid no-smoking rule, and during the journey staff will distribute sweets and the occasional cup of water. If you're unlucky, you'll get to see a video as well.

Tickets must be bought before boarding and these buses leave according to a timetable – on the dot. It is worth booking in advance, as demand can be high. In the cities and bigger towns the competing companies share a bus station, where you'll find rows and rows of booths, each one belonging to a different company and displaying the times and destinations of its various services. The form is that you quickly shop around to see who has the next bus going to your destination and then see if you can get a seat on it. In practice you don't have to look too hard because bus company staff loudly try to drum up competition for any remaining seats. Usually you won't have to wait more than half an hour for a departing bus.

Ticket prices differ little between the companies, with the greatest variation only ever being about S£5 or S£10 at most. Some companies, however, are notably better than others in terms of service – the cleanest, smartest and most modern buses are those belonging to Qadmous, Al-Ahliah and Al-Ryan.

In some small towns, eg Tartus and Hama, there is no central luxury bus station and it is a matter of tracking down each company's office. In such cases we've located the offices of the better companies on the relevant maps.

Karnak

The orange-and-white buses of the state-run Karnak company were once the deluxe carriers on the Syrian highways. But the company failed to move with the times and with so many rival companies now employing

---

Caution

It can be considered offensive for men to sit next to women on buses – at least next to more elderly and conservative women. If a male traveller only finds free seats next to local women, it would be prudent to remain standing. Often passengers will rearrange themselves so that women sit together, or with family members, and free the spare seats.

---

faster, sleeker vehicles, it looks a poor cousin by comparison. The other problem is that the Karnak network is shrinking and there are fewer services than there used to be. Generally, from any given town there are only one or two services a day to the major destinations and you must book a day in advance. Karnak buses are perfectly acceptable and if you don't mind having to leave at a particular time they are usually a good 20 to 30% cheaper than the luxury buses.

Bus & Minibus

At the bottom rung of the ladder are those buses and minibuses of a hard-to-determine vintage that formed the bulk of Syria's public bus system until the end of the 1980s. While it would appear that they are destined for extinction, for now they are the most colourful, crowded, slowest and cheapest way to get around.

This class of transport is usually kept well away from the shiny new vehicles of the private companies, and most towns and cities have a separate 'old' bus/minibus station and a new 'luxury bus' station.

On the outside, these big old buses and slightly smaller, boxy minibuses look fairly plain, and a little travel-worn and battered, but on the inside they are decorated with an extraordinary array of gaudy ornaments (including plastic fruit and plants, lights and mirrors). The driver usually has just enough uncluttered window to see some of the road ahead. Then there's the cassette player, without which no bus or minibus would be complete. The sound is invariably tinny, the tapes worn out and the volume loud.

These buses are far less comfortable than the more modern alternatives but, if the distance is short, this is no real hardship.

Buses connect all major towns, while the minibuses work on short hops and serve more out-of-the-way places. They have no schedules and leave when full, so on the less popular routes you may have to wait for an hour or so until they fill up. Virtually all these buses have their destinations written in Arabic on the front of the bus; if you can't read Arabic, you will just have to ask and allow yourself to be swept along to the right bus.

Sometimes you are obliged to buy tickets for preallocated seats – those right up the front behind the driver are not numbered but titled *khususi* (special), a spot sometimes assigned to foreigners.

If you find yourself being shunted around by passengers or the conductor as they point to your ticket, it will be because you've actually bought a seated ticket and chosen the wrong seat. On popular routes one reason for all this agitation is that people holding tickets get a seat, while those who pay when they embark must stand.

Journey times are generally longer than with the other buses, as people are set down and picked up at any point along the route. This has earned these buses the nickname of 'stop-stops' among some locals. Conversations on buses will often lead to an invitation to someone's house or village, so try to keep your schedule flexible enough to make the most of Syrian hospitality.

Fares are cheap. For instance, the five hour trip from Damascus to Aleppo costs as little as S£60 – less than US$1.50. Often you will be charged marginally more on minibuses that cover the same route as their bigger siblings.

Microbus

The term microbus (pronounced 'meecro-baas' or just 'meecro'*)* is a little blurred, but in general refers to those modern (mostly Japanese) little vans that are white with a sliding side door, and squeeze in about 12 passengers. These are used principally on short hops between cities (such as Homs to Hama, Damascus to Quneitra or Der'a to Bosra) and many routes to small towns and villages. They are increasingly replacing the clattering old minibuses with which they compete, and are generally more expensive (because they take fewer people). They too leave when full, but because they are smaller and there is no standing room, departures are more frequent. Again, destinations are usually posted somewhere on the front, and in some cases the fares are posted inside, but all in Arabic only.

In most (but not all) cases you pay for the trip on the microbus. The etiquette is admirable. On a request by the driver, the passengers start passing money towards the front of the bus, with one of them becoming the *de facto* conductor. One advantage of this is that you can wait to see what other people are paying before putting in your bit (don't forget, however, that some may pay less for getting out before the final stop). This trust system means you generally need not fear being ripped off.

Holiday Fares

Fares cost up to 25% extra on virtually all buses and microbuses on official holidays (this does not apply to normal Fridays).

TRAIN

Syria has potentially an excellent railway network with more than 2000km of track connecting most main centres. The main line snakes its way from Damascus north to Aleppo via Homs and Hama before swinging south-east for Deir ez-Zur via Raqqa. At that point it turns north-east to Hassake and finally to Qamishle. Trains also operate on a couple of secondary lines, one of which runs from Aleppo to Lattakia, and then down the coast to Tartus and on to Homs and Damascus. The rolling stock is a fleet of slowly ageing trains supplied by Russia in the 1970s.

However, despite the large areas covered, train travel is just not an option. The first drawback is that there are never more than three services a day between any given destinations (and often fewer) and almost without exception they arrive and depart in the dead hours of morning. Not only does this disrupt your sleep but most journeys are made in complete darkness so you don't see any scenery. To compound matters, the stations are nearly all awkwardly located a few kilometres from the centre of town and are poorly catered to, with little or no public transport. Unless you really are a train travel enthusiast you are better off with the more practical, if admittedly more prosaic, buses.

On the trains, 1st class is air-con with aircraft-type seats; 2nd class is the same without air-con. Sleepers *(manaama)* are also available.

For details on the Hejaz Railway linking Damascus with Amman see the Getting There & Away chapter.

SHARE TAXI

Share taxis, which are also called service taxis (pronounced 'servees'), are usually old American Desotos and Dodges from the 1950s and 60s. There's a chronic shortage of spare parts but ingenuity and improvisation keep them running. Although more modern vehicles have begun to appear, most drivers persist with their old favourites – largely for their robustness and size (good for squeezing people in). See the colour section 'Retro Road Fleet' in the Damascus chapter between pages 128 and 129.

Share taxis only operate on some major routes and in some cases seem to have succumbed to competition from microbuses. They can cost a lot more than the buses. For instance, the trip from Aleppo to Hama costs S£150 per person, while on the old minibus you're looking at S£25. Unless you're in a tearing hurry, or you find yourself stuck on a highway and it's getting late, there's really no need to use them.

CAR
Road Rules

Traffic runs on the right-hand side of the road, while the speed limit is generally

60km/h in built-up areas, 70km/h on the open road and 110km/h on major highways.

The roads are generally quite reasonable in Syria, but in the backblocks you will find that most signposting is in Arabic only. Always take care when driving into villages and other built-up areas, as cars, people and animals all jostle for the same space.

Long-distance night driving can be a little hairy, as not all drivers believe in using headlights. Beware also of the mad overtaker. Some people appear to consider it a test of their courage to overtake in the most impossible situations.

Rental

For a long time Europcar was the only car hire firm in Syria, but there are now several major international companies, including Avis, Budget and Hertz. Damascus is the main car rental centre but cars can be hired via rental desks at the Cham hotels in Aleppo, Deir ez-Zur (see Places to Stay in those sections for addresses), Lattakia (☎ 041-428 700, fax 428 285) and Safita (☎ 043-525 982, fax 525 984).

Rental rates are not particularly cheap and are about on par with those you might find in Europe. Budget's cheapest standard rate, for example, is US$45 a day for a Ford Fiesta or something similar, including all insurance and unlimited kilometres. Rental for a week is US$259. Chamcar's cheapest is an air-con Renault Clio for S£1400 (roughly US$30) per day including insurance but with only a 115km allowance. Unlimited kilometres would be S£2400 (US$50). Most of the rental companies also insist on a minimum rental term of between three and five days.

A plethora of local companies has appeared since the early 1990s but be careful with these, as many charge ridiculous rates and don't offer full insurance – if you are involved in an accident you could end up having to foot the bill. Another problem with local agencies is that their cars are not always well maintained and are prone to breakdowns. Back-up services are also inefficient and their fleets are small, which means you could be left hanging around for

a day or two waiting for your hire car to be fixed or replaced. One exception is Marmou in Damascus, although it's not particularly cheap – for a small car like a Mazda 323 (no air-con) you'll be looking at US$55 a day, which includes unlimited kilometres and insurance, but with a five day minimum rental period.

You need to be at least 21 years old to rent a car in Syria, although some places require that you be 23. Most companies will require a deposit in cash of up to US$1000, or you can leave your credit card details.

Cars & Drivers An alternative option that is sometimes available (notably in Hama) is to hire a car and driver for a day. We managed to get a big old Mercedes taxi to ferry us around for almost 12 hours covering something like 350km for US$50 – and no insurance necessary, no deposit, and the luxury of lounging in the back while someone else drove. You should be able to arrange a car and driver through your hotel but make it clear how many hours you want to be out and where you wish to go, and get a firm agreement on this and the price beforehand.

Fuel

If you are driving a car in Syria you'll be better off if it runs on diesel *(mazout)*, which is widely available and dirt cheap at S£2.66 per litre. Regular petrol *(benzin)* costs S£6.85 a litre and super (sometimes referred to as *mumtaz*) costs S£20.40 a litre. The latter is fairly widely available, but you can forget about lead-free petrol.

Customs

If you are travelling without a *carnet de passage en douane*, you will want to avoid crossing borders as much as possible because of the costs and red tape involved. On the off chance that you bring a vehicle into Syria without a carnet, and then need to leave Syria briefly and return, it is possible to do so without taking your vehicle out of the country. The most likely reason for doing this is heading to Amman to get a Lebanese visa.

To do this, you need to go to the customs *(jumruk)* building on Sharia Filasteen in

Damascus to get a paper (S£10 revenue stamp) allowing you to leave Syria and return without getting into trouble for not having your vehicle (details of which are scribbled into your passport when you first arrive). You may be obliged to have the vehicle impounded during your absence.

The customs building is also the place to go if you stay more than a month and need to renew your Syrian third party insurance or customs waiver (see also Bringing Your Own Vehicle in the Getting There & Away chapter).

BICYCLE

A growing number of independent travellers are choosing to cycle through Syria as part of a wider bike tour around the Mediterranean, or indeed overland from Europe to Asia. This can be hard work for several reasons. Syrians are not used to long-distance cyclists, which means you need to pay extra attention on the roads. The extreme temperatures, especially in summer, need to be taken into account. You should also have a very complete tools and spares kit, as you cannot rely on finding what you need on the way, although there are bicycle repair workshops in both Damascus (in the Christian Quarter of the Old City on Straight Street) and Aleppo (just off Sharia al-Maari, near Bab al-Faraj), which are marked on the relevant maps.

On the plus side, those cyclists we met said they were having a ball, receiving fantastic welcomes everywhere they went – being showered with invitations to stop and eat or drink and frequently being offered accommodation for the night.

Roads are generally good except the Aleppo-Damascus highway (Highway 5), which is made dangerous by the heavy volume of traffic. Two cyclists we met avoided this by detouring west via Idlib and then down to Apamea and Hama. And as they point out, you have more chance of meeting Syrians on secondary roads like these. From Homs to Damascus there is only one route, but a frontage road runs alongside the highway and cyclists are likely to have this to

themselves most of the time. We've also heard from a cyclist who looped out along the Euphrates to Rasafa, from where he managed to cycle across the desert down to Qasr al-Heir al-Sharqi (he says you need a good compass and about 10L of water).

Practicalities

Carry a couple of extra chain links, a chain breaker, spokes, a spoke key, two inner tubes, tyre levers and a repair kit, a flathead and Phillips screwdriver, and Allen keys and spanners to fit all the bolts on your bike. Check the bolts daily and carry spares. Fit as many water bottles to your bike as you can – it gets hot.

Make sure the bike's gearing will get you over the hills, and confine your panniers to 15kg maximum. May to mid-June and September to October are the best times for cycling; in between, bring lots of extra water. In your panniers include: a two person tent (weighing about 1.8kg) that can also accommodate the bike where security is a concern; a sleeping bag rated to 0°C and a Therm-a-Rest; small camping stove with gas canisters; MSR cooking pot; utensils; Katadyn water filter (2 microns) and Maglite. Wear cycling shorts with chamois bum and cleated cycling shoes. Don't fill the panniers with food as it is plentiful and fresh along the route.

HITCHING

Although generally speaking Lonely Planet does not advocate hitching because of the small but potentially serious risk it involves, unless you have your own transport hitching cannot be avoided if you want to see some of Syria's more remote sites. In fact, as so many locals don't own cars, it is an accepted means of getting around. National courtesy dictates that often the first vehicle along will stop for you. In the months we spent on backroads and dusty lanes out in the middle of nowhere, we rarely ever had to wait more than 10 minutes or so for a lift. And it was not just cars that stopped; we rode in the back of trucks, frequently on tractors, and in a couple of uncomfortable instances three of us squashed up on one motorbike or scooter!

Hostage to Hospitality

At the risk of sounding ungrateful, the problem with hitching in Syria is not getting a lift but getting rid of it when you've got to where you're going. Several times we were delivered to our destination only to have our driver insist we come in for tea, meet the family, look at some photos, even watch some TV ... On one particular occasion the kind and enthusiastic soul who picked us up on the desert road decided it would be much more fun to come sightseeing rather than go back home for lunch. And so for the next few hours he happily chauffeured us around, adding a good 60km or so to what would otherwise have been his normal 8km drive home.

All of this is wonderful as long as you're not in any kind of hurry. Anybody with rigid schedules and a strict quota of four sites a day should probably stick to buses, but for anyone with a more relaxed attitude to sightseeing, then standing at the roadside and taking pot luck is a fine way to experience the country through its people rather than just its old stones.

It was all great fun and an excellent way to meet people. No pay was ever expected and on the few occasions we proffered money it was unequivocally refused.

It still needs to be said, however, that despite the hospitality of Syrians, we still do not recommend that women should hitch unaccompanied by a male.

LOCAL TRANSPORT
Bus

All the major cities have a local bus and/or microbus system but, as the city centres are compact, you can usually get around on foot. This is just as well because neither the buses nor the microbuses have signs in English (and often no signs in Arabic), though they can be useful (and cheap) for getting out to distant microbus or train stations, especially in Damascus.

Service Taxi & Taxi

Taxis in most cities are plentiful and cheap. In Damascus they have meters, although not all drivers use them – a cross-town trip should never cost more than S£25, although from the centre to Mezzeh you'd be looking at more like S£40. In Aleppo a cross-town ride should not cost more than S£15. There is a flagfall of S£3 everywhere. Where they don't use a meter, you'll have to negotiate the fare when you get in.

It's a real surprise to find that all taxi drivers are not sharks. In Syria, if you get into a taxi and ask how much it is to the bus station (or wherever) you will often be told the correct fare and bargaining will get you nowhere. This is not, however, an invitation to drop your guard.

Although they are not in evidence in Damascus, some other cities, notably Aleppo, are served by local service taxis that run a set route and pick up and drop off passengers along the way for a set price. For the outsider, there is no obvious way to distinguish them from the normal taxis – both are yellow, although you can generally bet the big, old lumbering American relics are service taxis.

If you can read Arabic, it's easy. Regular taxis have a sign on the doors reading *'Ujra medinat Halab, raqm ...'* (City of Aleppo Taxi, Number ...), while service taxis a similar-looking sign reading *'Khidma Medinat Halab'* (City of Aleppo Service) followed by the route name.

Should you end up sharing with other people and the taxi doesn't take you exactly where you want to go, you're probably in a service taxi.

ORGANISED TOURS

If time is important or you're just in Damascus for a couple of days, several travel agents in the area around the Cham Palace Hotel offer half-day and one-day excursions as far afield as Palmyra and Bosra. They operate mainly in spring and summer, and you're looking at around US$35 per person for the transport – if there is sufficient demand to fill a microbus.

Damascus

Until the beginning of the 20th century, Damascus could still boast it was the 'Pearl set in Emeralds'. However, the emeralds, or green fields watered by the Barada River, have long since been submerged in the urban sprawl that is home to some six million people. It is nevertheless still the bright light in Ash-Sham, which loosely translates as southern Syria. Words change their meaning, and 'Dimashq ash-Sham' (the modern Arabic for Damascus) is often simply referred to as Ash-Sham by locals.

Syria's capital and by far its largest metropolis, Damascus is a city of fascinating contrasts. Veiled women in traditional garb mix with country Bedouin ladies and other city folk sporting trendy western-style fashions. Old men in *jalabiyyas* and *kufeyyas* shuffle past go-ahead young public servants in natty suits and pushy young hawkers in the crowded *souqs* of the Old City.

Beyond the timeless oriental bazaars and blind alleys of the Old City stretches the largely modern administrative and commercial district, with its seemingly lawless traffic and the hustle and bustle you'd expect of a busy capital. Above it all, like a permanent leitmotiv, Arabic pop music wafts from music stands and cassette shops at every turn, sweeping you along with its unmistakable rhythms.

The city owes its existence to the Barada River, which rises high in the Anti-Lebanon Range (Jebel Libnan ash-Sharqiyya). The waters give life to the Ghouta Oasis, making settlement possible in an otherwise uninhabitable area.

HISTORY

Damascus claims to be the oldest continuously inhabited city in the world, although its northern rival, Aleppo, hotly disputes this. Hieroglyphic tablets found in Egypt make reference to 'Dimashqa' as being one of the cities conquered by the Egyptians in the 15th century BC, but excavations from

Highlights

- **Damascene houses** – more like *objets d'art* than residences (see page 111)

- **Getting lost in the Old City** – the Umayyad Mosque is wonderful, as are the souqs and madrassas and khans, but the best thing is simply to wander and see where the next turn takes you (see page 122)

- **Steaming at the Nur ad-Din** – unfortunately it's a men-only experience, but a spell in the steam room at this particular hammam leaves you not just clean but purged (see page 137)

- **Fine dining** – some Old City restaurants have superb food and exceptional settings; you may find yourself spending the whole day in anticipation of your evening meal (see page 140)

- **Beer at the Damascus Workers' Club** – Damascus has few drinking venues but this one's a winner (see page 141)

- **Evenings at the coffeehouses** – our favourite Damascene pastime was to while away an hour or two, or three, at the end of each day at either the Ash-Shams or the An-Nafura (see page 143)

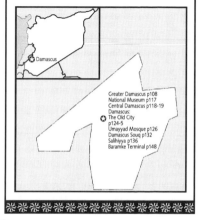

Greater Damascus p108
National Museum p117
Central Damascus p118-19
Damascus:
✪ The Old City
p124-5
Umayyad Mosque p126
Damascus Souq p132
Salihiyya p136
Baramke Terminal p148

the courtyard of the Umayyad Mosque have yielded finds dating back to the 3rd millennium BC. The name Dimashqa appears in the Ebla archives and also on tablets found at Mari (2500 BC).

Damascus has been fought over many times and some of the earliest conquerors include King David of Israel, the Assyrians in 732 BC, Nebuchadnezzar (circa 600 BC) and the Persians in 530 BC. In 333 BC it fell to Alexander the Great. Greek influence declined when the Nabataeans occupied Damascus in 85 BC. The Romans soon sent the Nabataeans packing in 64 BC and Syria became a Roman province.

Damascus was an important city under the Romans and it became a military base for the armies fighting the Persians. Hadrian declared it a metropolis in the 2nd century AD and during the reign of Alexander Severus it became a Roman colony. It was here that Saul of Tarsus was converted to Christianity and became St Paul the Apostle.

By the end of the 4th century AD most of the population had adopted Christianity. The Temple of Jupiter became a cathedral dedicated to St John the Baptist, whose head supposedly lies in a tomb inside the Umayyad Mosque.

With the coming of Islam, Damascus became an important centre as the seat of the Umayyad caliphate from 661 to 750. The city expanded rapidly and the Christian cathedral was turned into a mosque. When the Abbasids took over and moved the caliphate to Baghdad, Damascus was plundered once again.

After the occupation of Damascus by the Seljuk Turks in 1076, the Crusaders tried unsuccessfully to take it in 1148 before it finally fell to Nur ad-Din (Nureddin), a general of Turkish origin, in 1154. Many of the monuments in the city date from the time of his successor Salah ad-Din (Saladin), when Damascus became the capital of a united Egypt and Syria.

The next to move in were the Mongols who, after only a very brief occupation, were ousted by the Mamluks of Egypt in 1260. During the Mamluk period, Damascene

goods became famous worldwide and attracted merchants from Europe. This led to the second Mongol invasion under Tamerlane, when the city was flattened and the artisans and scholars were deported to the Mongol capital of Samarkand. The Mamluks returned soon after and proceeded to rebuild the city.

From the time of the Ottoman Turk occupation in 1516, the fortunes of Damascus started to decline and it was reduced to the status of small provincial capital in a large empire. The only interruption in 400 years of Ottoman rule was from 1831 to 1840, when it once again became the capital of Syria under the Egyptians, following the rise to power there of Mohammed Ali Pasha. Fearing the consequences of an Ottoman collapse, the west intervened and forced Ibrahim Pasha, Ali's lieutenant, to withdraw from Syria.

By 1878 the city's population had grown to 150,000, great improvements had been made in sanitary conditions and a transport system was built. By 1908 Damascus had a network of tramlines and was connected by rail to Beirut and Medina.

The Turkish and German forces used Damascus as their base during WWI. When they were defeated by the Arab Legion and the Allies, the first, short-lived Syrian government was set up in 1919.

The French, having received a mandate from the League of Nations, occupied the city from 1920 to 1945. They met with a lot of resistance and at one stage in 1925 bombarded the city to suppress rioting. French shells again rained on the city in the unrest of 1945, which led to full independence a year later when French and British forces were pulled out and Damascus became the capital of an independent Syria.

ORIENTATION

There are two distinct parts to Damascus: the Old City and the rest. The Old City is tightly defined by its encircling walls, while modern Damascus sprawls around it and stretches off in all directions climbing the slopes of Jebel Qassioun (Mt Qassioun) to

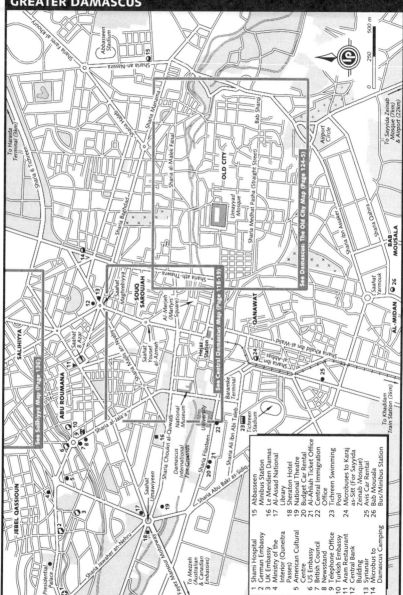

GREATER DAMASCUS

Map labels:

To Harasta Terminal (3km)
Abbasseen Stadium
Sharia Fares al-Khoury
Sharia an-Nassira
Sharia Manama
Sharia Halib
Sharia Baghdad
Bab Sharqi
To Sayyida Zeinab Mosque (7km) & Airport (22km)
Sharia al-Malek Faisal
OLD CITY
Umayyad Mosque
Sharia Medhat Pasha (Straight Street)
BAB MOUSALA
Sharia Qahira
Sharia ibn Asaker
Sharia Khalid ibn al-Walid
Airport Circle
See Damascus: The Old City Map (Page 124–5)
SALIHIYYA
JEBEL QASSIOUN
See Salihiyya Map (Page 136)
SOUQ SAROUJAH
Saahat Maghrebiyya
Sharia ath-Thawra
Al-Merjeh (Martyrs') Square
QANAWAT
AL-MIDAN
Saahat Yarmouk
See Central Damascus Map (Page 118–19)
ABU ROUMANA
Saahat 8 Azar
Saahat Yousef al-Azmeh
Sharia Maisaloun
Sharia an-Nasr
Sharia al-Jala'a
Sharia Choukri al-Quwatli
National Museum
University
Hejaz Station
Baramke Terminal
Sharia ibn al-Abbas
Sharia Ali ibn Abi Taleb
Sharia Filesteen
Damascus International Fair Grounds
Tichreen Stadium
Sharia Abu Bakr as-Siddiq
Saahat Umawiyyeen
To Khaddam Train Station (3km)
To Mezzeh (Australian & Canadian Embassies)
Presidential Palace
To Damascus Camping
Sharia Jawaher an-Nehru
Feraz Namour Motorway

Legend:

1 Shami Hospital
2 German Embassy
3 UK Embassy
4 Ministry of the Interior (Quneitra Passes)
5 American Cultural Centre
6 US Embassy
7 British Council
8 Newsstand
9 Telephone Office
10 Turkish Embassy
11 Aram Restaurant
12 Central Bank Building
13 Syrianair
14 Microbus to Damascus Camping
15 Abbasseen Minibus Station
16 Le Meridien Damas
17 Al-Assad National Library
18 Sheraton Hotel
19 National Theatre
20 Budget Car Rental
21 Al-Ahliah Ticket Office
22 Central Immigration Office
23 Tichreen Swimming Pool
24 Microbuses to Karaj as-Sitt (For Sayyida Zeinab Mosque)
25 Avis Car Rental
26 Bab Mousala Bus/Minibus Station

the north and petering out on the plains to the south. However, all the parts that are of interest to a visitor are contained in something like two square kilometres and finding your way around on foot is no problem. Be warned, though, official street signs do not always correlate with the commonly known names of various streets and squares – we give both where appropriate.

The heart of the city is Saahat ash-Shohada (Martyrs' Square), which the locals tend to refer to as 'Al-Merjeh', a name dating from Ottoman times and meaning something along the lines of 'pasture' or 'park'. Any pastoral qualities are long gone as today Al-Merjeh is just an ugly chicane for cars to speed through, but most of the cheap hotels and restaurants are around here.

The rest of what could be considered as 'downtown' Damascus lies north and west of Al-Merjeh. The main street is two blocks west and begins at the Hejaz train station as Sharia Said al-Jabri and then cuts a kilometre-long swathe north to the grand entrance of the Central Bank building, changing its name enroute twice. Along here you'll find the post office, main tourist office, various airline offices and many mid-range restaurants and hotels. About halfway along this main street is Saahat Yousef al-Azmeh, a focal point for the modern city centre, into which all roads seem to run. The road that runs off to the west, Sharia Maysaloun, has most of the airline companies, the swish Cham Palace hotel and a scattering of restaurants that get more expensive the further west you go. At its extreme western end, Maysaloun joins Sharia al-Jala'a, which is the main thoroughfare through the wealthy diplomatic district, known as Abu Roumana. Here you are already on the lower slopes of Jebel Qassioun; there's plenty of greenery and the air seems distinctly fresher and more breathable than down below.

By contrast, the old quarters of the city lie in the east on the lowest ground around the banks of the Barada River, which is now little more than a sluggish, foul-smelling drain. The Old City is separated from the new by Sharia ath-Thawra, one of several inhumanely wide avenues that slice apart Damascus and are a complete nightmare for the pedestrian. The main way in is via the covered Souq al-Hamidiyya, which leads directly to the Umayyad Mosque, the centrepiece of the Old City. South of the mosque is Sharia Medhat Pasha, the ancient 'Straight Street' (named such for obvious reasons), which bisects the Old City on an east-west axis.

INFORMATION
Tourist Offices
There are two tourist offices: the main one (☎ 222 2388) is on Sharia 29 Mai, just up from Saahat Yousef al-Azmeh, while there is a second, smaller place (☎ 221 0122) in the Ministry of Tourism building by the Takiyya as-Suleimaniyya, near the National Museum. The staff at both tend to be friendly and English-speaking and they do their best to answer any questions, but beyond some free maps they have little else in the way of information to hand out. The main office is open from 9 am to 7 pm daily except Friday, while the smaller office is open only until 2 pm.

Visa Extensions
For visa extensions, the central immigration office is on Sharia Filasteen, one block west of the Baramke bus station (see the Greater Damascus map). As with all government departments, it's open from 8 am to 2 pm every day except Friday. Go to the 2nd floor to fill in the three forms, for which you'll need three photos (across the road, a couple of photographers with ancient cameras can do some awful photos for you). You can get extensions of up to one month. It costs S£25 and will take one working day to process – you can pick up your passport at 1 pm on the following day.

There is another immigration office on Sharia Furat, just west of Al-Merjeh, but this only deals with re-entry visas, which are necessary if you are planning a visit to Lebanon and don't already have a multiple-entry visa. For further details see the Lebanon section in the Around Damascus chapter.

Foreign Embassies

See Embassies & Consulates in Syria in the Facts for the Visitor chapter for the addresses of foreign representations in Damascus.

Money

There are several branches of the Commercial Bank of Syria (CBS) as well as more straightforward exchange booths where you can change money much more easily. The booth on Al-Merjeh is open from 9 am to 6 pm Saturday to Thursday and 10 am to 2 pm on Friday and will change cash and travellers cheques. So will the booth opposite the Hejaz train station, which is open from 10 am until 5 pm seven days a week. Neither of these places charge any commission.

Of the CBS branches, No 5 on the corner of sharias Said al-Jabri and Jumhuriyya will change cash and travellers cheques, while branch No 8 on Sharia Bur Said deals in cash only. The banks are usually open 8.30 am to 12.30 pm. If you need to change money late in the evening, the bank branches in the Sheraton and Le Meridien Damas hotels are open from 9 am to 9 pm daily and take cash and travellers cheques.

The local American Express agent (☎ 221 7813, fax 222 3707) is on the 1st floor above the Sudan Airways office on Sharia Balkis, which is a small street running between sharias Al-Mutanabi and Fardous. The financial services on offer are extremely limited – it can't cash cheques, it can only replace stolen ones. The office is open 8.30 am to 8 pm Saturday to Thursday, and 9 am to 1.30 pm and 5 to 8 pm Friday. The postal address is PO Box 1373, Damascus.

Thomas Cook is represented by Nahas Travel (☎ 223 2000, fax 223 6002) on Sharia Fardous. Again, it can't cash travellers cheques, only arrange for replacements for any stolen (this can take anything up to 10 days). Nahas can arrange to have money wired to it (and hence to you) in a matter of hours and can also give you cash against a Visa card (it represents MasterCard and Visa in Syria). Travellers also report being able to get cash advances on a Visa card at a shop on the south side of Al-

Merjeh that has a prominent Visa/Diners Club/MasterCard sign outside.

To change money on the black market just walk down the Souq al-Hamidiyya.

Post

The central post office is an ugly, monolithic building on Sharia Said al-Jabri. It's open from 8 am to 7.30 pm every day, except Friday and national holidays, when it closes at 12.30 pm. The poste restante counter is to the left when you enter and is fairly efficient. You'll need to have your passport as proof of identity and there is an S£8 charge per letter for any mail. The poste restante window closes at 5 pm.

The parcel post office is outside and around the corner, while there's an express mail (EMS) service in the parking lot behind the main building. It operates 8 am to 5 pm daily except Friday. You can also have mail sent to you via American Express (see Money earlier in this chapter).

There's a DHL courier office (☎ 222 7692) on Sharia Omar bin Abi Rabea, near the post office, which is open 8 am to 9 pm daily.

Telephone & Fax

The telephone office is a block east of the Hejaz train station on Sharia an-Nasr and is open around the clock. However, you can't make operator calls and will instead be directed to the card phones on the street outside. As there are card phones at every major junction in Damascus and as the cards are sold throughout the city at places indicated by stickers on the phone kiosks, you really don't need to bother with the telephone office. If you do for some reason decide to go there to buy a phonecard then these are not sold at the counters inside the building but rather by the guys hanging around on the steps outside. For details of call costs, discount rates and so on, see Post & Communications in the Facts for the Visitor chapter.

Telegrams can be sent from this office during vaguely set daytime hours, as can faxes. For the latter you must present your

continued on page 115

THE HOUSES OF OLD DAMASCUS

TONY WHEELER

Damascus has a hidden treasure: unseen behind the walls of the Old City are hundreds of houses built around courtyards and featuring their own distinctive decoration. While outside the city walls the old buildings are being demolished to make way for the new, within the Old City these houses are, for the most part, undisturbed by developers. The unfortunate part is that much of this hidden treasure is in a sorry state of disrepair. The Old City was abandoned by the middle classes and the wealthy in the first half of the 20th century, and their once grand homes, now occupied by the poor who can't afford their upkeep, have been left largely to the ravages of time and the weather.

Domestic architecture in Damascus flowered during the 18th century, a prosperous time when, for many years, members of the powerful Al-Azem family were governors of the city. This is when most of the great palaces were built, or rebuilt, for though there are no complete houses to be seen in Damascus that are pre-18th century, parts of them go back much earlier. Treasure hidden in the 16th century was discovered in the walls of one, while Roman walls and stonework have been found in others.

The finest example of this architectural blooming is the Azem Palace which, happily for visitors to Damascus, is now a well preserved museum and is open to the public so that they can bear witness to the 18th century Damascene ideal.

The palace, like all Damascene houses, was constructed in stone on the first floor around the courtyards and in wood and mud on the floors above. It has always been a puzzle as to why, when the stone

Box: The Azem Palace displays fine banded stonework.

Right: A traditional striped stone arcade at the Azem Palace (now the Museum of the Arts & Popular Traditions of Syria). The dome of the Umayyad Mosque can be seen in the background.

ANDREW HUMPHREYS

quarries lay not far from the city, this fragile and impermanent method of building never changed. It has astonished visitors to Damascus throughout the centuries: 'A golden kernel in a shell of clay' is how one of them described a traditional house with its dazzling interior and mud walls.

The courtyard facades of these Damascene houses were laid in stripes of black basalt and white stone, and decoration was done in coloured pastework – an art invented by the Egyptian Mamluks but which became a speciality of Damascus craftsmen. (Coloured pastework is a technique in which a pattern is incised into stone and then filled in with pastes made from different coloured stones to give the effect of an immensely complicated stone inlay.) Courtyard paving and the ever-present fountains were made in plain-cut stone.

Inside the houses it was a different story – particularly in the grand reception rooms. In these, decoration ran riot with richly painted and gilded wood covering the walls and ceilings; with glittering mother-of-pearl inlay in stone; with marble mosaic for floors patterned like carpets; and with indoor fountains which cooled the air in summer. These rooms stunned European visitors to Damascus who, one after the other, described them as like something from *The Thousand and One Nights*.

There was no furniture in Damascene rooms, only divans or cushions covered with embroidered silk that were placed around the walls of the raised seating areas. Persian rugs overlapped on the floors. All bedding was stored in giant, built-in wall cupboards concealed behind painted doors, and the only free-standing piece of furniture was a huge mother-of-pearl inlaid chest in which a bride kept her trousseau.

Every family in Damascus had a house in the same style as the Azem Palace, varying from humble one courtyard versions with far less lavish decoration, to enormous three or even four-courtyard palaces owned by the grandest of the notables.

In the 19th century the decor of houses in Damascus changed dramatically because of the increased European influence on the Ottoman

TIM BEDDOW

Left: Coloured pastework and black & white stone stripes decorate the entrance (*'ataba*) of a reception room at Beit as-Siba'i.

Right: Stone carving adorning an arcade at Maktab Anbar. Maktab Anbar was built in the second part of the 19th century and shows western influences.

TIM BEDDOW

THE HOUSES OF OLD DAMASCUS

TIM BEDDOW

TIM BEDDOW

Top: The private reception room of Beit Shatta, one of Damascus' prettiest private houses.

Bottom: An ornate cupboard at Beit Nizam. A family would keep their bedding behind doors like these.

TIM BEDDOW

TIM BEDDOW

TIM BEDDOW

Top Left: Marble and painting for the entrance to the reception room at Beit Shatta.

Top Right: Old painted panels re-used in Beit Uruktanji, a house built in the 1930s outside the city walls.

Bottom: This house, Beit al-Quwatli, was the British consulate in the mid-19th century. It is now inhabited by several families.

TIM BEDDOW

TIM BEDDOW

Top: A traditional bride's chest *(sunduq),* inlaid with mother-of-pearl, at Beit Shami, the Historical Museum of Damascus.

Bottom: The main reception room at Beit Barudi, now under restoration by the architectural faculty of Damascus University. Western-style, the room has no raised seating platform.

empire, and the opening up of Damascus to the outside world. Following the lead set by Istanbul, it became the fashion to rearrange and redecorate 18th century houses in a more western way.

Ornament became much more florid with mirror work, more and more elaborate stone and wood carving, and wall paintings of landscapes (often Istanbul). Marble replaced plain cut stone for paving and fountains, and new canvas ceilings were stretched over the old painted wooden ones and decorated in a European style. Un-Damascene additions such as dining rooms were built; the traditional raised floors were levelled to be like European drawing rooms; more windows were let into previously blank facades; and western-style furniture began to appear.

Some of the grandest houses were built at this time by Christian and Jewish merchants who had prospered because of the region's increasing trade with the west, and who poured their wealth into ostentatious houses – houses like Maktab Anbar (Dar Anbar), now the offices of the Commission for the Old City, whose three courtyards can be visited during office hours.

By the beginning of the 20th century, new European-style suburbs were growing up outside the Old City and it became fashionable to move into a modern apartment or house in one of these areas. With the arrival of the motor car, this migration from the Old City speeded up, so that although 100 years ago every notable family lived in a traditional house in the Old City, now only one or two do.

Right: Stone stripes, coloured pastework and marble mosaic for the entrance *('ataba)* of another reception room at Beit as-Siba'i.

TIM BEDDOW

The abandonment of the Old City is understandable – access is difficult, parking impossible, the courtyard house is uncomfortable in winter and difficult to heat, cool and clean. Lifestyles have changed too; new generations don't want to live with their parents and grandparents, they want their independence.

Although the traditional way of life of the Old City may have disappeared, there is some hope that the houses may live on: it's only a decade since the first restaurants opened in the Old City and now there are at least a dozen, all in converted old residences. There's a small hotel on the drawing board, and several influential individuals who feel passionate about preserving the Old City have bought houses and are restoring them. Mme Nora Jumblatt, wife of the Lebanese Druze leader, Walid, who is herself a Damascene, has restored one of the most delightful houses in Damascus, Beit Mujallid. The architectural faculty of Damascus University has acquired Beit Barudi in Qanawat as their centre for Old City studies, while the Danish Institute has restored a marvellous palace, the Beit Aqqad, which is due to open in 2000.

Perhaps all this will inspire new and sensitive buyers for the old houses and persuade the authorities to take a more dynamic attitude towards the Old City, where a big investment would, if nothing else, be paid back quickly in increased revenue from tourism. One can only hope – Damascus is, after all, a city of sudden conversion.

Brigid Keenan, author of
Damascus: Hidden Treasures of the Old City **(see Books)**

TONY WHEELER

Left: Striped stone *(ablaq)* facades around the main courtyard at the Azem Palace.

continued from page 110

passport. For charges see the Post & Communications section in the Facts for the Visitor chapter.

Travel Agencies
Sharia Fardous in the city centre is where you'll find the bulk of Damascus' travel agencies. We haven't had dealings with any of them and so we can't make any recommendations. Local contacts have spoken favourably of Adonis Travel (☎ 223 6272, fax 222 3062) at 34 Sharia al-Mutanabi.

Bookshops
The Librairie Avicenne, one block south of the Cham Palace hotel, is possibly the best bookshop in the country as far as foreign-language publications are concerned – though that's not saying much. It has a good range of books on Syria, as well as a dusty old stock of novels in English and French (predominantly kids stuff and bodice-rippers), and a selection of days-old press, including the *Financial Times*, *The Times* and *Le Monde*. It's open from 9 am to 2 pm and 4.30 to 8.30 pm daily, closed Friday.

The Librairie Universelle, just off Sharia Yousef al-Azmeh, has a more current crop of novels plus shelf-loads of art books. Opening times are similar to those of the Avicenne. The Family Bookshop just south of Sharia Maysaloun on Sharia Majlis an-Nyaby is also worth checking for its eclectic old stock of (almost) contemporary fiction. It's open from 9 am to 1 .30 pm and 4.30 to 8 pm most days but 10 am to 1 pm on Friday and closed Sunday.

The Cham Palace, Sheraton and Le Meridien Damas hotels all have bookshops, each with a handful of standard airport novels and a selection of coffee-table books on Syria and the Islamic world.

Newsstands *Time* plus a few international papers are available intermittently at the bookshops at the five-star hotels and the Librairie Avicenne bookshop, usually two or three days old. There are also a couple of newsstands which sell a better-than-average range of magazines and foreign press, often stocking more than the bookshops; one of the best of these is on Sharia al-Jala'a near the British Council.

Cultural Centres
Bring your passport as many cultural centres require some ID before they'll allow you to enter.

American Cultural Center
(☎ 333 8443) off Sharia Mansour near the US embassy. Its library is stocked with books, newspapers, videos and also shows CNN news. It is open from 1.30 to 5 pm Sunday to Thursday. Don't be daunted by the massive security screen.
British Council
(☎ 333 8436, fax 332 1467) 10 Sharia al-Jala'a. This is only a teaching centre; it doesn't have a library and the newspapers in reception are usually weeks old, although it does occasionally host films and other cultural events.
Centre Culturel Français
(☎ 224 6181, fax 231 6194) off Sharia Yousef al-Azmeh. As with the British Council, the primary vocation here is language teaching but films and exhibitions are often organised too – you can pick up a program at the front desk. There's also a small library. The centre is open from 10 am to 1 pm and 4 to 7 pm daily, closed Sunday.
Goethe Institut
(☎ 333 6673, fax 332 0849) 4 Sharia Houboubi, off Sharia Maysaloun.

Film & Photography
There's a good Kodak shop on Sharia Mousalam al-Baroudi, 100m west of the Hejaz train station, which sells a wide range of quality film, and you can pay by credit card. It does developing in one hour at a cost of S£25 for the processing plus S£10 per print. Slides, the sales assistant claimed, could be done in one day at a cost of S£200 plus S£7 per transparency – considering that in London and elsewhere, slides generally take at least a couple of days, we didn't fancy putting this to the test.

For emergency camera repairs or spares try Pluto Photo Services on Sharia Maysaloun, just west of the Cham Palace hotel.

Laundry

There are at least two laundry shops on Sharia Bahsa, around the Al-Haramein Hotel, both of which charge a standard S£25 to S£35 per item and take a minimum of 24 hours to turn around your washing. If you're staying at the Sultan Hotel, it also operates a laundry service and charges about S£40 an item.

Medical Services

If you can, it is always a good idea to consult your embassy for referrals to recommended doctors or dentists. Damascus has several hospitals but among the better ones is the Shami Hospital (☎ 371 8970) on Sharia Jawaher an-Nehru, north-west of the centre; reports say that the treatment is good and some of the doctors speak English. There are numerous pharmacies dotted around Saahat Yousef al-Azmeh.

CENTRAL DAMASCUS

Most of what there is to see in Damascus is within the Old City. The modern city is short on sights and largely bereft of beauty – the main thing to do is to visit the National Museum and its neighbour, the Takiyya as-Suleimaniyya. The backstreets of the Souq Saroujah area are also worth a wander and, if you haven't already had enough of the splendours of traditional Damascene architecture, then the Historical Museum of Damascus is a beautiful place. If you have half a day to spare, it's also worth a walk around the old Salihiyya district on the lower slopes of Jebel Qassioun.

Al-Merjeh & the Hejaz Station

As the Place Merjeh, this untidy square that's now officially known as Martyrs' Square was the hub of 19th century Damascus. It was a tram terminus and park and the address of several of the city's better hotels. But in the last 40 or 50 years the focus of the city has shifted north and west and Al-Merjeh has been left behind. It has slid downmarket and though the place remains a busy centre of sorts the trade is in cheap eateries, pastry shops and low-rent hotels. Come evening there's even a tinge of the red light.

The martyrs referred to by the modern name were victims of the French bombardments in 1945. The rather curious bronze colonnade in the centre is nothing to do with them; instead, it commemorates the opening of the first telegraph link in the Middle East, the line from Damascus to Medina.

East of the square, the streets are filled with a profusion of small shops which at Sharia ash-Shohada degenerate into a small, ramshackle **bird market** mixing turkeys and chickens with canaries and parakeets and even falcons, all stuffed dozens to a cage.

A little south and west of Al-Merjeh, Saahat Hejaz (Hejaz Square) is another of the city's former grand spaces, created to show off the **Hejaz train station** that stands on its south side. Completed in 1917 the station was the northern terminus of the new Hejaz Railway, meant to ferry pilgrims down to Medina (see the boxed text 'The Hejaz Railway' in the Getting There & Away chapter). Compared with the grand transport palaces of Europe, the station is a fairly provincial affair but the interior of the building, though badly neglected and not improved any by the luridly painted presidential hagiography, still has a nicely decorated ceiling and upper gallery level.

The only trains that leave from here these days are summer services to the hills north of Damascus and the weekly service to Amman. Outside the station is a steam locomotive dating from 1908 that finds some use as a poster hoarding and a public water fountain erected at the same time as the station and still serving its intended purpose.

Souq Saroujah

Souq Saroujah is the most pleasant part of central Damascus in which to wander, a compact historical area of wonky streets lined with small shops, punctuated by medieval tombs, mosques and street furniture.

It was common practice in medieval times for the areas immediately outside the city walls to develop as burial places for the dead; you can still see this today with large areas of cemeteries lying to the south of the old cities of both Damascus and Aleppo. Occasionally, however, the needs of the living would overwhelm those of the dead. Such was the case with the area now known as Souq Saroujah. During the Ayyubid era the fields just north of the Barada River became a favoured location for the tombs and mausoleums of nobles, and for several hundred years this site served as an exclusive burial ground. As the city expanded under the Ottomans and space within the city walls was at a premium, the cemeteries became built over with the houses of well-off Turkish merchants and civil servants.

Unfortunately, the needs of the living are pressing once again, and many of the fine old houses have been demolished in the cause of redevelopment. Of the handful that remain **Beit al-Haramein** and **Beit al-Rabie** now serve as backpackers' hotels (where else but Damascus could you stay in an 18th century mansion – albeit one that's gone to seed – for as little US$3 a night?), while the **Beit Shami** is also open to the public as the Historical Museum of Damascus.

Historical Museum of Damascus

This is like a downmarket version of the Old City's Azem Palace. It's an attractive old house with eight richly decorated rooms off a central courtyard. A couple of rooms hold half-hearted displays of photos and diagrams relating to the Old City and there is a superb large-scale model of the same, but it's the rooms themselves which are of greatest interest. If you haven't already overdosed on inlaid marble and carved wood, then this place is worth a visit. It's open from 8 am to 2.30 pm daily except Friday, and admission is S£150 (students S£10).

The museum is a little difficult to find but it's off Sharia ath-Thawra, just where the flyover comes down north of Sharia Souq Saroujah – locate the two tall modern buildings and it's next to those. It's on Ministry of the Interior property and you have to pass through a guarded gate.

National Museum

This is the most important of Syria's museums and it could well be argued that you would profit from a visit before *and* after seeing the main sites around the country.

You enter through a shady garden that acts as an overflow for pieces that the museum, overburdened by riches, cannot house inside. Tickets are purchased at the gate and cost S£300 (students S£15). The museum is open from 9 am to 6 pm (4 pm in winter) every day except Tuesday; on Friday the museum also closes between 11.15 am and 1 pm for noon prayers. All bags and cameras have to be left in the office at the entrance.

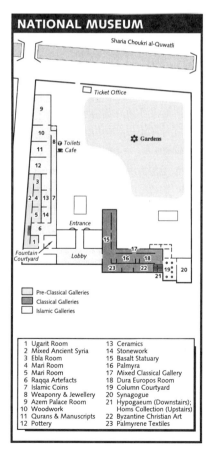

NATIONAL MUSEUM

Sharia Choukri al-Quwatli

Ticket Office

Gardens

Toilets
Cafe

Entrance

Fountain
Courtyard   Lobby

☐ Pre-Classical Galleries
■ Classical Galleries
☐ Islamic Galleries

1	Ugarit Room	13	Ceramics
2	Mixed Ancient Syria	14	Stonework
3	Ebla Room	15	Basalt Statuary
4	Mari Room	16	Palmyra
5	Mari Room	17	Mixed Classical Gallery
6	Raqqa Artefacts	18	Dura Europos Room
7	Islamic Coins	19	Column Courtyard
8	Weaponry & Jewellery	20	Synagogue
9	Azem Palace Room	21	Hypogaeum (Downstairs);
10	Woodwork		Homs Collection (Upstairs)
11	Qurans & Manuscripts	22	Byzantine Christian Art
12	Pottery	23	Palmyrene Textiles

DAMASCUS

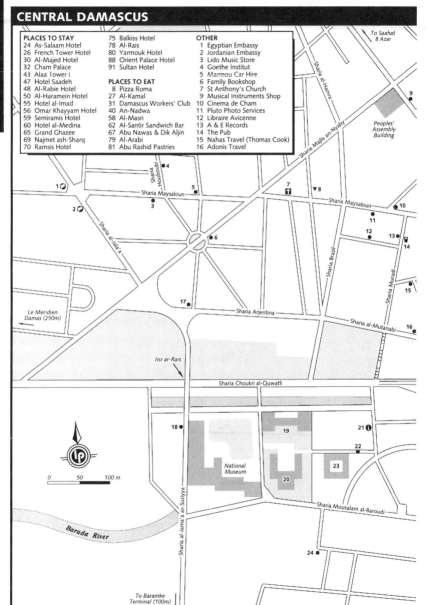

CENTRAL DAMASCUS

PLACES TO STAY
24 As-Salaam Hotel
26 French Tower Hotel
30 Al-Majed Hotel
32 Cham Palace
43 Alaa Tower i
47 Hotel Saadeh
48 Al-Rabie Hotel
50 Al-Haramein Hotel
55 Hotel al-Imad
56 Omar Khayyam Hotel
59 Semiramis Hotel
60 Hotel al-Medina
65 Grand Ghazee
69 Najmet ash-Sharq
70 Ramsis Hotel

75 Balkiss Hotel
78 Al-Rais
80 Yarmouk Hotel
88 Orient Palace Hotel
91 Sultan Hotel

PLACES TO EAT
8 Pizza Roma
27 Al-Kamal
31 Damascus Workers' Club
40 An-Nadwa
58 Al-Masri
62 Al-Santir Sandwich Bar
67 Abu Nawas & Dik Aljin
79 Al-Arabi
81 Abu Rashid Pastries

OTHER
1 Egyptian Embassy
2 Jordanian Embassy
3 Lido Music Store
4 Goethe Institut
5 Marmou Car Hire
6 Family Bookshop
7 St Anthony's Church
9 Musical Instruments Shop
10 Cinema de Cham
11 Pluto Photo Services
12 Libraire Avicenne
13 A & E Records
14 The Pub
15 Nahas Travel (Thomas Cook)
16 Adonis Travel

CENTRAL DAMASCUS

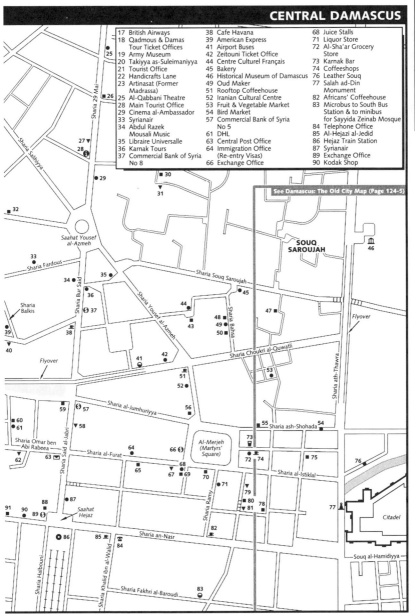

17 British Airways
18 Qadmous & Damas Tour Ticket Offices
19 Army Museum
20 Takiyya as-Suleimaniyya
21 Tourist Office
22 Handicrafts Lane
23 Artinasat (Former Madrassa)
25 Al-Qabbani Theatre
28 Main Tourist Office
29 Cinema al-Ambassador
33 Syrianair
34 Abdul Razek Mousali Music
35 Libraire Universelle
36 Karnak Tours
37 Commercial Bank of Syria No 8

38 Cafe Havana
39 American Express
41 Airport Buses
42 Zeitouni Ticket Office
44 Centre Culturel Français
45 Bakery
46 Historical Museum of Damascus
49 Oud Maker
51 Rooftop Coffeehouse
52 Iranian Cultural Centre
53 Fruit & Vegetable Market
54 Bird Market
57 Commercial Bank of Syria No 5
61 DHL
63 Central Post Office
64 Immigration Office (Re-entry Visas)
66 Exchange Office

68 Juice Stalls
71 Liquor Store
72 Al-Sha'ar Grocery Store
73 Karnak Bar
74 Coffeeshops
76 Leather Souq
77 Salah ad-Din Monument
82 Africans' Coffeehouse
83 Microbus to South Bus Station & to minibus for Sayyida Zeinab Mosque
84 Telephone Office
85 Al-Hejazi al-Jedid
86 Hejaz Train Station
87 Syrianair
89 Exchange Office
90 Kodak Shop

The facade of the museum is imposing – it is the entrance to the old Qasr al-Heir al-Gharbi, a desert palace/military camp west of Palmyra dating from 688, the time of the Umayyad caliph Hisham. It was transported to Damascus stone by stone and reconstructed, but looks somewhat cramped by the wings of the museum.

Within the museum, the exhibits are presented thematically and grouped into Pre-Classical, Classical and Islamic sections. Most of the exhibits are labelled only in French or Arabic and some have no explanation at all. (Neither is there any kind of guidebook available.) Devoid of any context, the endless procession of small, largely nondescript objects can become a bit numbing, but you should definitely see the synagogue and the hypogaeum, both in the east wing.

ANDREW HUMPHREYS

The National Museum has such an abundance of riches that some fine pieces are pushed out into the garden.

The museum lobby is devoted to Qasr al-Heir al-Gharbi, with large black and white photos of the palace with its facade still in situ – it can't help but strike you how much better the facade looked out in the desert than it does tacked onto the front of the museum.

Turning right and heading for the west wing you pass a very attractive fountain courtyard, constructed to resemble the type of inner sanctuary common to many of the more opulent Damascus dwellings built during the Mamluk and early Ottoman eras.

Across from the courtyard, ranging up the far west side of the museum, are the pre-Classical galleries.

Pre-Classical Galleries The first room (No 1 on the map) is devoted to finds from **Ugarit** and contains stone tablets inscribed with what is believed to be the world's earliest alphabet (see Ugarit in The Coast & Mountains chapter). The long gallery contains more finds from Ugarit, as well as from other sites. It leads into the **Ebla** room, which contains very little other than a couple of large photos, and then on to two rooms devoted to artefacts from the Mesopotamian city of **Mari**, in the extreme south-east of the country near what is now the border with Iraq (see Mari in The Euphrates River chapter). The incredibly distinctive statuettes in here with their fur skirts and lively black eyes date back to around the second millennium BC, making them roughly around the same age as the Great Pyramids of Giza.

Islamic Galleries The first room of the Arab-Islamic galleries (No 6 on our map) contains pottery and stucco panels recovered from the old Abbasid city of **Raqqa**, destroyed by Mongols in 1260. The long corridor running north begins with carved wooden fragments of a ceiling found at Qasr al-Heir al-Gharbi and goes on to coins and then some extremely badly lit heavy jewellery and wonderfully ornate weaponry that embodies the two traits for which the Mamluk dynasty was renowned: artistry and violence.

Off the far end is a large room devoted to the intricate style of woodwork that developed throughout the Islamic era as a result of the religious ban on figurative representations. The room is dominated by two great cenotaphs; the one nearest the entrance, decorated with a beautiful star motif, dates from 1250, while the second dates to 1265 and comes from the Khaled ibn al-Walid mosque in Homs. The other objects in here are domestic pieces of furniture removed from some of the old houses of Damascus.

North of the woodwork room is the **Azem Palace Room**, which is a reconstruction of a room from the Azem Palace in the Old City. Only parts of the room are original. It was closed at the time of our last visit but as you can visit the real Azem Palace if you wish, then this isn't a disappointment. The remaining rooms of the Islamic galleries are devoted to Qurans, ceramics and stonework.

Classical Galleries The Classical galleries are probably the most interesting part of the museum and make up the whole east wing. The first room (No 15 on the map) contains a large collection of statuary executed in the black basalt that is typical of the **Hauran region** monuments such as those at Bosra. There's also an excellent mosaic here recovered from Lattakia depicting the River Orontes in the form of a god.

Room 16 is full of busts from **Palmyra**. These are representations of the dead and they would have fitted as seals onto the pigeonhole-like chambers in which the body was stored. To see how this worked pass through the **Dura Europos** room, which contains jewellery and ceramics from this Roman site on the Euphrates, and down the stairs to the **hypogaeum**, which is an amazing reconstruction of an underground burial chamber from the Valley of the Tombs at Palmyra. Seeing this helps to make sense of the Funerary Towers at Palmyra and of some of the exhibits at the museum there (which is where this reconstruction truly belongs).

Where you go down to the hypogaeum is a staircase that goes up to the **Homs collection**, so named because much of it was found in and around that city. Alongside some exquisite gold jewellery, there are coins de-

picting Venetian Doges, the Roman emperor Philip the Arab, as well as Alexander the Great, among other historical figures. The staircase is usually roped off and you have to ask the permission of the curator in the entrance hall, but it's worth the effort.

The other thing worth seeing is the **synagogue**, which is across the colonnaded courtyard. This dates from the 2nd century and was discovered at Dura Europos (see The Euphrates River chapter), from where it was removed and reconstructed here. Other than its age, what is particularly interesting are the frescoes that cover the walls of the interior from floor to ceiling. Executed in a colourful naive style, they depict scenes from the Old Testament events, from the crowning of King Solomon through the reign of David, the story of Moses and the flight from Egypt. This is a real oddity in that depictions of the human form go against Talmudic traditions. While the frescoes are very faded (hence the low level of light in the room), it's remarkable that they've survived at all – something that occurred only because the synagogue lay buried under sand for centuries until its discovery in the 1930s.

Takiyya as-Suleimaniyya

Lying immediately east of the National Museum and just to the west of the post office, the Takiyya was built over six years, beginning in 1554, to the design of the Ottoman empire's most brilliant architect, Sinan. A favourite of the emperor Suleiman the Magnificent, Sinan would later go on to create the gorgeous Blue Mosque and Süleymmaniye that dominate the skyline of Istanbul.

The Takiyya (an Ottoman term for a Sufi hostel) is a much more modest affair than the Istanbul mosques and one that blends local Syrian styles (the alternating layers of black and white stone and honeycombed stonework over the main entrance) with typically Turkish features (the high central dome and tell-tale pencil-shaped minarets). It has two parts: the mosque to the south, and an arcaded courtyard with additional rooms on the north side that would have housed pilgrims. This former hostel area is now the Army Museum (see the next section) and its overspill of jet fighter planes unfortunately ruins the harmony of the complex.

Under the patronage of Suleiman's successor, Selim II, the Takiyya compound was extended with the addition of a small *madrassa*, or theological school. The madrassa, built around a central courtyard and fountain, now serves as the **Artisanat**, an appealing handicraft market where the former students' cells are now workshops and you can see all sorts of crafts being practised, from weaving to glass-blowing – see the Shopping section later in this chapter for more details.

Army Museum

An ill-considered and inappropriate use of the Takiyya, this museum has a mixed collection of military hardware from the Bronze Age to the near present. Exhibits range from flint arrowheads to a pile of the twisted remains of planes shot down in the 1973 war with Israel. An interesting anachronism is a display on the theme of Soviet-Syrian space cooperation. Hammers and sickles and smiling portraits of Mikhail Gorbachev seem to indicate the Syrians' desire to keep alive memories of the good old days.

The museum is open from 8 am to 2 pm daily except Tuesday; admission is S£15 (students S£5).

THE OLD CITY

Although settlement on this site dates back to perhaps as early as the 15th century BC and strong evidence of a Roman-era street plan occasionally shows through, the character of the Old City is essentially medieval Islamic. Unchanged from that time to an astonishing degree, the area is a labyrinth of twisting alleyways so narrow that the houses touch at the top.

Splendid mosques and *khans* (merchants' inns) and crushes of medieval facades hedge in rutted streets on which little Suzuki vans compete for the right of way with donkeys and carts and merchants with impossibly laden barrows. The sweet, pungent aromas of turmeric, basil and cumin mix with the odours of livestock and petrol. It's a maze-like area that is completely disorientating in that the casual visitor easily loses not just any sense of direction but also any sense of time.

With dozens of listed monuments and few signposts or other concessions to the visitor, the Old City can be a fairly daunting place. We've broken it down into seven loosely defined areas, each of which could take a couple of hours to explore:

In addition, if you are visiting the Old City intent on browsing the bazaars, refer to the additional information contained in the boxed text 'Shopping the Damascus Souq' on pages 132-3.

The souq aside, appropriate dress is always necessary for visiting this part of Damascus – legs and shoulders should be decently covered, otherwise custodians may baulk at allowing you inside mosques.

Also note that any given opening times should be interpreted as a rough guide only; caretakers are usually around from 9 am until early evening, but they do follow their own whims. Additionally, most mosques are closed to visitors during prayer times.

City Walls & Citadel

The old city wall, first erected in grand style by the Romans, has been flattened and rebuilt several times over the past 2000 years. What stands today dates largely from the 13th century. It is pierced by a number of gates (the Arabic for gate is *bab*, the plural is *abwab*), only one of which, the restored **Bab ash-Sharqi**, or East Gate, dates from Roman times.

The best-preserved section of the old city wall runs between **Bab as-Salaama** (Gate of Safety) and **Bab Touma** (Thomas' Gate) in the north-east corner; otherwise for most of its length the wall is obscured by new buildings constructed over and around it. And, because of this, there is no way to walk a circuit of the walls, nor is it possible to walk anywhere up on the ramparts.

The citadel itself forms part of the western wall, appearing as a shear dressed-stone cliff as you approach the Old City from the new. Originally the site of a Roman fort, it was expanded during the early Islamic period and further strengthened by Salah ad-Din's Ayyubid dynasty in the 13th century to resist Crusader attacks. Since that time, it has been destroyed and rebuilt no less than half a dozen times. Much of the destruction was wrought by the successive invasions of Mongols that periodically swept down from Central Asia during the 13th and 14th centuries, while the rebuilding was done by the Mamluks and, later, the Ottomans. As the fortification became redundant in any strategic sense, it passed into use as a barracks and then became a prison, a use that it served right up until 1985. Since then, it has been undergoing restoration work.

While the citadel remains closed to the public, if you take the small cobbled road that leads past its north face (turn off Sharia ath-Thawra by the large monument to Salah ad-Din) you pass under an arch beside Mamluk-era walls and gates that give a good impression of the scale and solidity of the structure. This is also a good alternative route to the Umayyad Mosque that avoids the crowds in the Souq al-Hamidiyya.

Souq al-Hamidiyya

Just south of the citadel is the gaping entrance to the Old City's main covered market, the Souq al-Hamidiyya. It's a wide cobbled street lined with glitzy small emporiums all vying for your eye. It's roofed over with a vault of corrugated iron that blocks all but a few torch beam-like shafts of sunlight and gives the souq the dimmed atmosphere and promise of Ali Baba's cave.

Although the street dates back to Roman times, its present form is a product of the late 19th century – the two-storey shops, the roof and the generously wide street are all due to a bit of civic smartening up that was

carried out in honour of the Ottoman sultan Hamid II (hence the name, Al-Hamidiyya).

The Hamidiyya is probably also the closest thing Syria has to a tourist trap. The first stretch is lined with souvenir shops containing some of the kitschest objects north of Cairo's Khan al-Khalili – how about a working telephone done out in fake mother-of-pearl inlaid wood? It's in this area that foreigners are most likely to be accosted by merchants. A lot of moneychanging goes on here, too.

Among the souvenir stalls in this first bit of the souq is the main rug and carpet market; for more information on what's sold where see the 'Shopping the Damascus Souq' boxed text on pages 132-3.

Temple Gateway At the far, eastern end of Souq al-Hamidiyya you emerge back into glaring sunlight at the spot where the western gate of the 3rd century Roman Temple of Jupiter once stood. The outer walls of the Umayyad Mosque, directly ahead, mark the position of the temple itself but here, on ground now occupied by stalls selling Qurans and all manner of religious memorabilia, was the *propylaeum*, or monumental gateway to the temple complex. What remain today are two enormous Corinthian columns to your left supporting a decorated lintel, and three more columns to the right. With all the commercial bustle at this point it's hard to view the ensemble – and it does not help that it's all draped with electric cables, telegraph wires and lights – but if you carry on into the open square beyond you get a pretty good view looking back.

Umayyad Mosque

The Umayyad Mosque is one of the most notable buildings of Islam, and certainly the most important structure in all Syria. In terms of architectural and decorative splendour it ranks with Jerusalem's Dome of the Rock, while in sanctity it's second only to the holy mosques of Mecca and Medina. It also possesses a history unequalled by all three.

Despite this weight of significance, the Umayyad Mosque is not an overbearing,

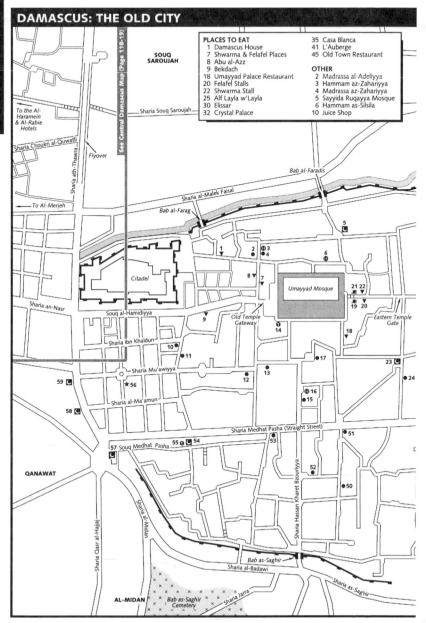

DAMASCUS: THE OLD CITY

SOUQ
SAROUJAH

PLACES TO EAT
1 Damascus House
7 Shwarma & Felafel Places
8 Abu al-Azz
9 Bekdach
18 Umayyad Palace Restaurant
20 Felafel Stalls
22 Shwarma Stall
25 Alf Layla w'Layla
30 Elissar
32 Crystal Palace

35 Casa Blanca
41 L'Auberge
45 Old Town Restaurant

OTHER
2 Madrassa al-Adeliyya
3 Hammam az-Zahariyya
4 Madrassa az-Zahariyya
5 Sayyida Ruqayya Mosque
6 Hammam as-Silsila
10 Juice Shop

See Central Damascus Map (Page 118-19)

To the Al-
Haramein
& Al-Rabie
Hotels

Sharia Souq Saroujah

Sharia Choukri al-Quwatli

Flyover

Sharia ath-Thawra

To Al-Merjeh

Bab al-Faradis

Sharia al-Malek Faisal

Bab al-Farag

Citadel

Sharia an-Nasr

Souq al-Hamidiyya

Old Temple
Gateway

Umayyad Mosque

Eastern Temple
Gate

Sharia ibn Khaldun

Sharia Mu'awiyya

Sharia al-Ma'amun

Sharia Medhat Pasha (Straight Street)

QANAWAT

Souq Medhat Pasha

Sharia Qasr al-Hajjaj

Sharia al-Midan

Sharia Hassan Kharet Bzouriyya

Bab as-Saghir

Sharia al-Badawi

Sharia as-Saghir

AL-MIDAN

Bab as-Saghir
Cemetery

Sharia Jarra

DAMASCUS: THE OLD CITY

11 Maristan Nur ad-Din
12 Madrassa an-Nuri
13 Azem Ecole
14 Toilets
15 Khan As'ad Pasha
16 Hammam Nur ad-Din
17 Azem Palace
19 An-Nafura Coffeehouse
21 Ash-Shams
 Coffeehouse
23 Mosque

24 Maktab Anbar
26 Madrassa al-Fathiyya
27 Hammam al-Qaimariyya
28 Mosque of Sheikh Farag
29 Hammam al-Bakri
31 Hammam al-Seikh Raslan
33 Joker Bar
34 Chapel of Ananias
36 Le Piano
37 Beit Nassan
38 Exchange Booth

39 Liquor Store/Bar
40 St Paul's Chapel
42 Bicycle Repair Shop
43 Khalil Haddad Craft
 Shop
44 Seibari Oriental
 Carpet Shop
46 St Mary's Church
47 Dahdah Palace
48 Vegetable Market
49 Al-Trabulsi Brasswork Shop

50 Beit Nizam
51 Minaret
52 Beit as-Siba'i
53 Khan Suleiman Pasha
54 Al-Qali Mosque
55 Toilets
56 Police
57 Mosque of Sinan
58 As-Siba'iyya Mosque
59 Ad-Darwishiyya
 Mosque

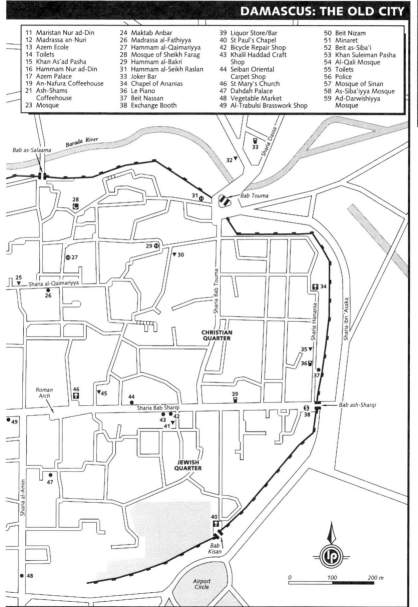

shuffle-in-silence sort of place. Unlike the cathedrals of Christendom, mosques were never built to inspire awe or trepidation in their users but rather to provide for spiritual needs. And so it is that the Umayyad Mosque is a peaceful place with plenty of shade and serenity offering a welcome respite from the heat and bustle outside.

The history of the site goes back 3000 years to the 9th century BC, when the Aramaeans built a temple to their god, Hadad (mentioned in the Book of Kings in the Old Testament). With the coming of the Romans the temple became associated with the god Jupiter and it was massively expanded.

A cousin to the great temples to Bel/Baal at Palmyra and Baalbek, the walls of the mosque as seen today were just the inner court of the temple. Around this was a large courtyard with four access points – traces of two of these grand gateways still exist and are described in the Souq al-Hamidiyya and North of the Mosque sections. After Constantine embraced Christianity as the official religion of the Roman empire, Jupiter was ousted from his temple in favour of Christ.

The former pagan shrine was replaced by a basilica dedicated to John the Baptist, whose head was said to be contained in a casket here.

When the Muslims entered Damascus in 636 they converted the eastern part of the basilica into a mosque but allowed the Christians to continue their worship in the western part. This arrangement continued for about 70 years. But, during this time, under Umayyad rule Damascus had become capital of the Islamic world and the caliph Khaled ibn al-Walid considered it necessary to empower the image of his city with 'a mosque the equal of which was never designed by anyone before me or anyone after me'.

Consequently, the Christians were elbowed out of the basilica while all the old Roman and Byzantine constructions were flattened and for the next 10 years over 1000 stonemasons and artisans were employed in the construction of a grand new Muslim cathedral. According to historical accounts, practically every surface wall was covered with rich mosaics, precious stones were set into the prayer niches, and the wooden ceil-

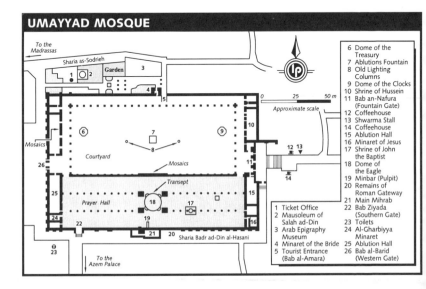

UMAYYAD MOSQUE

To the Madrassas

Sharia as-Sodrieh

Garden

0   25   50 m

Approximate scale

Mosaics

Courtyard

Mosaics

Transept

Prayer Hall

Minbar (Pulpit)

Sharia Badr ad-Din al-Hasani

To the Azem Palace

6 Dome of the Treasury
7 Ablutions Fountain
8 Old Lighting Columns
9 Dome of the Clocks
10 Shrine of Hussein
11 Bab an-Nafura (Fountain Gate)
12 Coffeehouse
13 Shwarma Stall
14 Coffeehouse
15 Ablution Hall
16 Minaret of Jesus
17 Shrine of John the Baptist
18 Dome of the Eagle
19 Minbar (Pulpit)
20 Remains of Roman Gateway
21 Main Mihrab
22 Bab Ziyada (Southern Gate)
23 Toilets
24 Al-Gharbiyya Minaret
25 Ablution Hall
26 Bab al-Barid (Western Gate)

1 Ticket Office
2 Mausoleum of Salah ad-Din
3 Arab Epigraphy Museum
4 Minaret of the Bride
5 Tourist Entrance (Bab al-Amara)

ing was inlaid with gold and hung with 600 lamps, also of gold. But since that time the mosque has been ravaged by invading Mongols, rocked by earthquakes and gutted by fire, most recently in 1893. Still, what remains is impressive enough.

Courtyard The northern part of the rectangular mosque is an expansive, open courtyard with a beautiful, white marble floor, flanked on three sides by a two-storey arcade. The fourth side is the facade of the prayer hall, dominated by a central section, which is covered by a gilding of golden **mosaics**. Much of this work is the result of 1960s renovations and you can only imagine how the courtyard area must have appeared when all the walls shimmered like this.

A larger expanse of mosaic also remains on the western arcade wall. Stretching some 37m in length and executed in shades of greens and limes on a background of gold, the mosaic depicts fairytale-like clusters of towers and domes, alternating with great spreading, heavily foliated trees. Scholars have yet to decide on what it all represents but Damascenes claim it's the Barada Valley and the paradise Mohammed saw in Damascus.

In the centre of the courtyard is an odd square-shaped **ablutions fountain** topped by a wooden-canopied pulpit, which is a fairly recent addition, while flanking it are two old columns which used to hold lamps to light the courtyard. The small octagonal structure on the western side, decorated with intricate 14th century mosaics and standing on eight recycled Roman columns, is the **Dome of the Treasury**, once used to keep public funds safe from thieves. It's counterbalanced by a domed structure on the east side built in the 18th century and known as the **Dome of the Clocks** because it's where the mosque's clocks used to be kept.

Minarets The courtyard is about the only place in the Old City from where you can actually see – at least partially – all three of the mosque's minarets. All date from the original construction but each has been ren-

ovated and restored at later dates by the Ayyubids, Mamluks and Ottomans. The one on the northern side is the **Minaret of the Bride**, the one in the south-west corner is the Mamluk-styled **Al-Gharbiyya minaret**, while the one on the south-eastern corner is the **Minaret of Jesus**, so named because local tradition has it that this is where Christ will appear on earth on Judgement Day.

Prayer Halls On the southern side of the courtyard is the rectangular prayer hall, its three aisles divided by a transept. The hall as you see it today is the Ottoman reconstruction that took place after the devastating fire of 1893. At the centre of the hall above the transept, resting on four great pillars, is the **Dome of the Eagle**, so called because it represents the eagle's head while the transept represents the body and the aisles are the wings. If you stand under the dome facing the *mihrab* (prayer niche) to the south and look up, you'll see eight names in Arabic. From the bottom right clockwise they are Allah, Mohammed and then the first four caliphs (who had been Companions of the Prophet), Abu Bakr, Omar, Othman and Ali. The last two names are Hassan and Hussein, Ali's two sons.

Looking somewhat out of place in the sanctuary is the green-domed marble-clad structure that is the shrine of John the Baptist (the Prophet Yehia to the Muslims). The story goes that during the building of the mosque back in the early 8th century a casket was discovered buried under the old basilica floor which contained the biblical character's head, still with skin and hair intact, and that's what's in the shrine. However, this is only one of several claimed final resting places for the gory relic and unless the saint was endowed with multiple heads, the authenticity of any such claims has to be seriously doubted.

The eastern side of the mosque contains another shrine and a claimed head, this one supposedly formerly belonging to Hussein, son of Ali and grandson of the Prophet. He was killed by the Umayyads at Kerbala in Iraq, but whether or not his head ended up here is more a matter of legend than fact – the Egyptians claim that they have the head buried underneath one of their mosques in Cairo. The shrine attracts large numbers of Shi'ite Muslims (Ali is the founder of Shi'ism – see Religion in the Facts about Syria chapter) and you may see black-clad Iranians arriving and making straight across the courtyard for this part of the mosque.

Visiting the Mosque The tourist entrance is through the northern Bab al-Amara. You buy your entrance ticket (S£10) from a small office just west of the gate. All women have to use the black robes supplied. Men are spared the robe but you won't be allowed in wearing shorts. As in all mosques, you must remove your shoes, and it's best to keep them with you. The mosque is open daily including Friday but you won't be admitted during noon prayers – roughly from 12.30 to 2 pm. The doors close in the evening after the final prayers. It's quite OK to take photos anywhere inside.

Mausoleum of Salah ad-Din In the small archaeological garden that lies along the north wall of the Umayyad Mosque are a few columns dating back to the original Roman Temple of Jupiter and a small white building topped by a rust-red dome which is the Mausoleum of Salah ad-Din. The famed, chivalrous adversary of the western Crusaders (for more on his life see History in the Facts about Syria chapter) died in Damascus in 1193 and the original mausoleum was erected on this site that same year. It was restored with funds made available by Kaiser Wilhelm II of Germany during his visit to Damascus in 1898.

As with the man himself, who was famed for his austerity, the mausoleum is a very modest affair. Inside are two cenotaphs – the walnut-wood one on the right, richly decorated with motifs of the Ayyubid period, contains Salah ad-Din's body, while the modern tomb in marble on the left was donated by Kaiser Wilhelm.

You supposedly need your ticket to the mosque to get into the mausoleum, but the caretaker doesn't seem too bothered with this. It's open from 10 am to 5 pm daily.

Arab Epigraphy Museum For most visitors this will be a case of a museum building being more engaging than its contents – the small calligraphic exhibit will attract only those with a particular interest. However, the 15th century Madrassa al-Jaqmaqiyya in which the collection is exhibited is a really fine example of characteristic Mamluk-era architecture. It's open from 8 am to 2 pm daily except Tuesday, and entry is S£100 (students S£25).

North of the Mosque
After leaving the Umayyad Mosque and Mausoleum of Salah ad-Din head west (see the Damascus: The Old City map) rather than south to the Souq al-Hamidiyya area. Not more than 100m along, on your right, you'll see two great old Quranic *madrassas*.

Al-Adeliyya & Az-Zahariyya Madrassas
Both of these teaching schools were erected in the 13th century during the ascendancy of the Ayyubids. On the left, the Madrassa al-Adeliyya was begun under Nur ad-Din and continued under a brother of Salah ad-Din called Al-Adel Seif ad-Din, whose grave it contains. Its facade is considered a classic example of Ayyubid architecture. It is now a library.

The Madrassa az-Zahariyya, opposite, was originally a private house belonging to the father of Salah ad-Din. Following the death in 1277 of the great Mamluk sultan Beybars, who went a long way to expelling the last of the Crusaders from the Levant – see History in the Facts about Syria chapter – it was converted into his mausoleum. Look for someone to open up the room where Beybars lies, as there are some interesting mosaics to inspect there. Apart from his burial chamber, the focal point of interest is again the entrance facade, with its alternate levels of black and cream stonework and complex decoration.

From the madrassas a good route is to head north and then bear right just past the

In sanctity, splendour and antiquity, Damascus' Umayyad Mosque is virtually unparalleled worldwide.

RETRO ROAD FLEET

Shiny new Mercedes and BMWs clog the streets and Hyundai has clearly made a major onslaught on the local market but new cars are a phenomenon of the liberated 1990s. For many years huge import charges ensured that Syria had one of the world's oldest car fleets. Remarkably, despite the influx of new cars most of the old ones seem to be surviving. There are lots of old Peugeot models from France, solid 50s and early 60s Benzes and Opels from the era of militaristic German model names like Kapitan or Admiral. You'll spot examples of now extinct British marques like Hillman, Austin or Humber. But most of all, Syrians love their American cars, most particularly Chevies. Many of these ancient vehicles are close to totting up a half-century on Syrian roads. Most of them bear the scars from navigating the dings and narrows of outrageous traffic but 10 minutes in Damascus or Aleppo will convince any visitor that mere survival is no mean feat. Many of these survivors, relics from an era when US cars were closely related to ocean liners, have been lovingly restored and often look movie-set new.

Tony Wheeler

Box: Early 50s Buick (photo by Tony Wheeler)

Left: 56 Chevrolet

Below: 57 Chevrolet

hammam; following this narrow alley will bring you to a small square addressing the main entrance of the Sayyida Ruqayya Mosque, a building that is well worth a quick visit, especially if you're a fan of chintzy decor.

Sayyida Ruqayya Mosque For centuries the mausoleum of Ruqayya bint al-Hussein ash-Shaheed bi-Kerbala (Ruqayya, the Daughter of the Martyr Hussein of Kerbala) was hidden among the clutter of tumbledown Damascene housing just to the north of the Umayyad Mosque. Not any more – it's now showcased in the most ostentatious hall in all Syria. In 1985, the Iranians (Ruqayya being a Shi'ite saint) began construction of a mosque around the mausoleum, designed very much in the modern Persian style. While the portico, courtyard and main dome are relatively restrained, and quite beautiful, the interior of the prayer hall is a riot of mosaiced mirrors. If they built mosques in Las Vegas this is what they'd look like. The whole complex strikes a very discordant note with the predominantly dusty yellows and greys of the rest of the Old City. Non-Muslim visitors are welcome any time outside of Friday prayers but women must wear the black cloaks provided.

From Sayyida Ruqayya head north to take a look at the **Bab al-Faradis**, one of the old city gates dating from 1241 – you can't actually see that much of the gate but the short stretch of market within the vaulted tunnel is quite atmospheric. If you then double back slightly and continue east you can reach the **Bab as-Salaama** which is the best preserved of the gates and a beautiful example of Ayyubid military architecture – unfortunately it is now draped with electric cables and telegraph wires.

From the As-Salaama gate head due south – the route will jink around with plenty of little side alleys, but don't turn – just keep straight on and eventually you'll connect with a main street running east-west, which is Sharia al-Qaimariyya. Almost in front of you should be the gate and fenced garden of the Madrassa al-Fathiyya.

Madrassa al-Fathiyya Built in 1742 in the Ottoman style, this is a gorgeous little place with a two storey arcade around a small central garden. Unfortunately, you can't enter the building proper as it's still in use as a Quranic school but you should at least be able to step inside the gate for a quick look around at the courtyard area.

If you walk west from the madrassa after 150m you come to a crossroads, either side of which you'll see the remains of the **triple gateway** that served as the eastern entrance to the compound of the Temple of Jupiter. Continue on straight ahead and you pass a clutch of shwarma stalls and two lazy coffeehouses (see Entertainment later in this chapter) before ascending a broad flight of steps that brings you up against the eastern wall of the Umayyad Mosque and what was the Roman-era monumental temple entrance (now the Bab an-Nafura, or Fountain Gate).

Following the street around will now take you along the mosque's southern walls (see the following section) and back, if you wish, to the Souq al-Hamidiyya.

South of the Mosque

South of the Umayyad Mosque is the heart of the souq with stretches of stalls devoted to spices, gold, sweets, perfume and fabrics – for a guide to what's sold where see the 'Shopping the Damascus Souq' boxed text on pages 132-3. If you can drag yourself away from the colourful and fragrant displays and the patter of the merchants, there are numerous wonderful bits of architecture to discover around here, including at least 18 khans – one or two of which are definitely worth seeking out – and a beautiful and tranquil small palace complex.

Azem Palace If you are only going to visit one old building in Damscus (beside the Umayyad Mosque) then it should be this, a stunning *tour de force* of all that's best about Damascene architecture.

The complex of buildings, courtyards and gardens that make up the palace were built from 1749 to 1752 as a private residence for the governor of Damascus, As'ad

Pasha al-Azem. It remained the Azem residence until the beginning of the 20th century when the family moved outside the Old City and the house was sold to the French to become their Institute of Archaeology and Islamic Art. The palace was badly damaged by rioters in the uprising against the French in 1925 but has since been beautifully restored.

As you enter, turn left then right, which will bring you through into the main outer courtyard with a pool and fountain and a variety of rooms and buildings around its edge. The first thing you'll notice is the mixed use of black basalt, limestone and sandstone, which creates a beautiful and subtle banding effect on all the facades and walls. This technique, known as *ablaq*, is a characteristic theme throughout Levantine and Egyptian architecture that was particularly popular under the Mamluks, but was also later adopted by Ottoman masons.

Each of the rooms is sumptuously decorated with wooden panelling, tiling and painted ceilings, the cumulative effect of which can be overwhelming. But before you reach the point at which you've had enough, do look in the rooms on the south side (to your right as you enter the courtyard); the one reached by the flight of stairs, featuring a central marble fountain, is the reception room and is probably the most impressive of all. The next room, on the other side of the snack kiosk, has a small corridor which leads back to a hammam complex, and that's quite interesting. The rooms also all contain displays with mannequins each on a different theme (a musical party, the pilgrimage, a wedding), which is why the palace is also known as the **Museum of the Arts & Popular Traditions of Syria**, but this is all pretty lame stuff and only distracts from the sublime architecture and interiors.

The Azem Palace is open from 9 am to 6 pm daily (4 pm in winter) except Tuesday; it is also closed for approximately two hours from 12.30 pm on Friday. Entry is S£300 (students S£15).

After leaving the Azem Palace it's worth making a quick detour west, past a glazed fruits shop and a herbal remedies place, to the Azem Ecole and, just beyond, the Madrassa an-Nuri.

Azem Ecole Built in 1770 by a member of the same Azem family responsible for the palace (who through successive generations governed Damascus from 1725 to 1809), this former madrassa is a little gem of Ottoman urban architecture. It has a beautiful tight little courtyard hemmed in by a three storey gallery, the upper floor of which is wood. Today, known as the Azem Ecole, it houses an expensive souvenir store (see Shopping later in this chapter) but you're not obliged to buy anything if you just want to go in and have a look around.

Madrassa an-Nuri Just 50m beyond the Ecole, at the start of a street devoted to gold and jewellery, you can easily pick out this building by its crimson, pimpled domes. The structure is fairly modern and not particularly noteworthy but inside is a surviving part of a madrassa dating from 1172 which houses the mausoleum of Nur ad-Din, the uncle of Salah ad-Din, who united Syria and paved the way for the latter's successes against the Crusaders in the latter 12th century. You don't need to enter the building to see the tomb chamber, instead you can walk down the narrow market alley beside the madrassa and peer in through a big iron grille opening in the wall.

Maristan Nur ad-Din Located 150m west of the Madrassa an-Nuri this is another of those fine buildings that has been pressed into service as a less than wonderful museum. At least in this case there is some connection between past and present function. The *maristan* was built in 1154 under the patronage of Nur ad-Din as a hospital and was the most advanced medical institution of the time. Remarkably, it stayed in use as a centre of healing right up until the 19th century. Now it serves as a **Science & Medical Museum**, filled with old medical and surgical odds and ends from Roman to Ottoman times, most of which look more like implements of torture. There's even an old electric-shock machine. It's easy to see why many patients carried good-luck charms. There's also a display of 100 or so medicinal herbs and spices used in ancient times – but what the room full of stuffed animals and birds is doing here is anybody's guess.

The maristan/museum is open from 8 am to 2 pm daily except Friday; admission is S£300 (students S£15). Labelling is in French and Arabic only.

Khan As'ad Pasha Along the vaulted souq running south from near the Azem Palace, and standing virtually side by side, are the Hammam Nur ad-Din (see Hammams later in this chapter), the most elegant of Damascus' old bathhouses, and the grand entrance to the Khan As'ad Pasha which, in our opinion, is the finest piece of architecture in the Old City. It was built in 1752 under the patronage of As'ad Pasha al-Azem. What makes it so special is the vast space the khan encompasses, achieved through a beautiful arrangement of nine domes supported by colossal grey and white piers. The fact that the central dome has collapsed allowing in a flood of sunlight actually improves the space. Although a lot of work recently went into restoring this khan, the authorities have yet to decide what to do with it – at the time of our last visit it was being woefully underused as an exhibition space.

Straight Street

Although it's now more commonly known as Sharia Medhat Pasha/Bab Sharqi, the main east-west street that bisects the Old City was historically known as Straight Street, from the Latin *Via Recta*. It was the main street of Damascus during Greek and Roman times, when it would have appeared something like the main avenues you can still see at Apamea or Palmyra. It was four times its present width and planted with a seemingly endless row of columns that supported a canvas street covering. During the early Islamic era, buildings started to encroach onto the street, to the point where today pedestrians have almost to flatten themselves against the shop fronts to allow a single lane of traffic to pass.

The street is busiest at the western end, where it's known as Sharia Medhat Pasha, and is largely devoted to the rag trade and lined by shops selling textiles and clothes. **Souq Medhat Pasha**, running parallel one block south, is full of more of the same.

Although there are few notable monuments or sites, the twisting narrow alleyways in this south-west corner of the Old City are particularly picturesque and tranquil and well worth exploring. One monument to look in on, though, is the **Khan Suleiman Pasha**, back on Sharia Medhat Pasha at the end of the souq – you can pick it out by its striped entrance. Built in 1732, it's a fairly modest khan of two storeys around a central courtyard that was formerly roofed by two domes; the domes collapsed at some point leaving the courtyard open to two great circular discs of sky.

The stretch of Straight Street around the junction with Sharia Hassan Kharet Bzouriyya is a pungent mix of spices and coffee, which gives way to a variety of shops ranging from butchers to brassworkers. In the sidestreets between here and Sharia al-Amin are some striking examples of old Damascene houses.

Damascene Houses A short loop off Straight Street takes in three excellent, finely decorated pieces of traditional domestic architecture of the kind described in the Old Houses of Damascus special section. Head south down Sharia Hassan Kharet Bzouriyya and take the first left for **Beit as-Siba'i**, built from 1769 to 1774. As was always the case, a blank facade belies an expansive, sumptuous interior. It's in an extremely good state of repair as for a time during the 1990s it served as the residence of the German ambassador. Now it stands empty and, as with many of these grand old places, the authorities don't quite know what to do with it. At present it serves occasionally as a set for historical TV dramas and as an atmospheric venue for ministerial functions.

Shopping the Damascus Souq

The Damascus souq is not as strictly ordered as its Aleppo counterpart – some lanes are predominated by certain types of trade, but generally everything's scattered everywhere. For instance the main **Souq al-Hamidiyya** is a mixture of all sorts from clothes to Qurans. However, there are some areas where certain wares predominate. Immediately on entering the Souq al-Hamidiyya from the west, off to the right are the rug and carpet shops. These items can be found cheaper elsewhere but this is where you'll strike the greatest concentration of them. As you come to the end of the first section of roofing, there's a great little passageway devoted almost purely to toiletries, which leads into household goods and toys and stationery.

The east end of Souq al-Hamidiyya features **clothes**, as does the area south, the **Souq an-Niswan**. Where Al-Hamidiyya ends and you hit the Quran sellers, turn right down a narrow fabric street and the first little passageway on your right leads to a **belly-dancing costumier**; the next right is a wonderful domed passageway that's part of an old khan.

The most aromatic and enchanting part of the whole bazaar is the dogleg **Souq al-Bzouriyya**, which is the covered area running south from the Umayyad Mosque. This mixes more jewellery with perfumes, spices, nuts and sweets, all illuminated in the evening by chandeliers hung in the passageway. It's an alluring place to linger with a few curious little places like the glazed fruits shop and, just around the corner, Dr Mounif Aidi's herbal remedy shop. Al-Bzouriyya gives way to the **Souq al-Attarine**, actually a stretch of Sharia Medhat Pasha (aka Straight Street) devoted to spices and coffee.

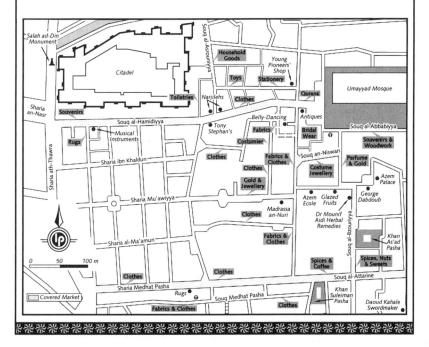

Shopping the Damascus Souq

Where to Buy

Give a wide berth to the souvenir shops on Souq al-Hamidiyya. A tale to illustrate why: we were looking for old books with hand-painted miniatures. They are rare, but we did find one or two in a ramshackle shop on Souq al-Abbabiyya. The seller wanted S£1500 but it was early in the day so we said, not bad, and continued looking. A few fruitless hours later we ended up in a large souvenir emporium on Al-Hamidiyya. The owner said he could lay his hands on what we wanted. He made a couple of phone calls and 15 minutes later a boy appeared with a package. No surprise that it was the two books we'd seen earlier, but out of perverse curiosity we were driven to ask, 'How much?' Three thousand, he replied. Some mark up.

On Souq al-Hamidiyya, **Tony Stephan's** at No 156 is worth a look. This place carries a range of merchandise from textiles through inlaid woodwork and jewellery to copper and brassware. Also, take a look at the **Azem Ecole**, a gorgeous sales space in a former madrassa (see the main text) full of beautiful items from Bedouin jewellery to silk products hand-woven on site. Prices are very high and you'll find cheaper elsewhere but few places match it for variety and quality.

We found prices at **George Dabdoub** on the small square in front of the entrance to the Azem Palace to be very fair, and the sales staff were knowledgeable and helpful without being pushy. Among other things, it sells jewellery, brass, icons, brocade and carpets.

Once you've looked around the souq and priced a few things, it's then worth checking the shops along Straight Street heading into the Christian Quarter (see the Old City map). The places down here specialise in one product and often have lower prices than the souq. For example, for brasswork visit the **Al-Trabulsi** workshop at 175 Straight Street or, for inlaid boxes and chests, go to **Khalil Haddad** at No 115. The selection and quality of carpets and rugs in this part of the Old City is also much better than you'll find around the Souq al-Hamidiyya – the rug sellers are just east of the Roman arch and a recommended one is the **Seibari Oriental carpet shop**. This is also the area to look for Damascene tablecloths, which sell down here for S£700 to S£800, compared to a starting price of S£1200 in the Souq al-Hamidiyya.

The Christian Quarter is also the area for antiques – and even antiquities. There are several places along Straight Street and a few on Sharia Hanania by Bab ash-Sharqi, but perhaps the most interesting is at the **Dahdah Palace** (see the main text), where the owner has a room full of 'finds' including coins, figurines and tiles recovered from demolished Damascene houses. Rummaging through this fascinating horde is very much like indulging in some amateur archaeology of your own.

However, our favourite Syrian souvenirs of all are to be found back in the heart of the souq, just north of Al-Hamidiyya at the **Young Pioneers' Shop**; here you'll find more Assad kitsch than the most ardent Baathist could ever dream of, from stickers to posters to button badges.

Shopping Hours

Shops in the souq start to close around 6 pm and by 7 pm nearly all the shutters are down. For a few hours, until about 10 pm, Souq al-Hamidiyya is taken over by street traders who use the pavement to lay out their wares of mostly cheap clothing and shoes. Most of the souq stays closed all day Friday, although the shops and businesses in the Christian Quarter close on Sunday instead.

Walking on past the As-Siba'i house and turning right at the T-junction brings you to **Beit Nizam**, another very similar 18th century house where, for a brief period in the late 19th century, worked the Victorian adventurer and diplomat, Sir Richard Burton. Its present fate is similar to that of Beit as-Siba'i. Both houses are open from 8 am to 2 pm Sunday to Thursday but many of the rooms are kept locked and in either case you can't view much more than the courtyard and peer through windows.

A two minute walk east through the back alleys (see The Old City map for directions) brings you to the **Dahdah Palace**, an 18th century residence owned by the elderly Mr Dahdah. If you ring the bell (No 9) his amiable wife, who speaks good English, may be free to show you around the many beautiful rooms, one of which operates as a dusty antique shop – see Shopping later in this chapter. They ask that visits be confined to the hours of 9 am to 1 pm and 4 to 6 pm.

And if you still aren't sated, you can back track to Sharia al-Amin and bear left along Straight Street, then right to the **Maktab Anbar** (Dar Anbar), which is a relatively late house, built only in 1867. It's huge, with three courtyards, and from 1920 it served for many years as a secondary school. These days it houses the offices of the team of architects responsible for the preservation and renovation of the Old City. It's open to visitors until 2 pm Sunday to Thursday.

Just east of the junction of Straight Street and Sharia al-Amin is a small **Roman arch** on a mean patch of grass, all that remains of what was likely a grand triple arch that once marked an important intersection. The arch now serves to mark the boundary of the Old City's Christian Quarter.

Christian Quarter

Like Aleppo's Armenian-Christian quarter of Al-Jdeida, this part of the Old City is slowly attracting the interest of entrepreneurs. Streets like Sharia Bab Touma and Sharia Hanania, just inside Bab ash-Sharqi, are beginning to acquire a number of chichi dining and drinking spots which, thankfully, are being carefully adapted so as not to clash with the very traditional surroundings.

There are a few churches in this area but the only one of any historical interest is the **Chapel of Ananias** (Kineesat Hanania), the old cellar of which is reputedly (but quite probably not) the house of Ananias, an early Christian disciple. He was charged to 'go into the street which is called Straight, and inquire in the house of Judas for one called Saul of Tarsus (St Paul) so that he might be able to touch him and restore Saul's sight' (Acts 9:11).

The entrance to the chapel is just inside the wall between Bab ash-Sharqi and Bab Touma. Take the last left before exiting the old city through Bab ash-Sharqi and follow it to the end. The chapel is in a crypt below the house where you (sometimes) pay to enter. It is open daily except Tuesday from 9 am to 1 pm and 3 to 6 pm. In the chapel, the story of Paul is told in a series of panels in Arabic and French.

Part way between the chapel and Bab ash-Sharqi is another fine old merchant's house, **Beit Nassan**, only this one isn't so old – it dates only to the beginning of the 20th century. As such, its layout and decor are not typical of the Damascene standard but it is attractive all the same, particularly the doors.

St Paul's Chapel in Bab Kisan purportedly marks the spot where the disciples lowered St Paul out of a window in a basket one night so that he could flee from the Jews, having angered them after preaching in the synagogues. You can't enter the Bab from the outside. Follow the driveway up to the new convent on the left and push open heavy wooden doors into the back of the Bab, now containing the small chapel.

SALIHIYYA

Strung out along the lower slopes of Jebel Qassioun north of the modern city centre, Salihiyya is a ramshackle old quarter of small shops, markets and Islamic architecture with a lovely small-town air about it. The district was first developed in the 12th century when Nur ad-Din settled Arab refugees here who had fled the Crusader

Richard Burton (1821-90)

Adventurer, explorer and scholar, translator of *The Thousand and One Nights* and *Karma Sutra*, Sir Richard Burton held the post of British Consul in Syria from 1869 to 1871. Although the consulate was in the city, the fact that the great gates were sealed at night made Burton, and his wife Isabel, feel claustrophobic. Instead, they chose to live in Salihiyya, which at that time was a Kurdish village of 15,000 inhabitants on the mountainside overlooking Damascus. Their house, as described in Isabel's letters, was flanked on one side by a mosque and on the other by a hammam and had a rooftop terrace where the Burtons would entertain guests. They also had a house in Bludan in the Barada Gorge and Burton would ride into Damascus once a week to attend to consular duties. But being the colourful, unconventional character that he was, Burton made enemies. After only two years into his post the foreign office in London felt compelled to remove him following numerous petitions of complaint, so ending what he would later refer to as the two happiest years of his life.

massacres in Jerusalem (1099). What grew up in the subsequent four centuries was a lively if straggly zone of mosques, mausoleums and other religious institutions. Though few of these places can be viewed from the inside, most of them are strung out along one particular street and passing by the domes and decorated portals makes for a great one or two hour walk.

The reason that few buildings here can be visited is that while ancient enough to warrant having preservation orders slapped on them, there are so many of these old monuments and the needs of the locals are so pressing, that they are all still in private service – albeit rarely for the purposes intended. So it is that the small 14th century **Tomb of Emir Kajkar** serves now as a Christian Union care centre, while the neighbouring **Tomb of Amat al-Latif**, which dates from 1243, harbours a human rights organisation. The **Madrassa Morsidiyya**, complete with the only surviving example of a square 13th century minaret in Damascus, is a kindergarten, while over the street a 14th century tomb with an elaborate *muqarnas* (stalactite-type stone carving used to decorate doorways and window recesses) doorway is obviously now somebody's home, judging by the satellite dish on the dome.

There are one or two hidden gems that are worth gaining access to, if at all possible. Tucked down a sidestreet called Sharia ibn al-Muqaddam, the 14th century **Jamaa al-Jedid** (New Mosque) was in the process of being rebuilt when we last visited, probably in honour of the tomb it contains within, which belongs to Ismat ad-Din Khatun, wife of first Nur ad-Din and then his successor Salah ad-Din. The burial chamber is richly decorated and certainly worth a look.

Back on the main street and just a little distance east, facing a small square is the modest **Mosque of Mohi ad-Din**. Architecturally undistinguished (although it does possess a beautiful late-Mamluk minaret), this is very much a community mosque with washing hanging from lines strung between the columns and men dozing in the shade of the prayer hall. It's also a popular centre of

DAMASCUS

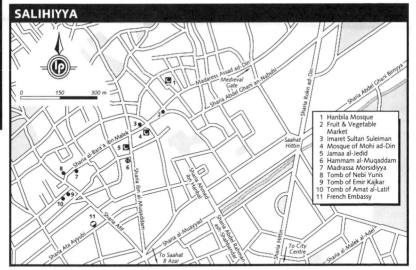

SALIHIYYA

0   150   300 m

Madaress Assad ad-Din
Medieval Gate
Sharia Abdel Ghani an-Nabulsi
Sharia Abdel Ghani an-Nabulsi
Sharia Rokn ad-Din
Sharia Abdel Ghani Birniyya
Sharia al-Bara'a Ibn Malek
Sharia Ahmed Ibn Hanbal
Sharia Ibn al-Muqaddam
Sharia Afif
Sharia Ata Ayyubi
Sharia al-Muayyad
Sharia Abdel Rahman ad-Shahbandar
Sharia Hittin
Sharia al-Malek al-Adel
Saahat Hittin
To Saahat 8 Azar
To City Centre

1 Hanbila Mosque
2 Fruit & Vegetable Market
3 Imaret Sultan Suleiman
4 Mosque of Mohi ad-Din
5 Jamaa al-Jedid
6 Hammam al-Muqaddam
7 Madrassa Morsidiyya
8 Tomb of Nebi Yunis
9 Tomb of Emir Kajkar
10 Tomb of Amat al-Latif
11 French Embassy

pilgrimage – buried here is the body of Sheikh Mohi ad-Din al-Arabi (died 1240) a great Sufi mystic whose writings are supposed to have greatly influenced Dante in his descriptions of hell. The tomb is down a flight of steps off the left-hand side of the entrance courtyard; the claustrophobic chamber is filled by a cenotaph enclosed in a glitzy silver casing and illuminated by fluorescent green light. It's not unusual to find large family groups picnicking happily down here.

As you leave the mosque, the **Imaret Sultan Suleiman**, just slightly back along and across the main street, is another building designed by Sinan (see Takiyya as-Suleimaniyya earlier in this chapter).

Historian Ross Burns in his excellent book, *Monuments of Syria: A Historical Guide,* also suggests the **Hanbila Mosque** is worth a visit for the Crusader columns in the courtyard and the pleasing simplicity of its minaret, but the main door was closed and locked when we visited and, despite a thorough search, we were unable to find anyone with the key.

Getting There & Away
To get up to Salihiyya walk north from Saahat 8 Azar (also known as Saahat Arnous) in central Damascus, up Sharia Jamal Abdel Nasser, cross a main road and continue on up Sharia Afif, past the French embassy on your left.

SAYYIDA ZEINAB MOSQUE
About 10km south of the city centre stands an extraordinary Iranian-built mosque on the site of the burial place of Sayyida Zeinab, granddaughter of Mohammed. The glistening gold of the onion-shaped dome topping the mausoleum and the brilliant shades of blue tile work that covers the edifice and its twin, freestanding minarets comes as something of a shock – in much the same way as do the great Shi'ite monuments of Kerbala in southern Iraq.

The main entrances to the sanctuary are on the northern and southern sides, and non-Muslims may enter the courtyard that surrounds the central mausoleum. This itself they may not penetrate, but you can have a look inside to the riot of colour that bedazzles the faithful. The latter kiss and stroke the silver grate surrounding Zeinab's tomb, seemingly in the hope of thus attracting to themselves some of the holiness of the much venerated descendant of the Prophet.

To get here, take a microbus for Karaj as-Sitt (S£5) from the microbus station on Sharia Fahkri al-Baroudi. At Karaj as-Sitt, which is a minibus station, you change vehicles for another that will take you on to the mosque (S£5). A taxi to the mosque and back should cost about S£150 to S£200 but as a foreigner you'll be lucky to get a driver to agree to that.

JEBEL QASSIOUN

To get a good view of the city, take a local microbus to Muhajireen from the lower end of Sharia Yousef al-Azmeh. Ride the bus to the end and then climb the stairs to higher up on Jebel Qassioun. A good time of day to visit is late in the afternoon when the sun is behind you.

ACTIVITIES
Hammams

If you only visit one hammam in Damascus then it probably should be the Hammam Nur ad-Din, in the covered street that runs between the Umayyad Mosque and Straight Street. Founded in the mid-12th century (though much remodelled since then), it is one of the grandest as well as the oldest functioning hammams in the country. It has an excellent, super-heated steam room, and the full deal of massage, bath and sauna with towel, soap and tea will cost you S£240. It's open from 9 am to 11 pm daily but it is strictly men only.

The Hammam az-Zahriyya, next to the madrassa of the same name, just north of the Umayyad Mosque, has also been in use since the 12th century but alterations over the centuries have completely deprived it of any charm. Nevertheless, the place is clean and well looked after and it does the job. A scrub, sauna, massage and tea will cost you S£175 (when we visited the masseur tried to con us into paying S£100 extra for his ser-

vices, so beware). It's open from 8 am to midnight daily.

More or less opposite the Minaret of the Bride at the rear of the Umayyad Mosque is the comparatively bland Hammam as-Silsila. It has cottoned on to tourists and charges S£300 for the whole package. Women generally can't get in, but mixed groups can arrange to take the place over for a hefty consideration in dollars. It's open from 9 am to 11 pm daily.

Heading towards Bab Touma is a much less touristed bathhouse, the Hammam Bakri. It opens daily from 8 am to midnight and charges about S£160 for the full scrub and massage. Women can get in by special reservation only.

About the only hammam we could find with a regular session for women is the Hammam al-Qaimariyya on Zuqqaq Hammam (Baths Lane), just north of Sharia Qaimariyya, 300m east of the Umayyad Mosque. It's very much a local establishment with no sign in English and no glamour. Women's hours are from midday to 5 pm daily.

For general information on hammam etiquette see the boxed text 'The Hammam' in the Facts about Syria chapter.

Swimming

The Olympic pool at the Tichreen sports complex just south-west of the Baramke terminal on Sharia Ali ibn Abi Taleb is open all year round from 6 am to 8 pm, although in the afternoons it is generally open to women only. A single entry ticket costs S£50 (if anyone's taking any notice) or you can get a monthly pass for S£500.

Otherwise, most of the big hotels open their pools in summer. They don't come cheap – the Cham Palace charges S£500 a day to nonguests.

Language Courses

It is possible to enrol in Arabic language courses in Damascus. Most people start off at the government Arabic Teaching Institute for Foreigners. For details see the Facts for the Visitor chapter.

PLACES TO STAY

The accommodation scene in Damascus is dire. At the lower end of the scale, there are two basic categories of accommodation: no star and two star. To qualify for two stars a hotel must have a lift and air-con in the rooms. Beyond that it doesn't matter – rooms can be dirty with just a few old battered bits of furniture, showers can be filthy and out of order and the place can be falling down, but a lift and air-con automatically confers two stars and a government-set room rate of US$17/23 for singles/doubles. With no-star establishments you have to climb stairs to get to your dirty room with its battered furniture and filthy shower and once there you get only a rickety ceiling fan to help move the rank air around.

You'll be glad to hear that there are a number of exceptions to this awful state of affairs but these places tend to fill up fast (particularly Al-Haramein, Al-Rabie and the Sultan) and you must book in advance.

PLACES TO STAY – BUDGET
Camping
If you really want to pitch a tent in an approved ground, **Damascus Camping**, also known as **Harasta Camping (☎ 445 5870)**, 4km out of town on the road to Homs, charges S£250 per person a day. It's basic but clean and has a toilet, shower and cooking facilities, but is hardly worth it, particularly when you consider the inconvenience of having to make your way into the centre and out again. A local microbus runs out there from along Sharia ath-Thawra. It is popular with some of the overland truck tours that make their way through here.

Hotels
With a couple of notable exceptions, the bulk of the cheap accommodation is to be found grouped around Al-Merjeh (Martyrs' Square). This is a good place to be as it's central to the sights and there are plenty of cheap eating places around. But beware, some of the hotels double as brothels and will accept foreigners only to later pressure them to take some female company. Some

will give you a bed and hit you for more than it's worth the next day, since you've taken up valuable space. To the best of our knowledge, none of the hotels we list below operate as brothels.

In any case, the true travellers' ghetto lies in the Souq Saroujah district in the pretty Sharia Bahsa, a little lane north off Sharia Choukri al-Quwatli. Here you'll find the hotels Al-Haramein and Al-Rabie, Damascus' two backpacker institutions.

Al-Haramein Hotel (☎ 231 9489, fax 231 4299, Sharia Bahsa) is an enchanting old Damascene house converted into a hotel. Rooms are extremely basic with no private bathrooms and there are only two terrible toilets for the whole building, but there are hot showers in the basement and the central courtyard is beautiful. At reception there are a couple of books filled with travellers' tips. Beds in share rooms cost S£150, while singles/doubles/triples go for S£200/325/425. You can also sleep on the roof for S£100. There's an additional charge of S£35 per shower. This place is *the* travellers' favourite in Damascus, so you have to book in advance to be sure of a room.

Al-Rabie Hotel (☎ 231 8374, fax 231 1875, Sharia Bahsa) is another old house with a courtyard that's even more attractive than that at Al-Haramein, however the rooms are not as good. Again, there are useful travellers' tips books at reception. Singles/doubles are S£200/350 with no charge for showers.

Hotel Saadeh, a couple of lanes east of Sharia Bahsa, is owned by the Al-Rabie and takes in the overspill but it's a semi-derelict building with absolutely foul rooms. While some rooms have individual showers, there are no communal facilities so you may have to traipse over to the Al-Rabie to wash. Beds are S£150 a throw or S£325 for a private double room.

The following hotels are all in the side-streets off and around Al-Merjeh. They are all very similar sorts of places, occupying upper floors of commercial buildings and reached by narrow staircases that lead up to pokey and fairly unwelcoming reception areas. With little to choose between them – including price – we've simply listed them in alphabetical order.

Balkiss Hotel (☎ 222 2506) two blocks east of Al-Merjeh is reasonably clean and the rooms on the top floor are extremely well lit (but hot in summer). Singles/doubles with ensuites are S£250/500.

Grand Ghazee (☎ 221 2481, Sharia al-Furat) just west of Al-Merjeh used to be a popular backpackers' alternative to Al-Haramein and Al-Rabie but standards have plummeted and now it's a very definite last resort with filthy beds and terrible bathrooms. Rooms are S£275/375.

Najemt ash-Sharq (☎ 222 9139, Al-Merjeh), on the south-west corner of the square above the juice stalls, is right in the thick of things and so can be noisy but it's relatively clean and a bit less seedy than most of the other places round here. Rooms with fan and bathroom are S£300/500.

Al-Rais (☎ 221 4252), one block east and south of Al-Merjeh, has been recommended by a couple of readers. It has basic rooms that contain nothing more than a bed but it comes with fresh sheets and the bathrooms are scrubbed regularly. A double with ensuite goes for S£400.

PLACES TO STAY – MID-RANGE

Although going upmarket a bit generally means a fairly hefty leap in prices, and not always a commensurate increase in quality, there are a few decent mid-range options. If you can't get into the Al-Haramein or Al-Rabie then our advice would be to push the budget a little and consider staying at one of the following (the cheapest are listed first).

Ramsis Hotel (☎ 221 6702, Al-Merjeh) has a foyer that's an antique piece – it's wonderful, especially the enormous radiogram. Unfortunately age has not lent charm to the rooms, which are spartan and grubby, although kept decently clean. Singles/doubles are the standard US$17/23.

Yarmouk Hotel (☎ 221 3283) is one of the better options among the proliferation of two-star joints in the sidestreets off Al-Merjeh. While the rooms are basic, they are clean and most have balconies with partial views of the square. Rooms are US$17/23.

Hotel al-Medina (☎ 221 9375, off Sharia Omar ben Abi Rabeea), aka the City Hotel, just south of Sharia Choukri al-Quwatli near the post office, is worth checking out; the foyer is a bit gloomy but the rooms are fine and better looked after than at most of the places around Al-Merjeh. Rooms are US$17/23.

Sultan Hotel (☎ 222 5768, fax 224 0372, Sharia Mousalam al-Baroudi), just west of the Hejaz train station, is quite easily the best of the cheaper mid-range hotels. Favoured by archaeologists, visiting academics, even minor diplomats and, of course, travellers, it's an extremely well run place with a desk staff that speaks English. There's a small library, a notice board and a decent reception/breakfast area with satellite TV. Some of the rooms are a bit shabby and only have a fan but others are air-con and fine, and they're all well maintained with newish bathrooms with hot water. Rates are US$18/24, or US$24/30 with breakfast.

As-Salaam Hotel (☎ 221 9764, fax 231 7457, south off Sharia Mousalam al-Baroudi) is a close second best to the Sultan. It has two floors of spotlessly clean air-con rooms all with newly fitted bathrooms. Rooms are US$17/24.

Hotel al-Imad (☎ 231 4225, Sharia ash-Shohada) at the north-east corner of Al-Merjeh is a good option – rooms are airy with air-con, and bathrooms are well looked after. The place is popular with tour groups so they're used to dealing with foreigners. Rooms are US$19/25.

French Tower Hotel (☎ 231 4000, fax 231 4002, Sharia 29 Mai) just north of the tourist office occupies the top floors of a modern apartment block. Air-con rooms are clean, bright and frilly with modern ensuite bathrooms. There's also a very nice breakfast terrace with views of northern Damascus and Jebel Qassioun. For the quality of the accommodation rooms are a bargain at are S£1200/1500.

Al-Majed Hotel (☎ 232 3300, fax 232 3304) just off Sharia 29 Mai, behind the

DAMASCUS

Cinema al-Ambassador, represents even more of a bargain; it's a new, very modern place with very comfortable spacious air-con rooms with fridge, satellite TV and spotlessly clean new bathrooms. At the time of writing it was only charging S£1500 a double. If your budget stretches to US$30 a night for accommodation, then this has to be the best deal in Damascus.

Alaa Tower I (☎/fax 231 1221) in an un-named side alley off Sharia Yousef al-Azmeh is one of a series of hotels of the same name, all of which offer decent value; modern, western-standard doubles with satellite TV and air-con go for US$40. If it is full, it will send you to one of its other six branches.

Orient Palace Hotel (☎ 223 1351, fax 221 1512, Saahat Hejaz), across from the Hejaz train station, has been around since the 1920s and depending on your level of enthusiasm it either retains plenty of period charm or resembles a gloomy 19th century medical institution. Rooms are big, though a bit fusty, they're clean and most have balconies. One distinct advantage is that the hotel is used to foreigners and is very professionally run. Doubles cost US$41.

Omar Khayyam Hotel (☎ 231 2666, fax 231 2668, Al-Merjeh) is a big old place with enormous, high-ceilinged rooms overlooking the square. However, the place is worn at the edges and far from luxurious, and is seriously overpriced with singles/doubles at US$42/52.

PLACES TO STAY – TOP END

At the time of writing, Damascus had nothing quite as charming as the hotels in the converted old houses in Aleppo's Al-Jdeida quarter but there are rumours that something similar is in the pipeline for the Old City. In the meantime, the Cham Palace is one of the better hotels in the national chain, while the Sheraton and Le Meridien are also quite good, if inconveniently located for sightseeing.

Semiramis Hotel (☎ 223 3555, fax 221 6797, Sharia Choukri al-Quwatli) is a modestly sized place with a good central location (though the views are lousy) that has recently

been refurbished. It has a pool and a popular Chinese restaurant. Singles cost US$110 to US$150 while doubles will cost you US$130 to US$170, plus taxes.

Le Meridien Damas (☎ 373 8730, fax 373 8661, Sharia Choukri al-Quwatli), about 10 minutes walk west of the city centre, has an attractive foyer and a shopping court, plus all the other usual amenities including a business centre, pool, health club and tennis courts. Singles range from US$205 to US$220 while doubles are from US$240 to US$260.

Sheraton Hotel (☎ 222 9300, fax 224 3607, Saahat Umawiyeen) is at the western end of Sharia Choukri al-Quwatli, 2km distant from the centre, which is a terrible location unless you have your own transport. Singles range from US$175 to US$260, doubles from US$205 to US$310, not including taxes.

Cham Palace (☎ 223 2300, fax 221 2398, Sharia Maysaloun) is the most conveniently located of the biggies. It's just one block west of Saahat Yousef al-Azmeh, right in the middle of the new city centre. Singles range from US$150 to US$210, while doubles go from US$160 to US$240, plus 10% taxes.

Two smaller Cham hotels, the *Jala'a* and *Tichreen*, further from the centre, have singles/doubles for US$90/110. The Tichreen is near the Damascus International Fair and the Jala'a is out west in the Mezzeh district.

PLACES TO EAT

Generally speaking, the cheapest restaurants are all around Al-Merjeh. Then there's a variety of slightly more expensive options scattered throughout the city centre, mostly within a few minutes walk of Saahat Yousef al-Azmeh, with the chichi, top-end places mostly all in the Old City.

Budget Dining

Central Damascus The sidestreets off Al-Merjeh are crowded with cheap eateries, mostly offering the staples of *shwarma* and *felafel*, while some of the pastry shops also do some good savouries (see Self-Catering later in this section). There are also a couple of good cheap juice places right on the square.

Juices cost anything up to S£50, depending on how huge your glass is. If you are staying at the Sultan or any other place in the vicinity of the post office, then *Al-Santir* is a good little toasted sandwich and juice bar handy for breakfast – there's no sign in English but it's the place next to the spectacles shop.

Al-Masri (Sharia Said al-Jabri) is an excellent, cheap lunch place heavily patronised by local office workers. The name means 'the Egyptian' and much of the menu is the kind of home-cooked fare you'd find in the backstreet eateries of Cairo, including no-frills dishes like *shakshouka* (fried egg and mince meat; S£65), *fuul* (mashed fava beans, garlic and lemon) and a variety of *fatahs* (bread soaked in humous and oil, topped with chickpeas and meat; S£80). It's filling.

An-Nadwa (Sharia al-Mutanabi), just off main Sharia Bur Said, is more like a work canteen than a restaurant and has a basic menu but the food (which is very average) is cheap with *kebabs* (lamb cooked on a skewer served with bread) at S£60 to S£80 and plenty of *mezze* (starters) all under S£20. Beer is also served and it's about the cheapest in town at S£36 (but send the 'complimentary' nuts back as they'll appear on the bill and cost more than the drink).

Pizza Roma, off Sharia Maysaloun, west of the Cham Palace hotel, is run by a guy who used to work for Pizza Hut in Abu Dhabi. He has adapted the idea and this takeaway or eat-in joint does an acceptable American-style deep-pan pizza for less than S£100 – though there's a choice of only two types.

Old City Since most people like to spend the bulk of their time in Damascus in the Old City, it's a logical place to look for a bite to eat too. Surprisingly then, there are only a couple of places where you'll have any luck finding something cheap and convenient (though there's no shortage of more upmarket options – described under Restaurants).

The best bet is the small alley east of the Umayyad Mosque; just past the two coffee-houses are a couple of very good *shwarma* places and a stall that does probably the best value *felafel* in town – a truly fat felafel with

salad will cost you S£25. There's another collection of felafel and shwarma hole-in-the-wall *eateries* in the covered market lane that runs north off Souq al-Hamidiyya just before you reach the mosque.

Restaurants

Most Damascus restaurants, unless otherwise stated, open around 11 am for lunch and serve through until midnight or 1 am. Reservations are rarely necessary.

Central Damascus The cheaper restaurants are in the Al-Merjeh area, while the better restaurants are dotted around the city centre. All are on the Central Damascus map except for Aram, which appears on the Greater Damascus map.

Al-Arabi, off the south-west corner of Al-Merjeh, is the name of two adjacent cheap restaurants, both run by the same management and sharing the same extensive menu with an unusually wide range of meat and vegetable dishes. The food is hit and miss and there are no prices given, but for a main dish plus a couple of mezze you can expect to pay S£200. Staff can be extremely rude but if you can get a table out on the pavement it's worth putting up with them.

Abu Nawas and *Dik Aljin*, on the south-west corner of Al-Merjeh, are two adjacent new eateries, both very clean and efficiently run, and with similarly short menus of mezze, kebabs and chicken. The meat is stored in refrigerated cabinets at the front of the restaurants and cooked there on open grills. A main meal with a couple of mezze and a cold Barada beer will come to exactly S£200, and no hidden extras are added to the bill. Both places also do good breakfasts.

Damascus Workers' Club (An-Nadi al-Umal), off Sharia 29 Mai, behind the Cinema al-Ambassador, is an unexpected delight amid the modernity of the city centre: a garden restaurant in the sprawling courtyard of an old house, complete with fountain and plenty of greenery. A lot of people just come here to drink but the food is extremely good – it's standard fare like mezze, kebabs and *shish tawouk* (spicy chicken on a skewer served with bread), but all very well done, and quite reasonably priced (two mezze, two kebabs and two beers came to S£385). It's open from 5 pm to midnight only.

Al-Kamal (Sharia 29 Mai), next to the tourist office, reminds us very much of a Parisian bistro with its air of busy efficiency, regular clientele (including unaccompanied women) and good value *plats du jour*. The menu features a lot of home-style dishes like mixed vegetable stews but the best are on the changing daily menu – try the *kabsa*, which is exotically spiced rice with chicken or lamb. Main dishes are in the region of S£90, while mezze are S£15 to S£30. No alcohol is served.

Aram (Saahat 8 Azar) does good traditional Syrian fare including *shinklish*, a tangy strong cheese and tomato salad that's a particular favourite of ours but is often hard to find. The restaurant itself is not that easy to locate either, as it's hidden up on the 3rd floor of a drab office-type building but it does have a good terrace overlooking the square. Prices are average – a bill for two came to S£350.

Old City It's only as recently as the 1990s that the first restaurants opened in the Old City. Prior to that, the souqs aside, the place was considered by the folk that dine out to be a bit beyond the pale. These days the story couldn't be more different. There are at least a dozen fine dining options, most of them in the Christian Quarter, and you can be sure there are many more to come. A couple of the places (notably *Abu al-Ezz* and *Damascus House* just north of Souq al-Hamidiyya) cater primarily to tourist parties and, quite frankly, they're awful – set menus only, rude staff and indifferent, overpriced food. Worse still, the interiors of these two places have been turned into ridiculous pantomime sets.

Umayyad Palace Restaurant (☎ 222 0826) south of the Umayyad Mosque, belongs to the same genre as the Abu al-Ezz but it has not unnecessarily tarted up the lovely old rooms that make up the dining area. It offers set meals only but the food is laid out buffet style and it is excellent. Lunch here is S£350 per person but we would recommend coming in the evening when, in addition to the food, there is superb entertainment included (see Entertainment later in this chapter) for an all-in price of S£700 per head. Expensive, yes, but worth it.

Alf Layla w'Layla (☎ 542 3021, Sharia Qaimariyya), or in English 'The Thousand and One Nights', is yet another place for tourists but it would seem that it doesn't get too much trade as the place is becoming a little run-down and scruffy. Although it does do set meals to order, there is an à la carte menu of Syrian standards with mezze from S£15 to S£50 and mains at around the S£100 mark.

Crystal Palace (☎ 542 0052, Sharia Qasr al-Ballur), just outside the Old City walls near Bab Touma, is a good moderately priced open-air restaurant. It's a garden-type affair, separated from the main road by vine-covered trellises, and is fairly small and intimate with friendly staff. The menu's composed of mezze (around S£30 each) and grilled meats (S£100), and the food, while not exceptional, is good. Beer is available, though araq is definitely the drink of choice with most of the patrons.

Old Town Restaurant (☎ 542 8088) in the Christian Quarter is one of the newest and most tasteful old house conversions. The main dining area is in an open courtyard with flagged flooring and striped stone walls, plenty of greenery and tasteful furnishings – unfortunately the effect is marred by the TVs and piano player. The menu is western with some pastas at the cheaper end (around S£125), moving up through steaks and the like. Local beer is S£65.

Elissar (☎ 542 4300, Bab Touma) offers a classy atmosphere and perhaps the best dining in Damascus. It's an enormous old house with tables filling the courtyard and two upper levels of terraces. While the menu of typical Syrian cuisine offers few surprises, the food is as good as it gets. Of course, it doesn't come cheap: entrées are in the region of S£60, while main dishes clock in at around S£250. Our bill for two was

S£800 (which included two local beers and a huge platter of complimentary fruit) but we considered it money well spent. Reservations are recommended.

Casa Blanca (☎ 541 7598, Sharia Hanania), near Bab Sharqi, is right up at the top end of the market, specialising in French cuisine with a menu inclined heavily towards steaks in sauces and seafood. The food is said to be superb, but then you'd expect nothing less with mains priced from S£350 to S£500.

Self-Catering

For the do-it-yourself crowd, there is a good *fruit and vegetable market* wedged in-between Al-Merjeh and Sharia Choukri al-Quwatli. For things like milk and cheese, there's a decent grocery store, the *Al-Sha'ar*, next to the coffeehouses just off the east side of Al-Merjeh, while for hot freshly baked bread go to the hole-in-the-wall *bakeries* at the north end of Sharia Bahsa, just north of the Al-Haramein and Al-Rabie hotels in the Souq Saroujah area.

Of the many pastry shops on the south side of Al-Merjeh, we think the best is *Abu Rashid*, down the alley at the south-east corner of the square and up at the top of the steps. We gorged ourselves on its sickly sweet pastries on numerous occasions, and it also does savouries like *kibbeh* (minced lamb patties), cheese or meat *boreks* (pastry triangles) and something called *ouzi sarrar*, which is a bit like a big, round samosa – rice, meat, peas and spices in a pastry ball.

Takeaway beer and araq are available from the Elias Hayek liquor shop on Sharia Ramy, just off Al-Merjeh – it's open until 8 pm daily except Friday.

Ice Cream

For one of the best ice creams you are likely to taste, head for *Bekdach* in the Souq al-Hamidiyya. There is at least one 'imitation' place before you get to it (they are both on the right heading towards the Umayyad Mosque), but wait for the best.

A bowl of ice cream, covered with pistachio nuts, or *sahlab* (a kind of smooth, sweet milk pudding) covered with same, costs S£25 and is worth every lira. That's all they serve, but they do it well.

ENTERTAINMENT
Coffeehouses & Cafes

The finest place to relax in Damascus is at either of the two coffeehouses nestled in the shadow of the Umayyad Mosque's eastern wall. *Ash-Shams*, on the north side of the street, occupies a former hammam, which makes for an excellent setting for a coffee and *narjileh* (water pipe) – although it's much more entertaining to sit out and watch the activity in the street.

The exception is each evening at 6 pm when a local *hakawiti*, or storyteller, takes up the chair inside. His performance is all in Arabic but it's still worth catching for the accompanying dramatic flourishes and the novelty of witnessing one of the last few practitioners of an art form that was once such a vital part of popular Middle Eastern culture – see the boxed text 'Keeping the Story Going' over the page. The *An-Nafura* (Fountain), on the south side of the street, is by far the older of the two coffeehouses and, if you're concerned about such things, it's also cheaper.

In central Damascus, there are a couple of coffeehouses on one of the sidestreets leading east off Al-Merjeh, although they are not particularly friendly places. You may feel more comfortable in the *Al-Hejazi al-Jedid*, a big, open-air coffeehouse just across from the telephone office on Sharia an-Nasr, near the Hejaz train station, or there's a very laid-back place over the road on the corner of sharias An-Nasr and Ramy that is heavily frequented by African students.

One place that's popular with travellers is the *rooftop coffeehouse* just south of Al-Merjeh and next to the Iranian cultural centre on the corner by the Choukri al-Quwatli flyover. The *Cafe Havana* on Sharia Bur Said is also quite interesting and has something of a history as a haunt for coup planners and other plotters in the days before President Hafez al-Assad got a firm grip on the country.

DAMASCUS

Keeping the Story Going

In one of the tales that make up the collection known as *The Thousand and One Nights*, a king commissions a merchant to seek out the most marvellous story ever. The merchant sends out his slaves on the quest and at last success is achieved – a slave hears a suitably wondrous story told in Damascus by an old man who tells stories every day, seated on his storyteller's throne.

Jump forward some 500 years or so from the time that the tales of the *Nights* were in popular circulation, and here in Damascus today there is still an old man who tells stories every day, seated on his version of a storyteller's throne. His name is Abu Shady and he's one of the last of the Syrian *hakawiti*, or professional storytellers.

Enjoying a fairly low-level status on a par with quack doctors, astrologers and charm sellers, storytellers were a common feature of Middle Eastern city street life as far back as the 12th century. With the spread of coffee-drinking during Ottoman times, the storytellers moved off the street and into the coffeehouse.

> He recites walking to and fro in the middle of the coffee room, stopping only now and then, when the expression requires some emphatical attitude ... Not unfrequently in the midst of some interesting adventure ... he breaks off abruptly and makes his escape ... the auditors suspending their curiosity are induced to return at the same time next day to hear the sequel.
>
> **The Natural History of Aleppo by Alexander Russell (1794)**

As with so many Arab world traditions, the art of public storytelling has largely failed to survive the 20th century, supplanted in the coffeehouses first by radios, then by television. According to Abu Shady, the last professional storyteller in Syria went into retirement in the 1970s. Abu Shady, who was a frequent member of the audience in coffeehouses as a boy, decided to revive the profession in 1990. Since then he's been appearing nightly, first at the An-Nafura, now at the Ash-Shams. Costumed in baggy trousers and waistcoat with a fez on his head, he recounts nightly from the tale of Sultan Beybars, a tale that is exactly 356 instalments long. And once that's finished he'll begin on the story of Antar ibn Shadad, another Islamic hero, and another epic that takes a year in the telling.

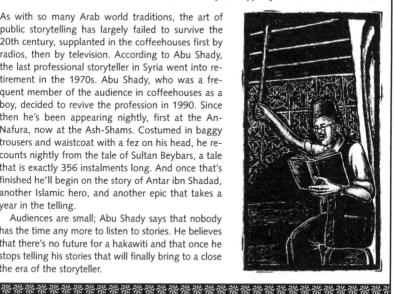

Audiences are small; Abu Shady says that nobody has the time any more to listen to stories. He believes that there's no future for a hakawiti and that once he stops telling his stories that will finally bring to a close the era of the storyteller.

Bars

While there's no shortage of restaurants serving alcohol, there are actually few dedicated bars. About the most convenient, and a popular haunt with locals and backpackers alike, is the **Karnak** above the Hotel Siyaha on Al-

Mosques of Damascus: colourful mosque built over the tomb of Sayyida Zeinab, Mohammed's granddaughter (top left); and the modern Sayyida Ruqayya Mosque (top right) with its beautifully decorated dome (bottom).

DAMIEN SIMONIS

ANDREW HUMPHREYS

TONY WHEELER

Damascus: Takiyya as-Suleimaniyya (top), once a mosque and a pilgrim's hostel, now houses an army museum; the ubiquitous president Hafez al-Assad (bottom left); Khan Suleiman Pasha, once a domed inn, now a striking monument to the travelling traders of the past (bottom right).

Merjeh – just head up the stairs in the street entrance off the square. You can eat here, but really it's more a serious drinking place with patrons knocking back the beers (S£50) or araq until two in the morning. You wouldn't bring your mother here, though. On the other hand, she'd probably love the *Damascus Workers' Club* – see Places to Eat. Though people do eat here, plenty take a table and order only beer (S£55). It's open until around midnight.

In the Old City there is a pokey little men-only liquor shop-cum-bar on Sharia Bab Sharqi, which is interesting for a quick beer but you are unlikely to feel very comfortable there. Round the corner but a different world altogether is the *Piano Bar*; however, this place is so uptight (there's a strictly enforced couples-only policy) and the beer so pricey (S£120 for the local stuff) that you probably wouldn't want to linger around here for too long, either.

You could try the *Joker Bar*, a dark little western-style place off Sharia Dassa, just outside Bab Touma. It was gloomy the night we visited but maybe it livens up on the advertised karaoke evenings. If not, then the nearby *Crystal Palace* is a restaurant that doesn't mind if you order alcohol only.

All the large hotels have bars, and two have the same name – *The Pub*. The Sheraton's version is popular with expats and one of the better places for meeting long-termers in Damascus, while the one in the *Al-Fardous Tower Hotel* features a little light jazz piano in the evenings to accompany your S£175 can of Carlsberg.

Discos & Nightclubs

Le Meridien Damas has a disco playing a mix of Middle Eastern and western pop. The entry cost of S£500 includes one drink. Subsequent tipples cost S£250 a throw. It's a similar story at the *Jet Set* disco in the Cham Palace hotel. Otherwise, the only alternative seems to be the sleazy nightclubs scattered around the city centre. These all charge between S£250 and S£400 admission and then on top of that it's S£150 to S£250 for a beer.

Cinema

Most of the cinemas around show pretty appalling fare. The exception is the *Cinema de Cham* at the Cham Palace hotel. This place regularly screens almost-current Hollywood releases in its two wide-screen auditoriums. Tickets cost S£150. The only way to find out what's showing is to drop by.

Theatre & Music

The *national theatre* (Saahat Umawiyeen) is at the western end of Sharia Choukri al-Quwatli, and there's another large *theatre* (Sharia 29 Mai), the Al-Qabbani, north of the tourist office. Not a lot goes on at either (see the Arts section in the Facts about Syria chapter) but you can ask at the tourist office for details of what's on. Otherwise, some of the cultural centres have fairly active programs of events and performances – for contact details see the Information section earlier in this chapter.

Traditional Dance

The Abu al-Ezz, Umayyad Palace Restaurant and possibly the Damascus House restaurants in the Old City include a floorshow as part of their fixed menu package (see Places to Eat). We visited the Umayyad Palace Restaurant one evening and along with the buffet we got whirling dervishes and musicians, plus a troupe of singers/ sword fighters/human pyramid builders (with the restaurant dwarf as the top of the pyramid). The dervishes all belong to one particular family and, along with one troupe in Aleppo, are among the last of their kind in Syria since Assad closed down all the Dervish colleges.

The Centre Culturel Français (see Information earlier in this chapter) also sponsors performances by local musicians – check their notice board for details.

SHOPPING

The best and most obvious place to shop in Damascus is the extensive souq, which is where you'll find spices, fabrics, handicrafts, gold and silver, jewellery, rugs, copper and brasswork and general souvenirs, all of which are covered in the boxed text

'Shopping the Damascus Souq', earlier in this chapter.

For more of the same, visit what the tourist office calls 'Handicrafts Lane', a small stone alleyway that's part of the Takiyya as-Suleimaniyya complex just south of Sharia Choukri al-Quwatli. Off the lane is the Artisanat, a Turkish madrassa that has been converted into workshops whose goods are sold on site. The whole complex, small though it is and limited in choice, is quite lovely and it is certainly worth taking a look even if you have absolutely no intention of buying anything.

For nontourist-oriented shopping, the main area is just north of the Cham Palace hotel in central Damascus, centred on Sharia al-Hamra and the pedestrianised Sharia Salihiyya. These two virtually parallel streets are full of mainly clothes shops, with everything from veil specialists to the likes of Benetton.

Note that most shops close early in Damascus, bringing down the shutters at 7 pm prompt.

Music
Damascus has a superb CD and cassette shop in Abdel Razek Mousali on Sharia Bur Said, just south of Saahat Yousef al-Azmeh. It specialises in CDs of the giants of the Arab world, artists like Umm Kolthum, Fairouz, Farid al-Atrache and Abdel Halim Hafez. The selection is superb and extensive and if it's not on the shelves you will probably find it in the back catalogue stored away in drawers.

Prices are cheap at S£300 for most CDs, or S£60 for cassettes. If you are interested in picking something up but not sure what to go for, see the Arts section in the Facts about Syria chapter.

For recordings of contemporary Arab world music and a limited selection of pirated tapes of western artists there's A&E Records, a cassette shop on Sharia Muradi, just off Maysaloun opposite the Cham Palace hotel. You should also check the Lido music shop towards the western end of Sharia Maysaloun.

Musical Instruments
If you are at all interested in Arabic music, or a musician yourself, you might be keen to visit the small workshop of a guy that makes *ouds*, the traditional Middle Eastern equivalent of the classical guitar. In a small, open-fronted space on Sharia Bahsa in Souq Saroujah he finishes and strings the shells, which are produced in another small, nearby workshop. Less well made models sell for around S£1500 (roughly US$30), while finer examples go for between S£4000 and S£5000 (US$80 to US$100). Ouds are also sold at a musical instrument shop just across from the People's Assembly building in the city centre, and at a few way overpriced places along the Souq al-Hamidiyya.

GETTING THERE & AWAY
See the Getting Around chapter for some advice on the best modes of transport between Damascus and the rest of the country.

Air
There are several Syrianair offices scattered about the city centre (for example, Sharia Fardous, on Sharia Said al-Jabri across from the post office, and up on Saahat Maghrebiyya); central sales and reservations numbers include ☎ 223 2154, 223 2159 and 222 9000. The telephone numbers for Damascus airport are ☎ 543 0201/9.

From Damascus Syrianair flies once or twice daily to Aleppo (S£600 one way, one hour), three times a week to Deir ez-Zur (S£600 one way, one hour), three times a week to Qamishle (S£900 one way, 80 minutes), and once a week to Lattakia (S£500 one way, 45 minutes). Return fares are exactly double the single fare.

For international flights to Damascus see the Getting There & Away chapter.

You'll find almost all of the airline offices and travel agencies for international travel on Sharia Maysaloun, opposite the Cham Palace hotel, or on Sharia Fardous, one block to the south.

Note, other than Syrianair and, in this case, British Airways (see Central Damascus map), airline offices are generally not marked on the maps in this book. Following, however, are the addresses of some of the larger carriers.

Aeroflot
(☎ 231 7952) Sharia 29 Mai
Air France
(☎ 221 8580) Le Meridien Damas
Austrian Airlines
(☎ 223 8297) Sharia Maysaloun
British Airways
(☎ 331 0000) Sharia Arjentine
EgyptAir
(☎ 223 2158) Saahat Hejaz, opposite the train station
Emirates
(☎ 231 3451) Sharia 29 Mai
Gulf Air
(☎ 222 1209) Sharia Maysaloun
Iran Air
(☎ 222 6431) Sharia Maysaloun
KLM (Royal Dutch Airlines)
(☎ 221 3395) 11 Sharia Fardous
Lufthansa Airlines
(☎ 221 1165) cnr of sharias Maysaloun and Muradi
Middle East Airlines
(☎ 222 4993) 88 Sharia Barada
Olympic Airways
(☎ 223 6660) Sharia Maysaloun
Royal Jordanian
(☎ 221 1267) Sharia 29 Mai
Swissair
same office as Austrian Airlines
Turkish Airlines
(☎ 223 9770) Sharia Maysaloun

Bus

There are two main bus stations in Damascus: Harasta, which has services to the north, and Baramke, which deals with services to the south, plus international services to Jordan, Lebanon, Egypt and the Gulf. In addition there are several small minibus and microbus stations serving specific regional destinations.

For a description of luxury, Pullman and Karnak buses and how they differ, see the Getting Around chapter.

Luxury Bus The Harasta terminal, from where all the northbound luxury buses go, is about 6km north-west of the city centre.

All the big private bus companies have their offices here, including Al-Ahliah, Qadmous and Al-Rayan. Prices are much of a muchness and average one-way fares include Aleppo (S£150, five hours), Deir ez-Zur (S£175, seven hours), Hama (S£90, 2½ hours), Homs (S£70, two hours), Lattakia (S£150, 4½ hours), Palmyra (S£130, four hours) and Tartus (S£110, three hours). There's a 24 hour left-luggage office at the far end of the booking concourse in unit 52.

To get up to Harasta you can take a microbus from Al-Merjeh (ask for 'karajat Harasta') for S£5 or a taxi will cost S£30 on the meter.

Some of the bus companies also have ticket offices in central(ish) Damascus: Al-Ahliah on Sharia Filasteen out past the immigration office, Qadmous and Damas Tour are under the Jisr ar-Rais flyover, west of the National Museum, while Zeitouni is under the Choukri al-Quwatli flyover, just east of Sharia Yousef al-Azmeh. Zeitouni aside, none of these offices is particularly convenient and as buses to almost all domestic destinations are so frequent it's pretty safe to just turn up at Harasta and buy a ticket for the next bus out.

Karnak Karnak services are split between the two big terminals; most domestic services go from Harasta, while international services go from Baramke, a conglomeration of bus, minibus, microbus and service taxi stations about a 15 minute walk to the south-west of Al-Merjeh. It's a big, bustling place that even has a reasonable cafeteria. Karnak's international service office here is in the south-western quarter of the terminal (see the map) and from the lot out the front services depart to destinations in Turkey, Lebanon, Jordan, Egypt and the Gulf – see the sections following.

Fares on Karnak's domestic Syrian services are generally a little bit cheaper than those on the luxury buses run by the private companies, but not always.

Note that although there is a Karnak office in the city centre it does not sell bus tickets, only tours.

Pullman The Pullman bus station is part of the Baramke terminal and from here rickety old vehicles run most of the main routes inside Syria at slightly lower rates than Karnak. Sample Pullman bus fares from Damascus are: Homs S£39; Aleppo S£86; Lattakia S£80; Deir ez-Zur S£110; and Raqqa S£130.

Minibus & Microbus There are several stations for minibuses and microbuses. From the Baramke terminal microbuses depart for destinations roughly south-east and north-east of Damascus including Khan Arnabah (for Quneitra) and Zabadani and all stops along the Barada Gorge.

From a large minibus station in the district of Bab Mousala (known as 'karajat Bab Mousala', or also 'karajat Der'a'), about 2km south of the Old City, services depart for the Hauran region including Suweida, Shahba and Der'a (for Bosra and the Jordanian border). Although there are microbuses to Bab Mousala from a stop on Sharia Fakhri al-Baroudi (one block south and east of the Hejaz train station) the easiest way to get to the depot is by taxi, which should cost about S£25 from the vicinity of Al-Merjeh.

A third minibus/microbus station exists in the north-east of the city called 'karajat Abbasseen', which is about 200m south of the Abbasseen stadium. This is where you come to catch transport to Ad-Dumeir, Seidnayya, Maalula and An-Nabk and all destinations to the immediate north of Damascus. Again, the

easiest way of getting here is by taxi which should cost about S£25 from the city centre.

To Turkey Karnak has a daily 10 pm departure from the Harasta terminal for Istanbul (S£1500, 30 hours), stopping enroute at Antakya (S£350) and Ankara (S£1200). There are also other regular buses from Harasta to Istanbul; for instance, the Seraj company has a daily 8 pm bus to Istanbul for S£1500. It may be necessary to book in advance for these buses.

Note, if you are on a tight budget then it's cheaper to get local transport to Aleppo and on to the border and then get Turkish buses once you're across.

To Lebanon Karnak has buses to Beirut (S£175, 4½ hours) every hour from 7.30 am to 4.30 pm, although in practice these times turn out to be somewhat theoretical – if they haven't sold enough tickets the bus is cancelled and all ticket holders have to hang around for the next one. They depart from the Baramke terminal.

To Jordan & Egypt Karnak has daily services to Amman at 7 am and 3 pm (actually the Jordanian JETT bus is making the return trip) departing from the Baramke terminal. The fare is US$6 or JD5 (no Syrian pounds accepted) and the journey takes six or seven hours depending on how long you're held up at the border. You can also go to Amman by train or service taxi – see the following sections.

For Egypt there's just one Karnak bus a week and that's at 8 pm Sunday from Baramke and it costs US$43, including the ferry fare from Aqaba to Nuweiba. The trip takes about 30 hours.

Train

While the Hejaz train station is right in the centre of town most trains nowadays actually leave from the dismal Khaddam station, way out in the wilds about 5km south of town. Travelling by train is not recommended – see the Getting Around chapter for the reasons – but for the perverse of nature, there

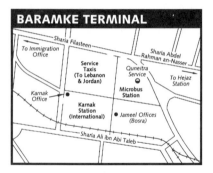

BARAMKE TERMINAL

Sharia Filasteen

To Immigration Office

Service Taxis (To Lebanon & Jordan)

Sharia Abdel Rahman an-Nasser

Quneitra Service

To Hejaz Station

Karnak Office

Microbus Station

Karnak Station (International)

Jameel Offices (Bosra)

Sharia Ali ibn Abi Taleb

are daily departures at 5.25 pm and midnight for Aleppo (S£85, 1st class; S£57, 2nd class, six hours) and at 12.30 am for Lattakia (S£90, 1st class; S£60, 2nd class; six hours). The 5.25 pm train also carries on to Deir ez-Zur (S£155, 1st class; S£105, 2nd class; 10 hours) and Qamishle (S£200, 1st class; S£135, 2nd class; 16 to 19 hours). Sleepers are available to both these destinations for S£455 and S£560, respectively. A shuttle bus runs between the Hejaz station and Khaddam station to meet trains. It leaves the Hejaz station at 4 and 11 pm.

The only trains leaving from the Hejaz train station are the 7 am Friday service south to Der'a (S£26, three hours), the summertime day-trippers' steam train to the mountain 'beauty spot' of Zabadani and the weekly service to Amman (stopping at Der'a). The latter departs at 7 am Monday and costs S£157 (one class for all). If you are catching this train, double-check the departure day – it has traditionally been Sunday but at the time of research it had been switched to Monday and whether this is a permanent change or not, nobody could say. (Also see Train under Jordan in the Getting There & Away chapter.)

Service Taxi

The main service taxi station is at the Baramke terminal, just south of the city centre. Taxis leave just as soon as they fill up throughout the day and night for Amman (S£400, five hours) and Irbid (S£250, 3½ hours) in Jordan, and Baalbek (S£250, 2½ hours) and Beirut (S£300, four hours) in Lebanon.

GETTING AROUND
To/From the Airport

The airport is 25km out of the city centre. You have to decide whether you want to wait for a bus or get off to an annoying start by paying though the nose for a taxi.

Bus Local buses leave for the airport every half-hour from next to the Choukri al-Quwatli flyover just west of Sharia Yousef al-Azmeh from 6 am to 11 pm. The trip costs

S£10 and takes about 45 minutes. Tickets are bought from the kiosk in front of the Express snack bar. In the reverse direction, coming from the airport the buses depart from a stand just outside the main terminal building.

Taxi Taxis from the airport are a rip-off. There's a pre-pay taxi desk inside the terminal but it asks an outrageous US$10 (S£460). However, if you bypass the desk, the taxi drivers will start the bidding at US$20. A fair price would be more like S£350. Walking away and standing at the bus stop can bring the price down dramatically.

Bus

Bigger town buses still operate but the microbuses are handier. Tickets cost S£5 or you can get a book of five at the ticket booths for S£20.

Microbus

Damascus' battered old city buses are ceding ground quickly to a mass onslaught by very nimble little microbuses (also known as 'servees').

The city is compact and you should not really have a great need to use either except in rare cases. The microbuses run set routes, and generally pick up and set down at marked stops, although the drivers are pretty flexible about this. The fare ranges from S£3 (if anyone has coins) to S£5.

The main central terminal is at Jisr ar-Rais, the flyover west of the National Museum. From here you can get microbuses to Bab Touma, Muhajireen, Mezzeh, Abbasid Square (or Abbaseen garage for Seidnayya and Maalula) and Harasta terminal, the north-east bus station. The latter two can also be picked up along Sharia Choukri al-Quwatli.

Microbuses for the south bus station near Bab Mousala leave from another station on Sharia Fakhri al-Baroudi, as do others that take you to the minibus for Sayyida Zeinab Mosque.

Route names are posted in Arabic on the front of the bus.

Car Rental

Of the internationally known companies, Europcar has desks in the Sheraton (☎ 222 9300) and Le Meridien Damas (☎ 222 9200) hotels, Avis (☎ 223 9664) is on Sharia Uthman bin Affan, some way south of the centre (you'll need to take a taxi to get there; see the Greater Damascus map), while Budget (☎ 224 6725) is on Sharia Filasteen west of the university and immigration office. Hertz operates through a local partner, Chamcar (☎ 223 2300 ext 9050, fax 221 2398), with offices at the Cham Palace hotel on Sharia Maysaloun.

Of the many local companies, Marmou (☎ 333 5959, fax 221 9316) is one of the best, well established and widely known; it has an office on Sharia Maysaloun in central Damascus.

For general information on rates and terms of rental in Syria see the Getting Around chapter.

Taxi

All the taxis are yellow, and there are hundreds of them. They are cheap and drivers in Damascus tend to be honest and use the meter – if they don't, then the usual fare for a cross-town ride is S£25. From Al-Merjeh to the embassies out in Mezzeh costs about S£40, while the ride from Harasta terminal to Al-Merjeh (and vice versa) is roughly S£30 on the meter.

Note, it's extremely difficult to find an empty taxi between 2 and 4 pm on working days. If you have a bus to catch round this time from Harasta, allow a good hour for getting up to the terminal.

Around Damascus

There aren't a lot of must-see sights around Damascus. Many visitors use the city as a base for exploring the southern regions of the country (see The Hauran chapter), otherwise most sights lie to the north-west, off the Damascus-Aleppo highway (Highway 5). This region is a bastion of Christianity and is dotted with several predominantly Christian towns and villages and plenty of remote monasteries. We'd certainly recommend that you make at least one day trip here, and you might even consider extending the visit by spending a night or two at the Mar Musa desert monastery.

The other picturesque region near Damascus is the Barada Gorge, incised into the Anti-Lebanon Range to the west. There are a handful of small towns in the gorge that are popular with day-tripping Damascenes – as there's not a lot to do or see, half the fun is in watching the locals at leisure. The other half is the ride up on what is possibly the Middle East's only working narrow-gauge steam train.

With peace restored in Lebanon, more and more travellers are also using Damascus as the base for a brief foray into this country, particularly to visit Baalbek, which is almost as close to the Syrian capital as it is to Beirut. With a bit of advance planning it is possible to visit the site in one long day, though considering the expense of transport and the necessary visas it would make more sense to extend the trip to an overnight stay at least.

AD-DUMEIR

The so-called Roman temple at Ad-Dumeir (or Ad-Dmeir), a dusty, nondescript little village some 40km north-east of Damascus on the Palmyra road, is something of a conundrum. Conventional wisdom has the temple dating from the 3rd century and dedicated to Zeus, but some maintain that it started life as a public fountain. There is also evidence that suggests the existence of an earlier Nabataean religious building on the same site.

Highlights

- **Maalula** – small but picturesque, this is perhaps Syria's prettiest village and there's a good short walk along the cliff tops (see page 153)

- **A night at Mar Musa** – a chance to feel monastic for a night or two with spectacular views to boot (see page 154)

- **Baalbek** – it ranks with the Pyramids, Petra and Palmyra as one of the Middle East's must-see sites and is definitely worth the trouble of travelling into Lebanon for (see page 156)

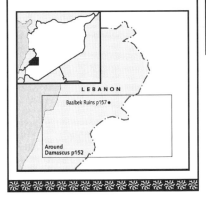

Whatever the case, the temple has been restored to quite an impressive state and is well worth a look. The squat, rectangular structure sits deep in a pit that resulted from intense excavations and subsequent reconstruction work. A local caretaker has the keys and will let you in (a small tip is recommended) – if he's not around when you arrive, someone will get him. You can see Greek inscriptions on the wall as you enter and again in several spots inside. There are also carved reliefs inside, one of which is believed to represent Philip the Arab (see The Hauran chapter).

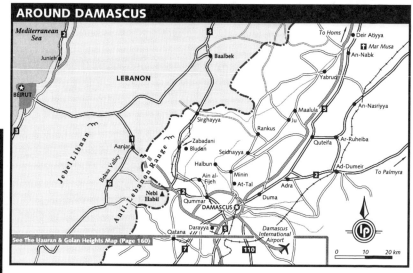

AROUND DAMASCUS

See The Hauran & Golan Heights Map (Page 160)

The temple is off the main drag about 100m east of the microbus stop. A few kilometres further east, just off the road to Palmyra, are the scant remains of a 2nd century Roman camp.

Getting There & Away

There are regular microbuses to Ad-Dumeir (S£15, 45 minutes) from the Abbasseen garage in north-east Damascus (see Getting There & Away in the Damascus chapter for more details).

SEIDNAYYA

At first glance you could just about mistake the modern Greek Orthodox convent, lording it over the Christian town of Seidnayya, for another Crusader castle. In fact, the convent stands on the site of one of the most important places of Christian pilgrimage in the Middle East, a status derived from its possession of a portrait of the Virgin Mary purportedly painted by St Luke. All manner of miracles have been attributed to this icon, to the extent that at the time of the Crusades, the Christians considered Seidnayya to be

second in importance only to Jerusalem. Veneration of the icon is still strong, but it is particularly fascinating that it attracts Muslim pilgrims as well as Christians.

According to William Dalrymple, writing in *From the Holy Mountain* (see Books in the Facts for the Visitor chapter), Muslims believe that spending a night in the presence of the holy icon is a sure way of becoming pregnant. The Virgin is also a healer and a guarantor of safety; when three Syrian cosmonauts were chosen to spend a month on the Russian space station, Mir, they came to Seidnayya to seek her blessing. On their safe return, they revisited the convent with a gift of a sacrificial sheep and a photograph of themselves in their spacesuits (which Dalrymple describes seeing in one of the convent guest rooms).

Legend has it that the convent was founded by the Byzantine emperor Justinian in the 6th century, probably on the site of an earlier Greek or Roman shrine, but it has been rebuilt so many times that there's little of antiquity remaining in the present structure. It's possible to identify bits of medieval masonry in the lower courses of some of the walls, but most of the structure dates from the 19th century. After ascending a flight of steps you enter through a small doorway and proceed across a courtyard to the main chapel – off to the left – which is crammed with modern icons and other testimonies of faith from the convent's visitors. The shrine containing the famed relic is to the right of the chapel in a small dark room. Lonely Planet author Pat Yale reckons this is one of the most evocative of all the shrines in the Middle East.

After visiting the chapels it's worth wandering through the courtyards and up the various steps to the roof, from which there are great views over the town and the plains beyond. St George's Day (6 May in 1999) is another day of celebration at the monastery, with lots of music and dancing.

The Feast of Our Lady of Seidnayya is held on 8 September each year, and if you are around at that time it may be worth attending the spectacle.

The town itself, although set in a spectacular position in the heart of the Anti-Lebanon Range, has little of obvious interest beyond the convent, and probably warrants no more than a half-day excursion. You could catch a microbus north to Maalula and combine the two places in a one-day trip.

Getting There & Away

There are regular microbuses to Seidnayya (S£12, 40 minutes) from the Abbasseen garage in north-east Damascus (see Getting There & Away in the Damascus chapter for more details).

MAALULA

Set in a narrow valley in the foothills of the Anti-Lebanon Range, Maalula is a beautiful little village in which the houses are pressed up against a cliff face, as if clambering on top of each other. Many are painted sandy yellow and silvery blue, lending the place a splash of brightness missing in most of Syria's concrete-grey villages. There is nothing specific to see but it's a lovely place to wander around.

Although some Muslims live here, most of Maalula's residents are Greek Catholics and the village is an age-old and important centre of Christianity. Until very recently, the people of the village spoke a dialect of Aramaic, the language spoken by Jesus.

Get off the minibus at the main intersection in the village, where there's a little traffic island and the road splits. Head right and then right again up the hill. The road then switches back and continues to climb steeply to the **Convent of St Thecla** (Deir Mar Takla), tucked snugly against the cliff.

The convent grew up around the shrine of St Thecla, said to have been a pupil of St Paul, and one of the earliest Christian martyrs. The convent itself is modern and of no particular interest. Carry on past it and enter a narrow cleft. Cut through the rock by the waters draining the plateau above the village, this deep, narrow groove is like a tunnel in places, a mini-version of the *siq* (gorge) in Petra (Jordan). In a couple of places it widens out and the sides slope more gently – these are popular picnic spots with the locals, especially on Friday. When you emerge onto the road at the top, turn left and follow the route along the top of the cliff for some good views of the village and valley below. The atmosphere is unfortunately spoiled by the ugly intrusion of the Safir Maalula hotel.

Just past the hotel is the **Monastery of St Sergius** (Deir Mar Sarkis), parts of which date to the 4th century AD. A very low doorway leads into the monastery, where there is a small Byzantine church with a circular altar that may predate Christianity – the evidence for this is a groove around the altar edge thought to have been used to catch the blood spilt during pagan sacrificial ceremonies.

The hillside south of the church is riddled with small cell-like caves with neat, square openings. It's thought that some of these caves date to the earliest years of Christianity, but now they serve as oversized garbage bins. If you continue down this way, the road loops back to the main intersection at the centre of the village, where you can pick up a minibus back to Damascus. If you want to

AROUND DAMASCUS

proceed on to Mar Musa, take a Damascus minibus and ask to be let off on the Damascus-Aleppo highway (just a 10 minute ride away); there, you need to flag down any bus or minibus going north (for Homs or Aleppo) and ask to be let off at An-Nabk.

Places to Stay & Eat

As Maalula is an easy half day trip from Damascus, it is hard to believe that many people would want to spend the money on the expensive hotel here. However, the *Safir Maalula* (☎ 012-770 250, fax 770 255) offers four star accommodation with singles/doubles at US$79/95 from 1 October to 31 May and at US$95/112 from 1 June to 30 September. You may also be able to stay overnight in the Convent of St Thecla.

There are a few small *snack places* in the centre of town and by the convent.

Getting There & Away

Minibuses (S£12, one hour) and microbuses (S£22, 50 minutes) run to Maalula from the Abbasseen garage in north-east Damascus, and departures are frequent.

MAR MUSA

At Mar Musa it's very much like the last 1500 years never happened. This monastery is a throwback to the 6th century heyday of Byzantine Christianity, when the deserts and rocky landscapes of the eastern Mediterranean hinterland provided shelter for thousands of tiny, isolated, self-sustaining pious communities. Mar Musa is one of the very few surviving desert monasteries in modern-day Syria. It is way off the beaten track, 14km from the nearest town, and the last stretch, along a steep-sided rocky gorge, must be walked. Entered through the tiniest of doorways, it's not until you are standing on the monastery's terrace that you realise the complex is perched high on the edge of a cliff, facing east over a vast, barren plain.

The monastery was founded, so the monks tell, in the 6th century by an Ethiopian royal named Moses (or Musa), who favoured a monastic life to the throne. He fled his outraged family, finding refuge first in Egypt and then Palestine, before founding several monasteries in present-day Syria, including this one based on the site of an old Roman watch tower. By the 11th century, the monastery was the seat of a local bishopric and it flourished until the 15th century, after which it went into decline and was finally abandoned in the 1830s. It was rediscovered by a former Italian Jesuit in the 1980s who, with the help of the local Syrian Catholic community, undertook to renovate the place and have it reconsecrated.

Since 1991 the monastery has been home to a small mixed group of monks, nuns and novices (who numbered just six at the time of our visit). As well as being mixed sex, Mar Musa is doubly unconventional in that it is also ecumenical, with both Syrian Catholic and Syrian Orthodox Christians represented within the community.

The pride of the monastery is its ancient church, which contains some beautiful frescoes, some dating to the 11th century.

Visitors are made very welcome and it's possible to stay overnight, or even longer. Basic accommodation (including bedding) and simple meals are free, but guests must take an active part in the community's life and help with cooking and other work.

Getting There & Away

To get to Mar Musa you will need to take a microbus to An-Nabk (S£35, 50 minutes), 80km north-east of Damascus on the road to Homs and Aleppo. Microbuses depart from the Abbasseen garage. If you're coming from Maalula on a Homs or Aleppo bus, you'll be dropped off on the highway at the An-Nabk turn-off, from where it's a 2km walk to the town centre. If you wait around, somebody is bound to pick you up and give you a ride in.

Once in An-Nabk, you have to sort out transport on to Mar Musa, which is some 14km north-east across some extremely stony terrain. You could attempt to bargain with the microbus drivers, but we couldn't get them to go below S£600. Instead, we walked 100m down the main street to the taxi office, where we managed to cut a deal for S£300 which included the ride there and back (30 to 40 minutes each way), plus a two hour wait.

Vehicles can't go all the way to the monastery; you must walk the last 1.5km along a winding path halfway up a steep-sided gully, which degenerates in places into a scramble over rocky outcrops. Make sure you are wearing good, strong footwear.

WEST UP THE BARADA GORGE

The Barada River flows into Damascus from the west, winding down from the Anti-Lebanon Range and through low foothills to reach the city. The valley through which it flows is extremely picturesque and Damascenes flock here on Fridays and throughout summer to escape the city and picnic by the river. For the traveller, however, the main attraction is the narrow-gauge train trip up the valley.

The antiquated wooden carriages are loaded with a great variety of people – from elderly veiled women with children and grandchildren in tow, to teenage boys sporting their latest western clothes and ghetto blasters – all being hauled by a groaning, wheezing Swiss-built steam train.

The train crawls as far as Sirghayya, a small village just short of the Lebanese border, but most passengers alight before that at **Zabadani**, which is only 50km from Damascus (though it takes the train three to four hours to get there). Its 1200m altitude means that Zabadani is considerably cooler than the capital during the summer months, making it a popular retreat. The hills around the town are clustered with holiday homes, while the main street is lined with chichi restaurants and cafes.

Bludan, 7km east of Zabadani and only accessible by microbus, is a more exclusive getaway spot for stressed-out Damascenes. Although pleasant enough, it really doesn't have too much to offer the traveller and probably isn't worth the extra effort.

The return train to Damascus departs about three hours after arriving in Zabadani. If that's too long a wait for you, you can catch a microbus down to Ain al-Fijeh to have a look around before picking up the

train (or another microbus), or simply ride all the way back to Damascus. On the way to Ain al-Fijeh you pass through Barada Gorge and it's just to the west of here, on the mountain of Nebi Habil that, according to local legend, biblical Cain buried Abel after slaughtering him.

Getting There & Away

The *Zabadani Flyer*, as it's known to expat wits, runs only during summer, leaving from the Hejaz train station at 8 am daily. The fare is S£12. Microbuses leave from the station next to the Karnak bus station. They take about an hour and cost S£20 to Zabadani and S£22 to Bludan.

Lebanon

Lonely Planet publishes a *Lebanon* guidebook, which offers complete coverage of the country, but as so many people visit Baalbek from Damascus, we've included some details here.

You can travel to Baalbek and back to Damascus in a day. It's about 2½ hours each way (including half an hour each way clearing immigration), so if you set off at 8 am you could have a decent few hours at the site and be back in Damascus by early evening. But that's a pretty gruelling way of doing things. It would be far more enjoyable to head off at lunch time one day, stay overnight in Baalbek, get up early to see the temples in the first morning light, and then head back to the border around noon.

Depending on where you stay, you may not even have to change any money. The service taxi both ways can be paid for in Syrian pounds, and the ticket kiosk at Baalbek also accepts Syrian currency. You may also be able to pay for your accommodation in US dollars. If you do need to change money there's a bank in Baalbek (see Orientation & Information later in the chapter).

For some up-to-date information on visiting Lebanon, check out the informative guest books at the Al-Haramein and Al-Rabie hotels in Damascus.

Visas

While Lebanon has no embassies or consulates in Syria (the Syrians don't recognise Lebanon as an independent entity), holders of passports from the following countries can get a visa at the border: Australia, Austria, Belgium, Canada, Denmark, Finland, France, Germany, Greece, Ireland, Italy, Japan, Malaysia, the Netherlands, New Zealand, Norway, Portugal, South Korea, Spain, Switzerland, the UK and the USA. A 48 hour transit visa is free, a 15 day single entry visa is US$16, and a three month visa is US$32. All other nationalities must obtain their Lebanese visa before arriving in Syria. For the latest information see the Lebanese foreign ministry-maintained Web site at www.emboﬂeb.org/waiver.htm.

It is vital to remember that if you have only a single entry Syrian visa you will not be allowed back into Syria from Lebanon. If you do not have a multiple entry visa, you must obtain re-entry permission in Damascus before making your trip. Do this at the passport and immigration office on Sharia Furat, 200m west of Al-Merjeh. They don't give you any kind of permit, but instead telegraph your details to the border post; when you pass through on the way back you will be issued a new visa (around US$18, depending on your nationality).

BAALBEK

The acropolis at Baalbek is one of the largest in the world; it is also the most impressive ancient site in Lebanon and arguably the most important Roman ruin in the Middle East. This World Heritage-listed site is stunning whether bathed in morning sunlight or floodlit at night.

The town of Baalbek, 86km north-east of Beirut, was originally named after Baal, the Phoenician god. The Greeks later called it Heliopolis, or City of the Sun, and the Romans made it a major worship site for their god Jupiter.

Orientation & Information

The modern town is small, with a population around 122,000, and is centred around a tiny square east of the Roman temples. It is easy to tour the whole town on foot and the ruins are close to the centre of town.

There are two main roads in Baalbek. If you are coming from Beirut, Rue Abdel Halim Hajjar is the road you'll arrive at first. Roman ruins will be on your left-hand side and the Palmyra Hotel on the right. It's also the street where you'll find banks, sandwich bars and the Ash-Shams Hotel. It intersects with the other main road, Ras al-Ain Boulevard, where there's the Pension Shuman, more sandwich bars, a service taxi office and riverside restaurants.

Bring cash with you: there are no ATMs in Baalbek, the banks don't change travellers cheques and the hotels don't accept credit cards. The BBAC bank will provide a cash advance on Visa or MasterCard for a US$3 minimum fee. The post and telephone office is about 1km from the ruins, just off Ras al-Ain Boulevard.

The Temples

The remains of the Temple of Jupiter and Temple of Bacchus are the sites that draw the crowds. There are only partial remains of the Temple of Jupiter, originally completed around 60 AD, but they do give you a feel for how massive this temple was. From the entrance to the ruins, you wander through a hexagonal forecourt and the Great Court, with its sacrificial altar, before reaching the temple itself, on a high platform at the top of a monumental staircase. The six remaining, oft-photographed columns which soar to 22m are awesome.

Adjacent to the Temple of Jupiter is the Temple of Bacchus, known in Roman times as the 'little temple'. Completed by about 150 AD, it is amazingly well preserved. Its features include an ornately decorated interior, a monumental doorway, and a portico with richly decorated walls and ceiling displaying scenes of the gods at work and play.

At the entrance to the site there is a new museum which has a voluminous amount of information in English, French, German and Arabic about the history of Baalbek. The chronology is a little unclear but it's

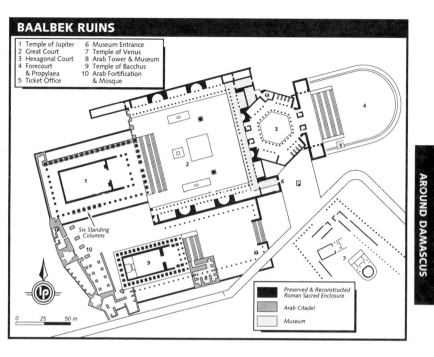

BAALBEK RUINS

1 Temple of Jupiter
2 Great Court
3 Hexagonal Court
4 Forecourt
  & Propylaea
5 Ticket Office
6 Museum Entrance
7 Temple of Venus
8 Arab Tower & Museum
9 Temple of Bacchus
10 Arab Fortification
   & Mosque

Six Standing
Columns

Preserved & Reconstructed
Roman Sacred Enclosure

Arab Citadel

Museum

0   25   50 m

AROUND DAMASCUS

definitely worth spending an hour or two
wandering through. At the corner of the
Bacchus temple is another museum, housed
in the 15th century tower added by the
Mamluk rulers, which has a good display of
sarcophagi.

The best time to visit the Baalbek site is
early in the morning when there are few
people around. Allow a few hours for both
the ruins and the museums, and bring food
and drink with you as neither is available
inside.

Guides can be organised at the ticket office and cost US$14 for about an hour,
though a lot of the information they provide
is covered in the museum. A ticket to the site
costs LL 10,000 (S£400, payable in Syrian
pounds) and it's open daily from 8.30 am
until 30 minutes before sunset.

When you leave the site check out the
Temple of Venus, near the entrance to the

main site. It's closed to visitors but you can
walk around the perimeter fence to admire
this comparatively delicate and exquisite circular temple, with its many fluted columns.

Places to Stay & Eat

The years of fighting kept tourists away from
Baalbek and there are still too few visitors to
spark a full-scale revival of the hospitality industry here. As a result, accommodation and
eating options are limited.

*Ash-Shams Hotel (☎ 373 284, Rue Abdel
Halim Hajjar)* has four basic but clean rooms
(with washbasins) that sleep up to five people. Beds cost US$6 per person and there's a
shared toilet and a hot water shower on the
1st floor. The dentist next door can provide
keys if there is no one at the hotel.

*Pension Shuman (☎ 370 230, Ras al-Ain
Boulevard)* has the very best views and the
hardest beds in town. It costs LL 10,000 per

person, about US$6, and there's a dingy shared bathroom.

Palmyra Hotel *(☎ 370 230)*, on the Beirut-Baalbek highway, is opposite the ruins on the right-hand side of the road just before Baalbek and is *the* place to stay. Built in 1874, the rooms are grand and feature high ceilings, antique furniture, freshly painted walls, immaculate bathrooms and wonderfully comfortable, huge beds. If you get the right room you only have to sit up in bed for a splendid view of the great temples framed in the window. There's an atmospheric if poky little bar and a shady garden where meals are served. Singles/doubles/triples with bathroom are US$38/53/65. There are cheaper rooms (which won't be mentioned when you check in, so ask) without the view and with shared bathrooms for US$20/25/30.

Even if you're not staying at the Palmyra you can dine in the garden; the food is the standard Levantine fare and, while not exceptional, it's good. A full meal for two with a few glasses of araq comes to about US$20.

Alternatively, there are lots of very cheap *eateries* on Rue Abdel Halim Hajjar where you can get a plate of *fuul* (fava bean paste) or *humous* (chickpea paste) and sandwiches for LL 1500, about US$10. ***Snack al-Ajami*** on Ras al-Ain Boulevard is a friendly snack bar which serves excellent shwarmas and cheese pizzas.

Getting There & Away

Although there are plenty of buses from Damascus to Beirut (see Getting There & Away in the Damascus chapter), the only direct route to Baalbek is by service taxi. These depart from the Baramke terminal, just south-west of the Hejaz train station. The official fare posted by the ticket office is S£175, but we couldn't find anyone who would take us for that rate and we had to pay S£250 per person – as did the Syrians sharing the car with us. Coming back, we got a service taxi from in front of Baalbek's Palmyra Hotel for exactly the same fare – S£250 (US$5 or LL 8000).

The Hauran

Much of the area from Damascus south to the Jordanian border, about 100km away, is fertile agricultural land, intensively farmed, particularly with watermelons. In late summer you'll see extraordinary quantities of melons for sale by the side of the road. Often, however, it looks more as though the farmers are trying to grow polythene bags – the fields are littered with them. Closer to the border, the crop fields become sparser until the agriculture dies out almost completely to be replaced by harsh, scrubby grassland. This is the area known as the Hauran, a basalt plain that straddles the Syria-Jordan border. Quarried and used locally for building, the black rock gives the villages and towns of the area a strange, brooding quality. You can see this most clearly in the Roman remains at Bosra, one of Syria's highlights and a must-do day trip from Damascus. Other places worth visiting include Suweida, with its excellent museum, and the ruins at Shahba and Qanawat, both close enough to Suweida to be visited on the same trip.

Transport is a bit of a problem in the Hauran; though it is easy enough to travel between Damascus and places like Bosra and Suweida, there's a distinct lack of transport linking the provincial towns. You could try hitching but you might find it easier to shuttle back to Damascus each time and cover the Hauran in a series of day trips.

The other popular trip south of Damascus is one for political enthusiasts only, and that's to visit the ghost town of Quneitra. Captured by the Israelis during the Arab-Israeli War of 1967 and deliberately destroyed on their withdrawal, it lies in the UN-monitored Golan Heights and requires special permission from the Ministry of the Interior for the visit.

DER'A

Although Der'a has been around since at least Byzantine times, when it was known as

HIGHLIGHTS

- **Theatre at Bosra** – after the Krak des Chevaliers, this is possibly Syria's single most impressive structure; if there's anything at all being performed here while you are in the country, do not miss it (see page 166)

- **Mosaics at Suweida** – every museum in the land has its mosaics but these 4th century gems from the site at Shahba are by far the most impressive (see page 167)

Adraa, the town only gained importance in the early 20th century when it became a station and junction on the Jerusalem-Haifa-Damascus-Medina railways and a major centre for Turkish armies in the Levant. If you've heard of the town at all, it's probably in connection with the Lawrence of Arabia story.

In the David Lean film of the same name, Der'a is where Lawrence (played by Peter O'Toole) is captured in disguise spying on the town. He's brought before the Turkish commandant whose sexual advances he rebuffs, earning himself a severe lashing with

THE HAURAN

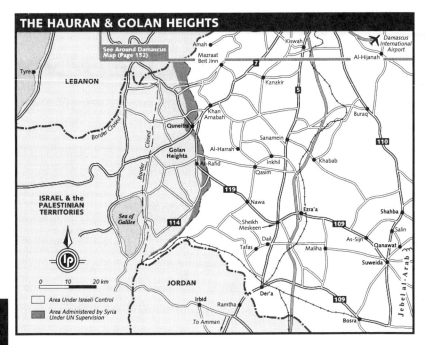

THE HAURAN & GOLAN HEIGHTS

See Around Damascus Map (Page 152)

Tyre

LEBANON

Amah

Mazraat Beit Jinn

Kiswah

Damascus International Airport

Al-Hijanah

Kanakir

Border Closed

Khan Arnabah

Quneitra

Golan Heights

Closed

Border

Al-Harrah

Az-Rafid

Sanamein

Buraq

110

Inkhil

Khabab

Qasim

119

ISRAEL & the PALESTINIAN TERRITORIES

Sea of Galilee

114

Nawa

Ezra'a

Shahba

Sheikh Meskeen

109

As-Sijn

Salin

Tafas

Dail

Maliha

Qanawat

Suweida

JORDAN

0   10   20 km

Area Under Israeli Control

Area Administered by Syria Under UN Supervision

Irbid

Ramtha

To Amman

Der'a

109

Bosra

Jebel al-Arab

THE HAURAN

a whip. These events are taken directly from Lawrence's autobiographical *Seven Pillars of Wisdom* and are supposed to have occurred in November 1917. However, it's the conclusion of several of Lawrence's biographers that the whole sadistic encounter never took place at all and was a complete fabrication on the part of Lawrence.

So the only potentially interesting thing about Der'a turns out to be a fiction.

You will probably have to visit Der'a enroute to the ruins at Bosra or if you want to go north to Ezra'a, but the bus stations are 3km out of town and most travellers just hop from one minibus to another and pass straight through – which is the recommended way to see Der'a. You'll also end up here if you want to tackle the Jordanian border by local transport – see the boxed text 'Crossing into Jordan' later in this chapter.

Information

There is a tourist office on the Damascus road (Sharia Damas), just north of the train line, and further up the road is a post office.

Things to See

There are a couple of sights worth a quick look if you have time to kill. About 2km south of the centre is the **Omari Mosque**, built in 1253 by the Ayyubids and loosely based on the Umayyad Mosque in Damascus, although far less grand. To get to it, head out along the Jordan road, then veer off to the left before crossing the stinking dribble that passes for a river. Follow the road up around the left side of the knoll and beyond; the mosque will appear on the left.

As you leave the mosque, take the side street almost directly opposite and, on your right, you'll see the remains of a **Roman theatre**. They are still being investigated.

Top: Maalula, only a half-day journey from Damascus, is a wonderful place to wander around.
Bottom: Baalbek, a 2½ hour journey from Damascus, is Lebanon's, and arguably the world's, most imposing set of Roman ruins.

DAMIEN SIMONIS

DAMIEN SIMONIS

GADI FARFOUR

In 2 AD Bosra was the capital of the Roman province of Arabia. Its ruins feature a *nymphaeum*, or public water fountain (top left), scattered colonnades (top right), and the magnificent amphitheatre (bottom) which would have seated 15,000 in its heyday.

Lawrence of Arabia

Born in 1888 into a wealthy English family, Thomas Edward Lawrence studied archaeology, which led him in 1909 and 1910 to undertake excavations in Syria and Palestine.

With the outbreak of WWI, Lawrence became an intelligence agent in Cairo. Highly regarded in this capacity, he adopted an attitude that was both unobtrusive and nonconformist. In 1915, as a specialist on Middle Eastern military and political issues, he recorded his ideas on the Arab question and these were taken into consideration by British intelligence. Supporting the cause of the Arab revolt and manifesting his own hostility towards French politics in Syria, Colonel Lawrence favoured the creation of a Sunni and Arab state. He also became the main architect of the English victory against the Turks. But it was the desert revolt of October 1918 that etched Lawrence's name into legend. At the side of Emir Faisal, who he made the hero of the Arab revolt, and of the English general Allenby, Lawrence conquered Aqaba. He then entered Damascus in triumph, marking the final defeat of the Ottoman forces. Syria then became a joint Arab-English state.

Returning to England, Lawrence defended his ideas at the peace conference and served as the special interpreter of the Hashemites. In 1921, following the conference in Cairo at which both Lawrence and Churchill participated, he was sent to Transjordan to help the emir Abdullah – the great-grandfather of the current king Abdullah II of Jordan – to formulate the foundations of the new state. Nevertheless, he later left this position and enrolled in 1922 with the RAF, under the assumed name of Ross, first as a pilot, then as a mechanic. He left the RAF in February 1935 and was killed in May of that year in a motorbike accident. He left behind him a myth – the myth of the man of the desert and the builder of empires, a myth magnified, and in part created by, David Lean's celebrated film, *Lawrence of Arabia* (1962).

The columns supporting the arcades in the Omari Mosque probably came from here.

Places to Stay & Eat

There is a handful of nondescript hotels in the centre of town. ***Hotel as-Salaam*** (*☎ 238 134, Sharia Ibrahim Hanano*) is about as cheap as you will find. Just S£150 will get you a bed in a grungy, shared room, and S£250 an equally unexciting double. Sharia Ibrahim Hanano runs parallel to the train tracks a block south of the station.

Hotel al-Ahram (*☎ 230 809, Sharia Ibrahim Hanano*) is marginally better than the As-Salaam. Again, S£150 will get you a bed in a very basic shared room. Overpriced but more comfortable doubles with bath cost S£700.

Orient Palace Hotel (☎ *238 304)*, aka the Al-Chark, is also on Sharia Ibrahim Hanano, about 150m east of Al-Ahram. It has easily the best accommodation in town and charges US$15/20 for good, clean rooms with bath.

There are a few small *felafel*, *chicken* and *shwarma places* along Sharia Ibrahim Hanano, and the *restaurant* at the Orient Palace Hotel isn't bad.

Getting There & Away
Bus The bus station lies about 3km east of the town centre, which is a real pain. Buses and minibuses to and from Damascus (Bab Mousala station) cost S£25 and take about

two hours, while microbuses cost S£50 and take 1½ hours. Minibuses to Bosra take up to 40 minutes and cost S£10, while microbuses cost S£15. Competition for the Damascus buses can be pretty tough in the afternoons.

There is a daily Karnak service between Der'a and Damascus. Tickets cost S£30 and the trip takes about 1½ hours. You can't pick up the Damascus-Amman (Jordan) bus here.

Train The diesel train for Amman passes through from Damascus at about noon on Sunday and costs S£150 (although this may now be Monday; see Getting There & Away in the Damascus chapter). The same train passes through on its way to Damascus (S£25) on Monday at 10.30 am. There is an additional service between Der'a and Damascus on Friday.

Getting Around
The bus station is linked to the town centre by a regular shuttle that costs S£1 and drops off on Sharia Ibrahim Hanano.

EZRA'A
If you have time to spare it's worth trying to squeeze Ezra'a into a trip to the Hauran. If you're heading for Bosra, for instance, you can go via Ezra'a and then on to Der'a.

Ezra'a has two of Syria's oldest functioning churches. The Greek Orthodox **Basilica of St George** (Mar Jirjis) has been in business since the 6th century and has remained in a remarkably unchanged state. An inscription above the west entrance (to the left of the current entrance), which begins 'What once was a lodging place for demons has become a house of God', dates to 515 AD and indicates that the church stands on the site of an earlier pagan temple. The church is basically an octagon within a square base, its interior graced by a series of attractively simple arches.

Virtually next door is the Greek Catholic **Church of St Elias**. It also dates from the 6th century but has been much altered over the years and consequently does not make the same impression as its Orthodox neighbour.

Crossing into Jordan

If you are looking for the best way to get between Damascus and Amman, then just stick with the regular twice daily bus. It's true, you could maybe knock a dollar or two off the fare doing it yourself by a combination of minibuses and service taxis, but the inconvenience renders the exercise uneconomical. However, if you are down in the Hauran already and don't want to double back to Damascus, crossing the border independently is straightforward enough, although it can involve a bit of hiking. Service taxis shuttle between the bus stations in Der'a and Ramtha (on the Jordanian side), and cost S£150 or JD2 per person.

Otherwise you will need to hitch or walk. Try to get a local bus from the bus station into the centre to save yourself the first 3km of walking. From there head south out on the Jordan road (it's signposted) and hitch or walk the 4km to the Syrian checkpoint. Once through formalities here, it's another 3 or 4km to the Jordanian checkpoint. The soldiers here may not allow you to walk the last kilometre or so to the immigration post, but are friendly and will flag down a car or bus for you. From Ramtha, minibuses go on to Mafraq, Irbid and Zarqa, from where you can proceed to Amman.

Getting There & Away

You can catch an Ezra'a minibus from the Bab Mousala station in Damascus or from the main bus station at Der'a, although you may have to change at Sheikh Meskeen, 15km west of Ezra'a. The minibus drops you off in central Ezra'a and the churches are 3km north – you will have to take a taxi.

BOSRA

The town of Bosra (or more properly Bosra ash-Sham) is a weird and wonderful place. Apart from having possibly the best preserved Roman theatre in existence – certainly the best theatre encompassed by an Arab fortress – the rest of the town is constructed almost entirely of black basalt blocks around and over old sections of Roman buildings. Altogether it's a strange mixture of architectural styles, and as the *Cook's Travellers' Handbook* of 1934 says, 'a zealous antiquary might find weeks of profitable enjoyment among the ruins'. That remains quite true to this day, though for most people one day is enough to see everything at a leisurely pace. It is possible to visit Bosra on a day trip from Damascus using public transport. Note that there's next to nowhere to eat in Bosra so it's worth packing your own lunch.

History

Bosra is mentioned in Egyptian records as early as 1300 BC (as Busrana) and during the 1st century AD it became the short-lived capital of the Nabataean kingdom, eclipsing Petra in the south. However, its historical importance was secured when, following Rome's annexation of the region, the renamed Nova Trajana Bostra became capital of the Province of Arabia and garrison for a Roman legion. A new road linked Bosra with both Damascus to the north and Amman to the south and the town grew as an important trading centre. The surrounding countryside was also something of a bread basket, providing a sound economic foundation for the Bosrans' wellbeing. When local boy Philip became emperor of Rome, he raised the town to the status of metropolis, and coins bearing his likeness were minted there.

During the Byzantine era, Bosra was the seat of a primate with 33 priests subject to him, and during the 6th century the largest cathedral in the region was built there. Prior to the town's fall to the Muslims in 634, tradition has it that the young Mohammed, passing through the town with his merchant uncle's caravans, encountered a wise Nestorian monk named Boheira. It's told that the boy and the monk engaged in theological discussions and the monk, recognising greatness in Mohammed, revealed his future vocation as the Prophet.

In response to two attacks by the Crusaders in the 12th century, both of which were repelled, the Ayyubids fortified the old Roman theatre, transforming it into a citadel. Throughout the Middle Ages, Bosra's position on the pilgrimage route to Mecca assured its continued prosperity, and because of the tradition of Mohammed and the monk, pilgrims often stopped here for up to a week. However, during Ottoman times declining security in the region led to pilgrims using a

Philip the Arab, native of the Hauran, became emperor of Rome in 244 AD.

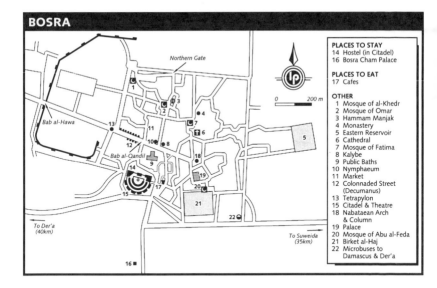

BOSRA

Northern Gate

Bab al-Hawa

Bab al-Qandil

To Der'a
(40km)

To Suweida
(35km)

0   200 m

PLACES TO STAY
14 Hostel (in Citadel)
16 Bosra Cham Palace

PLACES TO EAT
17 Cafes

OTHER
1   Mosque of al-Khedr
2   Mosque of Omar
3   Hammam Manjak
4   Monastery
5   Eastern Reservoir
6   Cathedral
7   Mosque of Fatima
8   Kalybe
9   Public Baths
10 Nymphaeum
11 Market
12 Colonnaded Street
    (Decumanus)
13 Tetrapylon
15 Citadel & Theatre
18 Nabataean Arch
    & Column
19 Palace
20 Mosque of Abu al-Feda
21 Birket al-Haj
22 Microbuses to
    Damascus & Der'a

route further to the west, through Der'a, and
Bosra lapsed into obscurity.

The town remains a backwater and is little more than an overblown village, completely overshadowed by the ruins of its
former grandeur.

Old Town

The minibus or microbus will probably drop
you off on the main Der'a-Suweida road,
east of the theatre (which you will have just
passed on the way in). The remains of the
old Roman town lie to the north of the theatre, covering an area about 1km by 500m.
Until quite recently much of the site lay
buried under the contemporary town but
there has been an ongoing project to relocate
the modern buildings and recover the
Roman-era structures.

Possibly the best way to approach the old
town is to walk around the north side of the
theatre and then bear right for the Bab al-
Qandil. (We recommend visiting the theatre
last of all, otherwise everything else is a little anticlimactic by comparison.) There is no
admission fee for the old town and as the

site is unbounded, there are no fixed opening hours.

The **Bab al-Qandil** (Gate of the Lantern)
is a triumphal arch, with one great central
arch flanked by two smaller arches. It dates
from the 3rd century AD and an inscription
on one pillar states that it was erected in
memory of the Third Legion, which was
garrisoned here. Through the arch you will
see a modern Bosran home, built from stone
scavenged from the ruins – which has at
least ensured that the building sits harmo-
niously amidst its ancient surrounds.

The gate marks an intersection with the
old town's main east-west street, the **decumanus**, which has been excavated to reveal its cobbled surface and parallel rows of
column bases. Some of the columns have
been re-erected. At the western end of the
decumanus rises the **Bab al-Hawa** (Gate of
the Wind), a plain, single-arched structure
that's flanked either side by the remains of
the Roman-era city walls.

Returning east, the large dilapidated
structure off to the right (south) is what remains of the **public baths**. Though the

building is in a bad state, it is possible to get some sense of how it functioned. You enter off the decumanus into a large octagonal room (with a collapsed ceiling) that would have served as the changing hall; from here you pass into the *frigidarium*, or cold room, which leads to a *tepidarium* (warm room) with a *calidarium* (hot room) to either side.

Almost opposite the baths are four enormous Corinthian columns set at an angle to the decumanus – this is what's left of the **nymphaeum**, or public water fountain. On the side of the street heading north you can see another column and lintel incorporated into a modern house. It is believed that this is what remains of a pagan sanctuary, or **kalybe**, built by a Bosran king to protect his daughter from death. A dismal failure it seems, as the daughter was brought a bunch of grapes in which a scorpion was hiding. It promptly stung and killed her.

This street leads north to the **Mosque of Omar**, claimed by some to have been built by (and named for) Caliph Omar, under whose leadership Syria was conquered in 636. This would make it one of the three oldest mosques in the world (the others are in Medina and Cairo). However, the mosque has been identified by historians as being wholly Ayyubid, which dates it to the 12th or 13th century. It's still in use as Bosra's main mosque and is currently undergoing extensive renovation.

Nearly opposite the mosque, the **Hammam Manjak** was only fully revealed in the early 1990s. Built in 1372 under the Mamluks, this odd little institution features a set of vaguely human-shaped cells for what look like individual showers. There's a small **museum** next door dealing with excavations past and present (closed on Friday; entry is free).

After walking around the hammam, head back south but bear left to the small **Mosque of Fatima** which is notable for a square minaret that stands separate from the main building. The mosque was built by the Fatimids in the 11th century and named after the Prophet's daughter. North of the mosque is the oldest **monastery** in Bosra, thought to have been built in the 4th century. Popular tradition has it that this is where Mohammed met the monk Boheira. The facade has been totally rebuilt but the side walls and apse are original. The square in front of the monastery is a makeshift **bazaar** where a couple of stalls sell a dusty collection of antiques and bric-a-brac.

South of the monastery lies the **cathedral**, in a sorry state of decay. It represents one of the earliest attempts to surmount a square base with a circular dome, but it was poorly built in the first place (circa 512 AD) and was rebuilt a number of times before its final demise. The emperor Justinian used the church as the model for cathedrals he built in Constantinople and Ravenna, both of which still stand. There's considerably less to look at here, with only the nave and two antechambers still standing, but many of the stones lying about the site are carved with religious symbols.

Continuing south, this small street intersects with the eastern end of the decumanus, marked by a **Nabataean arch and column**. As well as marking the edge of the Roman city, the gate was probably the main entrance to a Nabataean palace complex that archaeologists suspect lies immediately east of here, yet to be uncovered. Excavations have, however, been conducted on a Roman palace just to the south, beyond which is a

A cross adorns a fragment of stone found at Bosra's cathedral site.

THE HAURAN

GADI FARFOUR

massive Roman reservoir, 120m by 150m in size, which goes by the name of **Birket al-Haj** (Pool of the Pilgrimage) – a clear reference to the era when Bosra was a popular rest stop for pilgrims on their way to Mecca.

Citadel & Theatre

The citadel is a unique construction in that it began life as a massive Roman theatre which later had its fortifications grafted on. It's a wonderful experience to be lost in the dark, oppressive fortress halls and then to pass through a sunlit opening to find yourself suddenly looking down on a vast terraced hillside of stone seating.

The theatre was built early in the 2nd century AD when Bosra was the capital of the Roman province of Arabia. It's estimated that it would have seated 15,000 people and is a rarity among theatres of the time in that it is completely freestanding rather than built into the side of a hill. Buried under an accumulation of sand and long obscured by the addition of later buildings, the theatre's full glory was only laid bare in the 20th century. The stage is backed by rows of Corinthian columns and the whole facade was originally in white marble. The stage would have had a wooden roof, while the rest of the theatre would have been covered by silk awnings. As if this wasn't enough, it was the custom during performances to spray perfumed water into the air, allowing a fragrant mist to descend soothingly upon the spectators.

The citadel was built around the theatre in stages. The first walls were built during the Umayyad and Abbasid periods, with further additions being made in the 11th century by the Fatimids. Following Crusader attacks in 1140 and 1183, the Ayyubids strengthened the fortifications by constructing more towers between 1202 and 1251. The result is a ring of eight towers connected by thick walls that encircle the theatre like a protective jacket.

As it stands today, two of the towers contain museums. One, in the south-east of the citadel, houses a small and not terribly interesting archaeological display, while the other is one of those ubiquitous museums of popular culture and tradition, with scenes of Arab life depicted using mannequins and various exhibits of clothing and utensils. Both are often closed but this hardly matters as both are completely irrelevant to the real pleasure of wandering aimlessly up and down staircases, and venturing as far as you dare along the pitch-black corridors.

The citadel is open from 9 am to 6 pm (4 pm in winter) daily, and admission is S£300 (students S£25).

Places to Stay & Eat

Bosra has the most unusual accommodation in all Syria – a *hostel* in one of the towers inside the citadel. There are several rooms, each with four beds with adequate bedding. You can also bed down on mattresses in a room off the citadel's restaurant, but you would need your own sheets and as there didn't seem to be any price difference between this and a proper bed, it's hard to see why anyone would want to do this. There's a shower and toilet available and the cost is S£100 per person (in addition to the normal entrance fee). Travellers have reported that you can even stay here during the Bosra festival – see Special Events in the Facts for the Visitor chapter for details.

Bosra's only other accommodation is the expensive yet unappealing *Bosra Cham Palace* (☎ 790 881, fax 790 996), where singles/doubles cost US$100/120. It's a few hundred metres south of the theatre. Reservations are not normally necessary except during the biennial September festival, when they are essential.

Eating options are similarly limited. There's an attractive but pricey restaurant in the citadel, while on the north side of the square outside are a couple of *cafes* selling felafel and drinks but they charge over the odds. Otherwise, there are a few places along the Der'a-Suweida road east of the citadel and an expensive *restaurant* in the basement of the Bosra Cham Palace.

Getting There & Away

Direct Bosra buses (S£50, two hours) from Damascus' Baramke terminal are run by the

Jameel bus company but departures are infrequent – one every two to 2½ hours or so. It's probably more convenient to go via Der'a. You will have to change minibuses but it's simply a case of stepping off one and straight on to another. Damascus-Der'a-Bosra takes 1½ to 2½ hours and costs S£34 by minibus or S£65 by faster microbus. See Getting There & Away under Der'a earlier in this chapter for more details.

There are no buses of any sort from Bosra to Suweida and your only options are to take a taxi (possibly S£500) or to hitch.

SHAHBA

Lying about 90km south of Damascus, Shahba was founded as Philipopolis by the Hauran's most famous son, Emperor Philip of Rome. Building of the town began in 244 AD, the year of his accession, and it was laid out on wholly Roman lines on a grid pattern oriented to the cardinal points of the compass. Unfortunately, the building was halted abruptly when Philip was murdered only five years into his reign. The town continued to thrive for another hundred years or so, as the magnificent 4th century mosaics now held in the museum of nearby Suweida testify, but it was later abandoned. It came to life again only in the 19th century when it was settled by the Druze, who still account for almost the entire population. (For information on the Druze see People in the Facts about Syria chapter.)

The main north-south street of modern Shahba follows the line laid down by the ancient town's *cardo* (main north-south street), intersected by the east-west decumanus at the town centre and marked by a roundabout. If you head right along the partly intact cobbled decumanus, past four columns on the right (the remains of a temple portico), you'll see a number of buildings of interest on the left ranged around a large open space that was once the forum.

The best preserved of these buildings appears to have been a family **shrine**, dedicated probably to Philip's father, Julius Marinus. A set of stairs in the south-east corner gives access to the roof for a view over the site. The impressive structure on the west side of the forum is the remains of a palace facade. Just behind the shrine lies a modest **theatre**, with fish sculpted on the walls of the vaulted passages that lead to the seats.

Following the street that runs in front of the theatre 400m west, you reach a small **museum** in which the principal exhibits are some fine 4th century mosaics dug up in the town. The scenes depicted include the *Wedding of Ariadne and Bacchus* and *Orpheus Surrounded by Animals*. The museum is open from 9 am to 6 pm (4 pm in winter) daily except Tuesday, and entry costs S£150 (students S£25).

Getting There & Away

Minibuses (S£18, 1¼ hours) run from the Bab Mousala station in Damascus. You can also pick up minibuses or microbuses coming up from Suweida.

SUWEIDA

Capital of the Hauran, Suweida has a place in the hearts of many Syrians for two reasons: it's the centre of the viticulture industry (some of the country's best wines and *araq* come from round here) and it's also the birthplace of Farid al-Atrache, a giant of the golden age of Arab music (see Arts in the Facts about Syria chapter). However, for the casual visitor anything that might once have been of interest in this largely Druze redoubt has long been swept away by modern expansion. The one exception – a place that alone justifies the effort to get here from Damascus – is the museum.

Museum

The French helped to build and organise Suweida's museum, which opened in November 1991. It holds an impressive collection, covering periods in the history of the Hauran from the Stone Age to the Roman era. You can see prehistoric pottery, an extensive array of mostly basalt statuary, and a popular tradition section (the usual wax dummies in traditional garb and various other bits and bobs). The main attractions, however, are 4th century mosaics from

Shahba, displayed in the domed central hall. The best preserved and most remarkable is entitled *Artemis Surprised while Bathing*, while a depiction of Venus doing her make-up is also superb. The labelling is in Arabic and French only.

The museum is open from 9 am to 6 pm (4 pm in winter) daily except Tuesday. Admission costs S£300 (students S£25). To get to the museum, walk 1km directly east of the microbus station at the northern entry into the town. The outsized, modern and gleaming building is rather hard to miss.

Places to Stay & Eat

You really don't want to stay here if you can help it as the only accommodation is terrible. The *Rawdat al-Jabal Hotel (☎ 221 347)* is a grubby dive with beds in shared rooms for S£150, while the nearby *Tourist Hotel (☎ 221 012)* is hardly any better, yet charges US$20/25 for singles/doubles with thoroughly unappealing ensuite bathrooms. Both places are about 1.5km south of the museum on Sharia ash-Shohada, just east of the town's central square, Saahat Assad.

There are a few local eateries around the town centre; readers have recommended the *Al-Amir* for its cleanliness and good food – walk east from Saahat Assad, take the second right and it's about 200m down.

Getting There & Away

A minibus from Damascus (from the Bab Mousala station) takes 1¾ hours and costs S£22, or you can take a faster microbus for S£40. For the return trip, book ahead for the microbuses or be prepared for a long wait if you leave it later than about 3.30 pm, as there are very few running after that time.

QANAWAT

A 15 minute bus ride north-east of Suweida gets you to the town of Qanawat, once a member of the Roman-inspired Decapolis that included such cities as Jerash, Philadelphia (Amman) and Gadara (Umm Qais) in Jordan. The bus drops you at the most interesting monument, known as the **Seraglio**, which historians believe was a combination

of temples; the most intact building dates from the second half of the 2nd century AD. It was later converted into a basilica and the whole area given over to Christian worship. Admission costs S£150.

If you continue north from here (head left from the main facade), you will come to a riverbed where you can see remains of a **theatre**, a **nymphaeum** and a few other scattered relics.

Getting There & Away

To use public transport, you need to head about 1km towards the centre of Suweida from the northern microbus station. The Qanawat shuttle leaves fairly regularly from a side street off the main road, and about the only way you'll find it is by asking at regular intervals along the way for the Qanawat bus. The quick trip costs S£5.

Golan Heights

Few people have not heard mention of the Golan (or Jawlan) in news reports on the Middle East. The Golan Heights in the south-west of the country mark the only border between Syria and Israel. Originally Syrian territory, the Golan was lost to the Israelis in the Arab-Israeli War of 1967. After the war of 1973, a delicate truce was negotiated between Israel and Syria by then US Secretary of State, Henry Kissinger, which saw Syria regain some 450 sq km of lost territory. A complicated demilitarised buffer zone, supervised by UN forces, was also established, varying in width from a few hundred metres to a couple of kilometres.

In 1981 the Israeli government upped the stakes by formally annexing part of the Golan and moving in settlers. In Israeli eyes the heights are an indispensable shield against potential Syrian attack. The Syrians, of course, see things differently.

Since the Middle East peace process was kicked into gear with the 1991 Madrid conference, Israel and Syria have so far danced a reluctant tango with no tangible results yet. With peace signed between Israel and

Egypt, and Israel and Jordan, and the Palestinians slowly regaining some autonomy, Syria remains in some senses the odd one out. But its position, on the surface at least, is straightforward enough – Israel must execute a complete withdrawal from the whole of the Golan Heights before Syria will contemplate peace. The Syrian hard-line approach has been met by an equally intransigent response from Israel. Despite 1999's election of a moderate Israeli prime minister, it's hard to see the Golan stalemate being broken any time soon.

While general travel in this most politically sensitive of regions is not allowed, you can visit the town of Quneitra.

QUNEITRA

It is more than 20 years since a shot has been fired in anger here but the ruins of Quneitra, once the area's administrative capital, serve as a bitter reminder of conflict. Before the Israelis withdrew from Quneitra after the 1973 cease-fire, they evacuated the 37,000 Arabs here and systematically destroyed the town, removing anything that could be unscrewed, unbolted or wrenched from its position. Everything from windows to light fittings were sold to Israeli contractors, and the stripped buildings were pulled apart with tractors and bulldozers. It is reported that some graves were even broken open and ransacked.

Quneitra today is a ghost town. Demolished houses lie crumpled, and the empty shells of mosques and churches rise among strangely peaceful scenes of devastation. The main street banks and shops are lifeless, and the pockmarked local clinic has become the centrepiece for what has become something of a propaganda exhibit demonstrating the hard-nosed approach of the Israelis.

For some years, Quneitra has been under Syrian control within the UN-patrolled demilitarised zone. There is a UN checkpoint right in the town, and barbed wire on its outskirts marks the border between Syrian territory and Israeli-occupied land. From the town you can easily make out Israeli communications and observation posts on the heights to the west. Much of this area also has land mines.

Passes

To visit Quneitra you must obtain a pass from the Ministry of the Interior, just off Saahat Adnan al-Malki in the embassy district of Damascus. To reach it from the square, head west uphill with the steep grassy park on your right. Almost immediately you will see a flight of stairs going up – the office is just to the left at the top, signposted by T-shirted, machine gun-wielding guards. It's open from 8 am to 2 pm Sunday to Thursday and you must bring your passport. You should have the pass within about 15 minutes. You have the option of having the pass for that particular day or for the following day – if it's already past about 10 am ask for it to be for the following day, or you'll be really tight on time.

Getting There & Away

From Damascus, take a microbus from the microbus station at Baramke (S£20, one hour). They don't quite take you all the way, but will drop you off in Khan Arnabah, a small end-of-the-earth, UN-frequented town about 10km short of Quneitra. From here the odd minibus or microbus (S£5) makes the final run past the Syrian and UN checkpoints into Quneitra itself, or you can hitch. At the last checkpoint you'll be asked for your permit and presented with a 'tour guide' – actually a Syrian intelligence officer who probably won't speak any English but is there to make sure you don't wander off into any minefields.

THE HAURAN

The Coast & Mountains

Syria's 183km-long coastline is dominated by the rugged Jebel Ansariyya mountain range that runs along its entire length. Squeezed between the highland and the sea is a narrow coastal strip which widens towards the south, where the country is extremely fertile and heavily cultivated. The port city of Lattakia (Al-Lathqiyya), with its beach resorts, and the ruined ancient city of Ugarit (Ras Shamra), lie in the north. From here roads lead north to Turkey, east across the mountains to Aleppo, and south to Tartus, a secondary port that preserves remnants of its medieval Crusader past.

The mountains behind Lattakia contain Syria's only forests and these are easy on the eyes after the often monotonous interior. Excessive clearing of the forests for timber has led to large areas being reduced to scrub, although the government has laid aside some sections for preservation. Perhaps more interesting for the traveller is that much of this area was for centuries in Crusader hands. They left behind them a chain of hilltop eyries and precipitously located castles, the undisputed king of which is the stalwart Krak des Chevaliers.

The beaches along the coast have murky water and the sand is littered with garbage. Popular with Syrians on holiday, the foreign tourist would do better to save the beach experience for Mediterranean neighbours, such as Turkey or Israel.

LATTAKIA

Lattakia is not a typical Syrian town. A busy port since Roman times, it is less inward-looking than the rest of the country. The odd sign in Greek, and many more in Russian, point to the town's openness to the sea and its traffic with outsiders, while the results of this foreign exchange can be seen in wide, tree-lined boulevards and the occasional sidewalk cafe. In fact, there are a couple of blocks with an almost European air. Lattakia is one of the least conservative

Highlights

- **The cafe scene in Lattakia** – not a lot goes on in Lattakia but there are some excellent street cafes in which to while away lazy evenings (see page 175)

- **Qala'at Salah ad-Din** – another castle that, while not quite as impressive as the Krak, does benefit from a superb siting (see page 179)

- **Hosn Suleiman** – a minor site with a lovely setting tucked away up in the mountains (see page 189)

- **Krak des Chevaliers** – possibly the finest Crusader castle in the world (see page 190)

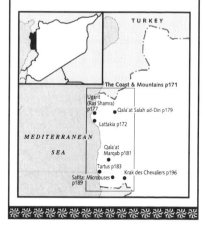

cities in the country. Helped by the influx of money that has come its way since local boy Hafez al-Assad became president, Lattakia has almost as many chichi bar-restaurants as the capital, while its inhabitants are snappy dressers, especially the girls – here, the *hejab* (headscarf) gives way to tight jeans and shoulderless tops and you may even see a miniskirt or two.

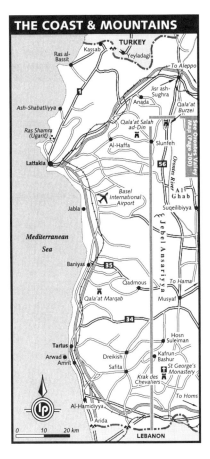

THE COAST & MOUNTAINS

fishing village. Alexander the Great passed through the town in 333 BC shortly after his renowned victory over the Persians at Issus, but it didn't become a settlement of any importance until the arrival of the Seleucids in the 2nd century BC. They gave the town its name, 'Laodicea', in honour of the mother of Seleucus I. During Roman times, Marc Anthony granted the town its autonomy and in the 2nd century AD it briefly served as the capital of the Roman province of Syria.

A string of serious earthquakes during the 5th and 6th centuries were precursors of further troubles. Lattakia was badly battered by the Crusader wars – it changed hands several times between the armies of the Christians and the Muslims and was sacked and pillaged by both.

Lattakia stagnated under the subsequent rule of the Ottomans and its harbour silted up. Rebellions by the local Alawites against the ruling administration gave the town little chance of regaining its former prosperity. Only since Assad came to power have the fortunes of the town boomed and it has become Syria's busiest port once again. However, the bizarre decision to site the terminal on the city centre seafront has done nothing to enhance the attractiveness of the town – in effect they have placed a huge concrete barrier between the town and the Mediterranean Sea, to which it owed its character.

Orientation

The chic main north-south street is Sharia Baghdad, home to the main bank, shops such as Benetton and a smattering of cafes and coffeehouses. The other main street is the downmarket Sharia 14 Ramadan, which begins at the northern end of Sharia Baghdad and then runs north-east for 1.5km to the tourist centre. The lower end of 14 Ramadan (also known as Saahat al-Sheikh Daher), marked by a statue of Assad, is where most of the cheap hotels and cafes are clustered. The train and luxury bus stations are almost 2km east of the centre; if this is where you arrive you can walk to the hotel area around Saahat al-Sheikh Daher, but it would be a lot less hassle to take a taxi (S£25).

Its comparative liberalism aside, Lattakia has no real attractions but does have a lively shopping district which comes to life in the evening, with some good restaurants and coffeehouses. As such, Lattakia makes a comfortable base for visits to the ruins of Ugarit, Jabla and Qala'at Salah ad-Din, even the northernmost beach of Ras al-Bassit.

History

Lattakia's history dates back to at least 1000 years BC, when it was a small Phoenician

LATTAKIA

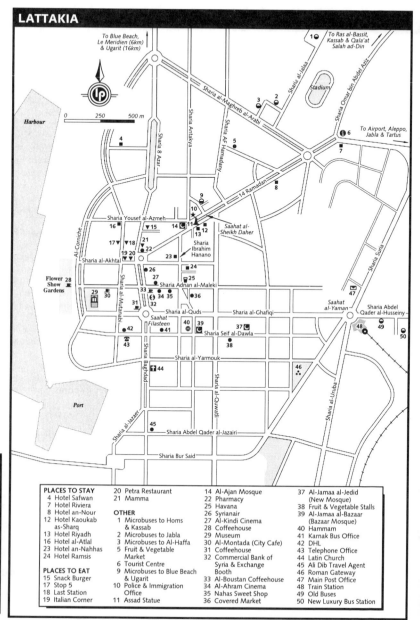

To Blue Beach,
Le Meridien (6km)
& Ugarit (16km)

To Ras al-Bassit,
Kassab & Qala'at
Salah ad-Din

Sharia al-Maghreb al-Arabi

Sharia al-Jalaa

Stadium

Sharia Omar bin Abdel Aziz

To Airport, Aleppo,
Jabla & Tartus

Harbour

0   250   500 m

Sharia Antakya

Sharia AF Hamdany

Sharia 8 Azar

14 Ramadan

Sharia Yousef al-Azmeh

Saahat al-
Sheikh Daher

Sharia
Ibrahim
Hanano

Al-Corniche

Sharia al-Akhtal

Sharia al-Maleki

Sharia Adnan al-Maleki

Sharia al-Mutanabbi

Flower
Show
Gardens

Sharia al-Quds

Sharia al-Ghafiqi

Sharia Suria

Saahat
al-Yaman

Sharia Abdel
Qader al-Husseiny

Saahat
Filasteen

Sharia Seif al-Dawla

Sharia Baghdad

Sharia al-Yarmouk

Sharia al-Quwatli

Sharia al-Uruba

Sharia al-Jazaer

Port

Sharia Abdel Qader al-Jazairi

Sharia Bur Said

PLACES TO STAY	20 Petra Restaurant	14 Al-Ajan Mosque	37 Al-Jamaa al-Jedid
4 Hotel Safwan	21 Mamma	22 Pharmacy	(New Mosque)
7 Hotel Riviera		25 Havana	38 Fruit & Vegetable Stalls
8 Hotel an-Nour	**OTHER**	26 Syrianair	39 Al-Jamaa al-Bazaar
12 Hotel Kaoukab	1 Microbuses to Homs	27 Al-Kindi Cinema	(Bazaar Mosque)
as-Sharq	& Kassab	28 Coffeehouse	40 Karnak Bus Office
13 Hotel Riyadh	2 Microbuses to Jabla	29 Museum	41 Karnak Bus Office
16 Hotel al-Atlal	3 Microbuses to Al-Haffa	30 Al-Montada (City Cafe)	42 DHL
23 Hotel an-Nahhas	5 Fruit & Vegetable	31 Coffeehouse	43 Telephone Office
24 Hotel Ramsis	Market	32 Commercial Bank of	44 Latin Church
	6 Tourist Centre	Syria & Exchange	45 Ali Dib Travel Agent
PLACES TO EAT	9 Microbuses to Blue Beach	Booth	46 Roman Gateway
15 Snack Burger	& Ugarit	33 Al-Boustan Coffeehouse	47 Main Post Office
17 Stop 5	10 Police & Immigration	34 Al-Ahram Cinema	48 Train Station
18 Last Station	Office	35 Nahas Sweet Shop	49 Old Buses
19 Italian Corner	11 Assad Statue	36 Covered Market	50 New Luxury Bus Station

Information

Tourist Offices The tourist centre (☎ 416 926) is in the foyer of a severe-looking municipal building at the fork at the end of Sharia 14 Ramadan. It is open from 8 am to 8 pm daily except Friday. The friendly staff (who speak English) will bend over backwards to help, even if they don't have that much information to offer.

Visa Extensions The immigration office is on the 3rd floor of the police building opposite the Al-Ajan Mosque on Saahat al-Sheikh Daher. Extensions are issued here on the spot. The office is open from 8 am to 2 pm daily except Friday.

Money The Commercial Bank of Syria is on Sharia Baghdad and is open from 8.30 am to 1.30 pm and from 5 to 8 pm daily except Friday. You can change cash and travellers cheques and commission is not charged.

Post & Communications The main post office is some distance from the centre, just north of the train station in a little alley off Sharia Suria. It's open from 8 am to 6 pm daily except Friday, but if you can hang onto your postcards it would be more convenient to post them elsewhere.

The telephone office is west of Sharia Baghdad on Sharia Seif al-Dawla. There are no operator calls except for emergencies; you must buy a phonecard and wait for a free phone. Phonecards are sold at the counters in the morning but sell out quickly; they are available later in the day from touts outside reselling at a small mark-up. You can also send faxes from here. The office is open from 8 am to 11 pm daily. If you need a courier, try the branch of DHL opposite the telephone office.

Medical Services There's an excellent pharmacy on the north side of the small square at the north end of Sharia Baghdad that contains a lot of recognisable, western products. It's also a good source for items such as toothpaste, shampoo and sanitary napkins.

Things to See & Do

Lattakia has precious little to show for its 2000 years or so of history. More or less the only existing monument is a right-angled **Roman gateway** on Sharia Bur Said southeast of the town centre. The monument is thought to date from the 2nd century and marks the site of a former eastern entrance to the town. There's also a **museum** near the waterfront, housed in what was once an old *khan* (merchants' inn), to which a second floor was added during the French Mandate. It contains some pottery and written tablets from Ugarit, chain-mail suits and a section devoted to contemporary art, but most descriptions are in Arabic only. It's open from 8 am to 6 pm daily except Tuesday. Entry is S£300, and at that price a visit is of questionable value.

In the evenings the **souq** area around Sharia al-Quds is lively and worth a wander around.

Beaches & Swimming Blue Beach (Shaati al-Azraq), 6km north of town, passes for Syria's premier coastal resort and might satisfy if you've never seen a beach before and know no better. Access to the best stretches is controlled by the Le Meridien and Cham hotels, but even here the sand is grey and the water a murky brown. Use of the beach is free to nonguests except in the high season. Le Meridien has pedal boats, jet skis and sailboards for hire. You can also use the hotel's pool from 9 am to 6 pm for a daily charge of S£250. To get to Blue Beach take a Shaati al-Azraq microbus (S£5) from behind the large white school building on Saahat al-Sheikh Daher.

Places to Stay – Budget

There are a lot of cheap options around central Saahat al-Sheikh Daher but few can be recommended. Sanitary conditions are near perilous in some of these places, with sheets yellowed with stale sweat, and shared showers and toilets pungent enough to make your eyes water. If you are on a tight budget, *Hotel an-Nahhas* on Sharia Ibrahim Hanano and *Hotel Ramsis* on Sharia al-Akhtal are probably the best of a very bad bunch. Both places charge around S£250 for a double. Women travellers beware – we've heard allegations of sexual harassment from people who have stayed there.

Hotel Kaoukab as-Sharq (☎ 478 452, *Saahat al-Sheikh Daher*) by the Assad statue is slightly better than most of the other cheapies in that it does at least provide clean sheets. Basic singles/doubles cost S£175/275, while rooms with shower and toilet cost S£325/425.

Hotel al-Atlal (☎ 476 121, *Sharia Yousef al-Azmeh*), 400m west of Saahat al-Sheikh Daher, is a quiet, family run establishment which provides freshly laundered sheets and a pleasant common area with a fridge stocked with soft drinks. It charges S£250 per person and hot water is available at all times in the shared showers.

Hotel Safwan (☎ 478 602, *Sharia Mousa bin Nosier*), just a little north of the centre off the Corniche, is possibly Lattakia's best budget deal. It's clean and all rooms have ensuite bathrooms with hot water on tap. The hotel charges S£250 per person in doubles, or S£700/1500 for three/five-person suites with their own kitchenettes.

Places to Stay – Mid-Range

Hotel Riyadh (☎ 479 778, *Sharia 14 Ramadan*) is a quiet and comfortable place with fairly modern air-con rooms, hot water and balconies. Single/double rooms cost US$24/28.

Hotel an-Nour (☎ 423 980, *fax 468 340, Sharia 14 Ramadan*) is similar in standard to the Riyadh but also has a comfortable lounge area and breakfast room. Rooms cost US$23/28, breakfast included.

Hotel Riviera (☎ 421 803, *fax 418 287, Sharia 14 Ramadan*), opposite the tourist centre, is a very smart, modern three star place with professional, friendly staff and rooms with air-con, hot water, satellite TV and fridge for US$52/56, including breakfast.

Places to Stay – Top End

Le Meridien (☎ 428 736, *fax 428 732*), about 6km north of town at Blue Beach

(Shaati al-Azraq), is the only international hotel in Lattakia's. It has 274 rooms plus all the usual amenities but it's a grim place and convenient only for the beach. Rooms cost US$90/115 plus 10% tax, but in the off season it's pretty easy to get a 25% discount.

To get to Le Meridien you pass Lattakia's *Cote d'Azur de Cham*. However, on our last visit we couldn't find an open gate in the barbed wire-topped fence, so we don't know if it's operating. It has such a foreboding, military air that you probably wouldn't want to stay there anyway.

Places to Eat

Budget The cheapest source of dining is around Saahat al-Sheikh Daher. A quick hunt will turn up the old faithfuls – felafel, chicken, kebabs and *shwarma* (sandwich of meat sliced off a spit). For something a bit different you could try *Mamma* (*Sharia 8 Azar*), a takeaway-style place that does reasonable pizzas (S£80 to S£120), as well as things like spaghetti bolognaise (S£65), burgers (S£80) and escalope (S£150). One block north of Mamma, tucked down a side alley, *Snack Burger* does a reasonable burger and chips for under S£100.

Restaurants There are a few restaurants along Sharia Baghdad and a couple of seafood places along the Corniche. In recent times many new places have opened around Sharia al-Mutanabi and it has acquired the nickname 'the American Quarter'.

Stop 5 (☎ 477 919, *Sharia al-Mutanabi*) resembles a bar more than a restaurant, with shelves of spirits, posters advertising happy hours, and a TV locked into MTV. Despite its obvious nouveau riche targeting, the food is surprisingly affordable and very good. A well marinated *shish tawouk* (marinated chicken grilled on skewers) is S£125, while a cheeseburger with fries and heaps of trimmings is S£95. Meals come with complimentary melon.

Last Station (☎ 468 871), across the street from Stop 5, is a little more formal and caters for a more mature crowd. It's definitely a restaurant as opposed to a bar-restaurant (though it does serve beer), however, its menu is a similar mix of international and Middle Eastern standards – the latter is mainly accounted for by variations on the kebab, and the two we tried were excellent and very good value at around S£120.

Petra Restaurant (☎ 468 388, Sharia al-Akhtal) is a bit confused: Middle Eastern name, starched-white Greek motif interior and a predominantly Italian/international menu. It's probably all supposed to add up to 'classy', which would be fine if the food were a bit better. As it is, it's fairly indifferent (spaghetti, pizza, steak and seafood starting at around S£100) but if you choose from the cheaper end of the menu it's passable enough. Beer is served.

Italian Corner Restaurant (☎ 477 207) on the corner of sharias Al-Mutanabi and Al-Akhtal offers a few Italian dishes (not terribly well prepared) and slightly better pizza (of sorts) from about S£85. However, it has a very pleasant covered terrace, which is a good place to sip local or imported beer, or even cocktails. Double-check your bill as we've received more than one letter complaining of overcharging.

Self-Catering There's a *fruit and vegetable market* just north of the big white high school on Sharia 14 Ramadan and another good selection of *stalls* selling fruit and vegetables along Sharia Seif al-Dawla. For bread and other groceries, there are a few little places down Sharia Ibrahim Hanano.

In summer, shops all over Lattakia sell luridly coloured but quite edible locally produced ice cream. *Nahas sweet shop* has an amazing range of local and imported chocolates and sweets. You'll find this shop up a side street, Sharia Sharia Adnan al-Maleki, not far from the bank. If you've been on the road for a while and have forgotten what Maltesers taste like, this is probably the only place in Syria where you're likely to be able to remind yourself.

Entertainment

Coffeehouses Among the more stylish of the cafes and coffeehouses along Sharia

Baghdad is the *Al-Boustan*, a great place for a kick-start morning coffee and not a bad place to while away the evening. Just down the street on Saahat Filasteen, a more *traditional coffeehouse* has pavement seating, and a fan-cooled interior in which to escape the heat on sticky afternoons. Just around the corner from the museum, *Al-Montada (Sharia Adnan al-Maleki)*, also known as the City Cafe, is a modern version of the coffeehouse – a restaurant-like facade fronts a large, fan-cooled hall that gets packed every night with locals sipping tea and coffee, watching TV, puffing on *narjilehs* (water pipes) and playing chess and cards. Foreigners are more than welcome.

Bars Havana, on the 1st floor overlooking a small square in the souq area, is probably the grittiest and most fun place for a beer. It serves the local Al-Chark only (S£35). Otherwise, you can drink without dining at Stop 5 and possibly at Italian Corner on the same street.

Cinema The *Al-Ahram* and *Al-Kindi cinemas* more or less face each other across Sharia Adnan al-Maliki, but they seem to only screen violent martial-arts movies.

Getting There & Away

Air Lattakia's international airport lies about 25km south of town, close to Jabla. This being Assad territory, the airport is among the rapidly expanding number of places across the country to be named after the president's son, Basel. A grand total of two flights a week depart here, both on Friday, one for Damascus (S£500) and the other for Cairo (hence the designation 'international'), which costs US$175 one way. The Syrianair office (☎ 476 863) is at 8 Sharia Baghdad.

Bus The new main bus station from where all the big luxury buses depart is on Sharia Abdel Qader al-Husseiny, about 200m east of the train station. The private companies all have their offices here and frequent services go to Damascus (S£150, four hours), Aleppo (S£100, 3½ hours) and Tartus

To Turkey on the Cheap

Although there are direct buses to Turkey from Lattakia, it is much cheaper to catch a bus from Aleppo. Alternatively, you can take a microbus to Kassab from the station near the stadium (S£25). You actually want to be dropped off 2km before Kassab, where the road passes within 50m of the border – ask the driver for 'Turkiyya'. Once across the border you'll have to haggle with any taxi driver you find (who will want Turkish currency – TL250,000 would be fair, which is about US$0.70) or try to hitch. You want to be taken on to Yayladag from where you can pick up a *dolmus* (minibus) for Antakya (TL250,000) and onward connections.

(S£35, under one hour). Buses also go to Antakya, Iskendrun, Ankara and Istanbul in Turkey, and to Amman, Beirut and Cairo.

Karnak buses also depart from this station but the booking office (☎ 233 541) is at the southern end of the town centre, on Sharia Seif al-Dawla just off Sharia Baghdad. Prices are slightly cheaper than the luxury buses but you need to book one day in advance. Karnak services include two a day to Damascus (S£125) stopping in Tartus and Homs, one day to Aleppo (S£65), and one service a day each to Beirut (S£175, with a stop in Tripoli), Antakya (S£200) and Istanbul (S£1500). The Karnak office is open from 7.30 am to 8.30 pm daily.

There's a second bus station between the luxury station and the train station from where old, clapped-out vehicles totter forth for Damascus (S£55) and Aleppo (S£40) – cheap, yes, but not recommended.

Microbus You'll find most microbuses around 1.5km north of the town centre near the stadium. From a large site, a confusion of services departs frequently for Baniyas (S£10, 45 minutes), Tartus (S£35, one hour), Homs (S£60, two hours) and Kassab (S£20, 1½ hours) for the Turkish border.

Microbuses for Al-Haffa (for Qala'at Salah ad-Din) and Jabla depart from a site near the junction of sharias Al-Maghreb al-Arabi and Al-Jalaa, on your left just before you get to the stadium.

Microbuses for Ugarit (Ras Shamra) and Blue Beach (Shaati al-Azraq) depart from a back alley down the side of the big white school on Saahat al-Sheikh Daher.

Train The station is 1.5km east of the town centre on Midan al-Yaman. There are three departures daily for Aleppo (S£67/40, 1st/2nd class). The trip takes 3½ hours on the 6.45 am and 3.30 pm trains, and 2½ hours on the 9 pm express. The route is beautiful and it may be worth passing up the greater convenience of buses just this once.

Service Taxi Service taxis to Beirut and Tripoli in Lebanon leave from a rank on Sharia 14 Ramadan outside the Hotel Kaoukab as-Sharq. They depart when full (and they fill up faster in the mornings) and the one way fare to Beirut is US$10 per person.

Ferry At the time of writing there were no longer any passenger ships or ferries calling at Lattakia. To check for possible changes, contact the Ali Dib travel agency (☎ 462 625, fax 470 111) on the corner of sharias Baghdad and Abdel Qader al-Jazairi – the staff are friendly and some speak English.

Getting Around
To/From the Airport A taxi to the airport from Lattakia will cost about S£300.

AROUND LATTAKIA
Few travellers ever visit Lattakia for its own sake; most stop over to make the easy half day trip to Ugarit or Qala'at Salah ad-Din, or both. If you are pushed for time, we'd recommend the latter, as much for its beautiful location as for the fortifications.

The scenery all around this region is lovely – it's extremely fertile country, full of orchards surrounded by high cypress hedges, and in season you'll encounter fruit stalls along the road selling apples and oranges.

THE COAST & MOUNTAINS

Ras al-Bassit & Kassab

The black sand beaches running north of Ras al-Bassit to the Turkish frontier are probably the best of a pretty uninspiring lot along the Syrian coast. Jebel al-Aqra, the ancient Mt Casius just over the border in Turkey, forms a dramatic backdrop and, if you're coming down the awful road from Kassab, the views are spectacular.

Outside the summer holiday period, the beach can be quite pleasant. There are not too many people around, the water is clean and so too (unusually enough) are the beaches. However, when the holiday crowds hit, get out.

Kassab itself is a popular mountain escape with Syrians, and is attractive enough. The route through here is among the most inviting ways to travel into and out of Syria – see the boxed text 'To Turkey on the Cheap' opposite.

Quite a few beach bungalows, cabins and 'chalets' are dotted along the beaches, but most are closed in the off season. There are also some inexpensive hotels in Kassab, but the only way to get to the beaches from there is to negotiate with taxi drivers.

Getting There & Away In summer there are one or two microbuses from Lattakia but the services are unreliable, especially for the return trip, and there is no service back after about 4 pm. Otherwise, you can catch a microbus up through the mountains to Kassab (S£20, 1½ hours) and negotiate your way down to the beaches by service taxi.

Ugarit (Ras Shamra)

Although there is not much to see today, Ugarit was once the most important city on the Mediterranean coast. Academics consider it to be the world's first international port, and evidence suggests that a settlement here was trading with Cyprus and Mesopotamia as far back as the 3rd millennium BC. Ugarit was at its peak around 2000 to 1800 BC, when it enjoyed a healthy trade providing the Egyptian pharaohs with timber and exporting the city's trademark

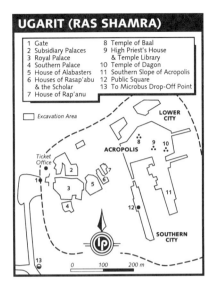

UGARIT (RAS SHAMRA)

1 Gate	8 Temple of Baal
2 Subsidiary Palaces	9 High Priest's House
3 Royal Palace	& Temple Library
4 Southern Palace	10 Temple of Dagon
5 House of Alabasters	11 Southern Slope of Acropolis
6 Houses of Rasap'abu	12 Public Square
& the Scholar	13 To Microbus Drop-Off Point
7 House of Rap'anu	

bronzework to the Minoans of Crete. With the immense wealth accrued from trade, the city's royal palace was developed into one of the most imposing and famous edifices in western Asia. Ugarit's wealth was matched by its learning and innovation. For instance, the palace had a piped water system and drainage, as did the houses of the well-to-do.

The most significant achievement of all, however, was the development of the Ugaritic alphabet. Tablets discovered at this site are inscribed with what is thought to be the world's earliest alphabet. Prior to those developed at Ugarit the two known systems of writing were hieroglyphics (developed by the Egyptians) and cuneiform (from Mesopotamia), both of which involved hundreds of pictograms that represented complete words or syllables. Ugaritic is a greatly simplified system of 30 symbols, each of which represents one sound. Some of the tablets discovered list these 30 letters in alphabetical order, providing a key for archaeologists to decipher the texts that were unearthed at the site. These include stock accounts, commercial records, diplomatic correspondence

A gold bowl found at Ugarit, once the most important city on the Mediterranean coast.

and descriptions of gods and religion. Taken together the texts are a fantastically important source of information on early life in Syria and the eastern Mediterranean region.

It's also thought that the Ugaritic alphabet may have been adopted and adapted by the Greeks and Romans, thus making it the ancestor of modern European alphabets.

Ugarit's fall was swift and occurred around 1200 BC at the hands of the Philistines. The city never recovered; the invasions had heralded the beginning of the Iron Age, and Ugarit was left behind by the changing technology.

The Site Ugarit was built in stone, so although the buildings are long gone the foundations and the lower courses of some walls are visible. It's still not that much to look at, and it doesn't help that the site is badly maintained – to the point where some parts are completely overgrown. There is absolutely no information or signposting. And, of course, the artefacts turned up by the digs that have been going on since the 1920s have been removed to museums in Lattakia, Aleppo and Damascus, as well as to the Louvre in Paris. It's another of those situations where you may find yourself a little aggrieved by the S£300 admission fee

(students S£30), wondering what on earth you are paying for and where the money is going. The site is open from 9 am to 6 pm (4 pm in winter) daily.

Things to See On the right of the track up to the ruins is the original entrance to the city, although now it looks more like a large drainage outlet. Once inside, you can gain an impression of the layout of the place from the low hill in the north-eastern quarter of the site that once served as Ugarit's acropolis. What you see stretched out below is a massive jumble of blocks with poorly defined streets and buildings. Among the ruins are vaulted tombs, wells and water channels. Water in fact played an important part in funerary rites. The dead had to have water near them, hence the elaborate wells and channels.

Two temples dominated the acropolis. One was dedicated to the storm god, Baal, the supreme deity for the Canaanites, Phoenicians and Aramaeans, was considered something apart from El, the father of all gods and creator of humankind, according to Ugaritic belief. The second temple was dedicated to Dagon, the father of Baal and the god associated with crop fertility.

What little remains of the **Temple of Baal** is found to the north-west of the acropolis, while the **Temple of Dagon**, of which only some of the foundations can be made out, is about 50m to the east.

Ugarit's **royal palace** and related buildings were in the west of the city, a short way south of the tourist entrance. Presenting itself now as something of a labyrinth, the main entrance in the north-western corner of the palace is marked by the bases of two pillars. Inside, the palace rooms are loosely organised around a series of courtyards. On the east side of the complex the royal gardens once thrived. It was in storerooms of the palace that a good many of the precious Ugaritic archives were unearthed. The area between the palace and the acropolis was given over largely to private housing.

The Mediterranean Sea is just visible through the trees to the west. It has receded

100m or so since Ugarit's heyday. Don't try to walk directly through to the water as this is a military area and you're likely to get a less than friendly reception. If you follow the road back a bit, you'll find some quiet stretches of water and beach, though they're usually too liberally strewn with garbage to be very tempting. There are a few little shops where you can buy a drink.

Getting There & Away Local microbuses make the 16km trip to Ugarit (ask for Ras Shamra, which is the name locals know it by), every hour or so from Lattakia. Ask the driver where to get off for *al-athaar* (the ruins). Coming back you can flag down a microbus, or it's easy enough to hitch.

Qala'at Salah ad-Din

Although it is much less celebrated than Krak des Chevaliers, TE Lawrence was moved to write of Qala'at Salah ad-Din, 'It was I think the most sensational thing in castle building I have seen'.

This sensational aspect is largely due to the site – the castle is perched on top of a heavily wooded ridge with near precipitous sides dropping away to surrounding ravines.

As you approach from Al-Haffa, your first sighting is from the top of the ridge to the north, and the distance across to the castle is almost less than the depth of the valley between. The road then slithers down the valleyside in a tight coil of switchbacks, crossing a stream at the bottom before

winding its way back upwards. Nearing the top, the road turns sharply right to enter a flat bottomed narrow canyon with sheer vertical sides – the castle sits up on the right, its heavy walls continuing where the rock leaves off to form one towering cliff of stone. Incredibly, the canyon is man-made, a niche laboriously hacked out of the hump of the mountain to separate the castle from the main spine. In the middle of the canyon, the freestanding needle of stone (28m high), which looks like a pharaonic obelisk, once supported a drawbridge.

The fortifications were begun by the Byzantines in the latter part of the 10th century. The site was chosen for its proximity to the main route between Lattakia and Aleppo – movement along which it effectively controlled – and for its command of the coastal hinterland plains. The Crusaders took over in the early 12th century and the construction of the castle as you see it today was carried out some time before 1188, the year in which the Crusaders' building efforts were shown to be in vain. After a siege of only two days the armies of Salah ad-Din breached the walls and the western knights were winkled out of yet another of their strongholds.

Unlike many other strategic sites, control of which seesawed between the Crusaders and the Muslims, this one stayed in the hands of the Islamic armies. As its importance declined, the castle was abandoned. A small village occupied the lower courts at some point but the remoteness of the location

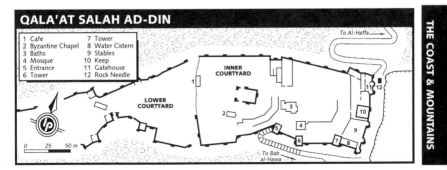

QALA'AT SALAH AD-DIN

1 Cafe
2 Byzantine Chapel
3 Baths
4 Mosque
5 Entrance
6 Tower
7 Tower
8 Water Cistern
9 Stables
10 Keep
11 Gatehouse
12 Rock Needle

To Al-Haffa

INNER COURTYARD

LOWER COURTYARD

0   25   50 m

To Bab al-Hawa

eventually caused this to be deserted too. The name Qala'at Salah ad-Din was officially adopted in 1957. Beforehand the castle was known as Qala'at Sayhun, a corruption of Robert of Saône, one of the original Crusader builders.

Tour Today, entrance to the castle is via the high tower on the south-eastern side. As you pass through the tower into the castle's interior, turn right. Both of the **two-storey towers** that anchor the walls have internal staircases that lead up to the roof. To the left of the furthest tower a doorway leads into a pillared room that served as **stables**. Through a doorway in the south wall of the stables is an old **water cistern**.

North of the stables is the largest and most heavily fortified of the castle's towers, the **keep**, or *donjon* (dungeon), with 5m-thick walls. It was always assumed that any attack would come from along the ridge to the east. In fact, when the attack came, Salah ad-Din split his forces: half occupied the defenders here as expected, but a second force bombarded the northern walls with catapults from the hilltop across the valley. The missiles breached the walls of the lower courtyard and the Crusaders, who were of insufficient number to defend such a huge fortress adequately, were unable to stop the Muslims streaming in. An intact staircase gives access to the roof, from where the views down into the canyon are vertigo-inducing.

The ruins to the north of the keep include the **gatehouse**, from where the drawbridge was lowered onto the **rock needle**. Heading back, you pass on your right the remains of an Ayyubid **bath** complex and a Mamluk **mosque**. Continue past the entrance and you'll reach, on your right, the remains of a small **Byzantine chapel**, before coming to a walled drop down to the lower courtyard. This area is completely overgrown and not really suitable for exploring.

For photographs, the best view of the castle is from a siding about 200m up the road leading east to Bab al-Hawa.

The castle is 24km east of Lattakia and is a very easy half day trip. It's open from 9 am to 6 pm (4 pm in winter) daily except Tuesday and admission costs S£300 (students S£30).

Getting There & Away Take a microbus from Lattakia to Al-Haffa (S£10, 30 minutes). From there the castle is about a 4km walk, or you could hitch. Keep heading east along the main road out of town and follow the signs. Alternatively, you can haggle with a taxi driver; one will probably be waiting around where the microbuses stop. The local price is S£20 per person but you'll have to be a good bargainer to get that – even with the advantage of fluent Arabic we could get no better than S£50 for two. The microbus drivers at the station in Lattakia offered to take us to the castle and back for S£200, which wouldn't be a bad deal for a group of four.

Slunfeh

This is an odd place. Though this is a small village high up the mountains and kilometres from anywhere, it has become a major resort, crowded with chichi new villas, holiday complexes and enormous restaurants. The reason for its popularity is that during summer this is about the coolest place in Syria. So, ministers and high-ranking members of the government – Assad included – keep residences up here, and in recent years the oil-rich Gulfies have started flocking here too. There's absolutely nothing to do or see in Slunfeh but if you are passing through by car it's worth pulling over for a quick wander around.

East of Slunfeh the road continues to climb – passing on your right the village helipad – until it reaches the crest of the easternmost ridge of the Jebel Ansariyya. The views from up here are incredible. The mountain slope falls away steeply to the Al-Ghab plain far, far below, part of the Orontes Valley which stretches out green and flat to end abruptly in another neatly walled mountain range.

Jabla

Located only 30 minutes south of Lattakia, the Phoenician settlement of Gabala was part of the kingdom of Arwad (see Tartus later in this chapter). It had some importance under the Byzantines and was fought over by the Crusaders, Salah ad-Din and the Mamluks but these days it is just a small market town. It is worth a quick look for its fairly dilapidated **Roman theatre** (open from 9 am to 2 pm daily except Tuesday, admission S£200). The theatre is 200m south of the microbus station, perhaps further if you stroll along the coast road. There is a good coffeehouse perched over the rocks just past the two little fishing boat harbours as you head south. It is a perfect spot to have a coffee, smoke a narjileh and watch the sun go down over the Mediterranean. Up on the promenade you may strike a rare sight indeed – women in traditional dress also sitting around enjoying a narjileh.

Although a couple of cheap hotels huddle by the theatre, transport between Jabla and Lattakia is regular; staying overnight hardly seems worth it. The microbus costs S£11.

BANIYAS

Lying south of Lattakia, about halfway to Tartus, Baniyas is a busy port town completely dominated by a large oil refinery. The only reason to stop here is to visit the old Crusader fort of Qala'at Marqab, 6km south of town.

Getting There & Away

Microbuses to and from Lattakia cost S£15 and take about an hour. Competition for a place on these can be fierce, especially in the mornings, and you have to pay for an assigned seat at a booth just to get on. The microbuses from Tartus take only 30 minutes and cost S£11.

QALA'AT MARQAB

After Krak des Chevalier and Qala'at Salah ad-Din, this is probably the third most impressive of Syria's castles. It's not as complete as Krak or as strikingly located as Salah ad-Din, but set out on a spur it does command almost limitless views over the Mediterranean to the west and over the valleys dropping away to the east and south.

The original castle was a Muslim stronghold, founded possibly as late as 1062. During the early 12th century it passed into Crusader hands and was part of the principality of Antioch before being sold in 1168 to the Knights Hospitallers. It was the Hospitallers who gave the castle its present shape, concentrating their fortifications on the southern flank where the gentler slopes made the site most vulnerable. Their work was well done (according to TE Lawrence, Marqab combined 'all the best of the Latin fortifications of the Middle Ages in the East') and the castle stood up to two major assaults in the 13th century. Salah ad-Din, who in 1188 successfully captured the nearby castle that now bears his name, did not even bother with Marqab but just marched right by, preferring to concentrate on easier targets.

Historians suspect that the main reason for its eventual fall in 1285 to the Mamluk sultan Beybars' successor Qalaun, was (as with the breaching of Qala'at Salah ad-Din) a lack of the necessary manpower needed for the extensive defences. Qalaun brought down

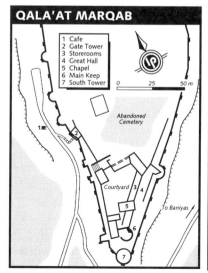

QALA'AT MARQAB

1 Cafe
2 Gate Tower
3 Storerooms
4 Great Hall
5 Chapel
6 Main Keep
7 South Tower

0   25   50 m

Abandoned Cemetery

Courtyard

To Baniyas

Marqab by 'mining'; his soldiers dug under the foundations of the castle walls and towers, propping up the tunnels with wooden beams. By lighting a fire and burning the beams, the tunnels collapsed and brought down the defences above them. Following the Crusaders' surrender, the Mamluks repaired the castle – you can identify their handiwork in the telltale white bands of the south tower – and continued to use it until they lost power to the Ottomans, who had little use for castles and kept it as a prison.

Things to See & Do The walls and towers are the most impressive elements of the remains, and the interior of the citadel is gradually being overrun by the slow march of vegetation. The entrance is now through the **gate tower** in the west wall. After entering, turn right and walk down between the inner and outer walls and then up the short flight of stairs on the left to what was the central courtyard and the focus of activity in the castle. Across from where you enter the courtyard is a Gothic-style **chapel** with two fine doorways and partial frescoes depicting the Last Supper.

Keep heading south past the chapel to the three storey semicylindrical **main keep**. An internal staircase leads up to the roof from where you can clearly make out the castle's concentric plan (like at the Krak) and enjoy some superb views of the coast. To the north and east are the barely distinguishable remnants of **storerooms** and possibly dining and living quarters.

Although it is possible to access the large wilderness that is the northern part of the castle (where there are the remains of a cemetery and an old Arab village) we don't recommend it as the area is snake infested.

The castle is open from 9 am to 6 pm (4 pm in winter) daily except Tuesday and entry is S£300 (students S£30).

Getting There & Away

Take a microbus (S£5) from Baniyas for Zaoube – it goes right past. You may have to wait a while for a microbus, and hitching is your best bet on the way back.

TARTUS

Tartus, Syria's second port, is an easy-going – some might say dead – town with what could be a reasonable beach if it weren't so covered in litter. Its principal attraction is the compact remnants of the old city (known to the Crusaders as Tortosa), which only covers about 500 sq m but is nevertheless a fascinating little warren. There's also the once fortified island of Arwad, which lies 3km offshore – this would be a marvellous place if it weren't for the rubbish and the stench it gives off. Syrians love Tartus for its beaches but anyone game to pick through the junk on the sand and to go for a dip should note the occasional dribble of sewage into the sea. Even if the beach was twinkling with pristine cleanliness, the jumbled strip of half finished bunker-style concrete housing and slums that form the backdrop is hardly conducive to Mediterranean daydreaming.

Just south of Tartus is the virtually untouched Phoenician site of Amrit, and not far inland the white, soaring heights of the Safita, the Crusader keep. Tartus is also a good base from which to visit the beautifully preserved Crusader castle, the Krak des Chevaliers. Alternatively, you could visit the Krak enroute from Tartus to Homs or vice versa, as long as you don't mind carting your gear around with you all day at the site.

History

Tartus seems to have been first established by the Phoenicians as a service town for the island of Arados (now called Arwad) and given the name Antarados (meaning 'Anti-Arados' or 'Opposite Arados'). It wasn't until the time of the Byzantines that Antarados became important – it's said that the emperor Constantine preferred the Christian community on the mainland to the pagans on the island, and the town became known as Constantina. With the collapse of the Byzantine empire, the town passed into the hands of the Arabs, from whom it was wrested in 1099 by the Crusaders.

Under the new name of Tortosa, the town was strategically important for the Crusaders as it kept their sea links open with Europe.

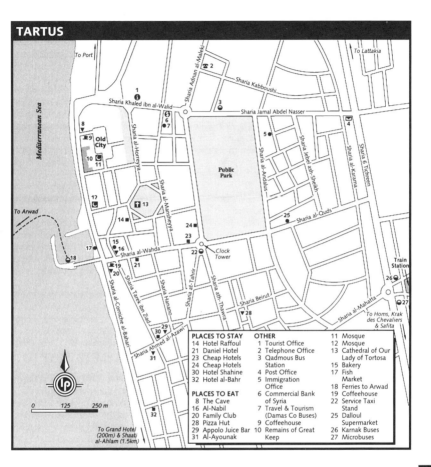

TARTUS

To Port
To Lattakia
Sharia Adnan al-Maleki
Sharia Kabboushi
2
1
Sharia Khaled ibn al-Walid
3
Sharia Jamal Abdel Nasser
Mediterranean Sea
8
6
7
5
9
Old City
10
11
Public Park
Sharia al-Horreya
Sharia Jebel ash-Sheikh
Sharia al-Andalus
Sharia 6 Tichreen
Sharia al-Karama
12
13
Sharia al-Mansheya
14
25
Sharia al-Quds
To Arwad
24
23
15
16
17
22
Clock Tower
Train Station
18
21
19
20
Sharia al-Wahda
Sharia Tarek Ibn Zaid
Sharia Hanano
Sharia at-Tahrir
Sharia ath-Thawra
Sharia Beirut
26
27
Sharia al-Mahatta
To Homs, Krak des Chevaliers & Safita
Sharia al-Corniche al-Bahri
28
29
30
Sharia Ahmed al-Azawi
31
0   125   250 m
32
To Grand Hotel (200m) & Shaati al-Ahlam (1.5km)

PLACES TO STAY	OTHER	11 Mosque
14 Hotel Raffoul	1 Tourist Office	12 Mosque
21 Daniel Hotel	2 Telephone Office	13 Cathedral of Our
23 Cheap Hotels	3 Qadmous Bus	Lady of Tortosa
24 Cheap Hotels	Station	15 Bakery
30 Hotel Shahine	4 Post Office	17 Fish
32 Hotel al-Bahr	5 Immigration	Market
	Office	18 Ferries to Arwad
PLACES TO EAT	6 Commercial Bank	19 Coffeehouse
8 The Cave	of Syria	22 Service Taxi
16 Al-Nabil	7 Travel & Tourism	Stand
20 Family Club	(Damas Co Buses)	25 Dalloul
28 Pizza Hut	9 Coffeehouse	Supermarket
29 Appolo Juice Bar	10 Remains of Great	26 Karnak Buses
31 Al-Ayounak	Keep	27 Microbuses

They turned the place into a fortified stronghold and built a cathedral in honour of the Virgin Mary, who had long been associated with this site. In 1152, after Muslim forces had briefly taken Tortosa, control of the town was given to the elite Knights Templar.

In 1188, Salah ad-Din led another Muslim assault and forced the Crusader knights to fall back to the donjon, the town's last defence. This they held, and eventually the Muslims withdrew. The Knights Templar set about refortifying the town and also defending the approaches with a series of castles. These precautions enabled them to hold Tortosa against a further two major attacks by the Mamluks but eventually, as the last of the Crusader strongholds elsewhere in the Holy Lands fell, the Christian knights realised their days were numbered and retreated to Arwad. There they maintained a garrison for 12 years before finally departing for Cyprus.

The town subsequently languished – hence its modest size – and only really began to flourish once Syria gained independence. With the subsequent partitioning off of Lebanon and the handing over of the Antakya region to Turkey, Syria found itself with only one functioning port (Lattakia), thus making it necessary to revive Tartus.

Information

Tourist Offices The tourist office (☎ 223 448) is on Sharia Khaled ibn al-Walid, north of the old city, and is open from 8 am to 2 pm daily except Friday. The staff have a few of the usual brochures, but are happy to help in whatever limited way they can.

Visa Extensions The immigration office is just south of Sharia Jamal Abdel Nasser, one block east of the park (it's well signposted and is on the 2nd floor). For a visa extension you need two photos, must fill in two forms and pay S£30 for an excise stamp; the extension will be processed in less than an hour. The office is open from 8 am to 2 pm daily except Friday.

Money The Commercial Bank of Syria is on a corner just east of the tourist office on Sharia Khaled ibn al-Walid. It changes cash and travellers cheques (S£40 commission) and is open from 8 am to noon daily except Friday.

Post & Communications The post office is at the junction of sharias Jamal Abdel Nasser and 6 Tichreen, about a 15 minute walk from the centre of town. It's open daily from 8 am to 8 pm (2 pm on Friday). The telephone office is on Sharia Adnan al-Maleki, just north of the junction of sharias Khaled ibn al-Walid and Ath-Thawra, and is supposedly open 24 hours except on Friday when it closes at 8 pm. Buy a phonecard from the desk and queue for one of the card phones. There are also a couple of card phones at the post office.

Old City

The old city is basically the Crusader fortress of Tortosa restructured and adapted as a residential quarter. Although little of

the fortress remains it's not too hard to identify the traces. Sharia al-Horreyya, which runs along the east side of the old city, follows the line of the old **moat** and there's still a large depression in the ground. The houses rising up on the other side bear a strong resemblance to a fortress wall. Round on the seaward face, you can clearly pick out the lower storeys of the **great keep** into which the Crusaders retreated while Salah ad-Din lay siege to the town in the 12th century. It's currently being converted into an exhibition centre.

Inside the old city, the main square is what would have been the castle's **courtyard**. The edges are built up with newer structures – which all blend with an admirable degree of harmony – but the whole area is honeycombed with low archways, narrow lanes and stairways that seemingly lead nowhere. The fact that there's a busy mosque, local shops and coffeehouses, and that the area buzzes with people going about their daily business, accounts for much of its charm. Disturbingly, the area is earmarked for major repackaging as a tourist drawcard. It's to be hoped that the redevelopment strikes a balance between living town and museum.

Cathedral of Our Lady of Tortosa

Don't be put off by the rather austere exterior of the 12th century Cathedral of Our Lady of Tortosa, as the interior is all graceful curves and arches and houses a good little museum. A chapel dedicated to the Virgin Mary is thought to have stood on this site as early as 367 AD. It is from that chapel that an altar and icon that became the object of pilgrimage here supposedly survived to be incorporated into the cathedral.

The fortress-like appearance is due to the fact that the cathedral stood outside the walls of Tortosa and so was designed with defence in mind. You can see arrow slits in the towers at the east corners. The only decoration is the five arched windows (which were finished shortly before the Mamluks took over the city in 1291) and the rebuilt doorway.

The interior consists of a nave with aisles on either side. Fragments of earlier buildings have been incorporated into the construction; most obvious are the Corinthian-style capitals used in two pillars in the nave. The second pillar on the left of the nave is built on top of a rectangular structure containing an arched passage. This is believed to have been the entrance to the original chapel where pilgrims made their devotions to the icon of the Virgin Mary; the Crusaders took this with them when they finally abandoned the city.

Items on display in the museum come from various sites including Ras Shamra, Arwad and Amrit, although unless you read Arabic you'll be at a loss to identify them. The sarcophagus in the central apse dates from the 2nd century AD, during the Roman era, as do the four to the left of the entrance. The headless statue in the nave is of Bacchus, the Roman god of revelry. Left of the sarcophagus, in the apse, is a mural taken from the Krak des Chevaliers and depicting Christ, Mary and St Simon.

The cathedral is open from 9 am to 6 pm (4 pm in winter) daily except Tuesday, although it has been known to open then too. Entry costs S£300 (students S£30).

Arwad

This small island, 3km south-west of Tartus, would be a real gem if only it weren't so filthy. As it is, you'd almost think it was an offshore garbage dump.

Founded by the Canaanites and at one stage occupied by the Egyptians, the island has a long and eventful history. In Phoenician times it was a prosperous and powerful maritime state, with colonies on the mainland at Amrit, Baniyas and Jabla. It gradually declined in the 1st millennium BC and was of little importance by the time it became part of the Roman empire. During the Crusades it assumed strategic importance and in 1302 it was the last Frankish outpost to fall to the Muslims.

Today, Arwad is an interesting, somewhat claustrophobic place to wander around. There are no cars or wide streets, only a maze of narrow lanes that jog and jink between tightly packed buildings. Little is left of the island's defensive walls, but two forts

remain; the one that you see off to the right as you come into the harbour is closed to the public, but there's another on the island's highest point that houses a small **museum**. Nothing is labelled but the attendants are eager to show off their English and guide you around. It's open from 9 am to 4 pm daily except Tuesday, and entry is S£300. To find the museum just head directly inland from the harbour and you'll come across it sooner or later – the whole island only measures 800m by 500m.

The stalls down by the boat harbour sell the most amazing array of tacky souvenirs, from shell-encrusted ashtrays to plastic toys. You can get an expensive cup of tea at the waterfront cafe, but if you want a more reasonably priced snack, wait until you stumble across one of the small shops in the tangle of lanes.

Getting There & Away Small boats head out to the island every 15 minutes or so from the small marina at Tartus. The return trip costs S£20 (pay on the island) and takes about 20 minutes each way. The last boat leaves the island around sunset – don't get stranded, as there is no accommodation.

Shaati al-Ahlam

Shaati al-Ahlam (Dream Beach) is just less than 2km south of the centre and is supposed to be the best stretch of beach around here. That said, for most of the year little attempt is made to keep the beach clean, making it anything but a dream. In fact, at times there seems to be more rubbish on it than on the beaches closer to town. However, it is a little more relaxed than Tartus and women should feel less inhibited about swimming (although bikinis are a definite no-no – a one-piece swimsuit with a T-shirt over the top is about as bare as you can go).

Places to Stay – Budget

Decent accommodation is thin on the ground in Tartus. There are several cheapies (around S£150 a bed) clustered around the junction of sharias Ath-Thawra and Al-Wahda but these are very, very dire – bedding down on one of the mattresses in these places could be the start of a long-lasting relationship with a dermatologist. There are a couple of places near the seafront too, *Ambassador* and *Blue Beach*, which were formerly quite grand but have been allowed to fall into such a bad state of repair that they are now little better than dosshouses; however, the owners still have the nerve to ask for S£800 a double (because the rooms have sea views).

Daniel Hotel (☎ 312 757, fax 316 555, Sharia al-Wahda) is one of Syria's better budget hotels. Rooms are large and the beds are big, with clean sheets. The ensuite bathrooms are aged but the creaky plumbing delivers constant hot water. Staff are friendly too and during summer they organise half day trips to Krak des Chevaliers and to an island beyond Arwad for swimming. Singles/doubles cost S£250/500.

Hotel Raffoul (☎ 220 616 or 220 097, Saahat Manchieh), across from the cathedral, is a converted apartment with 10 rooms. Two rooms have ensuite bathrooms, while the rest share facilities. It's quiet and very well looked after. Rates are S£200 per person. If the hotel is locked up (and it usually is), inquire at the grocer on the corner.

Places to Stay – Mid-Range

Unfortunately, even if you are prepared to shell out more cash, the choice of hotels hardly improves.

Hotel al-Bahr (☎ 221 687, Al-Corniche), south of town on the seafront, is a fairly decrepit old place where the rooms have no aircon or ceiling fan – all you're paying for is the sea view, which comes very expensive at US$18/25.

Hotel Shahine (☎ 222 005, fax 315 002, Sharia Ahmed al-Azawi) is a modern, eight storey place one block back from the sea – rooms on the 3rd floor and above all have good sea views. Rooms with air-con, ensuite and fridge are very decent and clean, and cost US$32/34 plus tax.

Grand Hotel (☎ 315 681, fax 315 683, Al-Corniche), about 800m south of the centre on the seafront, is fairly modern with garish pink rooms that benefit from good sea views

and newly fitted bathrooms. Doubles cost US$40 and credit cards are accepted.

Places to Eat

Budget The usual cheap restaurants and snack places (for felafel, shwarma, grilled chicken) are clustered around the clock tower and Sharia al-Wahda and south down Sharia ath-Thawra. There's also a cluster of cheap eats places along Sharia Ahmed al-Azawi, which is the place for local youth to hang out. *Al-Ayounak*, a snack bar at the seafront end of this street, is run by a friendly guy who lived in Sydney for 17 years. Just over the road and a block east, *Appolo* (its own spelling) is a very good juice bar (lemon S£25, orange S£30, cocktails S£40).

Al-Nabil, one block inland from the small marina, specialises in heavily spiced and salted baked fish but also does more regular dishes like chicken and kebabs for around S£100. Local beer (S£50) is available too.

Pizza Hut, just off Sharia Beirut east of Ath-Thawra, may have the name, logo and shiny red plastic furniture, but the pizzas are thoroughly Syrian. That's not to say that they're bad, and in fact they may make a welcome change from shwarma, kebabs and the like. Prices range from S£115 to S£180 and beer is available.

Restaurants The local speciality, not surprisingly, is fish, but what may take you aback is the price. It's sold by weight and starts at S£400 per kilogram (which will be a meal for two) and can shoot up to four times as much, depending on the type of fish. About the cheapest place to eat fish is probably the no-frills *Al-Nabil* (see the Places to Eat – Budget section earlier), but most locals head over to Arwad for one of the open-air fish restaurants around the harbour. At somewhere like *Arwad Seafood Restaurant* you're taken to the fridge to select your fish and it's then either baked or grilled for you and served with complimentary bread, humous and salad. You'll be lucky to get away with a bill of S£600 for two.

In Tartus, *The Cave* has an open-air dining section on the seafront corniche but the bulk of the restaurant is nestled in below the old city walls. The decor is suitably cave-like and nicely done, but the food is pricey. Only seafood is available, with fish starting at S£400 and calamari at S£350. It's open from 10 am to 11 pm.

Family Club Restaurant, below Blue Beach Hotel on the waterfront, has a menu of Middle Eastern standards such as kebabs and chicken. While the food is nothing exceptional it's a pleasant place to sit in the evening, and beer is available. Expect to pay around S£200 for a meal. The *Veneica* next door is similar, but on a recent visit we had a very bad time at this restaurant involving extremely rude staff and a bill that was complete fiction.

Self-Catering The very good, modern and small *Dalloul supermarket* just east of the public park on Sharia al-Quds has groceries and western toothpaste, shampoo and sanitary napkins. For freshly baked bread, rolls and croissants, there's a small *bakery* next to Al-Nabil restaurant. A *store* a couple of doors from the Daniel Hotel sells beer.

Entertainment
There's a *cinema (Sharia ath-Thaura)* south of the clock tower, but don't count on finding anything to watch there. The best bet for an evening in Tartus would be to settle into a *coffeehouse* and soak up the surroundings; there are a couple of boisterous places at the seafront end of Sharia al-Wahda or, much better, there's a good one tucked inside the old city, just on the right as you enter from the seafront near The Cave restaurant.

Getting There & Away
Luxury Buses Qadmous has a station just off the big roundabout north of the park. It has frequent services to Damascus (S£110, four hours), Aleppo (S£115, four hours), Lattakia (S£35, one hour) and Homs (S£40, one hour). There are also four buses a day to Damascus run by the Damas bus company, represented in Tartus by Travel & Tourism, on Sharia al-Uruba just south of Sharia Khaled ibn al-Walid.

Karnak The Karnak office is east of town just off Sharia 6 Tichreen (the main highway) by the train station. It has just one bus a day to Damascus (S£100) and one to Homs (S£40), as well as a daily service to Beirut (S£150) via Tripoli (S£100) departing at 7.15 am.

Microbus Microbuses depart from the main highway in front of the train station. To Lattakia costs S£35 and takes just over an hour; Baniyas is S£11 and 30 minutes away. There are also plenty of buses heading for Homs (S£23, 1½ hours) and Damascus (S£53, four hours). You can also get a microbus to Safita (S£8, 45 minutes) from here.

Train The only train for Damascus leaves at 1.30 am and costs S£67/S£45 (1st/2nd class) and you have to change at Homs. Another train leaves at about 4 am for Lattakia, which is where you must change for Aleppo.

Service Taxi Service taxis congregate around the clock tower. Demand is not very high so you may have to wait quite a while for one to fill up. They charge much higher than bus prices. Destinations include Damascus, Homs and Lattakia, as well as Beirut and Tripoli.

Getting Around
Although you're not likely to use them very often, the local buses can make life a little easier. A ticket booth is located about 200m north of the clock tower. A pink ticket valid for four rides (punch a corner at a time) will cost S£10. From the stop just south of the clock tower buses head south to Shaati al-Ahlam in summer.

AROUND TARTUS
Tartus is a good base from which to explore the mountainous hinterland and there are several interesting sites to head for. Closest to town is Amrit, although as with many of Syria's pre-Classical sites, this is really one for the keen amateur archaeologist. However, it's also a good place if you just fancy

THE COAST & MOUNTAINS

doing a spot of walking. The best thing to do is head inland and up into the hills. The local transport hub up there is Safita, a nice little hilltop town with an impressively sized Crusader keep. From Safita you can push on to Hosn Suleiman – there isn't that much there but the scenery along the way is beautiful and it's satisfying to get so far off the beaten track, passing through tiny villages that rarely see any foreigners.

Tartus is also a convenient base for full day trips to the castles of Qala'at Marqab to the north, on the way to Lattakia, and to Krak des Chevaliers, on the road to Homs. It takes only about 1½ hours to get to either of these places. Providing you get a reasonably early start, it wouldn't be too ambitious to combine Safita and Krak in one busy, castle-filled day.

Amrit

Two quite odd-looking monuments, erected as long ago as the 6th century BC, dominate the mysterious ancient site of Amrit, which is 8km south of Tartus. Known later to the Greeks as Marathos and conquered by Alexander the Great in 333 BC, Amrit had fallen by the wayside by the time it was incorporated into the Roman empire.

The so-called **meghazils** (spindles) stand in what was once a necropolis and, although no one is entirely sure how to explain the origins of this settlement, it appears that Phoenicians from Arwad made the area a kind of satellite or religious zone. The taller of the monuments has four lions carved in a Persian style around the base. Both towers stand above underground funeral chambers – you'll need a torch (flashlight) to poke around them – and betray a curious mix of Hellenistic, Persian and even Egyptian influences in their decoration.

About a kilometre to the north you will find the remains of a **temple** built to serve a cult centred on the springs here. The main feature is a deep basin cut out of the rock, which would once have formed an artificial lake. The water that filled the basin came from the nearby spring and was considered to have curative powers. Just 50m to the

north you can make out the shape of a small stadium.

The sea sparkles invitingly to the west, but most of the land around here belongs to the armed forces. This may change, as plans are afoot to create a US$70 million tourist complex. As yet the only evidence of this is a scarcely credible sign announcing its imminent appearance. Although the complex may allow sun lovers to get onto largely untouched beaches, such a development would be of dubious benefit to the area.

Getting There & Away Take the Al-Hamidiyya microbus (S£5) from Sharia 6 Tichreen near the train station in Tartus and ask to be let off at the track leading to Amrit – mention you want al-athaar. The track leads off towards the sea from the main road. After about 1.5km you will pass an army post (there are firing ranges around here). Some 200m further on, immediately after passing some communication towers, you can see the temple remains in the distance on the left – these are reached by turning onto the dirt track by the sign reading 'Rest Camp'. Continue along the paved road and take the dirt track beside the sign announcing 'Amrit Touristic Project'. This will bring you to the meghazils.

To get back to Tartus, return to the main road and flag down a microbus.

Safita

This restful mountain town is dominated by a striking white keep, all that remains of the once-powerful Crusader-era **Castel Blanc**. Originally built in the early 12th century as part of the outlying defences of Tartus, the castle was rebuilt and strengthened after damage sustained in an attack by the Ayyubid ruler Nur ad-Din (Nureddin). It was garrisoned by the Knights Templar until 1271 when they were driven out by the Mamluk leader Beybars, who shortly after went on to take Krak des Chevaliers.

From the very chaotic central town intersection where you will be dropped by most microbuses, take the road leading uphill to the west. After about 200m you'll see the keep ahead of you. Continue until you see a cobbled lane off to the right and follow it under the arched gate of what remains of the castle's defensive perimeter. Two steep, cobbled lanes lead up to the keep, and you enter from the western side.

At 27m high, the keep is the largest of all surviving Crusader towers. The design and function of the Safita tower reveals a great deal about the lives of its former occupants, the so-called military monks. Most obvious is its great simplicity – the tower consists of just one single lower floor and one great upper floor (plus a sub-floor passage that leads to a cistern for water storage). The lower level was a grand church with an elegant barrel-vaulted ceiling and an apse in the east wall. Only the arrow slits in the walls betray the room's military function.

The church still operates, now catering for the local Syrian Orthodox community. Stairs in the south-west corner lead to the upper level, which consists of a large hall divided by elegantly carved stone pillars. This room probably served as a dormitory for the knights, who lived in monastic conditions. Another flight of steps takes you to the roof, from where the tower was defended. To the south-east you can make out the Krak (the two were thus linked in the Crusaders' chain of communications) and, to the south, the snowcapped peaks of northern Lebanon.

The keep is supposedly open daily from 8 am to 1 pm and from 3 to 6 pm, but this is not strictly adhered to. Entrance is free, but you should leave a tip of S£50 or S£100 on the plate on the table.

Right next to the keep, *Restaurant al-Burj* has excellent views over the surrounding countryside. Stop for lunch if you can.

Getting There & Away The microbus from Tartus costs S£10 and you pick it up just south of the traffic circle in front of the train station. The journey takes about 45 minutes.

From Safita, microbuses for Hosn Suleiman (S£20) depart from Sharia Maysaloun, 100m south of the town's main intersection. There are also microbuses to Homs

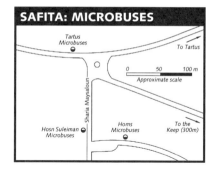

SAFITA: MICROBUSES

Tartus Microbuses

To Tartus

Sharia Maysaloun

0   50   100 m
Approximate scale

Hosn Suleiman Microbuses

Homs Microbuses

To the Keep (300m)

(S£35) from a side street off Maysaloun. If you want to go to the Krak des Chevalier from here, take a Homs microbus (you'll have to pay full fare) and ask to be let off at the junction for Qala'at al-Hosn.

Hosn Suleiman

A worthwhile excursion north of Safita will take you 25km along some of the highest mountain ridges of the Jebel Ansariyya to a remarkable and imposing testament to thousands of years of religious fervour. Outside the village of Hosn Suleiman you are confronted by temple walls constructed of huge stone blocks, some of them as large as 5m by 3m. What makes them all the more striking is the fact that they were here, high in the mountains, days distant from anywhere, at a time when travel was by foot or on horse.

Although evidence suggests the site has been home to temples of one religious persuasion or another since the Persian occupation of the Levant, what you can see was erected mainly under Roman domination in the 2nd century AD.

Four gates permit entry to the site. A partially collapsed *cella*, the focal point of worship and offerings in the temple, rises from the centre of the site. If you've already been to Palmyra you'll recognise the layout from the Temple of Bel there.

The gates themselves preserve the most intact decoration, with columns, niches as well as inscriptions (the clearest of these can be observed above the east gate). The east and west gates both display the same sculptural adornments. The figure of a bearded man stands above the lintel, while the same area on the inside is dominated by figures depicting two youths and a lion's head. As you pass through each gate, look up to see the outspread wings of an eagle.

Across the road are the less extensive ruins of what appears to be another temple compound, but little is known about its history or function.

Getting There & Away Microbuses (S£20) run at irregular intervals from Safita to Hosn Suleiman, taking about 40 minutes. Most go right past the site so just holler to be let out when you can see the ruins. As some microbuses terminate in the village, you have a better chance of picking up one to the ruins if you head back down the road on which you arrived and wait. Coming back, just stand on the road and flag one down.

KRAK DES CHEVALIERS

Author Paul Theroux described the Krak des Chevaliers as the epitome of the dream castle of childhood fantasies of jousts and armour and pennants. TE Lawrence simply called it 'the finest castle in the world'. Take their word for it, the remarkably well-preserved Krak des Chevaliers (Qala'at al-Hosn) is one of Syria's prime attractions and should not be missed. Impervious to the onslaught of time, it cannot have looked a great deal different 800 years ago, and such is its size and state of completeness that you could easily spend several hours here absorbed in exploring.

History

The fort is in the only significant break in the mountain range that stretches for 250km between Antakya (Turkey) and Beirut (Lebanon). Anyone who held this breach, known as the Homs Gap, that lies between the southern end of the Jebel Ansariyya and the northern outreaches of the Anti-Lebanon, was virtually assured of authority over inland Syria by controlling the flow of goods and people from the ports through to the interior. Even today, this gap carries the major road link from Homs to Tartus, as well as the oil pipeline from the fields in the far east of the country to the terminal at Tartus.

The first fortress known to have existed on this site was built by the Emir of Homs in 1031. He was briefly displaced in 1099 by the hordes of the First Crusade passing through on their push south to Jerusalem, and then given the complete push 11 years later when the Christian knights, now established in the Holy City, began to extend their gains throughout the region. Around the middle of the 12th century the First Crusaders were replaced by the elite Knights Hospitaller and it is they who built and expanded the Krak into the form in which it exists today. (For more on the Hospitallers and castle building see the special section on Crusader Castles in this chapter.)

They built well and despite repeated attacks and sieges, the Krak held firm. In fact, it was never truly breached. Instead, the Crusaders simply gave it up. By 1271, when Beybars marched on the castle, the knights at the Krak were a last outpost. Jerusalem had been lost and the Christians were retreating. Numbers in the castle, which was built to hold a garrison of 2000, were depleted to around 200. Surrounded by the armies of Islam and with no hope of reprieve, Krak must have seemed more like a prison than a stronghold. Even though they had stores of supplies to last for five years, that must have seemed too long a sentence for the Crusaders and after a month under siege they agreed to depart the castle under terms of safe conduct.

To guard against their return, Beybars garrisoned the castle with his own Mamluk troops and further strengthened the defences. Wandering around today, it is possible to distinguish the Frankish aspects of the castle, with their Gothic and Romanesque building styles, and those of the Arabs – there are some beautiful, typically Islamic geometric designs carved into some of the structures on the upper levels of the main complex.

continued on page 196

CRUSADER CASTLES

GADI FARFOUR

The Crusader castles that rise from the Syrian hill-tops and mountain crags remain the clearest legacy of the 200 year struggle for the 'Holy Land' between the Christians of Europe and the Muslims of the east. The monumental proportions and intricate craftsmanship still discernible in the enduring fortifications scattered across the countryside are a testimony to the vast scope of this conflict and to the engineering ingenuity of the combatants.

The Europeans who embarked on the First Crusade at the end of the 11th century were predominantly Frankish and the basic traditions of Crusader castle construction can be traced to their homelands. Throughout Western Europe fortification technology had developed from the days of Roman camps and forts, through the Middle Ages and the era of rulers like Charlemagne. However, there was no standard blueprint for Frankish castle construction. The nature of castle construction was dictated more by the topography of a chosen site than by any strict adherence to a building pattern. The greatest skill of the Frankish engineers was the ability to adapt designs to suit the demands of specific terrain, whether it was a precipitous mountain peak or a harbour-side promontory. This was equally true in Syria, where the fortifications in coastal towns like Tartus and the impregnable hilltop castle of Krak des Chevaliers bear the unmistakable stamp of Crusader technology but are fundamentally different in design, appearance and function.

It is likely that the Crusaders learned more about military architecture during the lengthy march to the Holy Land. They must have been amazed by the walls of Constantinople, and they discovered first-hand the effectiveness of ancient Byzantine fortifications during their long sieges of Nicaea (1097) and Antioch (1098). It is also interesting to

Box: The lintel decoration at Krak des Chevaliers.

Right: Krak des Chevaliers, like Qala'at Marqab, was protected by two lines of castle walls. The round, projecting towers gave the Crusader garrison a wide field of defensive fire.

TIM BEDDOW

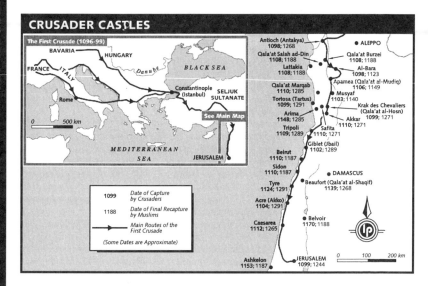

CRUSADER CASTLES

The First Crusade (1096-99)

BAVARIA   HUNGARY

FRANCE   ITALY   Danube   BLACK SEA

Rome   Constantinople (Istanbul)   SELJUK SULTANATE

See Main Map

MEDITERRANEAN SEA   JERUSALEM

0   500 km

Antioch (Antakya) 1098; 1268   ● ALEPPO

Qala'at Salah ad-Din 1108; 1188   Qala'at Burzei 1108; 1188

Lattakia 1108; 1188   Al-Bara 1098; 1123

Qala'at Marqab 1110; 1285   Apamea (Qala'at al-Mudiq) 1106; 1149

Tortosa (Tartus) 1099; 1291   Musyaf 1103; 1140

Arima 1148; 1285   Krak des Chevaliers (Qala'at al-Hosn) 1099; 1271

Tripoli 1109; 1289   Akkar 1110; 1271

Safita 1110; 1271

Giblet (Jbail) 1102; 1289

Beirut 1110; 1187

Sidon 1110; 1187   ● DAMASCUS

Tyre 1124; 1291   Beaufort (Qala'at al-Shaqif) 1139; 1268

Acre (Akko) 1104; 1291

Caesarea 1112; 1265   Belvoir 1170; 1188

Ashkelon 1153; 1187   JERUSALEM 1099; 1244

0   100   200 km

1099   Date of Capture by Crusaders

1188   Date of Final Recapture by Muslims

Main Routes of the First Crusade

(Some Dates are Approximate)

speculate upon possible Armenian influences on the Crusaders. The path of the Crusaders brought them into contact with Armenian populations in the principality of Antioch and also in Edessa. The Armenians had a tradition of constructing true castles, rather than city defences, on elevated or mountainous locations. Armenian castles were frequently built with an outer wall that closely followed the line of the cliff face, with round towers spaced regularly along it. These features can be seen in the Syrian Crusader castles of Qala'at Salah ad-Din and Qala'at Burzei, and it is likely that the technology or inspiration came, at least in part, from the Armenians.

Why Build Castles?

Following the conquest of Jerusalem in 1099, the Crusaders faced a crisis of human resources. It is estimated that of the 150,000 Crusaders who embarked on the journey, only 40,000 reached Jerusalem. Many of these returned home after the city was captured because they believed they had fulfilled their religious duty of liberating the Holy Land. It was to overcome this lack of manpower that the Crusader nobles began constructing their network of coastal fortifications and hinterland castles. The virtue of these great strongholds was demonstrated clearly during the rampaging campaign of Salah ad-Din in 1180 when the hopelessly outnumbered Crusader forces retreated to Krak des Chevaliers and the Muslims, who did not have the resources or the time to conduct a siege, had no option but to reluctantly pass

Top: Qala'at Salah ad-Din was one of the first castles to suffer from the Crusaders' lack of adequate resources. The castle, located high in the Jebel Ansariyya, was too isolated to allow full protection. It was stormed by Salah ad-Din in 1187 and was never recaptured by the Crusaders.

GADI FARFOUR

Centre: Musyaf is the best preserved of the Ismaili (Assassin) castles in Syria. The Ismailis managed to ensure their own survival during the volatile years of the Crusades by playing off the superior Muslim and Christian forces against each other.

ANDREW HUMPHREYS

Bottom: The black, volcanic stone of Qala'at Marqab gives the castle a dark, brooding appearance. Marqab withstood attacks against the Crusaders for more than 100 years, only falling when the castle could no longer be properly garrisoned.

ANDREW HUMPHREYS

TIM BEDDOW

Top: The tower and great gateway of the Aleppo Citadel are protected by box/slot defences, or machicolations. These are very similar in design to examples from Krak and suggest a transfer of technology between the Muslim and Crusader forces.

ANDREW HUMPHREYS

TIM BEDDOW

Centre Left: The double fortification walls at Krak made the castle almost impregnable. Note also the projecting round towers that gave the defences a wide field of fire.

Centre Right: The finely crafted arches and vaults that adorn the buttresses at the Hospitaller fortress of Krak are one of the castle's distinguishing features.

PATRICK SYDER

Bottom: A view of Krak from the south-west allows the best understanding of the many defensive features that made the fortress almost impervious to attack.

on by. Of course, once the army had moved away from the castle walls, the Crusaders sallied forth again and recaptured the local area on which they then levied taxes.

Krak des Chevaliers sometimes boasted a garrison of more than 2000 but such was the ingenuity of its design and the quality of its construction that it could be defended by a fraction of that number. Even when the Muslims managed to control the surrounding lands, the castle itself remained impregnable – in the words of the Arab historian Ibn al-Athir, Krak was 'a bone stuck in the very throat of the Muslims'.

The pattern of castle ownership, like the style of castle construction, changed markedly during the 200 year period of the Crusades. Initially, individual nobles attempted to create small, self-ruled estates in the Holy Land similar to those of Western Europe. But as the tide turned in favour of the Muslims, the survival of independent foreign states and eventually of the whole Crusading movement became increasingly precarious. As the plight of the Crusaders became ever more desperate, the defensive capacities of the great castles became even more important.

The Master Castle Builders

Increasingly, castle ownership and renovation became the responsibility of the two great elite military orders, the Knights of St John (or Hospitallers), and the Order of the Knights Templar. Most of the castles that can still be seen in Syria today were controlled by the

Right: The base of the inner defences at Krak was set in a massive glacis – a sloping embankment of stone that protected and re-inforced the towers and walls.

ANDREW HUMPHREYS

Templars or the Hospitallers in the 13th century and it was the knights who redesigned and expanded the fortifications, sometimes to a truly remarkable extent. Take for example the coastal town of Tortosa (modern Tartus); the site offered little in the way of natural defences so the Templars built on a massive scale. Originally the sea came right to the walls of the castle's main tower, or donjon, and the castle was protected on its landward side by two deep ditches and two heavily fortified walls.

When Salah ad-Din captured the surrounding town of Tortosa in 1188 he was unable to storm the castle itself. Tortosa never fell in battle to the Muslims but was abandoned by the Templars after the fall of the city of Acre in 1291. The ruins of the great donjon can still be seen in Tartus today, although it survives only to the first floor and is frequently concealed behind the washing-lines and drying clothes of the current inhabitants.

The architecture of the great Hospitaller castles, particularly Krak des Chevaliers and Qala'at Marqab, was distinctly different to that of the Templars. The dominating, rectangular donjons favoured by the Templars (the best example of which is at Safita) were not used as extensively by the Hospitallers. The Hospitallers favoured great, round towers that often projected boldly from the castle walls to allow the defenders a wide field of vision and fire.

Both Krak and Marqab were effectively two castles in one, with the main castle being fully enclosed by a complete outer circuit of heavily fortified walls and towers. The upper windows of the towers were wide enough to allow large defensive weapons to be deployed from within.

CHRISTOPHER WOOD

Left: Although badly deteriorated, the loggia at Krak is an example of the Crusaders' ability to craft fine, graceful structures in stone.

Castles after the Crusaders

In 1291 the last of the Crusaders abandoned the castle of Tortosa and sailed to the fortified offshore island of Arwad. Eleven years later they left this final refuge and departed the Holy Land forever. In some ways the Crusading movement can be seen as a failure. The knights came to protect their shrines and pilgrim routes from the Muslims, but when the last Crusader sailed from the coast the whole region was in Muslim hands.

Equally, it can be argued that the Crusaders did remarkably well to maintain an active foreign presence for more than 200 years, despite their isolation, lack of resources and inability to harness the support of the Christian populations in the east. There is no doubt that the key to the Crusaders' stubborn resistance was their construction and use of great fortifications.

Castle building did not, of course, end with the Crusaders. Hard-won experience led to the adoption of the use of large-scale fortifications by the Muslims. Late in the 12th century, rulers like Nur ad-Din built various styles of defences at Damascus, Homs, Aleppo, Bosra and elsewhere, while the Ayyubid rulers of the early 13th century also undertook an extensive program of fortification. Not surprisingly, there are many similarities between the styles of Muslim and Crusader construction – the defensive openings, or machicolations, that project from the tower overlooking the approach to the gate of the Aleppo citadel represent a device constructed by Muslims that is identical to Crusader workmanship at Krak des Chevaliers.

Military architecture in Western Europe underwent a revision in the years following the Crusades. But although many subsequent Western European castles incorporated design features that were conceived in the Holy Land, these fortifications never rivalled the size and splendour of the Crusader fortresses. Never improved upon, the great Crusader castles, of which Syria boasts the finest examples, represent the ultimate triumph of the art of defensive fortification construction.

Jeremy Smith

A Postscript

While the Crusades may be long-distant history, conflict in the Middle East continues as an ever-present reality. Some 900 years on since they were applied, modern-day warriors still have cause to appreciate/curse the Crusaders' construction skills. During the 1982 Israeli invasion of Lebanon, Palestinian forces holed up in Beaufort Castle, a defensive outpost first taken and rebuilt by the Crusaders in the 12th century. The castle was finally only relinquished by the Palestinians in the face of repeated air raids and a commando assault. Since then, the Crusaders' superb skills in site location continue to be vindicated as the Israeli army maintains Beaufort as an observation post.

continued from page 190

The Outside Wall

The castle comprises two distinct parts: the outside wall with its 13 towers and main entrance; and the inside wall and central construction, which are built on a very rocky platform. A moat dug out of the rock separates the two walls.

The main entrance leads to a sloping ramp with steps wide enough to allow the garrison's horses to ride up. The first tower on the left was a guard room and, next to it, the long hall served as stables – it's now a dark storeroom filled with building equipment. The ramp continues up to a point where it turns sharply to the right and leads to the inner fortress.

The **tower** at this point is massive, with a doorway leading out to the moat through a 5m-thick wall. On the outer wall above the

doorway are the figures of two lions facing each other, supposedly symbols of the English Crusader king, Richard the Lion-Heart.

The moat here is usually full of stagnant water. When the castle was occupied, this water was used to fill the **baths**, which you can get down to by a couple of dogleg staircases over in the corner to your left. These lead into a tight little complex of rooms and you'll recognise the layout if you've ever visited a *hammam* (bathhouse); there's a central chamber with a stone fountain and off it, private little washrooms, a couple of which still contain stone basins. This was a Mamluk or later addition to the Krak.

The cavernous room on the southern edge of the moat measures 60m by 9m and the roof is formed of one single vault – quite an impressive feat in stone. It was most likely used as a stable. From the roof of this great hall you can gain access to the three towers

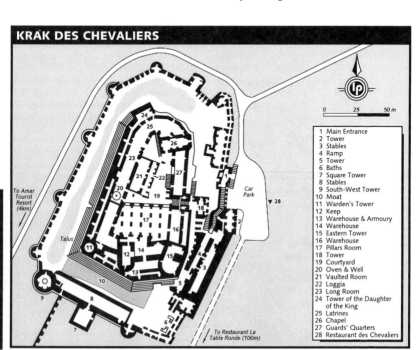

KRAK DES CHEVALIERS

To Amar Tourist Resort (4km)

Talus

To Restaurant La Table Ronde (100m)

Car Park

0   25   50 m

1 Main Entrance
2 Tower
3 Stables
4 Ramp
5 Tower
6 Baths
7 Square Tower
8 Stables
9 South-West Tower
10 Moat
11 Warden's Tower
12 Keep
13 Warehouse & Armoury
14 Warehouse
15 Eastern Tower
16 Warehouse
17 Pillars Room
18 Tower
19 Courtyard
20 Oven & Well
21 Vaulted Room
22 Loggia
23 Long Room
24 Tower of the Daughter of the King
25 Latrines
26 Chapel
27 Guards' Quarters
28 Restaurant des Chevaliers

THE COAST & MOUNTAINS

that punctuate the southern wall. The **square tower** bore the brunt of the attack in 1271 and was rebuilt by Beybars. So too was the **south-west corner tower**; its central pillar, which supports the upper level of the tower, bears an inscription in Arabic recording Beybars' full title: 'Al-Malek az-Zaher Rukn ad-Dunya w'ad-Din Abu al-Fath Beybars' (the Manifest King, Pillar of the World and the Faith, Father of the Victory)!

Walking around between the two walls from the south-west tower, you reach the **Tower of the Daughter of the King** in the north-western corner, unusual in that it is wider than it is deep. On the facade are three rows of triple-pointed arches. A large projecting gallery, where rocks were hurled at assailants, is concealed in the face. The eastern face of this tower has a rear gate opening onto the moat.

The Inner Fortress

Continue around and enter the inner fortress through the tower at the top of the access ramp into an open courtyard. The **loggia** on the western side of the yard is the most impressive structure in the Krak. It has a Gothic facade of seven arches, two of which are open doorways. The other five arches are windows, each subdivided by a delicate pillar with an acanthus-leafed capital.

The openings lead to a large **vaulted hall**, which was probably a reception room. On the far side of this is a 120m-long room running the length of the western wall. A few latrines are visible at the northern end. In the middle of the room are the remains of an **oven** measuring more than 5m in diameter. This area probably doubled as a storage area and granary, stockpiled with provisions against the sieges the Crusaders expected.

The **pillars room** has five rows of heavy squat pillars and is vaulted with fist-sized stones. It has been suggested that it was used as a refectory. Several nearby rooms were warehouses. In one are the remains of massive pottery oil jars and in another there's an oil mill, more oil jars and a well.

Back in the courtyard, the **chapel** has a nave of three bays of vaults. It was con-verted to a mosque after the Muslim conquest and the *minbar* (pulpit) still remains. The staircase that obstructs the main door is a later addition and leads to the upper floors of the fortress.

The upper floor of the Tower of the Daughter of the King was a cafe but at the time of our last visit it had closed. You can make your way over to the round tower in the south-west corner which is known as the **Warden's Tower**; this was where the Grand Master of the Hospitallers had his quarters. From the tower's roof are some magnificent views – if the haze clears – across to the snowcapped peak of Kornet as-Saouda (3088m) in the Anti-Lebanon Range to the south and the valley of the Nahr al-Kebir (Big River) to the east. To the west you should be able to make out the solitary pale figure of Safita's Castel Blanc.

For the best view of the Krak itself, take the road that leads to the Amar Tourist Resort; five minutes walking gets you onto the ridge of an adjacent hill from where you can look back to see the castle laid out in profile.

Krak des Chevaliers is open from 9 am to 7 pm (5 pm in winter) daily except public holidays. Entry costs S£300 (students S£30). A torch would be handy to explore some of the darker passages. Anybody passing through enroute to Homs, Tartus or anywhere else should have little trouble leaving their packs at reception.

Places to Stay & Eat

The Krak is an easy day trip from Tartus or Hama (see the Orontes Valley chapter), which both offer better accommodation possibilities. The only budget option here is *Restaurant La Table Ronde* (☎ 031-734 280), about 200m south of the castle's main entrance, which is primarily a restaurant but also has four basic and grubby rooms containing three beds for S£700. You can also camp here (S£150 to pitch a tent and use the shower). The restaurant owners are also building a hotel with fine views of the castle. When open it will probably charge about US$20 per person for a decent room plus breakfast.

Otherwise, *Amar Tourist Resort* (☎ *031-730 512)*, about 4km down the road past the Krak, is a popular resort-style hotel with expensive rooms, pool and restaurant. It's open only in summer, when a suite with two bedrooms and kitchenette costs C1350. The only other possibilities are the hotels on the road to St George's Monastery.

About the best value for food and drink is *Restaurant La Table Ronde* where a decent buffet meal costs S£200. There's also *Restaurant des Chevaliers*, opposite the Krak entrance, but the food here is poor and overpriced.

Getting There & Away
The castle lies some 10km north of the Homs-Tartus highway. It is roughly halfway between the two towns and can be visited on a day trip from either, or enroute from one to the other. Alternatively, the Cairo and Riad hotels in Hama both run day trips.

From Homs there are several microbuses to the village of Hosn leaving before noon (S£20, 1½ hours); they will drop you right at the Krak. Otherwise, there are a few others that will take you to within a few kilometres, leaving you to hitch the rest of the way or catch a local microbus. If you are staying in Hama, add on another 45 minutes each way between Hama and Homs.

The other alternative, and the only choice from Tartus, is to catch one of the buses shuttling between Tartus and Homs and alight at the turn-off on the highway. Tell the driver where you want to go and with luck you'll be charged less than the full fare to Homs (which is S£30). From there you will have to

hitch or pick up a passing local microbus (S£10 from the junction up to 'al-qala'a').

To return, wait for a microbus at the Krak or walk back down through the village and out to the road that leads to the Homs-Tartus highway. You have a better chance of picking up passing traffic late in the day from here than from the Krak or the village.

AROUND KRAK DES CHEVALIERS
St George's Monastery
The first Greek Catholic church on this site, in a valley to the west of the Krak, was built as early as the 5th century. The second church went up in the 12th century, and today houses an exquisite 300-year-old iconostasis carved in Aleppo. In the new church you can admire another iconostasis, fashioned about 150 years ago. The new monastery, Deir Mar Jirjis, is open from 9 am to 8 pm daily. To get there, take the road from the highway towards Nasira and 4km after the turn-off for Hosn and the Krak take a fork to the left. About the only way to do this trip is by hitching (if you don't have your own vehicle). Alternatively, you could arrange to go by taxi from the Krak; there and back, plus an hour or so waiting time, should cost no more than S£200.

About 2km before the monastery is one of Syria's better hotels, *Al-Wadi Hotel* (☎ *031-730 456, fax 730 399)*. It charges a hefty US$60/72 for singles/doubles, with breakfast. Closer to the main road is the unfriendly *Funduq ar-Riyadh* (☎ *031-730 402)*, which has doubles only for an excessive S£800. It also has a restaurant.

Orontes Valley

In Arabic, the Orontes River is known as Nahr al-Assi, the 'Rebel River', because it flows from south to north, unlike most of the other rivers in the region which flow in the reverse direction. It has its headwaters in the mountains of Lebanon near Baalbek and flows down the Bekaa Valley to enter Syria just south of Homs, near Tell Nabi Mend, the ancient site of Kadesh. Around 1300 BC, the Egyptians clashed with the Hittites at Kadesh in a pre-Classical war of the superpowers.

It's unclear whether any significant settlement existed at that time on the site of what is now Homs, but almost ever since, travel writers have been dismissing the place as drab, depressing and uninteresting.

Flowing north, the Orontes swings east, passing under the main Homs-Hama highway before looping through the attractive riverside town of Hama. It is here that, historically, the current has been harnessed to languidly turn the city's giant water wheels. The river used to flow north-west from Hama only to seep away into the swamps of the Al-Ghab plain. The swamps have long been drained and the river now emerges from the valley to pursue its course northwards into Turkey, finally entering the Mediterranean beyond Antakya.

HOMS

Homs, Syria's third largest city, has a history stretching back to the 1st millennium BC and at one time gave birth to a dynasty of Roman emperors. Sadly, there's little evidence today of any kind of pedigree. The sole major boast of modern Homs is a huge oil refining industry. Renowned for being dim and vulgar, Homsies are also the butt of Syrian humour – it's popularly said that the only thing refined about Homs is its oil. Still, the city remains an important crossroads where routes east to Palmyra and west via the Homs Gap to Tartus and the coast intersect with the main north-south Aleppo-Damascus highway. As such, most travellers

Highlights

- **Accommodation in Hama** – for the dedicated budget traveller this is as good as it gets: three-star-style rooms for as little as five bucks a head (see page 208)

- **Dining in Hama** – spend the money you save on accommodation on dining; as far as mezze, kebabs and araq go, Hama has some great eating options (see page 209)

- **Apamea** – perhaps Syria's second most impressive archaeological site after Palmyra and definitely one for fans of colonnades (see page 212)

- **View over the Al-Ghab** – the single best view in Syria is from the heights of the Jebel Ansariyya gazing down on the valley below, though how you get up there is another matter (see page 212)

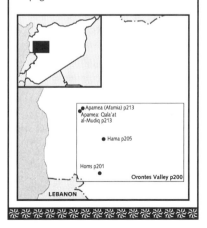

have to pass through Homs at some stage. The shortage of things to see is compounded by a lack of decent budget accommodation,

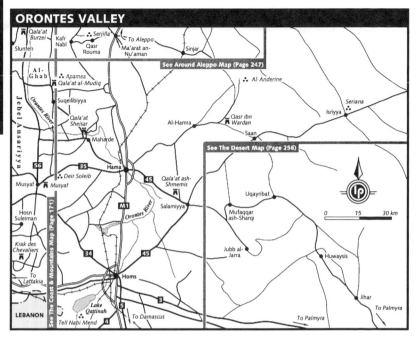

ORONTES VALLEY

so few choose to hang around, instead treating the city as a bus interchange. But if you do have time to kill, the city has a good buzz about it and the extensive souqs are well worth exploring.

History

Digs at the *tell* (artificial hill) which lies just to the south of the centre of the modern city, indicate that there were settlements on this site in pre-Classical times; however, Homs only gained importance during the Roman era. Formerly known as Emesa, the town benefited from close ties with Palmyra, 125km to the east.

Its regional importance was further enhanced around 187 AD when Julia Domna, daughter of an Emesan high priest, married a Roman garrison commander, Septimius Severus, who six years later would become emperor of Rome. They founded a Syro-Roman dynasty that spanned four emperors (reigning from 211 to 235).

Unfortunately it was a dynasty most noted for its rapid decline into depravity. Most notorious of all was Elagabalus, whose four year reign of chaos was abruptly terminated when he was assassinated by his own Praetorian guards who were seeking to restore some order to the empire.

Under the Byzantines, Homs became an important Christian centre (to this day it still has a very large Christian population). After falling to the Muslims in 636, led by the general Khaled ibn al-Walid (see the boxed text later in this section), Homs then became an equally fervent centre of Islam.

Information

Tourist Office There is a small information booth (☎ 473 898) in the park on Sharia al-Quwatli. There is no printed information here and the people running it, who seem to know very little, lock up shop and disappear all the time. Officially, it's open from 8 am to 2 pm and from 5 to 8 pm daily except Friday.

Visa Extensions For visa renewals, go to the 3rd floor of the multistorey administration building (marked immigration office on the map) at the end of a tiny side lane north of Sharia al-Quwatli. This place houses everything from the passport office to the traffic police and is chaotic to say the least. At street level there are passport photo places and a booth (on the left) where you will inevitably have to buy revenue stamps for your visa extension forms. The visa office is open from 8.30 am to 2 pm daily except Friday.

Money A few blocks north of Sharia al-Quwatli is the main branch of the Commercial Bank of Syria, where you can change cash or travellers cheques from 8 am to 12.30 pm daily except Friday. On our last visit, a big new branch of the Commercial Bank had yet to open on Sharia al-Quwatli. Otherwise, there is a foreign exchange booth

close to the souq that also takes travellers cheques and is open from 8 am to 8 pm daily, Friday included (though it shuts for a few hours in the early afternoon for lunch).

Post & Communications The new post office is on Sharia Abdel Moniem Riad, 150m north of the clock tower roundabout. It's open from 6 am to 5.30 pm daily except Friday. The telephone office is on Sharia al-Quwatli just east of the clock tower roundabout; there are several card phones inside and cards are available from the counter. It's open daily from 8 am to 8 pm except Friday, when it closes at 1 pm.

Khaled ibn al-Walid Mosque

Built in the first decade of the 20th century, Homs' best-known monument isn't exactly old but it is quite an attractive example of a Turkish-style mosque. The black-and-white banding of stone in the courtyard area is particularly striking, if a little overdone. Inside the prayer hall over in one corner is the domed mausoleum of Khaled ibn al-Walid who conquered Syria for Islam back in 636

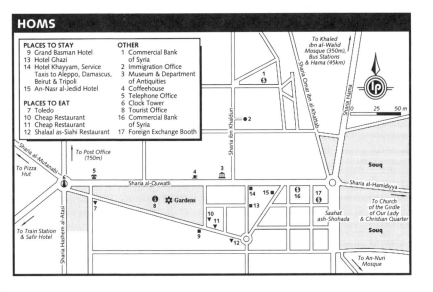

HOMS

PLACES TO STAY
9 Grand Basman Hotel
13 Hotel Ghazi
14 Hotel Khayyam, Service Taxis to Aleppo, Damascus, Beirut & Tripoli
15 An-Nasr al-Jedid Hotel

PLACES TO EAT
7 Toledo
10 Cheap Restaurant
11 Cheap Restaurant
12 Shalaal as-Siahi Restaurant

OTHER
1 Commercial Bank of Syria
2 Immigration Office
3 Museum & Department of Antiquities
4 Coffeehouse
5 Telephone Office
6 Clock Tower
8 Tourist Office
16 Commercial Bank of Syria
17 Foreign Exchange Booth

Khaled ibn al-Walid

Bearing the colourful, if bloody, title 'The Sword of Allah', Khaled ibn al-Walid is revered as the warrior who brought Islam to Syria. With an intrepid band of 500 camel-mounted soldiers, Al-Walid had earlier begun Islam's first campaign outside Arabia – in Iraq. He was having a deal of success when Abu Bakr, the caliph, ordered him to head west. He marched for 20 days along a circuitous desert route to evade observation, appearing as if out of nowhere in the vicinity of Damascus. He immediately attacked local forces from the rear, sowing disorder and panic among Byzantine troops. Al-Walid's terms of surrender were so modest that the invaders were favourably accepted by the local population.

A year later, the Byzantines returned in force, with an army of some 50,000. Months of skirmishes culminated in the great Battle of Yarmouk in August 636, in which Al-Walid triumphed and Islam was firmly established in the eastern Mediterranean. It is recorded that Al-Walid lived out the rest of his life in Homs, although there's a degree of doubt as to whether he is actually buried in the mosque that bears his name.

(see the boxed text above). The mosque is in a small park off Sharia Hama, 500m north of Sharia al-Quwatli.

Museum

The city's main museum is housed in the gloomy Department of Antiquities building on Sharia al-Quwatli. It contains a rather lacklustre archaeological collection comprised of artefacts unearthed in the Homs region and none of the exhibits is labelled in English.

It's open from 9 am to 1.45 pm and from 2.45 to 6 pm (4 pm in winter) daily except Tuesday. Admission is a totally unwarranted S£300.

Souq & Christian Quarter

Lying east of Sharia al-Quwatli, the souq in Homs is unusually large and busy and although it lacks the charm that age has conferred on the souqs of Aleppo or Damascus, its narrow lanes are free of souvenir stalls, hassle and any other indication that foreign tourists before you have ever wandered this way before.

Several of the passageways converge on the impressive main entrance of the **Mosque of an-Nuri**, which is worth a quick look inside. It's thought that it stands on the site of an ancient sun temple, and if you look closely at the columns you'll see from the capitals that some of them are clearly Roman.

If you push on east through the souq you come into the Christian Quarter, which is full of old buildings and is possibly the most interesting part of Homs in which to explore. One place definitely worth searching out is the Syrian Orthodox **Church of the Girdle of Our Lady**, or Kineesat Umm Zumaar. In 1953, the patriarch of Antioch, Ignatius Aphraim, declared a delicate strip of woven wool and silk found in the church six months earlier to be a girdle worn by the Virgin Mary. The story is that it had survived intact since the Ascension of Mary into Heaven, preserved in one container or another in a church on this spot. You can ask a caretaker to see the girdle but don't expect much; it is a fairly flimsy affair. To get there, follow the extension of Sharia al-Quwatli east through the souqs. Turn right at the second street after a building marked 'Archevêché Syrien Catholique' (Syrian Catholic Archbishopric) and you'll see the church at the end of the street.

Places to Stay – Budget

The cheap hotels are on or around Sharia al-Quwatli between the tourist office and the souq.

Hotel Ghazi and *Hotel Khayyam* are next door to each other on a side street off Quwatli and are equally unappealing. Singles/doubles at each are S£175/275 plus S£35 for a shower.

An-Nasr al-Jedid Hotel (☎ 227 423), entered from a side street just off Sharia al-

Quwatli, is about the best of the budget hotels. Its owner is a polite old guy who speaks English well and with whom you can have a long chat in the big, old, musty lounge. It's a bit grubby and basic but the sheets are clean and one of the showers along the corridor can be cranked up to give out some hot water (S£50 per shower). Singles/doubles cost S£200/300.

Grand Basman Hotel (☎ *225 009*) has rooms with bath and fan for US$15/22. The entrance is in the middle of a small shopping arcade. It's not bad, but as is so often the case with budget hotels charging dollars, it's overpriced and tends to be a haunt for some dubious passing trade.

Places to Stay – Top End
Safir Hotel (☎ *412 400, fax 433 420, Sharia Ragheb al-Jamali*) is 2km north-west of the centre – go south-west from city centre but then hang a right and go north. The Safir is one of Syria's best five-star hotels and, according to reports, in quality and service beats the Cham hotels hands down (see Places to Stay – Mid-Range & Top End in the Hama section later). It has a lovely bar area, a decent restaurant and a bookshop with a selection of titles on Syria and the Middle East. Singles/doubles are a reasonable US$77/92 and credit cards are accepted.

Places to Eat
The cheap restaurants are grouped together one block south of Sharia al-Quwatli and have the regular fare: kebabs, chicken, felafel, humous and salad. One of the better is *Shalaal as-Siahi Restaurant*, which is a really busy place with a takeaway section downstairs and seating upstairs. It has a menu in English and does *shwarma* (sandwich of meat sliced off the spit), hamburgers and juices.

Toledo, facing Sharia al-Quwatli across the gardens where the tourist office is sited, is also OK; it serves a variety of stews, soups and rice dishes and the bill will come to about S£250 a head. Beer is served.

If you fancy playing it safe, there's another imitation *Pizza Hut* restaurant (see Places to Eat in the Tartus section of The Coast & Mountains chapter) down at the western end of Sharia al-Mutanabi, a few minutes walk from the clock tower roundabout. The restaurant at the Safir Hotel (see previous Places to Stay – Top End entry) is also reputedly very good, though pricey.

On Sharia al-Quwatli there is a big shady coffeehouse called *Majmu ar-Rawda as-Siyahi* (something along the lines of Tourist Garden Association), where you can sit down for a drink and *narjileh* (water pipe), but food is not served.

Getting There & Away
Bus There are two bus stations: the Karnak station, which is about 1.5km north of the city centre up the Hama road, and a new luxury bus station, which is about 1km further. To get to the luxury station from the Karnak station, turn right out of the main entrance and walk 500m to a large roundabout; bear right there and the luxury bus station is 400m straight ahead. To get to the luxury station from the city centre in a taxi should cost about S£25.

To get to Krak des Chevaliers you need to catch a Tartus bus or minibus and ask to be let off on the highway at the castle junction – tell the driver you want 'Qala'at al-Hosn'. See the Krak des Chevaliers section in The Coast and Mountains chapter.

Luxury Bus There are all the usual bus companies and among them they probably send out a bus for Damascus (S£70, two hours) about every half hour. Services to Aleppo (S£75 to S£85, 2½ hours) and Hama are no less frequent, although the latter journey takes takes only half an hour and microbuses are much more frequent. There are also buses to Tartus (S£40, one hour) and Palmyra (S£70, two hours).

Karnak Buses operating from the Karnak station closer to town leave three times a day to both Damascus (S£60) and Aleppo (S£75). There is one service to Palmyra (S£65), one to Tartus (S£40), two to Lattakia (S£65, two hours) and three a day to Beirut (S£250).

Minibuses Battered old minibuses go everywhere from Karnak station, for fares that are considerably cheaper than the bigger buses, but they're generally cramped and uncomfortable with nowhere to put baggage. The fare to Hama on one of these is S£10, to Tartus is S£17, and to Palmyra is S£22.

Microbus Bright, new microbuses also shuttle in and out of the luxury bus station, most of them going to Hama (S£17, 40 minutes); they depart as soon as they're full and you can generally turn up at any time, climb straight in, and expect to be away in less than 10 minutes.

Train The new train station is a good half hour walk from the centre. Take the street heading south-west of the clock tower until it merges with the main road, Sharia Tarablus. At the second set of lights turn left down a side street, Sharia al-Mahatta, and head to the rather grandiose station at the end. There are two departures a day (all in the early hours of the morning, of course) south to Damascus (S£47/34, 1st/2nd class) and north to Aleppo (S£45/32). The Aleppo trains go on to Deir ez-Zur and Qamishle, in the north-east of the country.

Service Taxi All the service taxis gather around the corner of the Al-Khayyam Hotel on Sharia al-Quwatli and run to Damascus, Aleppo, and Beirut and Tripoli (Lebanon).

HAMA

With the Orontes River flowing through the centre, its banks lined with trees and gardens and gardens, groaning *norias* (water wheels), Hama is one of Syria's more attractive towns. While there's not an awful lot to see, the peaceful atmosphere, good restaurants and excellent hotels combine to make it a very pleasant place to spend a few relaxing days. Use the comforts of Hama as a base for excursions to some of the very worthwhile sites further north up the Orontes Valley (see Around Hama later this chapter), or to places further afield like the Krak des Chevaliers (see The Coast & Mountains chapter) or the Dead Cities (see the Aleppo chapter).

History

Although Hama's history is not that well documented, we do know that it Hama has occupied a position of importance for centuries. Excavations on the city's central *tell* have revealed that it was settled as long ago as the Neolithic Age, and there are historical references to an Aramaean kingdom of Hamah (or Hamath), which traded with Israel during the reigns of biblical David and Solomon (1000 to 922 BC). Occupied later by the Assyrians, Hama joined Damascus in a revolt against their foreign conquerors in 853 BC, defeating the troops of Shalmenaser. Under Sargon II, however, the Assyrians got their revenge in 720 BC and the city was razed and its citizens deported. By the time of the Seleucids, the Greek dynasty established by one of Alexander's generals, the town had been renewed and rechristened Epiphania after the ruler Antiochus IV Epiphanes (reigned 175 to 164 BC). It remained an important Roman and Byzantine centre until its capture by the Arabs in 637 AD.

The town prospered under the Ayyubids (the descendants of Salah ad-Din) but was often fought over by rival dynasties in Damascus and Aleppo, which it lay between. Finally, under the tutelage of the Mamluks, the Arab poet Abu al-Feda was made sultan of the city.

The most recent chapter in Hama's history has been one of the country's saddest. It was here in 1982 that the repressive nature of Assad's regime was most brutally demonstrated. The details of what happened that bloody February are hazy at best but it appears that about 8000 government troops were moved in to quash a rebellion by armed members of the then outlawed Muslim Brotherhood – a rebellion that by all accounts was ill-conceived and unpopular. Fighting lasted three weeks and the level of destruction was immense. Only those who knew the city before this calamity can fully measure the damage, although as recently as

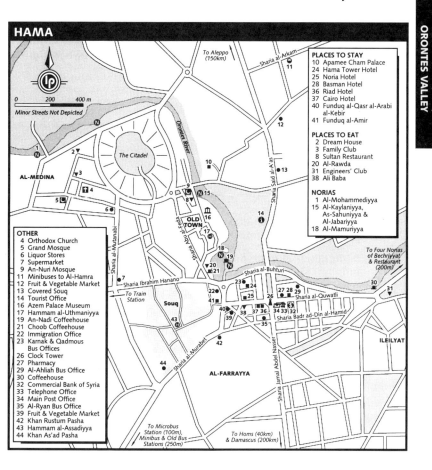

HAMA

0   200   400 m
Minor Streets Not Depicted

To Aleppo
(150km)

Sharia al-Arkam

Sharia al-A'as

Sharia Said al-A'as

The Citadel

Orontes River

AL-MEDINA

OLD
TOWN

Sharia Abu al-Feda

Sharia al-Mutanabi

Sharia Ibrahim Hanano

To Train
Station

Souq

Sharia al-Buhturi

Sharia al-Quwatli

Sharia Badr ad-Din al-Hamid

Sharia al-Murabet

AL-FARRAYYA

Sharia Jamal Abdel Nasser

ILEILYAT

To Four Norias
of Bechriyyat
& Restaurant
(200m)

To Microbus
Station (100m),
Minibus & Old Bus
Stations (250m)

To Homs (40km)
& Damascus (200km)

PLACES TO STAY
10 Apamee Cham Palace
24 Hama Tower Hotel
25 Noria Hotel
28 Basman Hotel
36 Riad Hotel
37 Cairo Hotel
40 Funduq al-Qasr al-Arabi
   al-Kebir
41 Funduq al-Amir

PLACES TO EAT
2 Dream House
3 Family Club
8 Sultan Restaurant
20 Al-Rawda
31 Engineers' Club
38 Ali Baba

NORIAS
1 Al-Mohammediyya
15 Al-Kaylaniyya,
   As-Sahuniyya &
   Al-Jabariyya
18 Al-Mamuriyya

OTHER
4 Orthodox Church
5 Grand Mosque
6 Liquor Stores
7 Supermarket
9 An-Nuri Mosque
11 Minibuses to Al-Hamra
12 Fruit & Vegetable Market
13 Covered Souq
14 Tourist Office
16 Azem Palace Museum
17 Hammam al-Uthmaniyya
19 An-Nadi Coffeehouse
21 Choob Coffeehouse
22 Immigration Office
23 Karnak & Qadmous
   Bus Offices
26 Clock Tower
27 Pharmacy
29 Al-Ahliah Bus Office
30 Coffeehouse
32 Commercial Bank of Syria
33 Telephone Office
34 Main Post Office
35 Al-Ryan Bus Office
39 Fruit & Vegetable Market
42 Khan Rustum Pasha
43 Hammam al-Assadiyya
44 Khan As'ad Pasha

1955 travel writer Robin Fedden could write in his book *Syria: An Historical Appreciation* that Hama was 'extraordinarily unspoilt' with houses that overhung the water and an extensive old town in which modern buildings barely intrude; this is no longer the case. The heart of the old town was completely razed and what was once narrow streets and souqs is now occupied by the Apamee Cham Palace Hotel.

Obviously this event is something the government would much prefer to pretend never happened, so it's prudent not to discuss the subject – not that anyone is likely to bring it up.

Information

Tourist Office The tourist office (☎ 511 033) is in a small building in the gardens in the centre of town, just north of the river. Apart from the usual free map, the staff here don't have anything much to tell you and they certainly aren't as well tuned in to travellers' needs as the staff at the Cairo and

Riad hotels. The office is open from 8 am to 2 pm daily except Friday.

Visa Extensions The immigration office is hidden away up three flights of stairs in a building just opposite the footbridge in the centre of town. There's a small sign saying 'passports' in English next to a pharmacy near the traffic island. You need four photos and S£50; the whole process takes about 30 minutes. The office is open from 8 am to 2 pm daily except Friday.

Money The Commercial Bank of Syria on Sharia al-Quwatli, just east of the clock tower and next door to the post office, is open from 8.30 am to 12.30 pm daily except Friday. It accepts cash and travellers cheques (no commission) at the exchange counter on the 1st floor. For a small transaction fee the Noria Hotel is able to give cash advances on Visa cards.

Post & Communications The main post office, open daily from 8 am to 6 pm (1 pm on Friday), is on the corner of sharias Al-Quwatli and Jamal Abdel Nasser. The postbox is an anonymous wooden box inside on the left. Behind the post office is a semi-open air phone office where, it seems, the card phones are accessible 24 hours; however, the office from where you buy the phonecards is only open 8 am to noon and from 5 to 7 pm daily.

Norias

Hama's most distinctive attractions are its norias, centuries-old wooden water wheels up to 20m in diameter. They were first built in Ayyubid times as an aid to irrigation. The land around the Orontes is considerably higher than the river itself, which is deeply incised into its rocky bed. The norias scooped water from the river and deposited it into aqueducts. The water then flowed to nearby fields and gardens.

Of the more than 30 norias that characterised medieval Hama, only 17 remain, and these date from late Mamluk and Ottoman times. They still turn today, although only

during summer; at other times the waters of the river are diverted into more modern irrigation schemes elsewhere, reducing water supplies. The wheels and blocks on which the norias are mounted are wooden, and the friction between the two produces a mournful groaning that carries around all of central Hama.

The most **central norias** are right in the middle of town with parks and cafes around them; proportionally, Hama probably has more green areas than any other town or city in Syria. This is a really pleasant spot and a great place to relax in the evenings, when the norias are lit up. The most impressive wheels, however, are about 1km upstream at a place known as **The Four Norias of Bechriyyat**. As the name suggests, there are four norias here – two pairs on a weir that spans the river. It's unfortunate that this weir also collects all the rubbish and debris that happen to be drifting down the river: everything from plastic bottles to dead sheep.

TONY WHEELER

One of Hama's wooden *norias* (water wheels) framed in the arch of an aqueduct.

Still, in the centre of town, on the west bank of the river are two decent restaurants with terraces looking across to the wheels (see Places to Eat later in this section).

About 1km from the centre in the other direction, west, is the largest of the norias, known as the **Al-Mohammediyya**. It dates from the 14th century and used to supply the Grand Mosque with water, and part of its old aqueduct still spans the road. Beside the noria there is a small stone footbridge across the river that leads to an uninteresting area of parkland.

Old Town

Much of Hama's old town was destroyed in the 1982 bombardment but there is a small remnant along the west bank of the river, just north of the two central norias. Follow the road that leads by the Al-Rawda restaurant, then swing off to the right just before what looks like an arched gate but which is in fact part of the old aqueduct connected to the **Al-Mamuriyya** noria. Follow the lane as it runs parallel to the aqueduct and then turns north. This area of basically two parallel narrow, twisting alleys, may seem derelict (yet still very attractive). However, it's slated as a tourist development zone and within the next couple of years you can expect it to spawn hotels, restaurants, handicraft shops and the like.

At present, the main thing to head for is the **Azem Palace Museum**, which Ross Burns, author of *Monuments of Syria*, regards as 'one of the loveliest Ottoman residential buildings in Syria'. The museum is housed in the Beit al-Azem, the former residence of the governor, As'ad Pasha al-Azem, who ruled the town from 1742. The palace has strong echoes of the more grandiose building of the same name in Damascus, which is hardly surprising as the latter was built by the same man upon his transfer to the capital. Burns singles out the *haramlek* (women's quarters), the area to the right when you enter, as being particularly noteworthy. Stairs from here lead up to what is known as the Royal Hall, where it is supposed As'ad Pasha had his sleeping quarters.

It took a pounding during the 1982 uprising but has largely been repaired and has a splendid mirrored ceiling. Back on the ground floor, another door leads into a small museum containing artefacts discovered in the citadel. The most interesting of the exhibits is a vivid 3rd century mosaic found near Hama, depicting a group of female musicians. The museum is open from 9 am to 6 pm (4 pm in winter) daily except Tuesday. Entry is S£300 (students S£30) and it's well worth a visit.

Just north of the museum is **An-Nuri Mosque**, built by the Muslim commander Nur ad-Din (Nureddin) in the 12th century. The building is more interesting from the outside than from the inside. If you cross the bridge beside the mosque you have a very picturesque view of the river and three norias, which are, from east to west, the Al-Kaylaniyya, the As-Sahuniyya and the Al-Jabariyya.

Citadel & Grand Mosque

For a good view over the city, walk up to the park on top of the citadel. Danish archaeologists did extensive work on this tell and found evidence of continuous settlement since Neolithic times, particularly during the Iron Age, but apart from a few unrecognisable fragments, nothing remains as all the stone was long ago carted off for use in other buildings. The area has been landscaped and developed into a picnic and recreation area, with a small cafe; it's popular with locals, particularly on Friday.

About 400m south-west of the citadel is Hama's **Grand Mosque** which, after being almost completely destroyed in the fighting of 1982, has since been faithfully restored. It was originally built by the Umayyads in the 8th century along the lines of their great mosque in Damascus. It had a similar history having been converted from a church that itself had stood on the site of a pagan temple. Also, as in Damascus, there is a domed treasury in the wide courtyard, raised on eight Roman/Byzantine columns. The two minarets are beautiful, particularly the square one next to the prayer hall.

Souq

Hama was never a great trading centre and today its main souq (off Sharia al-Murabet) is modest with hardly any of the great commercial *khans* (merchant's inns) that fill the old cities of Aleppo or Damascus. The two noteworthy khans Hama does possess have long since been pressed into other uses: **Khan Rustum Pasha** (1556), just south of the town centre on Sharia al-Murabet, was for a long time an orphanage (currently undergoing restoration); while **Khan As'ad Pasha** (1751), also on Sharia al-Murabet, is now a local Ba'ath Party branch. Both places are thus off limits to casual visitors.

The souq, while it may not be the most exciting you'll ever encounter, nevertheless does have everything a traditional oriental market should have: covered passageways, lots of intriguing cul-de-sacs, and noise, colour and smells. It is a great place to go for a wander in the morning and, with little on offer for tourists, it is unlikely anyone will so much as say 'boo' to you.

Aside from the main souq, there are also the remnants of an older souq, north of the river off Sharia Said al-A'as. Just past the tourist office on the opposite side of the street, a single passageway of what was formerly an extensive covered bazaar runs parallel to the road. The rest of the bazaar was destroyed in 1982.

Activities

Hammams Although still in working order, the attractive Ottoman-era Hammam al-Uthmaniyya (bathhouse) rarely opens these days as its location in the deserted old town means it gets very little custom. However, the Hammam al-Assadiyya in the souq does good business and is open from 6 am to 10 pm daily. It's a men only, no-frills place and use of the facilities costs S£100. The proprietor of the Assadiyya is also responsible for the Uthmaniyya and if you are interested he will open up the baths for you.

Swimming You can use the pool at the Apamee Cham Palace hotel during summer for S£200 a day (see Places to Stay – Mid-

Range & Top End later in this chapter). There is also a public swimming pool near the Four Norias restaurant (see under Restaurants in Places to Eat later in this chapter), about 600m east of the town centre, which only charges S£25. Women, however, are likely to feel uncomfortable here.

Places to Stay – Budget

There are really only two budget options in Hama but both are superb.

Cairo Hotel (☎ *222 280, fax 511 715, Sharia al-Quwatli*) near the clock tower is possibly the best budget hotel in Syria. Rooms are spotlessly clean with fridge (stocked with soft drinks) and satellite TV, and the ensuite bathrooms and shower units are new and have constant hot water. There's a good breakfast area which, by the time you read this, may have been moved up on to the roof. The manager is extremely friendly and speaks English. A bed in a dorm room is S£175, while singles/doubles are S£300/450. There are also some doubles without bathroom for S£350 and a couple of triple rooms for S£550. If you don't mind having no shade to retreat to in the heat of summer, a mattress on the roof will cost you S£100. The hotel also runs a variety of day trips – see the previous Organised Tours entry.

Riad Hotel (☎ *239 512, fax 517 776, Sharia al-Quwatli*) is in direct and not necessarily friendly competition with the neighbouring Cairo. Its rooms are equally good and the management are trying hard to match the Cairo, innovation for innovation – so there's a good breakfast, free tea on arrival, staff falling over themselves to be helpful, student discounts and numerous organised excursions (again, see Organised Tours under Around Hama). A bed in a shared room will cost S£150, while ensuite doubles go for S£400. You can also sleep on the roof for S£100.

It's unlikely, but if both the Cairo and Riad hotels are booked out, you're down to two flophouses where S£125 gets you a filthy bed (but the bugs come free). Look for *Funduq al-Amir* at the end of Sharia al-Quwatli (actually on a lane called Hadat Abi Taleb) or

Top: Hama, one of Syria's most attractive towns, is famous for its centuries-old wooden *norias* (water wheels), built to provide water for the town and for irrigation.
Bottom: In the arid region east of Hama there are villages full of these mud-brick beehive houses.

GADI FARFOUR

SUSANNAH FARFOR

ANDREW HUMPHREYS

In 2 AD Apamea was a flourishing city of 500,000; now it's one of Syria's top ancient sites.

TONY WHEELER

This Roman mosaic was unearthed in Apamea and is now on display in its museum.

ANDREW HUMPHREYS

Qala'at Sheisar, an Arab fortress near Apamea

TONY WHEELER

Approaching the entrance of Qala'at Sheisar

Funduq al-Qasr al-Arabi al-Kebir ('Hotel' in English) near the vegetable market just south of Sharia al-Quwatli.

Places to Stay – Mid-Range & Top End

Noria Hotel (☎ 512 414, fax 511 715, Sharia al-Quwatli) is run by Badr Tonbor, who also owns the Cairo and has a passion for the hotel business. It's an extremely comfortable place with good service, a smart reception, central air-con and excellent food. Rooms are among the highest quality in this price bracket that you are likely to find in Syria. All rooms have private bath and colour satellite TV; singles/doubles are US$18/28 and there are also triples and suites available.

Hama Tower Hotel (☎ 226 864, fax 521 523) is in the centre of town one block north of Sharia al-Quwatli and occupies the top floors of a tower block overlooking the river. The views are great but the hotel is badly maintained – despite having been open for only a couple of years the rooms are already grubby and worn. We were asked US$31 for a double with ensuite but rates seemed negotiable.

Basman Hotel (☎ 224 838, fax 223 910, Sharia al-Quwatli), opposite the Commercial Bank of Syria, plays host to lots of long-term residents, and scenes in the foyer can sometimes make the place seem more like a refugee centre. It's definitely a last resort. Singles/doubles/triples with fan, bath, TV and balcony are US$17/23/28.

Apamee Cham Palace (☎ 525 335, fax 511 626) is across the river from the citadel, well away from the buzz of the town centre. It's a disquietingly gloomy place with a mausoleum air about it. Singles/doubles cost US$100/120 plus tax. If you find yourself booked in here our advice would be to cancel and switch to the Noria.

Places to Eat

Although you can find it outside Hama, *halawat al-jibn* is a not-too-sweet dessert speciality of the city. It is a cheese-based, soft, doughy delicacy drenched in honey or syrup and often topped with ice cream. A lot of places around Sharia al-Quwatli sell it – a few sell nothing else.

Budget Dining In the couple of blocks along Sharia al-Quwatli west of the Cairo Hotel and in the side streets running north to the river are all the usual cheap kebab and chicken restaurants. There's about half a dozen of them here so if one doesn't have what you want, just try next door. *Ali Baba* on Sharia al-Quwatli (sign in Arabic only but look for the painted Ali Baba figure) is said to do some of the best felafel in Syria; it also has basics like *fuul* (fava bean paste) and humous.

Restaurants There are some excellent dining options in Hama and, outside Damascus and Aleppo, you'll eat the best food in Syria here.

Dream House (☎ 411 687) is a fairly new place in the Al-Medina quarter, two blocks north of the orthodox church. It's a bit large and soulless (and MTV doesn't do anything for the atmosphere) but it is very clean and smart and the food is good. The menu starts with pizzas and filling burgers with fries and salad (S£100 to S£130) and ranges up to steaks, fillets and oriental grills (S£120 to S£170). It's open from 10 am to 1 am, and is a good lunch option.

Sultan Restaurant benefits from a wonderful setting in part of a Mamluk-era complex. The main dining room is bare stone with wooden ceilings and has a central fountain but, best of all, right outside is one of the great old norias providing a groaning aural backdrop to your meal. The menu is limited to *mezze* (a shared meal of a variety of small starters) and several varieties of kebab (S£70 to S£80), which are merely OK. The bill comes laden with surcharges, which tends to sour the experience a little, but it's still worth a visit, especially if you can get the little wooden balcony in the far room. To get here, pass through the low, vaulted tunnel beside the An-Nuri Mosque.

Family Club (Nadi al-A'ili) is an open-air terrace on the 1st floor at the rear of a building a block north of the orthodox church (the club is run by the church). It's used as a social and drinking club by the wealthier citizens of Hama and is a frequent venue for weddings and parties. Anybody is welcome to show up though, and it's definitely worth a visit because the food is excellent. There's no menu as such, you just have to ask for what you want – they have a huge array of mezze available plus kebabs (see the Food section in the Facts for the Visitor chapter and use that to make your orders). Prices are reasonable and for a substantial meal for two you'll be looking at around S£400 to S£500. Alcohol is served and narjilehs are available too.

Engineers' Club (Nadi al-Mohandiseen) is in the wealthy Ileilyat quarter, just east of the town centre off the road that follows the course of the Orontes – it's an open-air garden; the set up is very similar to that at the Family Club and most of the same comments apply.

Four Norias is just over half a kilometre east of the centre on the banks of the river beside – what else – four norias. It's a large open-air place popular with groups and families and gets pretty lively on summer evenings. Food is the standard mezze and kebabs and is good, if not quite as good as that at the Family Club. The setting, however, is better. Beer and araq are served.

Al-Rawda (The Garden) on the west bank of the river has a fine setting overlooking norias. The food is only average, the prices are not, and don't be surprised if the waiter deducts a tip for himself before giving you the change – not that there'll be much change from S£300 for a meal of kebabs, chips, salad and humous. Occasionally, there are dance performances and a band.

Self-Catering For fruit there's a good little *market* just off the western end of Sharia al-Quwatli, while for groceries there's a good western-style *supermarket* at the junction of sharias Ibrahim Hanano and Al-Mutanabi which, though small, is well stocked. You can get takeaway beer at a couple of liquor stores at the north end of Sharia al-Mutanabi, near the citadel.

Entertainment

Coffeehouses For just a tea or coffee, and maybe a narjileh and a friendly game of backgammon, you can't beat the open-air *Choob coffeehouse* next to the Al-Rawda restaurant. It's set in a garden of shady eucalyptus trees and has views of the river and norias. It is a great place to escape the heat. Every so often a waiter will come around with a shiny silver coffee pot and very small cups; this is Arabic coffee, strongly flavoured with cardamom and quite bitter. It is drunk in tiny doses that you just knock back in one hit – a real heart-starter. When you've had enough, hand the cup back with a quick jiggle of the wrist. Bear in mind that this is not a free service and the guy will expect a tip on your way out.

There is also another open-air coffeehouse, *An-Nadi*, next to the big city centre noria and facing the Choob across the river; and a third near the Engineers' Club on the eastern edge of the town centre.

Bars Our research didn't turn up any dedicated drinking venues but the thing to do is enjoy a long leisurely meal at somewhere like the *Family Club* or the *Four Norias* and then linger after the food with a bottle of raki or another few beers.

Getting There & Away

Karnak & Luxury Bus Hama has no bus station as such. Instead, there are several bus company offices in the town centre and the buses pull up outside. The Karnak office is on the riverfront road just east of the roundabout, hidden inside Cafeteria Afamia. It runs three daily buses to Damascus (S£75), two a day to Aleppo (S£60) and two a day to Beirut.

Virtually next door to Karnak is Qadmous bus company office. Al-Ahliah has its office, with adjacent cafeteria, on the riverside road just east of the main bridge. Al-Ryan is one block south of the Cairo Hotel on Sharia Badr ad-Din al-Hamid. All three of these companies have better buses than Karnak but the fares are more expensive. Al-Ahliah has the most extensive services with 20 buses a day for Damascus (S£90, three hours), 15 for Aleppo (S£65, 2½ hours), five for Raqqa (S£145, three hours), four for Homs (S£20, 40 minutes), two for Tartus (S£70, one hour 50 minutes) and one for Lattakia (S£100, three hours). To this, Qadmous bus company adds six daily services to Beirut (S£300, four to five hours).

Minibus The minibus and old bus stations are on the southern edge of town about 1.5km from the centre; you walk down Sharia al-Murabet to where it joins with the main Damascus road and then turn towards the left. Conversely, if you arrive in Hama at the old bus/minibus station and want to walk into town, head left on the main road, bear right at the fork and Sharia al-Murabet will be the first street on your right.

Regular minibuses go to Salamiyya (S£7, 45 minutes), Homs (S£10, 30 minutes), Suqeilibiyya (for Apamea, S£10), Musyaf (S£10), Maharde and other surrounding towns. Buses leave from here for Aleppo (S£25), Damascus (S£32, 2¾ hours) as well as for Lattakia.

For Al-Hamra (S£15) there's a separate minibus station north of the river on Sharia al-Arkam – head up Sharia Said al-A'as, past the tourist office and take the fourth street on your right. In all, it's about a 10 minute walk from the centre.

Microbus The main microbus station is a 10 minute walk from the centre of town at the south-western end of Sharia al-Murabet, in a triangular site at the junction with the main Damascus road. They run to Salamiyya (S£13), Homs (S£17) and also to Suqeilibiyya (S£20).

Train The train station is at the far western end of Sharia Ibrahim Hanano, about 1.5km from central Hama; all bar one of the trains leave and arrive at indecent hours of the morning. Trains to Damascus (S£57/40, 1st/2nd class, four hours) stop in Hama at 2.30 and 4.30 am, while services in the opposite direction, for Aleppo (S£34/23, 2½ hours), stop at 9 pm and 3.40 am. At least

one of the Aleppo trains goes all the way to Qamishle.

Service Taxi Service taxis leave from near the microbus station.

Getting Around
Local buses may come in handy for getting to and from the bus and train stations, both of which are uncomfortably far from the town centre. Buses leave from Sharia al-Buhturi beside the bridge. You pay the S£2 fare on the bus. Alternatively, a yellow taxi will cost S£25 to either the old bus and minibus station or the train station.

AROUND HAMA
There are three main excursions to make from Hama around the Orontes Valley. You can travel north up to the Roman-era ruins of Apamea, west up into the hills to the Assassins' castle of Musyaf, or east out to the Byzantine ruins of Qasr ibn Wardan. Each of these trips takes about half a day but could be stretched by adding in extras, such as stopping off at Qala'at Sheisar on the way to Apamea, or swinging past Qala'at ash-Shmemis on the way back from Qasr ibn Wardan.

If you are comfortable in Hama you could also use it as a base for visiting Krak des Chevaliers (via a change of bus at Homs – see Getting There & Away in the Krak des Chevaliers section of The Coast and Mountains chapter). The Dead Cities are only 60km north of Hama and can be reached by microbus. See the Ma'arat an-Nu'aman and the Dead Cities sections of the Aleppo chapter for more details.

All these trips can be done fairly easily through a combination of public transport and hitching, or alternatively you could take advantage of the organised tours offered by Hama hotels.

Organised Tours
Hama's Cairo and Riad hotels both run excursions with flexible itineraries, determined by the wishes of the group. The most popular options are full day trips involving two or

three scattered locations like Apamea and Musyaf or the Dead Cities combined with Qala'at Salah ad-Din, which string together places that would be hard to get to in one go using public transport. Prices are typically S£500 per person (not including admissions) based on four people sharing the transport, which is not cheap but if you're pushed for time this may be a good way of doing things.

Al-Ghab

From Hama the Orontes River flows northwest for 50km and then into the Al-Ghab plain, a vast green valley stretching between Jebel Ansariyya to the west and Jebel az-Zawiyya to the east. It's said that in ancient times the pharaoh Thutmose III came here to hunt elephants, and a thousand years later Hannibal was here teaching the Syrians how to use elephants in war.

Under the Seleucids the plain must have been both rich and fertile as it supported large cities such as Apamea, but as the population dwindled (see Dead Cities in the Aleppo chapter) the untended land degenerated into swamp. However, with World Bank help, in recent times this low-lying area of some 40 sq km has, been drained and had irrigation ditches dug, returning it to its former status as one of the most fertile areas in Syria.

The view over the Al-Ghab from the ruins of the ancient city of Apamea is great, but by far the best – and most uplifting panorama in all of Syria – is from the top of the Jebel Ansariyya. It's impossible to get up there without your own transport (forget hitching: hardly any traffic comes this way) but if you are driving, or being driven, from Apamea to Qala'at Salah ad-Din via Slunfeh then you will take this route.

Qala'at Burzei

One for completists only, at Qala'at Burzei you will find the minimal remains of a once sizable Crusader castle. The castle was built in the 12th century but fell to Salah ad-Din not long after, in 1188. The most intact part of the ruins is the watch tower that guarded the eastern approach, and you can also pick out the keep on the far western side. It's a bit of a scrabble to get up to the ruins, so wear decent footwear.

The site is about 4km north of the turn-off for Slunfeh on the Jisr ash-Shughur road (No 56) and is accessed by a side road off to the west. You could probably hitch here easily enough from Apamea (Qala'at al-Mudiq).

Apamea

If it weren't for the unsurpassable magnificence of Palmyra, Apamea ('Afamia' in Arabic) would be considered one of the unmissable highlights of Syria. As it is, Apamea is like a condensed version of Zenobia's pink sandstone desert city, but built in grey granite and transposed to a high, wild grassy moor overlooking the Al-Ghab plain.

The site has no set opening hours as it's unfenced and there's nothing to stop anyone wandering across it at any time. However, there is an admission fee of S£300 (students S£25) payable at one of two ticket offices. Although the ticket offices are easily avoided, officials patrol the site checking tickets.

History Founded early in the 3rd century BC by Seleucus I, a former general in the army of Alexander the Great, Apamea became an important trading post and one of the four key settlements in the empire to which he gave his name. It was connected by road to another key Seleucid town, Lattakia (Laodicea), which served it as a port. Seleucus had great skills as a diplomat; while Laodicea was named after his mother, he also took due care to keep things sweet with his Persian wife, Afamia, by naming this settlement after her.

As a result of the rich pasture of the Al-Ghab, Apamea was renowned for its horses. According to Greek historian Strabo, the city had some 30,000 mares and 3000 stallions, as well as 500 war elephants.

Apamea was seized by the general Pompey for the Romans in 64 BC, and only entered into its true golden era in the 2nd century AD, after much of the city was rebuilt after an earthquake in 115 AD. The results of this reconstruction are what you see at the site today.

In its heyday, Apamea boasted a population of about 500,000 (120,000 free people) and was notable enough to be visited by Mark Antony, accompanied by Cleopatra, on his return from staging a campaign against the Armenians on the Euphrates River. Prosperity continued into the Byzantine period but then the city was sacked by the Persians in 540 AD and again in 612. Barely a quarter of a century later Syria was seized by the Muslims and Apamea fell into decline. It assumed importance during the Crusades when the Norman commander, Tancred, took possession of the city in 1106, but the occupation was short-lived and Nur ad-Din won the city back 43 years later. Eight years on the city was all but flattened in a devastating earthquake.

The site wasn't abandoned completely – a nearby hilltop which had served as an acropolis under the Seleucids and Romans became a citadel under the Mamluks, sheltering a small village which later became a popular stopover for pilgrims on their way south to Mecca. The village, which takes its name Qala'at al-Mudiq from the citadel, has long since outgrown its fortified walls and now tumbles down the hillside to the main road, which is where you'll be let off if you're arriving by microbus.

Mosaic Museum Just off the main road at the foot of the hill is a restored Ottoman khan

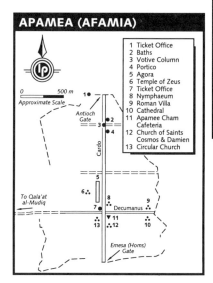

APAMEA (AFAMIA)

0   500 m
Approximate Scale

1 Ticket Office
2 Baths
3 Votive Column
4 Portico
5 Agora
6 Temple of Zeus
7 Ticket Office
8 Nymphaeum
9 Roman Villa
10 Cathedral
11 Apamee Cham Cafeteria
12 Church of Saints Cosmos & Damien
13 Circular Church

Antioch Gate
Cardo
To Qala'at al-Mudiq
Decumanus
Emesa (Homs) Gate

that dates from the 18th century and was used as a trading post on the route to Mecca from Constantinople. It is now a museum devoted to the mosaics unearthed up at Apamea during excavations. The mosaics are housed in the former stables around the central courtyard, along with an odd assortment of architectural bits and pieces. The most impressive, located in the south-west corner of the khan, are two large mosaics found in cathedral ruins at the eastern end of the main east-west boulevard. Unfortunately, the few labels are all in Arabic. The museum is open from 8 am to 2.30 pm daily except Tuesday and entry is S£150 (students S£15).

To get to the site from the museum just follow the trail up the hill. Ignore the guys on motorbikes who offer to show you the way or give you a lift and who say that it's too far to walk – it's not; from where you encounter the hustlers at the top of the hill it's only about 400m to the ticket office at the centre of the cardo.

Theatre On your right partway between the museum and the site proper you'll pass, on

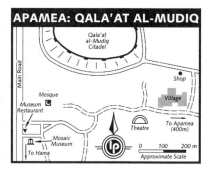

APAMEA: QALA'AT AL-MUDIQ

Qala'at al-Mudiq Citadel

Main Road
Shop
Mosque
Village
Museum
Restaurant
Theatre
To Apamea (400m)
Mosaic Museum
To Hama

0   100   200 m
Approximate Scale

your right, a hollow filled with the barest vestiges of what was a 2nd century AD theatre. After serving as a convenient quarry for the neighbouring village for centuries, the remains are less than impressive, yet archaeologists believe that this may once have been the largest theatre in the Roman empire, bigger even than that at Bosra (see The Hauran chapter). Close up it's impossible to see how this could be, but if you get up to the citadel and look back at the theatre ruins you do get a better idea of the area it once covered.

Cardo The main feature of the ruins is the north-south running *cardo*, or main street, marked out along much of its length by parallel colonnades. At 2km this cardo is longer than that at Palmyra and longer than the Roman-era Via Recta (Straight Street) in Damascus. The columns, originally erected in the 2nd century AD, bear unusual carved designs and some have twisted fluting, a

An example of Apamea's columns featuring the unique twisted fluting.

feature that's unique to Apamea. Interestingly, had you visited this site as little as 50 years ago, there would have been little to see – in what's termed 'reconstructive archaeology', the columns have been recovered from where they once laid overgrown with weeds and scattered about the site, and have been re-erected as colonnades by a Belgian team that has been working here since the 1930s.

Several lesser cross-streets, or *decumani* (Roman era main east-west streets), intersected the cardo and the main surviving decumanus now serves as the modern access road to the site. At this junction are a ticket office and the ludicrously pricey Apamee Cham Cafeteria.

From this intersection heading north you'll immediately notice that you are walking on the original uncovered paving of the cardo, very visibly rutted by the wear of chariot wheels. Off to the right are the remains of a *nyphaeum*, or public water fountain, while a little further on and off to the left two rows of column bases lead to a pile of stone blocks that were once part of the entrance to the *agora*, or forum. Continuing up the cardo you come to an impressive and beautiful portico set forward of the main colonnade and composed of taller columns crowned by a triangular pediment. Just beyond the portico you'll pass by the base of a large votive column in the middle of the street: this would have marked an important intersection.

Beyond the column is the best restored section of the cardo with raised paved areas either side of the street, and behind them the lower portions of facades which would most likely have been shops – you get a very clear idea of how the cardo must have looked in its heyday. Finally, you reach the northern end, bounded by the recently restored Antioch Gate (the southern end of the cardo is marked by the Emesa, or Homs, Gate), beyond which once stretched the ancient city's necropolis.

Decumanus Back at the intersection by the cafe, it's worth following the decumanus to the east, where on your left after about 400m are the remains of a Roman villa with an impressive entrance and colonnaded courtyard; and on the right is a cathedral from about the 5th century. The two outstanding mosaics now on display in the museum were discovered underneath the cathedral. The original church, which some references claim was built to house relics of the 'true cross', was raised over an earlier pagan temple and later expanded after earthquakes rocked the area in the 6th century. By that stage it had become the seat of the area's archbishop.

Citadel The citadel of Qala'at al-Mudiq which sits atop a spur just west of the ruins of Apamea is, typically, more impressive from the outside. It dates from the 13th century and occupies what had been the acropolis of the ancient city. Inside is the tumbledown village of Qala'at al-Mudiq, where local hustlers will try to sell you glass and coins from the ruins. A few of the pieces are obviously old and most are just as obviously made in the local workshop, so if you're interested, it's a case of buyer beware. It's quite an unkempt, grimy little place – especially after rain – but it's worth visiting for the views out over the Al-Ghab and of the ruins and theatre.

Getting There & Away Minibuses (S£10) and microbuses (S£20) regularly run the 45km from Hama to Suqeilibiyya, and from there microbuses go on to Qala'at al-Mudiq (S£10). The whole trip takes about an hour except on Friday when you can wait ages for a connection.

There is little point asking people where 'Apamea' is. Use the Arabic, Afamia, pronounced 'ah-FAM-iya'.

Qala'at Sheisar

About halfway between Hama and Suqeilibiyya the ruins of Qala'at Sheisar rise above the escarpment on the right and a small ruined noria groans away slowly by the river on the left. You can hop off the Hama-Suqeilibiyya microbus here to have a look at the castle, an Arab fortification that at one time dominated the east bank of the Orontes.

It was built by the Fatimids and later used as a base for attacks against the Crusaders at nearby Apamea. In return, the Crusaders tried to take Sheisar a couple of times but failed, so the two opposing fortified camps coexisted in an uneasy stalemate. After sustaining heavy damage as a result of the same 12th century earthquake that flattened Apamea, the Mamluks restored the castle and established a garrison here. With the rise of the Ottomans the place was abandoned as a military base and fell into disrepair. Locals dismantled it piecemeal to build with the stone.

Today only the northern gate complex and the main defensive tower, or donjon, are still reasonably well preserved. There's a track leading up to this area from the main road, just beside where it crosses the Orontes.

Maharde

If you are visiting Sheisar on the way back from Apamea and it's getting on for early evening, the exclusively Christian town of Maharde offers an uncommon nocturnal experience in its version of the Italian *passeggiata*, or evening stroll. About a half dozen so-called cafeterias buzz in the early evening with a mixed crowd of men and women enjoying a coffee or beer until about 8 or 9 pm. Just the sight of both sexes (not a veil to be seen) mingling apparently so freely seems wholly out of place. Outside, the main drag fills with the town populace parading self-consciously up and down in a slow and deliberate fashion. It is clear men and women still keep some distance from one another, unless married or family, and for many it appears this is an opportunity to take a look at possible future life partners. Whatever the ins and outs of it, the scene is one not often played out in other Syrian towns.

There are a few good little bars and restaurants in town. One in particular to look out for is *Restaurant Atlal*.

Musyaf

The solid castle of Musyaf, in the foothills of Jebel Ansariyya, about 40km west of Hama, was long the easternmost bastion of a string of castles held by the Ismaili Assassins for more than a century from 1140. While it's far from being the most impressive of Syria's many forts, the outer walls are intact and suitably imposing, especially viewed against the mountain backdrop, and it has colourful historical associations.

It's not known when the first fortifications were erected on this site but there was

The Assassins

The Ismailis were an extreme Muslim sect who leaned towards the mystical. They were little loved by orthodox Sunnis, who regularly persecuted them. Not surprisingly perhaps, since the doctrine of these followers of Ismail (the 8th century son of the sixth imam) included murder as a means of removing obstacles to the propagation of their faith. Under their charismatic 12th century leader Sinan, known to the Europeans as the Old Man of the Mountain, the surrounding Muslims and Crusaders came to fear and respect the Ismailis.

The Ismaili Assassins, so called – according to one account – because they smoked hashish (an Arabic word from which 'assassin' is said to be derived) before embarking on their murderous exploits, attempted on a couple of occasions to kill both Nur ad-Din and Salah ad-Din, two of Islam's principal champions against the Crusaders. Among the Christian rulers to end up on the wrong end of their poison-tipped swords was Raymond II of Tripoli, who bit the dust around 1150, and Conrad de Montferrat, king of Jerusalem, about 40 years later.

By the late 13th century, however, Sultan Beybars had not only all but finished off the Crusader presence in the Levant, but had also taken the Ismaili fortresses and stripped the group of any political importance.

Anyone interested in knowing more should get hold of a copy of The Assassins by Bernard Lewis.

definitely a castle of some sort here in 1103 because it was seized by the Crusaders. They didn't have enough manpower to garrison it and by 1140 it had passed into the hands of the mysterious Ismaili sect, more colourfully known as the Assassins (see the boxed text).

As Shi'ites, the Ismailis were at odds with Syria's ruling Sunni Ayyubid dynasty and they waged guerrilla warfare. They successfully assassinated several important Sunni figures and in 1175 and 1176 made two attempts on the life of Salah ad-Din himself. The warlord's immediate response was to meet the Ismaili threat head on and in the same year as the second attempt on his life, he laid siege to their stronghold of Musyaf. What happened next is unknown and is the source of an intriguing legend, for almost as soon as it was begun Salah ad-Din called off the attack. The story has it that in the midst of his camp, surrounded by his personal guards, Salah ad-Din woke suddenly one evening to see a shadowy figure slip out of his tent and found at the foot of his bed a dagger and a note of warning from the leader of the Assassins.

Some sort of agreement must have been reached between the two parties because Salah ad-Din did not attack the Ismailis again and their attempts on his life ceased. It wasn't until 100 years later and the campaigns of the Mamluk warrior sultan Beybars that the Assassins were finally driven out and Sunni orthodoxy was secured in Syria.

The entrance to the castle is via a flight of stairs at the south, which leads up into the main keep. Admission costs S£150 and it's supposed to be open from 9 am to 6 pm (4 pm in winter) daily except Tuesday, but it's anybody's guess whether you'll find the caretaker around when you arrive. If he's not there, go around to the tea stall on the east side of the castle (the opposite side to the town) and the guy there will be able to find him for you.

Minibuses to/from Hama and Homs cost S£10 and S£15, respectively. Microbuses cost S£18.50 and S£25.

Deir Soleib

The site of Deir Soleib, 4km south of the Hama-Musyaf road, is very reminiscent of places like Qalb Lozeh west of Aleppo or some of the other Dead Cities in that region. It contains the well preserved remains of a 6th century Byzantine basilica, featuring three columned aisles, a completely intact apse and a baptistry with a cross-shaped font in the southern annexe. About 2km to the east, accessible only by foot, is another much more ruined church.

Assuming you don't have your own transport, about the easiest way to get here is to take a Hama-Musyaf microbus and ask to be dropped at the turn-off. From there it's about an hour's walk, or you should be able to hitch. Coming back, the flow of microbuses dries up in the early afternoon, although you shouldn't have too much trouble hitching a lift back to Hama.

Qasr ibn Wardan

Qasr ibn Wardan lies about 60km north-east of Hama on a road that goes to nowhere. This route mirrors the Orontes' path west and, in contrast to the fields and fertility of the Al-Ghab, out this way there's little more than baked earth and dust.

Erected by the Byzantine emperor Justinian in the mid-6th century as part of a defensive line that included Rasafa and Halabiyya on the Euphrates, Qasr ibn Wardan was a combined military base, palace and church. Its appearance, however, would seem to belie any defensive function; rather than a frontier outpost it looks more like a modestly grand public building that would be more at home on some city square.

One theory for this is that Qasr ibn Wardan was a base from which to consolidate control over the local Bedouin population and as such it was meant to impress upon the nomads the strength and status of their would-be overlords.

The complex consists of an adjacent church and palace. The palace, asssumed to have been home to the local governor, is the building closer to the road and the caretaker will usually open this up first. The best pre-served part is the south facade, constructed of broad bands of black basalt and yellow brick, through which you enter into a hall with rooms off to either side. Many of the stones lying around are carved with symbols and you can pick out variously a jar, some scales, a sheep and a fish. In the courtyard two large stones are carved with a sundial and a calendar. On the north side of the courtyard were the stables while on the east side, to the right as you enter, is a small bath complex.

The church is similar in style to the palace but smaller. Its basic form is square, and it was once capped by a large dome (long since disappeared) and ringed by galleries on three sides. The fourth side is rounded off by the semicircular and half-domed apse common to many early Byzantine churches. Stairs in the north-west corner lead to an upper gallery, which originally would have been reserved for women.

Admission to the site is S£150, payable to the caretaker who lives in the house at the side of the road. If you walk into the courtyard someone will see you and run to get him – meanwhile you'll probably be sat down and offered strong syrupy coffee or tea.

Around Qasr ibn Wardan Beyond Qasr ibn Wardan another 25km of rough road leads north-east to Al-Anderine, another Byzantine settlement of which precious little remains today. The defensive settlement was dominated by a cathedral, but only a few pillars still stand. Back in the other direction, between Qasr ibn Wardan and the village of Al-Hamra, lie the hamlets of Sarouj and Twalid Dabaghein where you'll see plenty of good examples of beehive houses – see the boxed text on the next page.

If you're hitching ask to be dropped off to wander around and then pick up another lift later. The Cairo and Riad hotels in Hama both include a visit to beehive houses as part of their organised trips out to Qasr ibn Wardan.

Getting There & Away Although public transport doesn't go all the way out to Qasr ibn Wardan, it's still relatively easy to get

ORONTES VALLEY

Beehive Houses

ANDREW HUMPHREYS

'[They] are like no other villages save those that appear in illustrations to Central African travel books' – that was Middle Eastern adventuress Gertrude Bell writing on beehive houses in the early years of the 20th century. Her words hold true today. These structures are the ultimate in simplicity – white-washed conical mud-brick structures of one chamber, accessed by a single, small opening. But they're also well adapted to the climate; the thickness of the walls and lack of windows mean that the darkened interior remains a constant temperature, equally impervious to the heat of summer days and the cold of winter nights.

Although the appearance and building method of the beehive houses has changed little since Bell's time, there are far fewer of the structures these days. Concrete boxes have taken over. Those that still exist are often used for storage of hay and fodder rather than as family dwellings. You'll see them east of Aleppo on the dusty plains as you head out to the Euphrates, and in the arid areas east of Hama, where in villages like Sarouj and Twalid Dabaghein, people still inhabit these dwellings. One of the beehives in Sarouj is kept as a 'reception' house, complete with rugs, cushions and the painted chest which traditionally held all a family's valued possessions. This is where you'll be brought for tea if you sign up for a Qasr ibn Wardan trip with one of the hotels in Hama.

there under your own steam. Take a minibus from Hama – they go from a dirt site north of the river (see Getting There & Away in the previous Hama section) to Al-Hamra (S£15, 45 minutes). From Al-Hamra you have to hitch the remaining 20km and although there's not much traffic going this way, whatever there is will most likely stop and take you on. We had to wait only about 10 minutes for a ride out and about the same for the ride back.

Qala'at ash-Shmemis

Perched atop what for all the world looks like an extinct volcano, the ruins of the 13th century Arab fort of Qala'at ash-Shmemis are in an arid region about 32km south-east of Hama on the road to Salamiyya. As often

tends to be the case, the castle is far more impressive from a distance than close up. Once you are up at the top you can't easily get to the ruins as they sit in a crater with sides steep enough to put off all but the most intrepid. If you are game, use the entrance on the right, ignoring the narrow vertical slit in the rock wall that is just a cave. You may, however, prefer to content yourself with the views, which are pleasing rather than spectacular.

Salamiyya The town of Salamiyya itself, 3km further south-east of Qala'at ash-Shmemis, is a sleepy sort of backwater with a long history. It dates to Roman times when it was known as Salamias. Later, it became a stronghold of the Ismailis. If you take the time to wander around, parts of the old defensive walls can still be seen, while the oldest parts of the central Ismaili mosque date from the 16th century.

Getting There & Away Minibuses (S£7) and microbuses (S£13) connect Hama regularly with Salamiyya. To reach the castle, ask to be let off shortly after it comes into view north of the road. It takes about half an hour to walk out to it. Alternatively, you can combine Shmemis with Qasr ibn Wardan; on the way back from Al-Hamra heading toward Hama ask to be let off at the turn-off for Salamiyya.

You then need to pick up a lift south along this road, which goes right past the castle (the castle is still the better part of a kilometre away but this is as close as the road gets). After hiking up for the view, the simplest thing is to return down to the road and hitch on to Salamiyya from where you can

catch a microbus back to Hama from the main street.

Isriyya Only the main temple remains of the ancient desert settlement of Seriana. Apart from a missing roof, the temple is largely in one piece. Dating from the 3rd century AD, the stone employed is the same as that used in much of the construction in Palmyra. Seriana was in fact an important way station in the imperial Roman road network, with highways to Palmyra, Chalcis, Rasafa and Homs (ancient Emesa) all meeting here.

Getting There & Away Getting to Isriyya can be a bit trying. From Salamiyya you could hire a service taxi for about S£600 one way. Otherwise, you could take a microbus the first 45km north-east to Saan (S£10). From there you have another 45km of road to travel, and may still be obliged to deal with a service taxi for the remainder of the trip.

Aleppo

With a population nudging three million, Aleppo (Halab) is Syria's second largest city. It's a city of commerce and since Roman times it has been an important trading centre between Asia and Europe. Caravans arrived from Mesopotamia, Persia and India to be met by merchants from Venice and Genoa, who had a presence in Aleppo as early as the 13th century. They were followed in the 16th century by the British and French. A sense of how well known the city became to the west can be found in the fact that it receives mention at least twice in the plays of Shakespeare – in *Macbeth* the witches say of a sailor's wife, 'Her husband's to Aleppo gone'.

The long presence of a strong corps of merchants from Europe (not to mention French occupation in the interwar mandate years) may go some way to accounting for the vaguely European feel of Aleppo's more well-to-do areas, with their tree-lined boulevards, parks and upmarket restaurants. Ironically, it was under the French Mandate after WWI that the city lost much of its remaining significance as a commercial centre, cut off from southern Turkey, which it had served as a trading outlet until then.

The city is quite unique in that it's estimated somewhere between 20 to 30% of its population is Christian, representing perhaps the greatest concentration of Christians anywhere in the Middle East. The numbers were swollen in the 20th century by thousands of Armenians and other Christian minorities driven out of Anatolia by the Turks. In certain quarters of the city you'll see as many signs in the condensed-looking script of Armenian as in Arabic.

In a still more intriguing quirk of recent history, Aleppo was a beneficiary of the crumbling of the USSR. During the 1990s, a steady stream of traders from the former Soviet republics bustled through Aleppo on large-scale shopping sprees. The trade has lessened in recent years but you'll see plenty

Highlights

- **Shopping the souq** – while not the largest nor grandest, Aleppo's souq is arguably the most vibrant and untouristy in the whole Middle East (see page 229)

- **Steam at the Hammam Yalbougha an-Nasry** – one of the most attractively restored hammams in all Syria, and it's open to women too (see page 237)

- **Beit al-Wakil** – bust your budget ... trade in your air ticket home ... a night at this hotel is a night living out a *Thousand and One Nights* fantasy, with added air-con and minibar (see page 239)

- **Qala'at Samaan** – the hilltop remains of a sumptuous Byzantine cathedral dedicated to an ascetic who lived his life on top of a pillar (see page 247)

- **Dead Cities** – the shells of ancient towns and villages scattered across the landscape (see page 252)

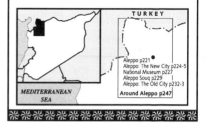

Aleppo p221
Aleppo: The New City p224-5
National Museum p227
Aleppo Souq p229
Aleppo: The Old City p232-3
Around Aleppo p247

of signs in Russian along the city centre shopping streets. At some of the cheaper hotels there are still a great many ex-Soviet citizens who have stayed behind to ply a different trade – as in Turkey to the north, prostitutes from the once-great socialist empire do a thriving business here.

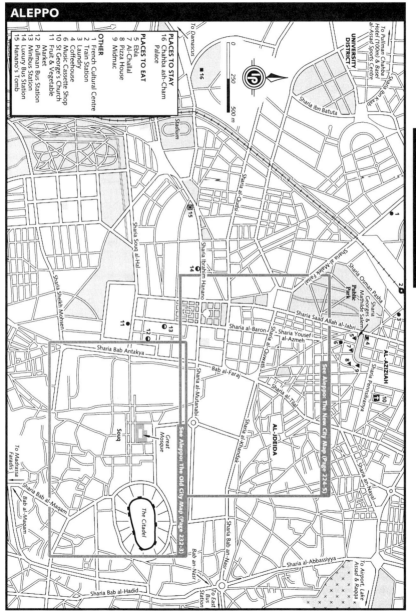

ALEPPO

PLACES TO STAY
16 Chahba ash-Cham Palace

PLACES TO EAT
5 Ebla
7 Al-Challal
8 Pizza House
9 Midmac

OTHER
1 French Cultural Centre
2 Train Station
3 Laundry
4 Coffeehouse
6 Music Cassette Shop
10 St George's Church
11 Fruit & Vegetable Market
12 Pullman Bus Station
13 Minibus Station
14 Luxury Bus Station
15 Hanano's Tomb

To Pullman Chahba Hotel (100m) & Basel al-Assad Sports Centre

UNIVERSITY DISTRICT

To Damascus

Sharia ibn Batuta

Stadium

Sharia al-Quds

Sharia Ibrahim Hanano

Sharia Souq al-Hal

Sharia Sheikh Mohsen

Sharia Bab Antakya

Sharia al-Malek Faisal

Sharia Orman Pasha

Sharia Georges & Mathilde Salem

Public Park

Sharia Saad Allah al-Jabri

Sharia al-Baron

Sharia Yousef al-Azmeh

Sharia al-Quwatli

AL-AZIZIAH

Sharia Pensilvanya

Bab al-Faraj

Sharia al-Tilal

Sharia al-Mutanabi

Sharia al-Khandak

AL-JDEIDA

Souq

Great Mosque

See Aleppo: The Old City Map (Page 232-3)

See Aleppo: The New City Map (Page 224-5)

The Citadel

To Madrasa Faradis

Sharia Bab al-Maqam

Bab al-Maqam

Sharia Bab an-Nasr

Bab an-Nasr

Sharia al-Abbassiyya

To East Bus Station

To Airport, Lake al-Assad & Raqqa

Sharia Bab al-Hadid

0   250   500 m

Most recently, a new breed of local investors and entrepreneurs have been applying their money to the city's most bountiful architectural heritage to create a new wave of boutique hotels and restaurants, which promises to turn Aleppo into one of the most attractive city destinations in the Middle East.

HISTORY

Aleppo vies with Damascus for the title of the world's oldest inhabited city. In fact, a handful of other Middle Eastern towns make this claim too, but texts from the ancient kingdom of Mari on the Euphrates indicate that Aleppo was already the centre of a powerful state as long ago as the 18th century BC, and the site may have been continuously inhabited for the past 8000 years. Its pre-eminent role in Syria came to an end with the Hittite invasions of the 17th and 16th centuries BC, and the city appears to have fallen into obscurity thereafter.

During the reign of the Seleucids, who arrived in the wake of Alexander the Great's campaign, it was given the name Beroia, and with the fall of Palmyra at the hands of the Romans, it became the major commercial link between the Mediterranean to the west and Asia to the east. The town was completely destroyed by the Persians in 611 AD and fell to the Muslims during their invasion in 637. The Byzantines overwhelmed the town in 961 and again in 968 but they could not take the Citadel.

Three disastrous earthquakes also shook the city in the 10th century and the town and fortress were subsequently rebuilt by Nur ad-Din (Nurredin). In 1124 the Crusaders under Baldwin laid siege to the town.

After raids by the Mongols in 1260 and 1401, in which Aleppo was practically emptied of its population, the city finally came into the Ottoman Turkish orbit in 1517. It prospered greatly until another earthquake struck in 1822, killing over 60% of the inhabitants and wrecking many buildings, including the Citadel.

As long as four centuries ago European merchants – particularly French, English and Venetian – had established themselves here and set up factories, but the flood of cheap goods from Europe in the wake of the Industrial Revolution, and the increasing use of alternative trading routes, slowly killed off a lot of Aleppo's trade and manufacturing. Today the major local industries are silk-weaving and cotton-printing. Products from the surrounding area include wool, hides, dried fruits and, particularly, the pistachio nuts for which Aleppo is justly famous. In the souqs of Aleppo, artisans still manufacture the famous Aleppo soap, a unique mix of olive and laurel oils.

ORIENTATION

As in Damascus, there are two distinct parts to central Aleppo: the New City where you stay and eat, and the Old City, which is where you do your sightseeing. The New City is centred on sharias Al-Baron and Al-Quwatli, which are where you'll find most travel agents, airline offices, banks, cinemas and shops.

The main travellers' area is east and south of these two streets, bounded additionally by sharias Bab al-Faraj and Al-Maari. In this tightly hemmed quadrilateral you'll find most of the cheap hotels and budget places to eat. The National Museum is just to the south and the main bus station is only a few minutes walk west of that.

The Old City lies south-east of the New City, no more than a 10 minute walk. The two are separated by a couple of drab, wide avenues (sharias Al-Mutanabi and Bab Antakya) which feel more Murmansk than Middle East. The heart of the Old City is the compress of streets that make up the city's famed souq. The main thoroughfares of the souq run east-west, slipping by the south face of the Great Mosque and terminating at the massive earthen mound of the Citadel. While the souq stops at the Citadel, the Old City doesn't, it sprawls on in all directions. To the north it runs into the 16th and 17th century Christian-Armenian quarter of Al-Jdeida, an area with its own very distinct character which acts as a buffer between old and new Aleppo.

INFORMATION
Tourist Offices
The tourist office (☎ 222 1200), in the gardens opposite the National Museum, is next to useless and doesn't seem to be staffed half the time, though it is theoretically open from 8.30 am to 4 pm daily except Friday. It has a reasonable free map and little else. The tourist police are based here too and in front of the office is where tour guides congregate if you're looking for someone to arrange a trip in the region around Aleppo – see Around Aleppo later in this chapter for more information.

Visa Extensions
The immigration office for visa extensions is on the 1st floor of a building just north of the Citadel. You must bring *four* passport photos and then fill out forms in quadruplicate. The processing takes one to 1½ hours and there's a fee of S£25 but you may be given an extension of up to two months. The office (as you come up the stairs it's through the right-hand door in the facing wall) is open from 8 am to 1.30 pm.

If you don't have any suitable photos there's a bunch of small passport photo shacks across the road, any of whom can do them on the spot.

Money
Down on the corner of sharias Al-Quwatli and Bab al-Faraj is an exchange office open from 9 am to 7.30 pm daily. You can change travellers cheques (no commission) as well as cash. With cash, most currencies (including Turkish lira) are accepted.

If you have any trouble with cheques, go to one of the two branches of the Commercial Bank of Syria on Sharia Yousef al-Azmeh north of Al-Quwatli. Branch No 6 is marked by a big sign in English but the entrance is hidden away at the back of an arcade and the office is up on the 1st floor. It's open from 8.30 am to 1.30 pm daily except Friday. Branch No 2 is 100m further north, next to the Cinema Ugarit. It's open from 8.30 am to 6 pm but closed for lunch from 1 to 2 pm. Note that you will be required to

show the counterfoil receipts for your cheques (the ones that you are advised to always keep in a separate place). At both branches there is a commission of S£25.

To change on the black market head for the narrow compress of passageways in the souq, just south of the Great Mosque, where you'll be inundated with offers to take dollars off your hands.

Post & Communications
The main post and telephone office is the enormous building on the far side of the Saahat Saad Allah al-Jabri square, opposite Sharia al-Quwatli. It's open every day from 8 am to 5 pm (and until 10 pm for telephones; the counter is off to the left). The parcels office is around the corner to the left of the main entrance.

At the time of writing there were no phonecards or card phones anywhere in Aleppo and all calls must be placed with the operator, for which you'll need your passport. On top of the standard call charge, you have to pay an extra 'commission', equivalent to one minute's charge. There is a fax service – you pay for time used as you would for a phone call.

Alternatively, the DHL office just south of Sharia al-Quwatli in the hotel area will also place international phone calls and send faxes, but for a slightly higher price than the post office.

Bookshops
With little to choose from, the best bookshop in town is that at the Chahba ash-Cham Palace hotel. It has a reasonable selection of books about Syria and the Arab world, plenty of locally produced guidebooks, and a handful of novels in English and French. You can also get a limited range of international newspapers here but they'll be at least a week old. The problem is it's a S£35 to S£40 taxi ride out here. The bookshop at the Amir Palace hotel, which used to be quite decent, has now been given over to chocolate, hair combs and tacky souvenirs.

Librairie Said, on the corner of sharias Qostaki al-Homsi and Litani, has a small

ALEPPO

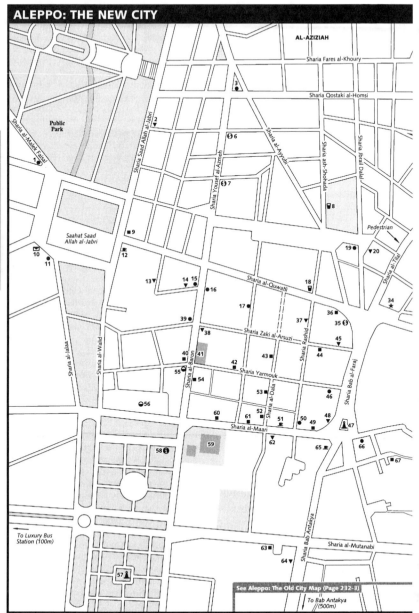

ALEPPO: THE NEW CITY

AL-AZIZIAH

Sharia Fares al-Khoury

Sharia Qostaki al-Homsi

Sharia Saad Allah al-Jabri

Sharia al-Malek Faisal

Public
Park

3

2

6

Sharia Yousef al-Azmeh

Sharia al-Ayyubi

Sharia ash-Shohada

Sharia Ibrail Dalal

7

8

Pedestrian

Saahat Saad
Allah al-Jabri

9

10

11

12

Sharia al-Tilel

19

20

13

14 15

16

Sharia al-Quwatli

18

34

Sharia al-Jalaa

Sharia al-Walid

17

39

38

40

41

55

54

42

43

Sharia Yarmouk

37

36

35

45

44

Sharia Zaki al-Arsuzi

Sharia Rashid

Sharia al-Baron

Sharia al-Dala

53

46

Sharia Bab al-Faraj

56

60

61

52

51

50 49

48

47

Sharia al-Maari

62

65

66

58

59

63

64

Sharia Bab Antakya

67

To Luxury Bus
Station (100m)

57

Sharia al-Mutanabi

See Aleppo: The Old City Map (Page 232-3)

To Bab Antakya
//(500m)

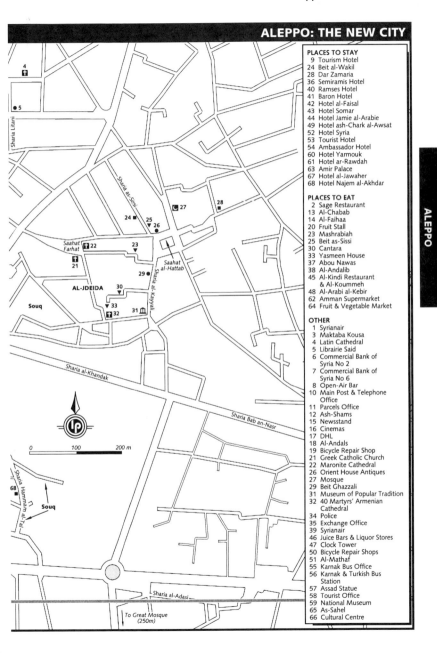

ALEPPO: THE NEW CITY

PLACES TO STAY
9 Tourism Hotel
24 Beit al-Wakil
28 Dar Zamaria
36 Semiramis Hotel
40 Ramses Hotel
41 Baron Hotel
42 Hotel al-Faisal
43 Hotel Somar
44 Hotel Jamie al-Arabie
49 Hotel ash-Chark al-Awsat
52 Hotel Syria
53 Tourist Hotel
54 Ambassador Hotel
60 Hotel Yarmouk
61 Hotel ar-Rawdah
63 Amir Palace
67 Hotel al-Jawaher
68 Hotel Najem al-Akhdar

PLACES TO EAT
2 Sage Restaurant
13 Al-Chabab
14 Al-Faihaa
20 Fruit Stall
23 Mashrabiah
25 Beit as-Sissi
30 Cantara
33 Yasmeen House
37 Abou Nawas
38 Al-Andalib
45 Al-Kindi Restaurant
& Al-Koummeh
48 Al-Arabi al-Kebir
62 Amman Supermarket
64 Fruit & Vegetable Market

OTHER
1 Syrianair
3 Maktaba Kousa
4 Latin Cathedral
5 Librairie Said
6 Commercial Bank of
Syria No 2
7 Commercial Bank of
Syria No 6
8 Open-Air Bar
10 Main Post & Telephone
Office
11 Parcels Office
12 Ash-Shams
15 Newsstand
16 Cinemas
17 DHL
18 Al-Andals
19 Bicycle Repair Shop
21 Greek Catholic Church
22 Maronite Cathedral
26 Orient House Antiques
27 Mosque
29 Beit Ghazzali
31 Museum of Popular Tradition
32 40 Martyrs' Armenian
Cathedral
34 Police
35 Exchange Office
39 Syrianair
46 Juice Bars & Liquor Stores
47 Clock Tower
50 Bicycle Repair Shops
51 Al-Mathaf
55 Karnak Bus Office
56 Karnak & Turkish Bus
Station
57 Assad Statue
58 Tourist Office
59 National Museum
65 As-Sahel
66 Cultural Centre

ALEPPO

selection of dusty old novels as well as the odd Syria coffee-table book.

Newspapers & Magazines

For newspapers and magazines in the city centre, you'll be lucky to find anything more than a yellowing copy of *Time* or the *Herald Tribune* – even the *Syria Times* hardly seems to make an appearance. Try the newsstand on Sharia al-Baron across from the cinemas or the Maktaba Kousa (sign in Arabic only), a small bookshop on Sharia Qostaki al-Homsi just east of the junction with Yousef al-Azmeh. The Chahba ash-Cham Palace hotel is another option (see Bookshops earlier).

Cultural Centres

The cultural centre just behind the clock tower on Bab al-Faraj is run by the Syrian Ministry of Culture and hosts occasional art and photographic exhibitions. There's a small French Cultural Centre (☎ 221 1518) at 40 Sharia al-Malek al-Faisal (the continuation of Sharia Kamel al-Ghazzi), north-west of the park, which is open from 10 am to 1 pm and 5 to 7 pm daily except Sunday.

Laundry

There is a laundry north of the public park near the train station but on the two occasions we visited it was closed.

Medical Services

There are a couple of good pharmacies on Sharia al-Quwatli, around the junction with Sharia Bab al-Faraj.

THE NEW CITY

There are few sights in the New City, which, for the most part, is a resolutely charm-free place. The exception is the National Museum, which is excellent and well worth visiting. The large public park north-west of the hotel district is also a pleasant place, nicely laid out with pathways meandering through well tended greenery and trees, and with an impressive fountain entrance off Sharia Saad Allah al-Jabri. If you're through with walking for the day this is as good a place as any to bring a book and find a bench.

Aleppo

The roads into other Syrian cities are always dominated by a statue of Assad, but in Aleppo I see nothing of the sort. At the entrance to a park modelled on the Jardin du Luxembourg in Paris, my eye is caught by a modest bust. Could that be Assad? 'Oh no, that's a poet,' Amira, a native Aleppine, informs me. Poets and monsignors are the local heroes. One-fourth of all Aleppines are Christians – many of them Armenians who fled from Turkey.

Leaves are blowing along the street. We drive past a cafe where people are sitting together under subdued lighting; a restaurant down the block is still serving lunch to a few late customers. A girl in a miniskirt walks past a woman wrapped in a black *abeyya*. I press my nose against the window and feast my eyes. Pastry shops, cafes, restaurants – it looks like Paris! Amira laughs. 'I knew you'd like Aleppo. All Europeans do.'

**From *The Gates of Damascus*
by Lieve Joris**

Up around the north end of the park is the district of **Al-Aziziah**, a fairly upmarket area developed during the 19th century and home to Aleppo's moneyed families, most of whom are Christian. Some of the domestic architecture around here is particularly fine and worth a look.

National Museum

Aleppo's main museum (☎ 221 2400), right in the middle of town, could be mistaken for a sports hall were it not for the extraordinary colonnade of giant granite figures that fronts the entrance. Stood on the backs of cartoonishly stylised creatures, the wide-eyed characters are replicas of pillars that once supported the ceiling of an 8th or 9th century BC temple-palace complex at Tell Halaf near the border with Turkey in the north-east of the country.

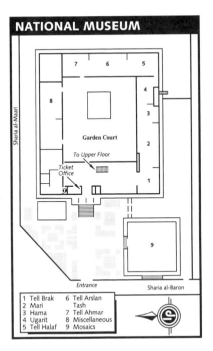

NATIONAL MUSEUM

1 Tell Brak
2 Mari
3 Hama
4 Ugarit
5 Tell Halaf
6 Tell Arslan Tash
7 Tell Ahmar
8 Miscellaneous
9 Mosaics

– although many of the best pieces went to the British Museum.

Mari This room contains some of the museum's best pieces, unearthed at Tell Hariri, the site of the third millennium BC city of Mari (see Mari under South of Deir Ez-zur, in The Euphrates River chapter). Look out particularly for the tableaux of delicate carved shell figurines of a general and his fettered prisoners and chariots, which attests to the high level of artistry existent at this early time; it's on the wall opposite case 4. Just past the tableaux, in the centre of the room, is a wonderful greened bronze lion. It's less refined than the shell figurines but it has a great doleful expression. Along with a twin, now in the Louvre in Paris, it was discovered flanking a temple doorway. Behind the lion are two fine, almost life-sized statutes, one in diorite representing the prince Ishtup-Ilum, and the other in limestone of the Lady of the Well Spring (pictured on the front of the S£50 note). The Lady has a hollow interior through which a pipe was run that spewed water out of the vase in her hands.

Hama These exhibits are of finds made from excavations at the citadel in Hama, which date back to around 1000 BC. Note the two lions which, like those at Mari, were set as guardians to ward off evil.

Ugarit Many of the objects in this room display evidence of the links between this one-time busy port (see Ugarit in The Coast & Mountains chapter) and Egypt. In case No 1 there are some bronze figures which are wholly Egyptian and may have been gifts from a pharaoh to the king of Ugarit. In case No 4, one of the alabaster vessels bears the name of Ramses II in hieroglyphs, while beside case No 5 is a limestone Egyptian obelisk – all presumably imports.

Tell Halaf This hall is dominated by more of the giant figures similar to those at the entrance to the museum; however, while those outside are replicas, some of these are the

The ticket office is just inside the building on the left, and the admission is S£300 (students S£15). There's a fairly decent guidebook to the museum for another S£200, although most of the exhibits have some sort of labelling in English. The museum is open from 9 am to 1 pm and from 4 to 6 pm daily except Tuesday.

From the entrance hall the exhibits are displayed chronologically in an anti-clockwise direction.

Tell Brak Tell Brak (see under The North-East in The Euphrates River chapter) is located 45km north of Hassake in far north-eastern Syria. It and other neighbouring sites were excavated by Sir Max Mallowan, husband of Agatha Christie. (See the boxed text 'Agatha Christie & Sir Max' in The Euphrates River chapter.) Most of the exhibits in this room are finds from his digs real millennia-old things. The figures are believed to represent gods and a goddess; the central one is thought to be Haddad, the weather god, who is symbolically linked to the bull (on which he stands). The colossi were originally flanked by two, similarly wide-eyed and comical sphinxes, and a replica of one stands over to the left. The large panels are plaster casts of originals which once adorned Tell Halaf's palace walls – the originals were destroyed during WWII when the German museum in which they were held was bombed in an air raid.

Tell Arslan Tash The best thing in here is the astonishing collection of ivory carving. The pieces were discovered in the remains of a palace at Tell Arslan Tash, an Aramaean city (ancient name Hadatu) in the north-east of the country, excavated by the French early this century. They are not Syrian in origin and have been identified as coming from Phoenicia and dated to the 9th century BC. For such a cold, hard medium, some of the pieces display a touching warmth and fluidity, such as the cow licking her calf and the grazing gazelles. Others, like the Ugarit pieces earlier, bear a strong Egyptian influence: there's a series depicting the birth of the god Horus from a lotus flower which is very similar to an alabaster carving of Tutankhamun emerging from a lotus on display in the Egyptian Museum in Cairo.

Tell Ahmar Tell Ahmar is the site of another ancient Aramaean city, on what's now the Syrian-Turkish border, 20km south of the crossing point of Jarabalus. The wall paintings displayed in this room were removed from the remains of a palace excavated by the French in the 1920s. They date from around the 8th century BC.

Miscellaneous These halls contain exhibits from digs in progress.

Upper Floor Up here is a modern art gallery which suffers from a lack of labelling and serves only to show that 20th century Syrian art has been heavily influenced by the various European movements. Of more interest is the Islamic arts hall which contains brasswork, coins, a Mamluk tomb and a superb 3m square model of the Old City of Aleppo.

Mosaic Hall There is a separate mosaic hall entered from the museum garden but at the time of our last visit it was closed to the public.

THE OLD CITY

At one time walled and entered only by one of eight gates, the Old City has long since burst its seams and now has few definable edges. Exploring its seemingly infinite number of alleys and cul-de-sacs could easily occupy the better part of a week, depending on how inquisitive you are. We would suggest tackling it over a couple of days: on the first visit dive into the souq and then escape from the crush into the sanctity and calm of the Great Mosque. Next time around, start with the Citadel before exploring down to the south and looping back up into the heart of the bazaar.

The Souq

Not as extensive as Cairo's Khan al-Khalili or as grand as Istanbul's Kapali Carsi, Aleppo's souq is nonetheless one of the finest in the Middle East. Its appeal derives largely from the fact that in a country yet to develop the concept of department stores, malls and high street shopping, the souq is still the main centre of local commerce. If an Aleppine housewife needs some braid for her curtains, a taxi driver needs a new seat cover, or the school kids need satchels, it's to the souq that they all come. Little here seems to have changed in hundreds of years and, unlike Khan al-Khalili or the Kapali Carsi, the local trade has yet to be displaced by the tourists.

Parts of the souq date from the 13th century, but the bulk of the area is an Ottoman-era creation. In among the souqs are numerous *khans* (merchants' inns) in which the bulk of the European commercial representatives were to be found. Unfortunately,

Shopping the Aleppo Souq

Generally speaking, Aleppo's souq is much less touristy than that in Damascus and, away from the central area just behind the Great Mosque, pressure to buy is low key. In fact, because Aleppo's souq is geared to local trade it's very likely that you won't find a lot to buy. Exceptions might be gold, silver and carpets as the choice is much better than in the capital.

Aleppo's bazaar is broken down into the usual demarcations – gold in one alley, spices in another, carpets in one corner, scarves across the way. The exception to this is the main **Souq al-Attarine**, which is a mix of everything – hardware to the west, select items of clothing to the east, spices and perfumes in the middle counteracting the stench from butchers' stalls.

South of Souq al-Attarine the laneways are given over almost exclusively to fabrics, clothing and shoes. Textiles have always been an important component of Aleppo's trade and places like the **Souq al-Jukh** still operate as major wholesale cloth markets.

North of Attarine the souq is at its most dense. Squeezed around the Great Mosque are veins of parallel narrow alleys that in places are barely wide enough for a single person. Some of the specialisations here are fascinating: the **Souq al-Hibal** is devoted to shops selling cord, braid and rope, while one lane south the **Souq at-Tabush** is filled with stalls selling nothing but buttons, ribbons and all manner of things necessary for a woman who runs up her family's clothes.

The **Souq az-Zarb** area is a good place to look for plain or gaudy *jalabiyyas*, the thin cotton gowns worn by women and men alike and which make excellent night dresses, or, as a souvenir, a *kufeyya*, the distinctive black-and-white or red-and-white headdress commonly worn by Palestinians and Jordanians.

Shopping Hours

Shops in the souq close around 6 pm. The souq is closed on Friday when the whole area is eerily deserted and many of the small passageways and khans are inaccessible, locked up behind great old wooden gates. In addition, some shops, such as many of those in the gold souq, are also closed on a Sunday.

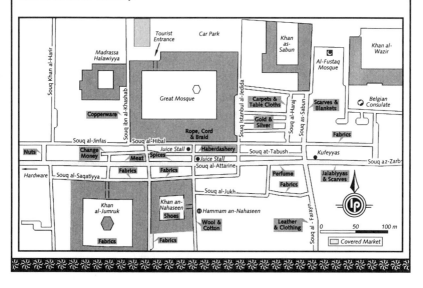

most are of limited interest because they are almost totally obscured by modern additions but it is worth noting their locations as several still boast portentously disposed gateways.

A walk through the souqs could take all day, particularly if you accept some of the many invitations by the stall owners to stop and drink *shai*. In fact, the polyglot sales patter and conversational tactics of the traders is astounding.

In his book *Cleopatra's Wedding Present*, Robert Tewdwr Moss describes a meeting in the souq with a young Aleppine who speaks fluent Cockney with a camp inflection that he claims to have picked up while working in a gay nightclub in London – it later transpires that 'James' has never even stepped foot outside Syria and his language comes from English travellers he's picked up. In *The Pillars of Hercules*, travel writer Paul Theroux gets tutored in Australian slang in the souq by a bunch of young Syrians, one of whom boasts that he's a 'ginger beer' who likes men, as do his friends. Is the Aleppo souq the great gay cruising zone of Syria? Well, we did get a wink and a smacked kiss blown in our direction but that was from a donkey.

Visiting the Souq It's worth visiting the souq at least a couple of times, including on a Friday, when, with all the shops closed, the lanes are silent and empty. Relieved of the need to keep flattening yourself against the wall to let the little overladen Suzuki vans squeeze by, you are free to appreciate architectural details that at other times you miss.

The most obvious way to enter the precincts of the souq is by heading for the Great Mosque, which these days marks the northernmost extent of the markets, but a more interesting approach is to enter from Bab Antakya, which is on the street of the same name about 500m south of the Amir Palace hotel.

Bab Antakya The 13th century Bab Antakya (Antioch Gate) is all but completely hidden by the swarm of busy workshops that

surround it, but you do definitely get a sense of 'entering' as you pass under its great stone portal and through the vaulted dogleg passageway. You emerge onto Souq Bab Antakya, the bazaar's bustling main thoroughfare, which runs due east to halt abruptly at the foot of the Citadel, almost 1½km distant.

Until the development of the New City in the 19th century this was the main street in Aleppo; before that, it was the *decumanus* (principal thoroughfare) of the Roman city of Beroia. A great triumphal arch is thought to have stood on the site of Bab Antakya and part of its remains were used in the construction of the nearby **Mosque of al-Kamiliyya**, which is 100m ahead on your left. Before then, however, if you take the first left after the gate, passing by a *hammam* (bathhouse), the steps here lead up onto the **ramparts** from where there are good views over the New City.

Khan al-Jumruk & Others Beyond the mosque, a corrugated iron roof blots out the sunlight and the souq proper starts. On your left are entrance ways to two adjacent khans, the **Khan at-Tutun as-Sughayyer** and the **Khan at-Tutun al-Kebir** – that's the little and big khans of Tutun, though in fact they're both the same size and both fairly modest in scale. From here on, virtually every building is a khan (see the special section 'The Souq' in the Facts for the Visitor chapter for some elaboration on what a khan is and how it functioned) and there are a few in particular that are definitely worth investigating.

At the point the street becomes spanned by stone vaulting, slip off to the right, then take a quick left to bring you to the great gateway to the **Khan al-Jumruk**. Completed in 1574, this is the largest and most impressive of Aleppo's khans. At one time it housed the consulates and trade missions of the English, Dutch and French, as well as 344 shops. Its days as a European enclave are now long gone but the khan is still in use, serving now as a cloth market. If you turn and look behind as you enter the courtyard you can find some evidence of its former grandness in the decoration on the interior facade of the gateway.

Immediately east of the Khan al-Jumruk, the much smaller **Khan an-Nahaseen** (khan of the coppersmiths), which also dates from the 16th century, housed the Venetian consul until the 19th century. Until fairly recently it also housed the Belgian consul. He lived in a house on the south side of the courtyard, reckoned to be the oldest continuously inhabited house in Aleppo. Its interior has been maintained pretty much as it was when it was built four centuries ago and it's filled with antiques and odd archaeological finds; to gain admission you have to apply to the Belgian consulate, which is close by in the Khan al-Kattin, just south of the Khan al-Wazir.

The Khan an-Nahaseen is now largely given over to footwear – but is still most definitely worth a look in. The entrance is off Souq an-Nahaseen, opposite the hammam of the same name.

If you carry on south down this street and out of the souq, after five minutes walking you'll come to the Bimaristan Arghan (see South of the Citadel later in this chapter), a place that should not be missed.

Around the Great Mosque The souq is at its most labyrinthine immediately south and east of the Great Mosque. This is where you'll find gold and silver and carpets and kilims – see the boxed text 'Shopping the Aleppo Souq' for more details.

Away from the glitter and sales patter, there are another couple of khans well worth a look. In the block east of the Great Mosque is the early 16th century **Khan as-Sabun**, largely obscured by a clutter of shops but with a very distinctive, richly decorated Mamluk facade. The **Khan al-Wazir** (Minister's Khan), just east of the Great Mosque, also has an interesting gateway, although inside it is not so inspiring. Nevertheless it transmits a good idea of the layout of the traditional khan. One single highly ornamental gateway leads into a quadrangle; the lower of the two storeys surrounding this courtyard served as warehouses while offices and sleeping quarters were found above.

Great Mosque

On the northern edge of the souqs is the Great Mosque (Al-Jamaa al-Kebir), the younger sibling (by 10 years) of the great Umayyad Mosque in Damascus. It's the work of Caliph Suleiman (715-17), brother of Caliph al-Walid, founder of the Damascus mosque. However, aside from the plan, nothing survives of Suleiman's original mosque as the building has been destroyed and rebuilt countless times. It was completely burnt down by fire as early as 1169 and constructed anew by Nur ad-Din.

The freestanding minaret was spared from the ravages of the fire and all subsequent destruction, and remains in original form as built in 1090 – although it does have a pronounced lean as a result of an earthquake. Standing 47m high, it's quite a beautiful thing, rising up through five distinct levels, adorned with blind arches, to the wooden canopied muezzin's gallery at the top.

While it's not possible to climb the minaret, you are allowed to visit the mosque. It used to be that non-Muslims had to enter through the west door, down the side alley, but it seems now you can enter through the main north gateway, by the base of the minaret. There's no admission fee but you have to remove your footwear, which will then be watched over by a custodian who customarily receives S£25.

You enter into the courtyard, the floor of which is decorated by a checkerboard of black and white marble geometric patterns. Under a strong sun, the reflected light is so harsh it hurts the eyes, while the marble is so hot that it burns your shoeless feet.

Inside the prayer hall is a fine 15th century carved *minbar* (wooden pulpit) and behind the grille to the left of it is supposed to be the head of Zacharias, the father of John the Baptist (for this reason the mosque is also known as Al-Jamaa az-Zakariyya). Notice the many padlocks fastened to the grille – they have been placed here temporarily by locals who believe that a few days soaking up the *baraka* (blessings) from the tomb will lend them additional strength.

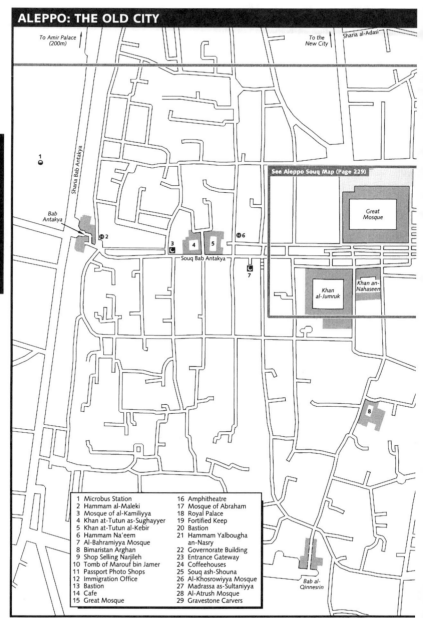

ALEPPO: THE OLD CITY

To Amir Palace
(200m)

To the
New City

Sharia al-Adasi

See Aleppo Souq Map (Page 229)

Great
Mosque

Sharia Bab Antakya

Bab
Antakya

Souq Bab Antakya

Khan
al-Jumruk

Khan an-
Nahaseen

Bab al-
Qinnesrin

1 Microbus Station	16 Amphitheatre
2 Hammam al-Maleki	17 Mosque of Abraham
3 Mosque of al-Kamiliyya	18 Royal Palace
4 Khan at-Tutun as-Sughayyer	19 Fortified Keep
5 Khan at-Tutun al-Kebir	20 Bastion
6 Hammam Na'eem	21 Hammam Yalbougha
7 Al-Bahramiyya Mosque	an-Nasry
8 Bimaristan Arghan	22 Governorate Building
9 Shop Selling Narjileh	23 Entrance Gateway
10 Tomb of Marouf bin Jamer	24 Coffeehouses
11 Passport Photo Shops	25 Souq ash-Shouna
12 Immigration Office	26 Al-Khosrowiyya Mosque
13 Bastion	27 Madrassa as-Sultaniyya
14 Cafe	28 Al-Atrush Mosque
15 Great Mosque	29 Gravestone Carvers

ALEPPO

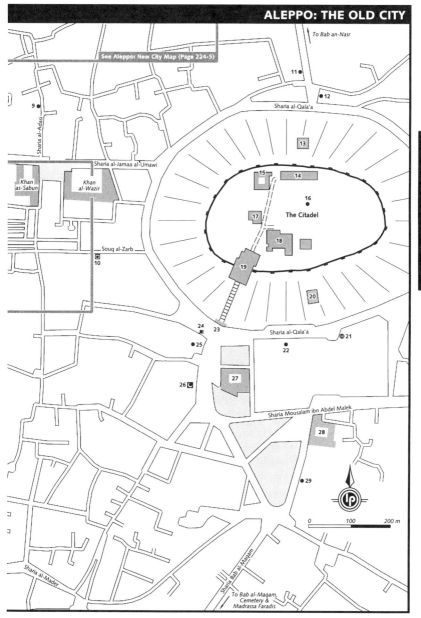

Madrassa Halawiyya Opposite the western entrance of the mosque, this rather dilapidated former theological college stands on the site of what was once the 6th century Cathedral of St Helen. The prayer hall opposite the entrance incorporates all that remains of the cathedral, which is a semi-circular row of six columns with intricately decorated acanthus leaved capitals. For several hundred years the cathedral and the Great Mosque (built in the cathedral's gardens) stood side by side, serving their respective faiths, who would appear to have worshipped in harmony. The cathedral was only seized by the Muslims in 1124 in response to atrocities committed by the Crusaders. The madrassa in its present form dates to 1245. The prayer hall is often kept locked but if you ask around someone will search out the custodian for you. There's also a recorded commentary available – something unique in Syria.

Citadel

Rising up on a high mound at the eastern end of the souqs, the Citadel dominates the city and was long the heart of its defences. It's probably just as impressive viewed from outside as from within, although the solidity and presence of the chambers in the main gateway is awesome and there are some good views from the ramparts.

The mound the Citadel stands upon is not, as it seems at first sight, man-made, it's a natural feature and one that originally served as a place of worship, as evidenced by two basalt lions unearthed here and identified as belonging to a 10th century BC temple.

It's thought that the first fortifications were erected up here at the time of the Seleucids (364-333 BC), but everything you see today dates from much later. The Citadel served as a power base for the Muslims during the time of the Crusades and it's at this time, during the 12th century, that the moat, 20m deep and 30m wide, was dug and the lower two-thirds of the mound were encased in a stone glacis. Much rebuilding and strengthening occurred during the period of Mamluk rule (1250-1517) and it's largely their work that survives.

To enter, you cross the moat by a **stepped bridge** on the south side, carried by eight arches. Any attacking forces would have been incredibly exposed on the bridge as they confronted the massive **fortified keep**, from which defenders could rain down arrows and pour boiling oil through the row of machicolations. The **bastion**, off to the right, was added in the 14th century to allow for flanking fire on the bridge.

Once through the first great gate, set on the right rather than dead in front to prevent charges with a battering ram, there is a succession of five further right-angle turns with three sets of steel-plated doors forming a formidable barrier to any would-be occupiers. Some of the doors still remain and one of the lintels of the doorways has carvings of entwined dragons; another has a pair of lions, echoing the millennia-old use of lions as guardians against evil, as seen in the National Museum.

Just before you pass the last door into the interior of the Citadel, a door to the right leads to the **armoury**. If you follow the path, which doglegs to the right and left, you'll see an entrance to your right leading to what is now called the **Byzantine hall**. Double back and head up the stairs. Here you enter the **royal palace** built in 1230 by Al-Malek al-Aziz Mohammed and largely destroyed 30 years later by the Mongols. You pass through what originally were the servants' quarters and an antechamber before entering the lavishly restored **throne room**, probably the highlight of the complex with its intricately decorated wooden ceiling.

There's little beyond the palace complex. Most of the area on the summit of the mound is covered by the rubble left in the wake of pillage and earthquakes, all overgrown by weeds. A path leads north and halfway along it is the entrance to a small 12th century **Mosque of Abraham**, attributed to Nur ad-Din and one of several legendary burial places for the head of John the Baptist. It retains little of its original charm. At the northern end of the path, opposite what is now a cafe, is the 13th century **great mosque**, a rather grandiose title for a building of its humble dimensions. The cafe is housed in what was the *thukna* (barracks) of an Ottoman commander, Ibrahim Pasha, and it's from here that you get the best views over the rooftops of the city. The replica Roman amphitheatre over to the east is new, clumsily built in concrete to accommodate infrequent opera and concert performances; ask at the ticket office for information.

The Citadel (☎ 362 4010) is open from 9 am to 6 pm daily except Tuesday. Admission is S£300 (students S£30).

South of the Citadel

If you want to get a feel for the Old City away from the commercial buzz of the souq or the tourist-coach crowds around the Citadel, you can strike off south and walk a loop that will take you down to the old southern gates, along the line of the walls, then back up toward the Great Mosque. This is an area full of mosques and khans, *madrassas* (schools of Islamic law) and mausoleums, and although we suggest a route that takes in a few of the most striking monuments, it's equally pleasurable to follow your own whims and lose yourself in the dusty, silent backstreets.

Virtually opposite the entrance to the Citadel is the **Madrassa as-Sultaniyya**, built in 1223 at around the same time that a lot of work was being done on the fortifications on the mound. The prayer hall of the madrassa has a striking mihrab with eye-catching ornamentation achieved through multicoloured marble inlays, but unfortunately this part of the building is often locked. Also here is the mausoleum of Al-Malek al-Zaher Ghazi, a son of Salah ad-Din, and one-time occupant of the Citadel.

Just across the road to the west is a low, multidomed mosque set in gardens, the **Al-Khosrowiyya Mosque**. Now used as a school for boys, the mosque is notable for being one of the earliest (1537) works of the Turkish architect Sinan – see Takiyya as-Suleimaniyya under Central Damascus in the Damascus chapter.

A couple of blocks east rises an earlier mosque built in a quite different tradition. The **Al-Atrush Mosque**, erected in the first decade of the 15th century, exemplifies the Mamluk tradition of combining mosque and mausoleum, often begun before the ruler destined for its grave died. Aqbogha al-Atrush was governor of Aleppo, and when the mosque was constructed it was also designed to serve as the local district's main Friday mosque. Alternating colours in stone and lavish ornamentation of the exterior mark Mamluk monuments such as this apart from their more sober Ayyubid predecessors and Ottoman successors.

If you now walk south, about 100m down you come to a stretch of street powdered white with dust and stone chippings – this is the residue of masons chipping names and inscriptions into the tall, white gravestones crafted at the workshop here. The cemetery where many of these stones end up is about 1km due south, beyond the old city gate of Bab al-Maqam. In the cemetery is what Ross Burns, author of the definitive guide to Syrian monuments, considers Aleppo's finest piece of Islamic architecture, the **Madrassa Faradis**. However, it's a fair distance away and unless you are particularly interested in this field, bear right instead then left at the next junction after the gravestone carvers.

This puts you on a long, narrow, looping street called Sharia al-Mader which, after a 10 minute walk, will bring you out at crossroads where you'll find, just 10m to your left, another of the great gates, the **Bab al-Qinnesrin**. This is a huge, solid, tunnel-like affair and easily the best preserved of all the Old City's gates.

If you now follow the road north it will lead you back into the heart of the souq but, before then, look on your right for the wonderful **Bimaristan Arghan** (it has railings out front with a little nameplate affixed).

The big wooden door of the bimaristan is often locked but if you shout the caretaker will open up. He'll lead you through into the main courtyard with its central pool overhung by greenery. It's a beautiful, serene space and one that is occasionally used by the Ministry of Culture for music recitals (see Entertainment). Diagonally across from where you entered the courtyard a doorway leads through to a series of tight, claustrophobia-inducing passages, one of which terminates in a small octagonal, domed courtyard. Off this are 11 small cells, a reminder of the bimaristan's previous function as an asylum – according to Ross Burns, these cells were where the dangerously insane were confined.

AL-JDEIDA

The Al-Jdeida quarter is the most charming part of Aleppo. It's a beautifully maintained warren of long, narrow, stone-flagged alleyways, occasionally arched, and with walls like canyons. The facades that line the alleys are blank because the buildings all look inwards into central courtyards. But every so often one of the studded black doors with their clenched fists for knockers is open and you can get a glimpse through into the private realms inside.

Much of the architecture here dates from the late Mamluk and early Ottoman period, which makes this quarter not quite as old as the Old City, hence its name Al-Jdeida, 'the new'. It developed as an area for prosperous businessmen, who were largely Maronite and Armenian Christians, getting rich on the city's virtual monopoly on east-west trade. They had money to spend and the houses here are some of the best examples of domestic Arab architecture in the Middle East (see the special section titled 'The Houses of Old Damascus' in the Damascus chapter).

Thankfully, unlike Damascus where much of that city's magnificent architectural heritage is crumbling away through neglect, Al-Jdeida is currently undergoing something of a rebirth. With the backing of a most enlightened city mayor and governor, private investors have recently been encouraged to purchase and renovate properties in the quarter and convert them to commercial usage. At the moment there are two really fantastic boutique hotels occupying former merchants' mansions (see Places to Stay

later in this chapter) and an ever-growing number of restaurants and bars sprouting in striped-stone courtyards and cellars.

Walking Tour

The best way to approach Al-Jdeida from the Bab al-Faraj area is to head on up the pedestrianised Sharia at-Tilal, which is a lively commercial street lined with clothes shops and boutiques. At the point where it's crossed by a small street that takes cars, turn right up to Saahat Farhat. On this wedge-shaped square are the main **Maronite Cathedral** and, to the south, a smaller **Greek Catholic Church**, both of which date only to the 19th century. Al-Jdeida is still very much the home of Aleppo's Christians and it is fascinating to wander around on a Sunday, when the area is busy with the faithful of five Christian faiths thronging together.

Squeeze down the alley to the left of the cathedral and follow it until you come to a stylised sculpture of two robed women set into a corner site; if you turn left here onto Sharia as-Sissi, then just off to the right is **Beit as-Sissi**, while 30m down on the left is **Beit al-Wakil**. Both of these are recycled old houses – the former is now a restaurant and bar, the latter a hotel and restaurant, but in both cases the management is happy to let visitors look around.

Beit al-Wakil was until quite recently a Greek Orthodox orphanage but it has since undergone three years of restoration and refitting under the watchful eye of the Ministry of Culture who ensured that all work carried out was faithful to the original building style. The domed reception is particularly fine and definitely worth a look. For further information on these two see Places to Stay, Places to Eat and Entertainment later in this chapter.

If you head south on Sharia al-Kayyali, 100m along is a door with a plaque identifying it as **Beit Ghazzali**. This is another fantastic house, built in the 17th century and until recently used as an Armenian school. Except for the caretaker and his family it's currently unoccupied while the authorities decide what to do with it. If you knock on the door you'll be let in to have a look around. A little baksheesh would be in order. If there's no answer, the people at the nearby Orient House antique shop also have a key.

Just a bit further down the street and around the corner from the narrow Harat al-Yasmin is yet another house, the Beit Ajiqbash (1757), but this one has been pressed into service as the **Museum of Popular Tradition** (☎ 333 6111), labelled Le Musée des Traditions.

It contains scenes of local life in bygone centuries and displays of clothing, tools, weapons, furniture and the like; however, the architecture totally overshadows any of the exhibits – the carved stonework around the windows and doors on the courtyard is particularly fine. From the roof you can see across to the Citadel in the south-east. It's open daily from 8.30 am to 2 pm except Tuesday and admission is S£150 (students S£10).

West of the museum, still on Harat al-Yasmin, is the entrance to the 15th century **40 Martyrs' Armenian Cathedral**. If you can, it is certainly well worth visiting here on a Sunday to observe the Armenian mass which, as performed here, is still pervaded with an almost sensuous aura of ritual and mystery. It starts at 10 am and lasts two hours.

West of the cathedral, the *hara* (alley) splinters into lots of smaller, serpentine passageways filled with clothes stalls, most of which eventually disgorge back onto Sharia at-Tilal.

ACTIVITIES
Hammams
The **Hammam Yalbougha an-Nasry** (☎ 362 3154) is one of Syria's finest working bathhouses and something of a state showpiece. It was originally constructed in 1491 but it had been destroyed and rebuilt several times before the latest restoration, completed in 1985. It's the excellent state of the interiors that makes the place so good rather than the actual bathing experience – the attendants have a tendency to hurry you along.

Note the sun clock inside the dome above the reception area with three intricate designs marking out four, eight and 12 o'clock.

Prices are clearly listed: entry is S£150, or it's S£365 for the whole package including massage, rubdown, soap, towels and tea. Women are admitted from 10 am to 5 pm on Monday, Wednesday (winter only), Thursday and Saturday; the rest of the time it's men only (Sunday, Tuesday and Friday, and from 5 pm until 2 am all other days). It's located just south-west of the Citadel's entrance.

Not to take anything away from the place, but the Yalbougha an-Nasry is something of a popular tourist stop. If that somehow detracts from the experience for you, there are other possibilities. **Hammam an-Nahaseen**, in the heart of the souq just south of the Great Mosque, has also been recently renovated, though not with the tourist in mind so most of the old architectural features have been obscured. It's used almost exclusively by bazaar traders and is for men only.

The same applies to **Hammam Na'eem** (also known as Hammam al-Jedida), a quiet and clean place just north of the main souq street. To find it, coming from Bab Antakya along the main souq street, take the first left after the start of the corrugated iron roofing and it's just ahead on the right.

Hammam al-Maleki, just off to your left immediately you enter the Old City via Bab Antakya, is very nontouristic. It's also battered and a bit scruffy. However, it is open for women from 12 to 6 pm daily. All of these hammams charge a basic S£150 for use of saunas and bathing, with usually a complimentary tea thrown in too.

Swimming
People wanting to cool off with a simple and relaxing swim can try the Basel al-Assad sports centre (☎ 266 6497), out west next to the Pullman Chahba Hotel. Men swim on Wednesday from 10 am to 2 pm and 3 to 6 pm and on Friday from 3 to 6 pm. Women get to use the pool on Monday from 10 am to 2 pm and 3 to 6 pm and on Thursday from 10 am to 2 pm. The other days are for families.

The Chahba ash-Cham Palace charges S£400 a day to use its pool, which is open in summer only.

ORGANISED TOURS

Ahmed Modallal (☎ 267 1719, fax 225 1606) is a genial guy with excellent English who guides Syria's expat and diplomatic community around the sites of Aleppo's Old City. We met him at the Great Mosque, where he claims his father was the *muezzin* for years. He certainly seemed to know his stuff and his prices were reasonable at US$5 per person for a two hour tour. You can set your own itinerary or he'll whisk you along on one of his own devising.

PLACES TO STAY

It's not as bad as Damascus, but finding decent accommodation in Aleppo is difficult. There is no shortage of cheap-end dives but getting a clean room with fresh sheets for a reasonable price can be problematic. There are one or two very good options but you have to book in advance to be sure of a bed. Otherwise, you can expect a grubby room with greying bed linen and a bathroom with broken fittings and very cranky plumbing. If you choose to upgrade, the few midrange options offer terrible value for money. The only good news comes if you can afford top-end – Aleppo has two of the country's most magical hotels in the Beit al-Wakil and Dar Zamaria.

PLACES TO STAY – BUDGET

The bulk of the budget hotels are in the block bounded by sharias Al-Maari, Al-Baron, Al-Quwatli and Bab al-Faraj. Note that hot water in these hotels generally comes only in the evening and/or early morning. Aside from the Tourist Hotel and the Al-Jawaher, there's little to choose between most of these places so we've simply listed them in alphabetical order.

The following list is far from exhaustive and includes only what we consider the better options.

Hotel ash-Chark al-Awsat (☎ 221 1630) on Sharia al-Maari, near Bab al-Faraj, is a huge place, notable for a large central courtyard on the ground floor; the better half of the rooms look onto this, the other half look onto the street. The rooms are not very well kept and the bathrooms are grossly unappealing – squat toilets and the rooms are so cramped that you virtually have to straddle the hole to stand under the shower head. Singles/doubles with bathroom are S£275/300, or S£200/250 without.

Hotel Jamie al-Arabie (☎ 222 0993) is on Sharia Zaki al-Arsuzi and is primitive and dirty, the haunt of the truly cash-strapped – it seemed to be full of no-wage Palestinians and Nubians. But it's one of the cheapest places there is at S£200/375 with bathroom, or S£175/275 without.

Hotel al-Jawaher (☎ 223 9554, fax 239 5542) behind the cultural centre, just off Bab al-Faraj, is second only to the Tourist Hotel in terms of cleanliness. The bathrooms are relatively new and in good condition, and there's a very comfortable common area with satellite TV. Singles/doubles/triples cost S£350/650/950. This place is always busy so you need to book in advance.

Hotel Najem al-Akhdar (☎ 223 9157), on Sharia Hammam al-Tal and also known as the *Green Star*, is buried off a busy market street south-east of the clock tower. It's a bit scruffy but still one of the better options in that it's frequented almost exclusively by travellers rather than Russian traders, and the management are friendly. Doubles with shower and toilet go for S£500.

Hotel ar-Rawdah (☎ 223 3896), on Sharia al-Maari one block east of the junction with Sharia al-Baron, has small doubles with an extremely cramped shower for S£500, or you can get a bed in a shared room for S£200.

Hotel Somar (☎ 221 2198), Sharia al-Dala, has pleasant rooms with their own showers and toilets and there's a nice little courtyard, but the management ask an outrageous and totally unwarranted US$23 for a double.

Hotel Syria (☎ 221 9760), also on Sharia al-Dala and a block south of the famed

Tourist Hotel, is not a bad option if you can't find board with Madame Olga. Sheets are changed regularly, the rooms have functioning ceiling fans and the bathrooms have hot water. Singles/doubles with bathroom are S£250/400, or S£200/350 without.

Hotel Yarmouk (☎ 221 7510) on Sharia al-Maari is a last resort sort of place. It's dingy and can be noisy but despite that it somehow continues to be popular with travellers. It charges S£250 per person, and doubles have private shower and toilet.

Tourist Hotel (☎ 221 6583), Sharia al-Dala, remains Aleppo's best budget option but with some serious reservations. While the place is outstandingly clean with immaculate bathrooms, this comes at a price – the eccentric proprietor Madame Olga is not above checking guests' rooms while they are out and then haranguing bemused individuals for their untidiness. Cleaners routinely 'tidy' guests' belongings, too. This might not bother everybody but we found it to be an objectionable invasion of privacy – especially when the cleaner threw away my unfinished bottle of deodorant! Rooms cost S£350 per person and booking in advance is essential.

PLACES TO STAY – MID-RANGE
There's really only one place to stay in this range: the ***Baron Hotel*** (☎ 221 0880, fax 221 8164) on Sharia al-Baron – see the boxed text on the next page.

You do have to be prepared for a bit of a trade-off: for heaps of character and an air of Gothic romance, you have to let go any attachments to more physical luxuries – the beds are old and squeaky, the air-con clatters like it was powered by diesel, the decor is spartan and the plumbing is antediluvian. Just put it all down to eccentric charm and enjoy it while you can. Rooms cost US$30/40 including breakfast in the grand dining hall.

Hotel al-Faisal (☎ 221 7768, fax 221 3719), on Sharia Yarmouk just around the corner from the Baron, is a new three star place that is very popular with tour groups. The rooms we saw were all extremely clean with central air-con and good ensuite bathrooms. Doubles are around US$30.

Ambassador Hotel (☎ 221 0231), on Sharia al-Baron just 100m south of the Baron Hotel, is a drab and dingy old place with extremely grim toilet/showers. We don't recommend it but if you've completely run out of other options then rooms are US$18/23.

Ramses Hotel (☎ 221 6700), opposite the Baron Hotel on Sharia al-Baron, dates from perhaps the 1950s and, as such, it's reasonably well looked after. Even so, and with air-con and breakfast included, rooms are very much overpriced at US$30/44.

Semiramis Hotel (☎ 221 9991) is just west of the exchange office on Sharia al-Quwatli. It has had a recent refurbishment and some of its rooms aren't bad at all, especially those with the brand new bathrooms. We were charged US$23 for quite a decent double but prices definitely do seem negotiable.

Tourism Hotel (☎ 225 1602, fax 225 1606) on the corner of sharias Al-Quwatli and Saad Allah al-Jabri, is a characterless place but the rooms are clean, many recently renovated. They come with air-con, fridge, TV and ensuite. A double is US$50 and this includes breakfast and taxes.

PLACES TO STAY – TOP END
The following are ranked in order of price but not necessarily quality. All accept credit cards.

Beit al-Wakil (☎ 221 7169, fax 224 7082), on Sharia Sissi in the Al-Jdeida quarter, is perhaps Syria's most romantic hotel. Opened only in 1998, it's a 450-year-old house lovingly restored and converted into a 19 room boutique hotel. Aside from two suites, the rooms aren't too exceptional but they do have delightful stone bathrooms complete with fonts taken from old hammams and they're arranged around a beautiful yellow-and-black striped courtyard. A second courtyard acts as a restaurant and bar. Rooms are US$80/100.

Dar Zamaria (Martini Hotel; ☎ 363 6100, fax 363 2333), just north of Saahat al-Hattab

ALEPPO

The Baron Hotel

Built at a time when travel invariably involved three-week sea voyages, a set of garden shed-sized trunks to be carried by porters and a letter of introduction to the local consul, the Baron belongs to a very different era. When it went up (1909-11), the hotel was on the outskirts of town 'in gardens considered dangerous to venture into after dark' and from the terrace guests could shoot ducks on the neighbouring swamp. The hotel was opened by two Armenian brothers and called the Baron because residents of Aleppo addressed the brothers as 'baron' (although some say the title meant little more than 'mister' in Armenian at the time).

The Baron quickly became noted as one of the premier hotels of the Middle East, helped by the fact that Aleppo was still a busy trading centre and staging post for travellers. The *Orient Express* used to terminate in Aleppo and the rich and famous travelling on it generally ended up staying in the Baron.

The old leather-bound visitors' book turns up names such as aviators Charles Lindbergh, Amy Johnson and Charles Kingsford-Smith, as well as TE Lawrence, Theodore Roosevelt and Agatha Christie, who wrote the first part of *Murder on the Orient Express* while staying here. Kept securely stashed in the safe, the visitors' book sadly isn't available for viewing but you can see a copy of Lawrence's bar bill displayed in the lounge.

in the Al-Jdeida quarter, is very similar to Beit al-Wakil in that it's a 17th century house, extensively renovated and converted into a luxury hotel with restaurant and bar. Perhaps the renovation hasn't been as faithful to the original as at Beit al-Wakil but only a purist would notice. Single/double rooms are US$75/100.

Pullman Chahba Hotel (☎ *266 7200, fax 266 7213*) is on Sharia al-Jama'a out in the west of town, opposite the University Hospital. It's a four-star-style place, not too big

Almost all Syrian towns have a *hammam* (bathhouse) usually located in the souq; few are as opulent as this, the Hammam Yalbougha an-Nasry in Aleppo.

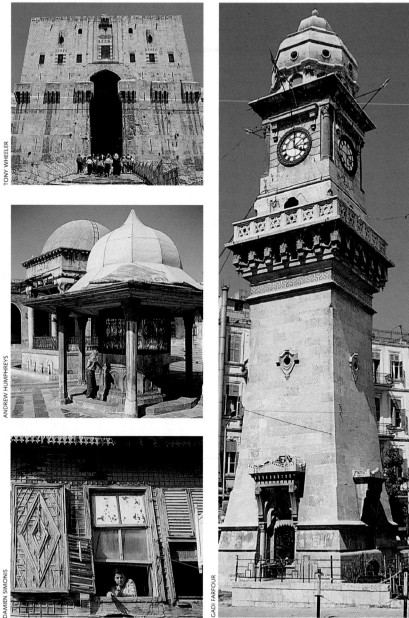

The dominating Citadel (top left) overlooks many of the treasures of Aleppo: the grandiose Great Mosque (middle left), the picturesque wooden houses of the Old City (bottom left) and the clock tower on Bab al-Faraj (right).

TONY WHEELER

TONY WHEELER

Qala'at Samaan, north of Aleppo, is a historical gem containing impressive remains of a ruined basilica, some beautiful hilltop views and a truly weird history.

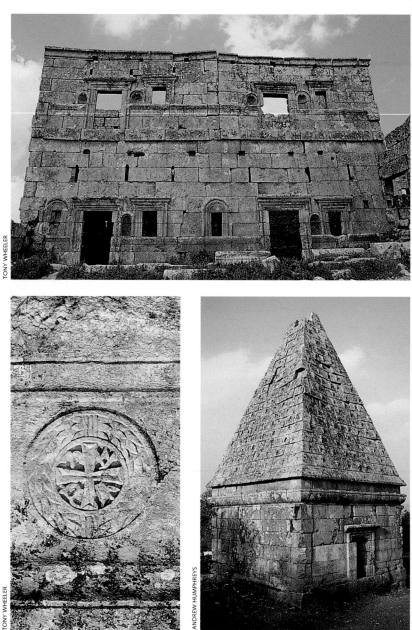

Sprinkled around Aleppo and reckoned to number about 600, Dead Cities such as Serjilla (top & bottom left) and Al-Bara (bottom right) are ghost towns from a once flourishing Byzantine empire.

but still a bit Siberian and gloomy. Rooms are US$80/100 plus taxes and, given the hotel's distance from the centre, have little to recommend them.

Amir Palace *(☎ 221 4800, fax 221 5700)* on Sharia al-Mutanabi is a standard, outwardly ugly, inwardly bland, four star hotel somewhat redeemed by its relative proximity to the places of interest compared with the other biggies. Rooms go for US$95/119 plus 10% taxes, which is typically out of all proportion to the quality of rooms or service.

Chahba ash-Cham Palace *(☎ 266 1600, fax 226 6719)* on Sharia al-Qudsi is also well out in the west of the city. It's Aleppo's showpiece five star tower, which has everything from tennis courts and a pool, right down to CNN plugged into each room. Room rates are US$160/190 plus taxes, and that does not include breakfast.

PLACES TO EAT

Generally speaking, the New City is the place for cheap eating, particularly the streets between sharias Al-Baron and Bab al-Faraj. It's all standard fare with little to excite.

For good dining you need to head north to the chichi district of Al-Aziziah. Crammed together on or near Sharia Georges & Mathilde Salem are about half a dozen classy restaurants, most with pavement tables occupied by young males sipping imported beer and toying with their mobile phones, while inside groups of jewellery-bedecked women in slinky evening wear chatter and pick at *mezze* (starters). We didn't get to visit all these places, so don't take it as a black mark if one or another isn't listed here. For top dining, however, head for the narrow alleyways of the Al-Jdeida quarter where there are several exceptional restaurants, a couple of which specialise in traditional Aleppine dishes. All these places benefit from postcard settings in the courtyards and halls of some of Aleppo's fine old houses.

Budget

In the block bounded by sharias Al-Maari, Bab al-Faraj, Al-Quwatli and Al-Baron are the cheapies offering the usual stuff – the price is more variable than the food so check before you sit down. There is a row of excellent juice stands at the Bab al-Faraj end of Sharia Yarmouk.

Al-Faihaa is a clean and immensely popular felafel place across from the cinemas on Sharia Al-Baron. It's takeaway only.

Al-Arabi al-Kebir is a small place, opposite the clock tower on Sharia Bab al-Faraj, serving a variety of Turkish-style stews or grilled meats with rice, bread and pickles. It's basic stuff and hygiene isn't necessarily a priority but you can eat well for under S£100.

Al-Kindi Restaurant on Sharia Zaki al-Arsuzi, just off Bab al-Faraj, is one of a cluster of similar kebab restaurants, all of which are none too hot on hygiene but offer reasonable food at budget prices. It has an extensive menu in English made up of kebabs (S£80 to S£85), grilled meats, and mezze in the S£15 to S£20 range. The mezze includes grilled cheese (E£20), a dish that will appeal to anyone who loves the crisp and greasy drippings left on the pan after grilling some overloaded cheese on toast. There's no beer and no desserts. Next door, ***Al-Koummeh*** offers more of the same.

Al-Chabab is an intimate open-air garden restaurant complete with lots of trees and greenery and a fountain, located in a side street off Sharia Al-Baron, just up from the Syrianair office. Though the food is nothing special (kebabs etc), it's a pleasant and inexpensive place to sit in the evenings and drink beer. However, as the Arabic name ('The Lads') suggests, it's largely a male hang-out – western women accompanied by men will be fine but solo women or female couples might feel uncomfortable.

Pizza House, just east of Sharia Georges & Mathilde Salem in the Al-Aziziah district, is a very Syrian take on the western Pizza Hut franchise. It may look copyright-infringing from a distance but get up close and you'll see that the menu is far from copycat, with a selection of pizza types that includes things like aubergine, vegetable, hotdog and Arabic sausage. They cost around S£125

ALEPPO

each and the place is open from noon to midnight. There's also a burger restaurant nearby with the name of **Midmac** – look for the yellow 'M'.

Sage Restaurant on Sharia Saad Allah al-Jabri, opposite the park, is a decent place for lunch, especially if you dine out at one of the pavement tables. It does sandwiches, omelettes and good burgers served with salad and fries for E£35 to E£50. The gloomy interior is a favourite haunt for furtive, romantic assignations. It's also somewhere that the rebellious *hejabi* (headscarf) girls go to smoke their cigarettes over ice creams.

Fountain Cafe at the Amir Palace Hotel is not exactly a budget option but it does offer a welcome air-con retreat from the heat and dust outside. Sandwiches (club, steak, chicken, mortadella, ham) start at S£125 and though a bit pricey, they're substantial and come with salad, crisps and other garnishings; one could stretch between two people for a light lunch. It also does excellent homemade iced milkshakes for S£70.

Restaurants

The following are listed with the cheaper options first. Note, the Al-Jdeida restaurants only start serving after 8 pm, and 9 or 10 pm seems to be the more normal time to turn up and dine.

Abou Nawas on Sharia Rashid is a city centre kebab restaurant but a cut above the Al-Kindi and neighbours. For a start, it has air-con and is clean. More notably, the menu stretches way beyond the usual foods to include the kind of dishes that are usually only ever served up at home such as *bamya* and meat stew and *fasoolyeh* (see Food in the Facts for the Visitor chapter). To help you select, you'll be invited into the kitchen to see what's cooking. A two course meal for two will come in at about S£250 to S£300. Visit if you can.

Al-Andalib on Sharia al-Baron is a rooftop restaurant one block north of the Baron Hotel in the New City. The atmosphere is boisterous and the place is packed most evenings with locals but you've got to be hungry to eat here. It's a set menu – a platter of kebab, huge amounts of salads, humous, baba ghanoug and fries – for an all-in price of S£200. The food is basic but fresh and it's good value for what you get but, given the choice, we'd have preferred less on the table and a smaller bill. There's also an insidious service charge of S£50. Beer is served.

Ebla and **Al-Challal** (☎ 224 3344) are two of the cheaper restaurants on Sharia Georges & Mathilde Salem in Al-Aziziah. Both have indoor and outdoor sections – in the case of the Ebla there's a lovely, old-world, canopied terrace with potted trees. Al-Challal is more chic and modern with lots of large glass windows. Its menu combines mezze and Middle Eastern grills (around S£120) with international dishes like escalope, steak diane (S£220) and an extremely delicious spaghetti bolognese (S£120). The menu at Ebla is somewhat similar but prices are more modest. Beer is served at both restaurants.

Yasmeen House (☎ 222 4462), off Sharia al-Kayyali, is the cheapest of the Al-Jdeida restaurants. It's set up for groups with bench-like tables in a large courtyard but nevertheless is attractive. The menu offers half a dozen nicely presented kebabs (all at S£160) accompanied by a house selection of mixed mezze (S£120) – although the staff didn't mind us specifying which mezze we would like. Half portions of everything are available, if you're not hugely hungry. The place is open from 8 pm nightly.

Mashrabiah (☎ 224 0249) on Sharia Farha in Al-Jdeida describes itself as a restaurant and pub and, although there's no bar as such, inside you could almost be in a small village tavern deep in rural England. Whether that's what you want in Aleppo is a different matter. The menu is fairly unexciting but reasonably priced: entrées range from S£30 to S£75, while mains start with kebab and kofta at S£115 and range up to S£250. It's quite possible to have a meal here for two for under S£500.

Beit al-Wakil (☎ 221 7169) and Beit as-Sissi (☎ 221 9411) in the Al-Jdeida quarter both have courtyard dining areas (and wood-panelled dining halls for the colder months) complete with jasmine and lemon trees and gently splashing fountains – you couldn't dream up better settings. Both places specialise in local variations on Levantine cuisine and the dishes change according to the season.

We were treated to cherry kebabs, stuffed deep-fried intestines, and mutton patties filled with feta cheese. There's no menu and we recommend just following the advice of the waiter. Local wine is available. Of the two restaurants, perhaps the food at the Beit as-Sissi doesn't quite match up to the high elegance of the surroundings but Beit al-Wakil is superb. Expect to pay S£600 to S£700 for a full meal for two, wine not included.

Cantara (☎ 333 6349) is yet another classy joint tucked away down an Al-Jdeida alley. We didn't get to try this one out but the menu was French haute cuisine and prices were quite high. It's open from 7.30 pm until midnight daily except Tuesday.

Self-Catering

For basics like bread, cheese, jam and biscuits, the Amman supermarket on Sharia al-Maari is a good place. It also sells toiletries like toothpaste, soap and shampoo. For fresh fruit, there is a fruit and vegetable market on Sharia Bab Antakya near the Amir Palace or there's an excellent fruit stall on Sharia Jbrail Dalal, 200m north of the Bab al-Faraj money exchange office.

We've already mentioned the juice bars on Sharia Yarmouk but if you take along your own container, like an empty mineral water bottle, they'll fill it up for you to take away. Among the juice stalls there are also two liquor stores where you can get Al-Chark beer for S£35 to take away.

ENTERTAINMENT

Aleppo is not a late city and there's not much going on beyond midnight. The better places to be are promenading around the Al-Aziziah area or ducking between the bar-restaurants in Al-Jdeida. The centre of the New City is decidedly sleazy at night with drunken men spilling out of the numerous clip joints making the area one to be wary of late at night.

Coffeehouses

Aleppo is not very good for coffeehouses. There are next to none in the Old City apart from a bank of three or four opposite the entrance to the Citadel. It's a great spot but don't the coffeehouse owners know it – you'll be charged several times the going rate for a shai or a narjileh (water pipe). Ask the price before you order and if you don't like it, getting up and making a move towards one of the other coffeehouses might bring it down.

Back in the city centre, Al-Mathaf on Sharia al-Maari, while definitely not picturesque or possessed of good views, is a decent enough, basic coffeehouse where the clientele are used to stray foreigners from the nearby hotels. It opens early and is good for a tea in the morning.

On the same street but across the road and closer to Bab al-Faraj, there's an upstairs coffeehouse called As-Sahel, right by the clock tower. The place is extremely grubby and we'd recommend that you stick to bottled soft drinks but it has a good view of the hectic intersection, and the antics of the drivers and pedestrians are good entertainment. The entrance is in the side street, through the reception of the awful As-Sahel Hotel.

Another good people-watching place is the Ash-Shams on Saahat Saad Allah al-Jabri, which is a busy venue for Aleppo's chess players.

If you are dining up in Al-Aziziah there's also a good, big post-prandial coffeehouse on the corner of Sharia Georges & Mathilde Salem, across from the park.

Whirling Dervishes

One of Syria's two remaining troupes of whirling dervishes frequently performs at the Bimaristan Arghan in the Old City (see South of the Citadel earlier in this chapter).

ALEPPO

For details of performance dates and times check with the tourist office.

Bars

Aleppo is Al-Chark territory, which is the less appealing of Syria's two local brews. Never mind, there are at least a few good venues in which to drink it, the most appealing of which has got to be the bar at the **Baron**. It's just a small room off to the left as you enter the hotel, with a few armchairs and six stools at a high dark-wood bar facing an arch of shelves half filled with half-empty bottles of spirits. It feels like a chapel and makes for a fitting place to commune with ghosts of guests past, like Lawrence. Alternatively, during the summer months the staff put some chairs and tables out on the terrace. Local beer is S£100, or you can pay S£150 for a can of whatever they have of the imported variety.

For fewer ghosts and more life, there's a huge **open-air bar** on Sharia ash-Shohada, just 200m north of Bab al-Faraj. With seating for a couple of hundred, it's a large garden with vines strung overhead and sploshing fountains, all walled around to protect innocent eyes from the site of alcohol being consumed. The place is also a restaurant but you're under no obligation to eat. A beer is S£55 and there doesn't seem to be any hidden service charge.

Plenty of Aleppo's restaurants don't object to patrons who only want to drink, and good options for a cold beer are the **Al-Chabab** and the terrace seating at some of the places along Sharia Georges & Mathilde Salem like **Al-Challal** (see Places to Eat). There's also the **Al-Andals on Sharia al-Quwatli**, hear the money exchange office, a grotty restaurant but fine for drinking, especially if you can get a window seat looking down on the street below (it's up on the 2nd floor).

For a vision of how Aleppo is developing, take a look at the underground bar at **Beit as-Sissi** in the Al-Jdeida quarter. Buried deep in former cellars, it's a cave-like grotto with goblin faces leering out of the rock walls – it could be a chill-out room at a Midsummer Nights Dream-themed club in London or New York.

Nightclubs

Sharia al-Quwatli in the centre of town is liberally sprinkled with an assortment of nightclubs where you'll be parted from anything up to S£500 to watch a third-rate floor show, be overcharged for booze and gain the attentions of a few Russian ladies wondering if you'd like to spend even more money.

Cinemas

There is no shortage of cinemas along Sharia Baron and its northern extension Sharia Yousef al-Azmeh. Most of what they screen is martial arts and trashy B-movies of the kind that go straight to video in the west. A lot of it is also so heavily censored that it's impossible to know what is going on – most of the slightly risqué stills used to entice the almost exclusively male customers belong to scenes removed from the film.

SHOPPING

The main place to shop in Aleppo is the souq, and information on where and what to buy is covered in the boxed text 'Shopping the Aleppo Souq', earlier this chapter. For souvenirs like narjilehs and inlaid backgammon boards, as well as toys and other nick-nacks visit Sharia al-Adasi, which is north of the main souq area; walk east from the front of the Great Mosque and then cut north (left) up the third lane.

For the same kind of wares, the souq area between Sharia al-Mutanabi and Bab al-Faraj, in the vicinity of the Hotel Najem al-Akhdar, is also worth a look.

If you want to browse in relative peace and quiet, try the Souq ash-Shouna, which is a regulated handicrafts market just behind the coffeehouses on the south-western side of the Citadel. Here you can take your time to inspect goods and quality with minimum fuss and everything has a fixed price. With these price tags in mind, you can then, if you choose, head out and see if you can bargain a lower price elsewhere.

For antiques and historical bric-a-brac take a look at Orient House which is on the 1st floor of the Beit as-Sissi building on Saahat al-Hattab in the Al-Jdeida quarter.

For music cassettes of Syrian and other Arab world artists there's a good place on Sharia Yousef al-Azmeh, up towards the Al-Aziziah area; it's on a corner and has pink painted window frames.

GETTING THERE & AWAY
Air
Aleppo has an international airport with some connections to Turkey, Europe and other cities in the Middle East, although it is not easy to find a travel agent who will organise international flights to Aleppo. Syrianair has flights to Istanbul every Friday for S£8030 (one way) and to Cairo every Tuesday and Wednesday for S£8811.

Internally, there are two or three flights most days to Damascus for S£602.

Syrianair has an office on Sharia al-Baron (☎ 224 1232) but if you are booking international flights you may well be directed over to its head office (☎ 222 0501) on Saahat Saad Allah al-Jabri. Most foreign airline offices are on Sharia al-Baron.

Bus
Aleppo has a confusing amount of bus stations. The main station, as far as travellers are concerned, is the one for luxury long-distance buses, located on Sharia Ibrahim Hanano about 800m west of the National Museum. The other important one is the station – actually little more than a parking lot – immediately north of the tourist office and behind the Karnak office on Sharia al-Baron. This is shared between state-owned Karnak buses and several private companies running services to Turkey and a handful of other international destinations.

South of the Amir Palace hotel is a vast area of dusty, rubbish-strewn bus bays stretching over half a kilometre. This area incorporates four adjacent stations serving, from north to south, city buses, old battered regular intercity buses, intercity Pullmans, and minibuses which cover the region around Aleppo. (For information on the distinguishing characteristics of these bus types, see the Getting Around chapter.)

There is also another station out to the east of the Old City running services to the east of the country but you shouldn't need to bother with this.

Luxury Buses More than 30 private companies, including the likes of Qadmous and Al-Ahlia, operate long-distance buses from the Ibrahim Hanano station and all have their own sales shacks around the edge of the bus bays. It's easy to shop around but there's not that much difference in prices. On average, you'll pay S£150 for Damascus (five hours), S£135 for Deir ez-Zur (five hours), S£65 for Hama (2½ hours), S£100 for Homs (3½ hours), S£100 for Lattakia (3½ hours), S£175 for Qamishle (eight hours), S£90 for Raqqa (three hours) and S£120 for Tartus (4½ hours).

In addition there are seven daily buses from here to Beirut (six hours) for S£300. Buses for Turkey go from the Turkish bus station next to the Karnak terminal.

Karnak The government-run Karnak bus office (☎ 210 2482) is on Sharia al-Baron diagonally opposite the Baron Hotel, and it's open from 7 am to 8 pm. The buses leave from around the back, almost opposite the tourist office. There are three buses daily to Damascus (S£130), six to Hama (S£60) and Homs (S£75), two to Lattakia (S£65), and one to Deir ez-Zur (S£125) via Raqqa (S£75). In addition there's a nightly service to Amman (S£450) departing at 10 pm, and three buses daily to Beirut (S£250) via Tripoli (S£175). It's advisable to book at least a day in advance for Karnak services.

Turkey & Other International Destinations Buses for Turkey leave from beside the Karnak bus station. There are four companies with sales offices at the station and between them they run at least five buses a day to Istanbul (about S£950, 22 hours) and more to Antakya (S£200 to S£250). Note that the Istanbul service involves a change of bus at Antakya. From the same station you can also get buses to Amman (S£450), Cairo (S£1000) and Riyadh (S£1200).

Pullman The Pullman bus station is south of the local city bus station behind the Amir Palace hotel. Different bays are allotted to various competing companies and you buy tickets in the large booking hall before boarding. Pullman buses are cheaper than Karnak but on a par in terms of quality (the trip to Deir ez-Zur, for instance, costs S£70) and more comfortable than the regular buses. Other fares include Damascus (S£90), Hassake (S£80), Qamishle (S£90), Beirut (S£250) and Tripoli (S£200).

Regular Buses The station for regular old buses is south-west of the Amir Palace hotel, off the southern extension of Sharia al-Baron. This is the cheapest and slowest transport you'll find. You buy tickets from a window, which supposedly ensures you a seat, but not always. Alternatively, you can hop on at the last moment and join the standing-room only squash. Buses to Damascus take six hours (S£60), to Hama a bit over two hours (S£25), to Homs about three hours (S£30), and to Lattakia three to four hours (S£30). There are also quite regular microbuses from here to Azaz (for Turkey).

Train
The train station is just to the north of the big public park, about 15 minutes walk from the central hotel area. Trains to Lattakia (3½ hours) depart at 7.25 am and 2.40 and 4.20 pm and tickets are S£55 in 1st class, S£35 in 2nd. There's a daily service to Damascus (seven hours) departing at 12.30 am which costs S£85/57 in 1st/2nd class seating, or S£325 for a sleeper. There's also a daily service departing at around 10.30 pm for Qamishle (8½ hours) in the north-east, via Deir ez-Zur. The fares to Qamishle are S£132/87, and S£350 for a sleeper.

At the time of writing the weekly service to Istanbul had been suspended but it was due to start up again. In theory it departs every Tuesday at midnight and takes 36 hours. There is no sleeper carriage and the 1st class fare should be around the S£500 mark.

Service Taxi
Next to the Pullman bus station is a service taxi stand. This is the expensive but fairly quick way to go. Sample fares include (for the whole taxi) Hama S£150, Damascus S£400 and Beirut S£700.

Car Rental
Europcar has a desk at the Chahba ash-Cham Palace, Pullman Shahba and Amir Palace hotels. For details of average rental rates see the Getting Around chapter.

GETTING AROUND
Everything in the city is reachable on foot, which is just as well because the city bus system is unfathomable. The city bus station is right behind the Amir Palace hotel, just off Sharia Bab Antakya, but there doesn't seem to be any posted information about routes. Should you think you need to take a bus to get somewhere, all we can suggest is that you ask a local. Tickets cost S£10 and are bought from the driver.

Taxi
Car buffs may like to ride in a regular taxi just for the hell of it. They are mostly enormous, lumbering old American limousines from the 1940s and 50s painted bright yellow and with plenty of polished chrome. An average across-town ride should cost no more than about S£25.

Some service taxis run set routes and pick up passengers for standard rates along the way, but it's difficult to tell them apart from the regular taxis (which multiple hire), until you're in one and find you can't go to exactly your chosen destination.

Around Aleppo

There are enough worthwhile sites around Aleppo to warrant at least two or three days exploring, if you can spare them. A day spent around Qala'at Samaan and another among the Dead Cities to the south could turn out to be highlights of your trip. The fact that these sites are out of the way, probably necessitating some hitching, is half the fun. However, you do need good weather as you're out in open, exposed countryside, which will turn to mud underfoot in rain.

CARS & GUIDES

Although all of the sites around Aleppo are accessible to some degree by public transport, if you're short on time it might prove worthwhile hiring a car and driver. It's easy enough to organise; just go along to the tourist office in Aleppo and before you get within a hundred metres you'll be intercepted by a 'guide' offering his services. In practice, many of these guys don't know that much about the sites they're offering to take you to and some of them speak virtually no English but that's not really an issue because you only want them for their wheels. The going rate is about US$40 for a full day, from early morning until early evening, although some travellers have reported being able to bargain drivers down to US$20.

However, if a driver agrees to such a low price it'll be with great reluctance and you can expect plenty of wheedling later for more cash – it's better to pay a fair price and save yourself hassle.

One driver/guide who has been recommended in readers' letters for his fairness and reasonable rates is a gentleman named Basheer Kadour (☎ 574 4043). With such an arrangement it's for you to dictate your own itinerary. As an idea of what's possible, with a car at your disposal you will be able to cover in a full day all the sites described in the North & West of Aleppo section or, alternatively, all the sites described lying south of Aleppo.

NORTH & WEST OF ALEPPO

The half-dozen major sites north and west of Aleppo are scattered across the Jebel Samaan in such a way that it is impossible to combine

them all into one trip without your own car. Qala'at Samaan, the jewel of the collection, is fairly accessible by public transport and from there it's possible to push on to Ain Dara and get back to Aleppo by minibus in one long day. Alternatively, you could combine Qala'at Samaan with Qalb Lozeh, if you do a little backtracking. Cyrrhus is more problematic and requires cash and time – if you are planning on visiting the Dead Cities to the south then it's probably not worth the expense to duplicate the experience here.

Qala'at Samaan

Qala'at Samaan is probably the must-see site of the many archaeological remnants that dot the countryside north of Aleppo. It's a ruined basilica, of which enough remains to impress, situated high up on a rocky outcrop bounded by valleys. The views are excellent.

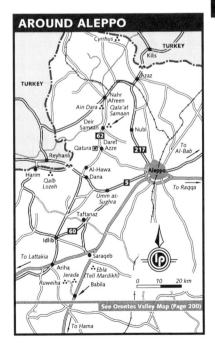

AROUND ALEPPO

The structure takes its name from a man named Simeon, who was one of Syria's most unusual early Christians. Born in 392 AD, Simeon was the son of a shepherd who opted at a young age for a life in a monastery. But finding monastic life insufficiently ascetic, he retreated to a cave in the barren hills where he lived under a regime of self-imposed severity.

Word got around of this extremely pious individual and people began to visit to seek his blessing. Simeon apparently greatly resented this invasion of his solitude and was driven to erect a 3m-high pillar on which he took up residence so that people couldn't touch him. The legend goes that as his tolerance of people got less he erected ever higher pillars. In all he's said to have spent close to 40 years on top of his pillars, the last of which was 18m in height. There was a railing around the top and an iron collar around his neck was chained to the stone to stop him toppling off in the middle of the night.

His increasingly eccentric behaviour eventually drew pilgrims from as far away as Britain and France, where he was known as Simon Stylites, a name derived from the Greek for pillar, *stylos*. The notion of stylism caught on and Simeon inspired a fashion for pious pillar-top dwelling that spread all the way to central Europe, where it eventually faltered in the face of a colder climate.

St Simeon would preach daily from his perch, and shout answers to his audiences' questions. However, he refused to talk to women and even his mother was not allowed near the column.

By the time of his death in 459, Simeon was possibly the most famous person in the 5th century world and his body was taken to be buried in the great Christian centre of Antioch (present-day Antakya). In addition an enormous church was built around the famous pillar. It had a unique design with four basilicas arranged in the shape of a cross, each opening onto a central octagonal yard covered by a dome. Beneath the dome stood the pillar. One basilica was used for worship, the other three housed the many pilgrims. Completed in 490 after 14 years of building, at the time it was the largest church in the world.

With the arrival of Islam in Syria, the Byzantine Christians were put on the defensive and the church complex was fortified, hence the name Qala'at, the Arabic for 'fortress'. It eventually fell to the Islamic Fatimid dynasty in 1017 and has apparently never been in use as a place of worship since.

Considering that, the church today is remarkably well preserved. The main Romanesque facade still stands, while behind it the arches of the octagonal yard are reasonably complete.

There's plenty of ornamental carved stonework to admire, although Simeon's pillar is in a sad state. It is nothing more than a boulder, reduced centuries ago by pilgrims chipping away at it for holy souvenirs.

The views of the barren hills to the west are stunning and the ruins of Deir Samaan can be seen down to the left at the foot of the hill.

The site is open from 10 am to 6 pm daily except Tuesday and entry is S£300. From Aleppo, Qala'at Samaan is an easy half-day trip; if you set off by 9 am you'll be back by early afternoon.

Deir Samaan Deir Samaan originally began life as the small Greek agricultural village of Telanissos. But like some ancient Corfu, during the first part of the 5th century it found itself being rapidly transformed by a steady influx of outsiders, in this case not tourists but their forerunners, pilgrims. As the antics of Simeon drew ever larger crowds, so the village expanded to provide hostelries, churches and three monasteries to accommodate the pilgrims (hence the new name of Deir Samaan, 'Monastery of Simeon').

With the building of the basilica on top of the hill the two were connected by a procession way (Via Sacra). A monumental arch remains part-way up the slope marking the old route. In the village there are skeletons of two of the monasteries, a church and the bazaar, plus 150m south of the arch there are two very impressive hostelries and a tomb chapel hewn out of rock and reached by a stone bridge.

Local people have taken up residence around the ruins and built their own dwellings – often with stone recycled from ancient Deir Samaan – but they don't mind if you wander around.

The ruins cover an extensive area at the foot of the hill of Qala'at Samaan and you can scramble down after viewing the basilica on top. Alternatively, at the point where the road forks at the foot of the hill, instead of bearing right up to Qala'at Samaan, swing left and the ruins are on either side of the road just 200m further on.

Getting There & Away Take a minibus from the minibus station in Aleppo (part of the complex of bus stations south of the Amir Palace hotel) to the village of Daret Azze (S£10). They depart every half hour or so and the journey takes 50 minutes. During the journey keep a look out for the 5th century Mushabbak basilica, which stands alone in fields off to the left about two-thirds of the way along the route. From Daret Azze it's around 6km to Qala'at Samaan. The minibus driver may well offer to take you on the extra distance or you can negotiate with a local taxi, but they're going to ask at least S£100. The cheapest option is to hitch. While there isn't much traffic on the road, any vehicle that comes by will invariably stop. We very easily got a tractor ride up to the site and a lift in the back of a pick-up on the return journey. The last minibus from Daret Azze to Aleppo leaves at about 8 pm.

Qatura

About 2km north of Daret Azze on the road to Qala'at Samaan is the turn-off to Qatura. Follow this road off to the west and you come to more ruins, which include some Roman-era tombs at Qatura. The tombs are cut into the rock and it's easy to scramble up to them. The last tomb on the road is carved with a reclining figure in much the same style as you see at Palmyra. You can also quite clearly make out the Latin and Greek inscriptions.

Getting There & Away See the directions to Qala'at Samaan earlier; when you pick up a lift out of Daret Azze you can ask to be let off at the Qatura junction and it's not much of a walk from there. Later you shouldn't have any trouble picking up either a lift onwards to Qala'at Samaan or back to Daret Azze.

Ain Dara

A thousand years before Christ, a Hittite temple dedicated to the goddess Ishtar stood on an acropolis off the present-day road that now leads north from Qala'at Samaan to the mainly Kurdish town of Nahr Afreen. The temple was destroyed in the 8th century BC, rebuilt and then gradually gave way to other constructions.

Excavations since the mid-1950s on the mound where the temple formerly stood have revealed the layout of the site and, most interestingly, some extraordinary basalt statues and reliefs, which litter the site. The single most impressive statue is a huge lion tipped over on its side. However, that said – and despite recent restoration efforts by a Japanese team – the site overall yields little and doesn't really repay the trouble taken to reach it. There's a small admission fee of S£100 (students S£15) collected by a local caretaker who will probably greet you and do his best to show you around.

Getting There & Away Ain Dara is around 18km north of Qala'at Samaan. You can continue hitching from Deir Samaan toward Nahr Afreen (note, you want the road that goes through Deir Samaan, not the one that leads up to Qala'at Samaan) and get dropped off at the turn-off to Tell Ain Dara. Alternatively, from Aleppo catch a minibus direct to Nahr Afreen (S£13) and from there take one of the irregular pick-ups to Ain Dara (S£10) which is 7km to the south. It will drop you at the turn-off just before the village; you can see the acropolis in the distance. Follow the road around (about 2km), or cut across the path and onion fields directly to the site.

Cyrrhus

In the remotest of spots, overlooking the Turkish border and deep in Kurdish territory, is the 3rd century provincial town of Cyrrhus (Nabi Houri to the locals). No one has lived here for ages and very little is left of the town today but it once held quite a strategic position for troops of the Roman empire and boasted a citadel, a theatre and a cathedral.

From the dusty town of Azaz (a windwhipped, putrid little dump) the road takes you through cheerful countryside, dotted by wheat fields and olive groves, across two 3rd century humpback Roman bridges on the Sabun River and past a Roman-era **mausoleum**. This pyramid-capped monument has survived well, partly because it was preserved by local Muslims as a holy site (the ground floor has been recycled as the tomb of a local Muslim prophet named Houri). Here you branch right off the road to the site, which is just 200m further on.

The easiest structure to distinguish, of what is a fairly decrepit bunch of ruins, is the amphitheatre. Of the town walls, colonnaded street and basilica in the north of the town, not very much remains, but it is quite good fun to scramble up through the ruins past the theatre to the Arab citadel at the top, from where you have sweeping views right across to the Turkish mountains. You can be virtually guaranteed of having this particular place to yourself.

Getting There & Away Minibuses run from Aleppo to Azaz (S£10), from where you have no real choice but to bargain with one of the taxis for the remaining 28km to the site. Do not be surprised to be hit for as much as S£800 for the ride there and back. You can try to hitch but there is precious little traffic on this road. The same taxis also run people to the Turkish border for S£100 (for the car, not per person). You could try to rent a minibus or microbus at the Aleppo bus station for the day to do Cyrrhus and Qala'at Samaan. This would probably cost about S£1000, which isn't so bad if you have a big enough group.

Qalb Lozeh

One of the very best preserved examples of Syrian-Byzantine ecclesiastical architecture, the church of Qalb Lozeh predates Saint Simeon by perhaps only a few decades. It was perhaps built as a stop-off point for pilgrims enroute to see Simeon on his pillar. The entrance to the church, flanked by two three-storey towers, and its walls, not to mention the semicircular apse, are almost completely intact. Even some stone slabs of the roof have been retained, but the once most impressive arch between the towers has, unfortunately, been lost forever. The simple elegance of the structure, clean lines of the columns around the apse and classical decoration make this church an obvious precursor to the Romanesque style that would later dominate, in its various forms, the breadth of European churchbuilding.

Getting There & Away Qalb Lozeh lies a short way south of the main road from Aleppo to the Turkish border and Antakya. To get there take a minibus from Aleppo to Harim, which is a small, attractive provincial town crowned by an Ayyubid castle. From Harim you'll need to negotiate for a taxi.

SOUTH OF ALEPPO

Ebla, Ma'arat an-Nu'aman, Jerada and Ruweiha are all just off the main Aleppo-Hama highway and are easily reached by public transport (plus a bit of hitching). They could all be visited in a single day trip. However, the most interesting sites are possibly Al-Bara and Serjilla and these really deserve a full day in themselves. If you have a car at your disposal you could see the whole lot in one go – see Cars & Guides earlier in this chapter. All of these sites can just as easily be visited from Hama.

Ebla

Lying about 60km south of Aleppo, the ancient city of Ebla (Tell Mardikh) is of enormous fascination to archaeologists and historians but considerably less so to most visitors.

The Italian teams that have been excavating the site since 1964 have discovered that it was one of the most powerful city-states in Syria in the late 3rd millennium BC (known as the Early High Syrian period), but was sacked before the close of the millennium, probably by Sargon of Akkad. In its heyday, Ebla probably controlled most of north-western Syria and it again rose for a relatively brief period from about 1900 to 1750 BC, before being destroyed in 1600 BC by Hittite invaders. Troops of the First Crusade passed by thousands of years later, when it was known as Mardic Hamlet.

In recent times, digs at Ebla have unearthed more than 15,000 clay tablets in a Sumerian dialect, providing a wealth of information on everything from economics to local administration and dictionaries of other tongues. However, only a small portion of the cuneiform secrets have as yet been unlocked.

The site lies over a rise about 1km beyond the village of Tell Mardikh. You buy your ticket (S£300, students S£15) outside the small museum dedicated to the story of the excavations, and then continue along the road and over the rise. The shallow remains of the city lie before you, dominated by the limestone *tell* (artificial hill) that once formed the core of the city's fortress. Before you go clambering all over the site, note that it is strictly forbidden to do precisely that. Stick to the ill-defined trails around the edge of the ongoing excavations. The most interesting ruins are probably those labelled 'Palace G', just west of the acropolis, which display remains of a royal staircase, walls and columned halls. Beyond that, and lots of trenches and holes in the ground, there's very little here to see at all and anybody who has paid the full whack of S£300 may find themselves wondering what on earth they shelled the cash out for.

Getting There & Away Take any Hama-bound minibus or microbus, or to be sure of not paying the full fare for Hama, one of the less frequent ones to Ma'arat an-Nu'aman (ask for Al-Ma'ara), and ask to be let off at the Tell Mardikh turn-off. From there it is a 20 minute walk through the village of Tell Mardikh to the site. It's quite likely that you may be offered a lift by one of the tractors buzzing between the archaeological digs and the village.

Ma'arat an-Nu'aman (Al-Ma'ara)

This lively little market town is nothing special in itself, although it was witness to a gruesome bit of history when the Crusaders disgraced themselves even more than usual. On 12 December 1098, under the command of Count Raymond of Toulouse, the Crusaders attacked the fortified Muslim town of Ma'arat an-Nu'aman, slaughtering thousands. But the horror was less in the carnage of killing than what followed: 'In Ma'ara our troops boiled pagan adults in cooking pots; they impaled children on spits and devoured them grilled', confessed one of the Crusader chroniclers. The food provisions the Crusaders had hoped to find in the town hadn't been there and, literally dying

Ma'arat an-Nu'aman was the scene of a bloodthirsty Crusader attack in 1098.

of starvation, they had resorted to eating the bodies of the dead.

The main point of interest here is the **Mosaic Museum** housed in the 16th century Khan Murad Pasha. Most of the mosaics covered the floors of the more important or luxurious buildings and private houses of the clusters of 5th and 6th century Byzantine towns, that are now collectively referred to as the Dead Cities. Not quite as old is the lovingly executed mosaic of Assad, which takes pride of place facing the entrance. The museum is about 50m to the north of the bus station, on the right side of a large square. It is open from 9 am to 6 pm daily except Tuesday and entry costs S£300 (students S£15).

Further north and off to the right is the **Great Mosque**, whose 12th century minaret was rebuilt after an earthquake in 1170. From the mosque, head to the right of the square and north for a few hundred metres – where the street opens out you'll see the sad remains of a medieval **Citadel**, which now serve as cheap accommodation for a few families.

Getting There & Away There are frequent minibuses to Ma'arat an-Nu'aman (S£17, one hour) from Aleppo's minibus station, off the southern stretch of Sharia al-Baron, sleeker and faster microbuses (S£25) from the microbus station a little further south. You'll find that bigger, older and lumbering buses also do this run (S£13), departing from the Pullman station.

THE DEAD CITIES

The main attraction of the region around Aleppo are the so-called Dead Cities, a series of ancient ghost towns among the limestone hills that lie between the Aleppo-Hama highway in the east and the Orontes River in the west. They date from the time when this area was part of the hinterland of the great Byzantine Christian city of Antioch. There are reckoned to be some 600 separate sites, ranging from single monuments to nearly whole villages complete with houses, churches, baths and even wine presses. Taken together they represent a great archive in stone from

which historians can put together a picture of life in antiquity.

The great mystery is why were the towns abandoned? It obviously wasn't because they were attacked and destroyed because there is no sign of damage or destruction. Some of the sites, especially Serjilla, have an almost Marie Celeste-like quality, as though their occupants had just vanished. The most current theory is that these towns and villages were emptied by demographic shifts; trade routes changed and the people moved with them.

Some of the Dead Cities form part of present-day villages with people inhabiting the ancient ruins or incorporating oddments of antiquity into the structure of their own homes. Travel author William Dalrymple describes this well in his excellent book *From the Holy Mountain* (1997):

> Carrying on through the trees, I began to climb over a small drystone wall that separated the land of two farmers; only when I was halfway over did I notice that the wall was made up of a pile of discarded doorjambs, carved tympana and inscribed lintels, an almost ridiculous richness of fine Byzantine sculpture piled up between the trees. Only in Syria, I thought, could a currency of this richness be so debased in value that it could be used for so humble a purpose as walling.

The number of sites is simply overwhelming and we can describe only a handful of the most interesting and most easily accessible. If you have the inclination, you could spend weeks pottering around this area, stumbling across Byzantine ghosts that have yet to be described in any guidebook.

Warning: beware of wild dogs while exploring the Dead Cities. William Dalrymple had to climb a wall to escape them, while a colleague of ours was bitten. Perhaps carry a stone or two to scare them off with.

Jerada & Ruweiha

Jerada is the closest of these twin Dead Cities to the Aleppo-Hama highway, which it overlooks from a position up on low rocky hills. The site is partially occupied, with some of the big old houses serving as barns for villagers who have built their own dwellings on the northern fringes of the ruins. These ruins include the extensive remains of noble houses, a 5th century Byzantine cathedral and a six storey watchtower. Some of the simple geometric designs on column capitals and lintels is vaguely reminiscent of Visigothic work done in Spain (the other extreme of the Mediterranean) at about the same time. About the only interruption you'll have here will come from the odd local who is more curious about you than you are about the ruins.

Hit the road again and follow it for another 2.5km or so across a barren lunar landscape to reach the even more striking, scattered remains of Ruweiha. The most imposing building here is the 6th century Church of Bissos, now home to a local family. Its transverse arches are thought to be among the oldest of their kind. Just outside, the domed mausoleum housing the body of Bissos (possibly a bishop) has since found its echo in similar designs throughout the Arab world. Few people live among the ruins now, although the occasional family gets up here for a Friday picnic.

Serjilla

Serjilla and Al-Bara (see following) are two of a cluster of five or more Dead Cities strung out on either side of a country lane that runs north from the green-domed mosque just outside Kafr Nabl. About 2km after the mosque you'll see a sign for **Shinshira** pointing off to your right, then after a further 2km just off to the left are the grey stone remnants of **Mahardiyya** buried within some straggly olive groves.

Both of these Dead Cities are really worth exploring, however if you're completely pushed for time, skip them and look out instead for the signposted turning to Serjilla, off to the right. If you are hitching, be warned, it's about a 4km walk from this junction down to Serjilla and next to no traffic comes along this way.

Serjilla is undoubtedly the most eerie and evocative of the Dead Cities. It has the greatest number of semi-complete buildings, all of which sit in a natural basin in windswept and hilly moorland. Although deserted for about 15 centuries, the stone facades are clean and sharp-edged and the surrounding ground is covered with short grass. There are no wild bushes or uncontrolled undergrowth – the place has quite a spooky air of almost human-maintained orderliness about it.

At its centre is a small plaza flanked by a two storey tavern and a large bathhouse. Now stripped of the mosaics that once decorated it, the latter building is quite austere but the mere existence of Christian-era baths is itself a source of curiosity. Virtually next door lies an *andron*, or men's meeting place, and further east a small church. Spreading away from this core are substantial leftovers of private houses and villas. In places you pass down narrow grassy lanes between high stone walls punctuated by carefully carved windows and doors, and half expect a householder to step out on a quick errand to fetch something from the market.

There's an admission fee of S£150 (students S£10) payable to a guard who hovers around the car park at the edge of the site.

Al-Bara

Al-Bara is the most extensive of the Dead Cities. It's also the farthest north from Kafr Nabl; you continue on beyond the turning for Serjilla and past another small Dead City called **Bauda**.

Occupying a good position on the north-south trade route between Antioch and Afamea and being surrounded by rich arable land, from humble beginnings in the 4th century AD Al-Bara rapidly became one of the most important centres of wine and olive oil production in the region. Even when the trade routes shifted in the 7th century (resulting in the abandonment of many neighbouring towns), Al-Bara prospered and grew. It boasted large villas, three monasteries and numerous churches – at least five can still be picked out among ruins that cover 6 sq km.

The town weathered the coming of Islam and remained predominantly eastern Christian – and the seat of a bishopric subordinate to Antioch – until its occupation by the Latin Crusaders in the very last years of the 12th century.

It was from Al-Bara that the Crusaders set out to perpetrate their horrible cannibalistic episode at Ma'arat an-Nu'aman in December 1098. Twenty-five years later they were driven out and Al-Bara reverted to Muslim control. It's thought that the town became depopulated in the latter part of the 12th century following a severe earthquake.

As it stands today, there's no obvious route around the site. Unlike at Serjilla, the land here is densely covered by trees and bushes and you have to squeeze through the undergrowth to discover the old buildings and ruins. Be careful where you tramp, though, as small plots are still intensively worked in among the ancient stones – the land remains good and olives, grapes and apricots still thrive here as in Byzantine times.

The most striking structures to look out for are a couple of **pyramid tombs**, 200m apart. Decorated with Corinthian pilasters and carved acanthus leaves, the tombs are a very visible testament to the one-time wealth of the settlement. The larger of the two still holds five sealed, decorated sarcophagi.

From the pyramids you can wander south past an underground tomb with three arches to a large, well preserved monastery, or clamber and scrabble over dry stone walls to head north to find the ruins of the five churches.

Take plenty of water and food as there's not much to be had in the town, although you will stand out so much that an invitation to tea is more than likely.

Getting There & Away

You need to take a microbus or minibus for Ma'arat an-Nu'aman (commonly referred to as Al-Ma'ara) – see that section above. For Jerada and Ruweiha ask to be let off at Babila, 7km before Al-Ma'ara. From where you are dropped off you can see the ruins over to the west, 3km away. If you start walking you're bound to be offered a lift before you get too far.

To get to Al-Bara, Serjilla and the other neighbouring Dead Cities, you stay on the minibus all the way into Al-Ma'ara where you then pick up a microbus for Kafr Nabl (S£5), some 10km away. From Kafr Nabl it's a further 6km on to Al-Bara. The microbus drivers will offer to take you for an outrageous price but your best bet is to start walking out of the village, following the main street, then after about 1.5km bear right at the large new mosque with the green dome; it won't be long before a passing car offers you a lift. Coming back, you do it in reverse.

The Desert

The Damascus-Aleppo highway marks roughly the division between the cultivable land to the west and the barren desert spreading eastward all the way to the Euphrates.

The wide fringe of the desert gets sufficient rain to maintain grazing for sheep and goats, and the people who live in this area traditionally built beehive-shaped houses as protection against the extreme heat (see the boxed text 'Beehive Houses' in the Orontes Valley chapter). You can see these houses on the road from Homs to Palmyra but increasingly concrete is taking over as the main building material, and the anonymous housing typical of much of the Middle East is asserting itself.

The desert proper extends south-east from Palmyra into Jordan and Iraq. Its Arabic name is Badiyyat ash-Sham and it is also known as the Syrian Desert. Rather than the seas of shifting sands that so excite the movie-inspired imagination, this desert consists of more prosaic stony plains. Rain is extremely irregular and it is not uncommon for two or three years to pass between rainfall.

Dotting this desert are the oases – the main one is Palmyra – that once served as way-stations for caravans travelling between the Mediterranean and Mesopotamia.

PALMYRA

Known to the locals as Tadmor (its ancient Semitic name), Palmyra is Syria's prime attraction and one of the world's great historical sites. If you're only going to see one thing in Syria, make it Palmyra. Even if you feel you have seen enough ruins to last you a lifetime and the thought of more is enough to make you groan, Palmyra really is special.

Although you can no longer expect to have the splendour of this place to yourself, the flow of tourists has not yet reached such proportions as to rob you of its magic. For much of the year you can still wander around the ruins pretty much by yourself, especially early in the morning. For this

Highlights

- **First light at Palmyra** – at 5.30 am you have three or more hours to view the ruins in photography-perfect light before the coaches turn up (see page 255)
- **Sunset at Palmyra** – avoid the crowds at the castle and perch on the hilltop behind the funerary towers to watch the site glow pink and orange (see page 263)
- **Coffee with the Bedouin** – if the invitation is offered, accept; it's not every day you get to share a brew with desert nomads (see page 265)

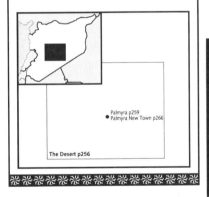

Palmyra p259
Palmyra New Town p266

The Desert p256

reason alone, try not to visit Palmyra as a day trip from Damascus or Hama – no matter how early you set off, you'll arrive too late to see the site at its best.

This oasis is in the middle of nowhere – 160km from the Orontes River to the west and 225km from the Euphrates to the east. This is the very end of the Anti-Lebanon Range, and the final fold of the mountain range forms a basin at the edge of which bubbles up the slightly sulphurous Efca Spring ('*efca*' is Aramaic for 'source'). Said

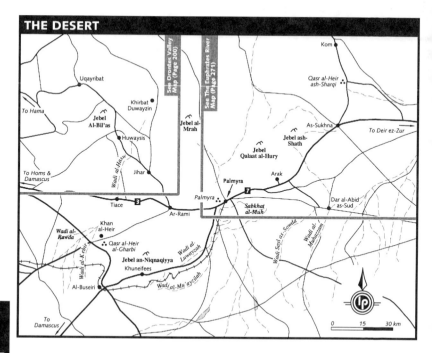

THE DESERT

[Map labels:]
Kom
Uqayribat
Qasr al-Heir ash-Sharqi
Khirbat Duwayzin
To Hama
Jebel Al-Bil'as
Jebel al-Mrah
As-Sukhna
To Deir ez-Zur
Huwaysis
Jebel ash-Shath
Jebel Qalaat al-Hury
Jihar
To Homs & Damascus
Wadi al-Hasw
Arak
Palmyra
Palmyra
Tiace
Ar-Rami
Sabkhat al-Muh
Dar al-Abid as-Sud
Khan al-Heir
Wadi al-Rawda
Qasr al-Heir al-Gharbi
Jebel an-Niqnaqiyya
Khuneifees
Wadi al-K'dir
Wadi al-Luweyzah
Wadi al-Mahassan
Wadi Seyl as-Sawda
Al-Buseiri
Wadi al-Mu'ayidah
To Damascus
See the Orontes Valley Map (Page 200)
See the Euphrates River Map (Page 271)

0   15   30 km

THE DESERT

to have medicinal qualities, it has now been closed because, according to the Palmyra tourist office, it has dried up.

The ruins of the city dating to the 2nd century AD cover some 50 hectares and have been extensively excavated and restored. Nevertheless, archaeologists continually make new finds. In 1994, for instance, a team of Belgian archaeologists stumbled across some Roman tombs south-east of the Temple of Bel. The new town is rapidly growing around the ruins, spreading especially towards the west, and now has more than 40,000 inhabitants. Nearby is an airforce base, and fighters scream over the ancient ruins on training runs (thankfully, they don't come in too low).

Tucked completely out of sight, and to the west of both the old and the new cities, is a high-security prison with an extremely grim reputation.

History

Tadmor is mentioned in tablets as far back as the 19th century BC, and from an early time was an indispensable staging post for caravans travelling from the Mediterranean to the countries of the Gulf. It was also an important link on the old Silk Road from China and India to Europe and the city prospered greatly by levying heavy tolls on the caravans.

As the Romans pushed the frontier of their empire further east during the 1st and early 2nd centuries AD, Tadmor's importance as a buffer between the Parthians and the Romans grew. The latter dubbed the city Palmyra (City of Palms) but the locals retained the old name of Tadmor (City of Dates), for reasons that will not escape the attention of the modern visitor. It appears that, in spite of the empire's growing influence, the city retained a considerable independence, profiting also from rerouted trade following the defeat of the Petra-based Nabataean empire by Rome.

The emperor Hadrian visited Palmyra in 130 AD and declared Palmyra a 'free city', therefore allowing it to set and collect its own taxes. Indeed, in 137 AD an enormous stone tablet was raised bearing the inscription 'Tariff of Palmyra' (now in the Hermitage in St Petersburg), setting out the taxes payable on each commodity that passed through the city; these included a tax on the activities of prostitutes, as well as charges for the supply of water.

In 212 AD, under the emperor Caracalla (himself born of a Syrian mother), Palmyra became a Roman colony. In this way, its citizens obtained equal rights with those of Rome and exemption from paying imperial taxes. During this period the great colonnaded street was enlarged, temples were built and the citizens grew extremely wealthy on the caravan trade – some even owned ships sailing in the Arabian Gulf. As internal power struggles caused a decline in the influence of Rome, Palmyra's rulers took it on themselves to further strengthen their independence.

The colony evolved into a kingdom that came to be ruled by Odenathus, a brilliant military leader who earned the respect and trust of Rome by defeating the army of its long-standing rivals, the Sassanians. In 256 the emperor Valerian bestowed upon Odenathus the title of 'Corrector of the East' and put all Roman forces in the region under his command.

The city's downfall began when Odenathus was assassinated in 267. His second wife, Zenobia (see the boxed text 'Zenobia' on the next page) took over in the name of their young son, Vabalathus. However, Rome was not keen to recognise them – particularly as Zenobia was suspected of involvement in her husband's death. The emperor dispatched an army to deal with the rebel queen. Rather than back down, Zenobia met the Roman force in battle and defeated it. She then led her army against the garrison at Bosra, then the capital of the Province of Arabia, and successfully invaded Egypt.

With all of Syria and Palestine and part of Egypt under her control, Zenobia declared her independence from Rome and had coins minted in Alexandria bearing her image and that of her son, who assumed the title of Augustus, or emperor.

The Roman emperor Aurelian, who had been prepared to negotiate, could not stomach such a show of open defiance. After defeating Zenobia's forces at Antioch and Emesa (Homs) in 271, he besieged Palmyra itself. Zenobia was defiant to the last and instead of accepting the generous surrender terms offered by Aurelian, made a dash on a camel through the encircling Roman forces. She headed for Persia to appeal for military aid, only to be captured by Roman cavalry at the Euphrates. The city then surrendered and got off pretty lightly, with only a fine for its insurrection.

Zenobia was carted off to Rome in 272 as Aurelian's trophy and paraded in the streets, bound in gold chains. She spent the rest of her days in Rome, some say in a villa provided by the emperor, although others claim she chose to starve to death rather than remain captive.

Whatever became of her, this was the end of Palmyra's prosperity. The city was destroyed by Aurelian in 273 following another rebellion in which the inhabitants massacred 600 Roman archers who were stationed there. In response, Aurelian's troops were particularly brutal, slaughtering Palmyra's residents and torching the city.

Palmyra was never able to recover its former glory and became a Roman outpost. The emperor Diocletian later fortified it as one in a line of fortresses marking the eastern boundary of the Roman empire. Justinian rebuilt the city's defences in the 6th century but by this stage it had lost all its wealth and continued to decline steadily with the drop in caravan traffic.

The city fell to the Muslims, led by Khaled ibn al-Walid, in 634 and from then on, despite the building of the castle, it dwindled to a small village beside extensive ruins – the result of a devastating earthquake in 1089.

THE DESERT

Zenobia

Claiming to be descended from Cleopatra, Zenobia imbues Palmyra with a wild romance. She was, it seems, a woman of exceptional ability and ambition. Fluent in Greek, Latin, Aramaic and Egyptian, she effectively turned Palmyra into an independent empire, wresting control of Egypt from Rome and marching deep into Asia Minor – although in doing so, she also assured her city's eventual destruction.

From her actions, she was obviously headstrong and wilful, but the 18th century historian Edward Gibbon also said of her in his *The Decline and Fall of the Roman Empire*:

She equalled in beauty her ancestor Cleopatra and far surpassed that princess in chastity and valour. Zenobia was esteemed the most lovely as well as the most heroic of her sex. She was of dark complexion. Her teeth were of a pearly whiteness and her large black eyes sparkled with an uncommon fire, tempered by the most attractive sweetness. Her voice was strong and harmonious. Her manly understanding was strengthened and adorned by study.

Apparently, she was also a ruler with a sense of humour. A merchant was to be punished for overcharging and was summoned to the theatre to appear in front of the queen and the public audience. The merchant stood alone in the arena and shook with fear, thinking that a wild beast was to be set upon him. When the beast was released the crowd roared with laughter – the merchant turned around to be confronted by a chicken.

After centuries of obscurity, Palmyra was 'rediscovered' in 1678 by two English merchants resident in Aleppo. The tales of Odenathus and Zenobia fascinated Europe, mainly because nobody had any idea that this once-important city had even existed. Throughout the 18th and 19th centuries a steady flow of intrepid visitors made the two- or three-day expedition out from Damascus to the desert, but it wasn't until the early 20th century that any scientific study began.

The first survey was carried out in the 1920s by the Germans, who at that time were close allies of the ruling Ottoman Turks, before French took over in 1929. Until then, Arab villagers had lived in the courtyard of the Temple of Bel, but they were removed to the fledgling new town.

Work intensified following WWII and it continues to this day.

Information

Tourist Office The tourist office is about halfway between the town and the site proper, near the Hotel Zenobia. It's open from 8 am to 2 pm and 5 to 7 pm (4 to 6 pm in winter) daily. At the time of our last visit there was talk of a new tourist office being opened on a site closer to town, near the post office.

Money There are no banks or exchange offices in Palmyra, so you'll need to bring enough cash for your visit. If, however, you run short it's not terribly difficult to find someone willing to change money on the black market, but be discreet. Failing that, it is possible to change money at the Palmyra Cham Palace Hotel (see Places to Stay – Mid-Range & Top End later in this chapter).

Post & Communications The post office is a very laid-back place with flexible opening hours – don't count on it being open after around 2 pm. There are a couple of card phones in front of the main entrance but the whole area is closed off after 2 pm.

The Ruins

Tempting though it may be to think of Palmyra as simply another Roman city, it is anything but that. Its layout does not follow classic Roman town planning at all, although Roman and Greek influences are obvious. Despite the power of its neighbours (Roman, Persian and Parthian)

Palmyra retained a distinct culture and its own language, a dialect of Aramaic.

Today, the unhurried traveller could easily spend a couple of days wandering around the main site, which spreads over a very large area, bounded by what have come to be known as Zenobia's walls. Then there are the funerary towers, as well as the 17th century Arab castle on the hill. It's highly recommended that you see the site both at sunrise, when the early morning light infuses the stone with a rich pinkness, and again at sunset.

Although there is no admission fee to the site, you can easily spend a lot of money visiting everything in Palmyra – the sum total of entry to all museums, the funerary towers and the Temple of Bel comes to S£1000, plus the cost of transport to the funerary towers (see the Funerary Towers section later for details). Those on a tight budget should make

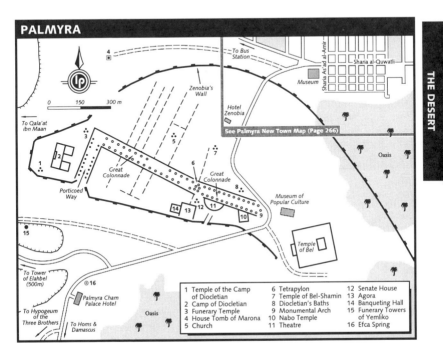

PALMYRA

THE DESERT

To Bus Station

Zenobia's Wall

Museum

Sharia As'ad al-Amir
Sharia al-Quwatli

Hotel Zenobia

See Palmyra New Town Map (Page 266)

To Qala'at ibn Maan

0   150   300 m

Oasis

Great Colonnade

Great Colonnade

Porticoed Way

Museum of Popular Culture

Temple of Bel

To Tower of Elahbel (500m)

16

To Hypogeum of the Three Brothers

Palmyra Cham Palace Hotel

Oasis

To Homs & Damascus

1 Temple of the Camp of Diocletian	6 Tetrapylon	12 Senate House
2 Camp of Diocletian	7 Temple of Bel-Shamin	13 Agora
3 Funerary Temple	8 Diocletian's Baths	14 Banqueting Hall
4 House Tomb of Marona	9 Monumental Arch	15 Funerary Towers
5 Church	10 Nabo Temple	of Yemliko
	11 Theatre	16 Efca Spring

An Expensive Precedent

Admission fees at Palmyra doubled in 1998, making the high cost of visiting Syrian sites a major conversational topic among travellers. This is nothing new. It is, in fact, a repeat of an odd situation that was first reported almost 200 years ago.

The Middle East has always attracted intrepid female explorers and adventurers – Gertrude Bell, Lady Jane Digby and Freya Stark to name just three – but Lady Hester Stanhope was one of the more extreme examples of the breed. She was the niece of a British prime minister and, as such, a one-time resident of 10 Downing St. On the death of her beloved uncle and her removal from the centre of British politics, Lady Hester decided to travel abroad and find herself a new court. Along with her retinue she travelled in the Middle East, interfering in local affairs but winning the admiration of the Arabs, who regarded her as a queen.

The intrepid adventurer, Lady Hester Stanhope

One of her greatest moments of glory was, in 1813, riding into Palmyra on an Arab stallion at the head of her travelling procession. On this occasion she was hosting a fete for the local Bedouins, during which she ordered that a silver dollar be given to all present. To the grand sheikh of the Bedouin she presented a piece of paper, handwritten, on which she directed him to charge a thousand piastres of every traveller who visited the ruins. 'This enormous tax', wrote traveller John Carne in *Letters from the East* (1826), 'which it is impossible to escape causes several travellers to leave Syria without seeing the finest ruin in the world'. One visitor who did attempt to evade the tax, reports Carne, had his hut set on fire by the Arabs.

At least the impecunious traveller of today is able to visit a great deal of the site for free and finds cash admissions barring the way only to a few selected sections, like the Temple of Bel and the museum. And if the traveller decides to give these sights a miss and hold back on the cash, the chances of having the hotel burned from under them are these days very slim.

the Temple of Bel their first priority, followed by the museum in the town.

Temple of Bel This temple complex is the most complete structure and single most impressive part of the ruins. Bel was the most important of the gods in the Palmyrene pantheon – at least, that's what historians assume from the prominence of his temple, although actually very little is known about Palmyra's deities. This god was most likely an imported masculine version of the Babylonian goddess Belili, the mother goddess, and identified with Jupiter of the Romans.

Raised on a slight mound, or *tell* (indicating the existence of a pre-Classical settlement on this site), the temple is entered through the ticket office, just north of the main monumental entrance. The keep-like form of the entrance was created by the Arabs in 1132 when they converted the temple into a fortress.

The complex consists of two parts: a huge walled courtyard and, at its centre, the temple proper or *cella*. Originally the court-yard was surrounded by a 15m-high wall but only the northern side is original, the rest being of Arab construction. The western wall, which contains the entrance and a small souvenir shop, was built out of fragments of the temple when it was fortified. A double colonnade used to run around three sides of the interior while the fourth (western) had a single row of columns much taller than the others. Some of these can be seen to the right and left of the entrance.

Just to the left of the entrance inside the courtyard is a passage that enters the temple from outside the wall and gradually slopes up to the level of the courtyard. This is where sacrificial animals were brought into the precincts. In front of the cella are the ruins of a banquet hall. The podium of the sacrificial altar is on the left, and the remains of another platform on the right were possibly used for religious purification ceremonies.

The cella itself dates from 32 AD – this date is part of a dedication inscription on a pedestal found inside (now in the Palmyra museum). The cella is unusual in that the entrance is in one of the sides rather than at an end, and is offset from the centre. Inside is a single chamber with porticoes at either end, whose ceilings were cut from single blocks of stone.

Both ceilings are highly decorated – the northern ceiling has a cupola featuring seven busts and signs of the zodiac, while the southern ceiling has a huge acanthus surrounded by linked swastikas. The stepped ramp leading to the southern portico suggests that it may have contained a portable idol used in processions.

Around the back of the shrine is a pile of old railway tracks that were used to remove trolleys of rubble during the original excavations. The temple enclosure is open from 8 am to 1 pm and 4 to 6 pm (8 am to 4 pm in winter) daily. Entry is S£300 (S£25 for students).

Great Colonnade This column-lined street formed the main artery of the town and ran north-west from the Temple of Bel entrance to a **monumental arch** – now the most prominent feature of the site – and then on for 700m or so, ending at the funerary temple. The section between the Bel temple and the arch no longer exists, although a handful of columns provide a reminder of it.

The main road from Palmyra to Damascus now winds through here and the heavy traffic that thunders through can hardly do the ruins any good. In fact it looks as though the keystone of the arch is ready to fall out at any moment.

Dating from the reign of Septimius Severus, when Palmyra was at its peak, the monumental arch is interesting in that it is actually two arches joined like a hinge to pivot the main street through a 30° turn. This slight switch in direction, and another just a little further west, are evidence of the city's unique development – a crooked street like this would be unimaginable in a standard Roman city.

The street itself was never paved, so that camels could use it, but the porticoes on either side were. The section between the arch and the *tetrapylon* (four groups of pillars) is the best restored and is impressive in its scale. Each column has a small jutting platform about two-thirds of the way up, designed to hold the statue of some rich or famous Palmyrene who had helped pay for the construction of the street. One of these statues has been replaced on its pedestal, virtually in front of the Museum of Popular Culture.

Nabo Temple The first ruin on the left as you pass the arch is a small trapezoidal temple built in the 1st century BC to the god Nabo, the Palmyrene god of destinies. All that's left are the temple podium, lower courses of the outer walls and some columns.

Diocletian's Baths Next up on the right is the site of baths built by Diocletian, marked out by the four taller columns that would have carried the entrance portico. The baths themselves exist only as trenches and as outlines.

THE DESERT

Theatre The theatre is on the south side of the street between two arches in the colonnade. Until the 1950s it was buried beneath sand but since then has been extensively restored – large sections now look just a bit too shiny and new.

Beneath the platforms on many of the columns are inscriptions with names for the statues that once stood there. It seems the statues were of prominent people such as emperors, princes of Palmyra, magistrates, officials, high-ranking priests and caravan chiefs.

The freestanding facade of the theatre is designed along the lines of a palace entrance, complete with a royal door and smaller doors on either side. From the rear of the theatre a pillared way led south past the senate house and *agora* (meeting place) to one of the gates in the wall built by Justinian.

During the annual Palmyra festival the theatre serves as a busy performance venue (see the Special Events entry later in this chapter).

Agora The agora was the equivalent of a Roman forum and was used for public discussion and as a market. Four porticoes surrounded a courtyard measuring 84m by 71m. The dedications of the statues that once stood on the pillars and walls provide important clues for historians. The portico on the north held statues of Palmyrene and Roman officials, the eastern one had senators, the western portico was for military officers while on the south side, merchants and caravan leaders were honoured. Today there is nothing left of the statues and most of the pillars are only 1m or so high.

Adjoining the agora are the remains of the **banqueting hall** used by the rulers of Palmyra.

Tetrapylon About one-third of the way along the colonnaded street is the reconstructed tetrapylon. Only one of these pillars is of the original granite (probably brought from Aswan in Egypt – many pieces of pharaonic statuary are carved from this same stone); the rest are just coloured concrete and

look pretty terrible – a result of some rather hasty and amateurish early reconstruction.

Each of the four groups of pillars supports 150,000kg of solid cornice. A statue once stood between the pillars on each of the four pedestals, one of them of Zenobia herself. Unfortunately, no vestiges of the latter have been found.

This monument marks a major intersection of the old city. From here the main street continues north-west, and a smaller, pillared street leads south-west to the agora and north-east to the Temple of Bel-Shamin.

Temple of Bel-Shamin Dating from 17 AD and dedicated to the Phoenician god of storms and fertilising rains, this small shrine stands near the Hotel Zenobia. Bel-Shamin was an import, like Bel, who only really gained popularity in Palmyra when Roman influence was at its height.

Although it is permanently closed, the six columns of the vestibule have platforms for statues, and displays some inscriptions. The column on the far left, dated 131 AD, has an inscription in Greek and Palmyrene that praises the secretary of the city for his generosity during the imperial visit of 'the divine Hadrian' and for footing the bill for the temple's construction.

Funerary Temple Beyond the tetrapylon the main street continues for another 500m. This stretch has seen much less excavation and reconstruction than elsewhere and is still littered with tumbled columns and assorted blocks of masonry. The road ends at the impressive portico of a funerary temple, dating from the 3rd century – the portico with its six columns stands as it was found but the walls are a relatively recent reconstruction. This was the main residential section of town and streets can be seen leading off to both sides. The area all around here has broken and scattered masonry everywhere, in places literally heaped into small hillocks of statuary fragments and decorated friezes and panels – it gives you a chance to look at the intricacy of the carving at extremely close quarters.

Camp of Diocletian South-west of the funerary temple along the porticoed way is Diocletian's camp. The camp was erected after the destruction of the city by Aurelian, possibly on the site of what had been the palace of Zenobia, although excavations so far have been unable to prove this. The camp lay near what was the Damascus Gate, which gave on to a 2nd century colonnaded street that supposedly linked Emesa (Homs) and the Euphrates.

Funerary Towers To the south of the city wall at the foot of some low hills is a series of tall, free-standing, square-based funerary towers. The towers contained coffins in niches like pigeonholes on five levels. The funerary niches, or *loculi*, were sealed with a stone panel carved with a head and shoulders portrait of the deceased – you can see dozens of these portraits in the museum at Palmyra and also in the National Museum at Damascus.

Nearest to the line marking what was the city wall is a series known as the **Towers of Yemliko**. The tallest of these – at four storeys high – is the most interesting. It dates from 83 AD and although it's kept locked you can peer in through the barred entrance. There is also an interesting carved lintel above the doorway. Even better, you can clamber up the hillside behind to gain a wonderful vantage point from which to survey the whole Palmyrene landscape.

As you head west back into the hills, there are plenty more of these funerary towers, some totally dilapidated, others relatively complete. The whole area goes by the name of the Valley of the Tombs.

By far the best preserved is the **Tower of Elahbel**, which lies about 500m west of the Yemliko group. Built in 103 AD, it has four storeys and could purportedly accommodate up to 300 sarcophagi. It's possible to ascend the stairs to visit the upper storey tomb chambers and to climb out onto the top of the tower.

On the way to Elahbel you'll notice the much excavated Tomb 36; the main museum has a detailed display of the tomb.

Visiting Elahbel can be a bit of a pain. At the museum in town an attendant with keys is prepared to go out to the tower four times a day (details posted at the museum), and tickets cost S£150. You are supposed to bargain with a local driver to take a group of people out – this should not cost more than S£200 and, given that you can walk out in less than 30 minutes, is a real pain. Your friendly museum attendant, however, will not budge unless you have organised the vehicle – a local form of state-assisted private enterprise. Recently, the trip over to Elahbel has started to take in a visit to the Hypogeum of the Three Brothers (see following), which makes it well worth doing.

Hypogeum of the Three Brothers A second, later type of Palmyrene tomb was the *hypogeum*, an underground tomb. The best example of a hypogeum is actually in the National Museum in Damascus – there the Hypogeum of Yarhai, which used to lie close to the Tower of Elahbel, has been beautifully reconstructed to illustrate perfectly how such tombs would have originally appeared. Here at Palmyra, the best of the 50 or more hypogea that have been discovered and excavated is the Hypogeum of the Three Brothers, which lies just southwest of the Palmyra Cham Palace Hotel (see Places to Stay later in this chapter).

The tomb is very modest in size but contains some beautiful **frescoes**, including portraits of the three brothers in oval frames. There are also three large sarcophagi topped by figures reclining on couches. You'll notice that these figures, like many in the Palmyra museum, are headless; the official Palmyra guide suggests that this is because early tomb robbers found they could quite easily sell the stone heads. However, it's also the case that in the days of early Islam, old statues and frescoes depicting people were often defaced because of the new religion's abhorrence of idolatrous images.

You can only get access to the hypogeum if you are accompanied by a museum guide – see the Funerary Towers section.

Qala'at ibn Maan

To the west of the ruins the dominant feature is the Arab castle, Qala'at ibn Maan, built in the 17th century by Fakr ad-Din the Maanite. You can't miss it – just jump the wall and head uphill. The castle is surrounded by a moat, and the footbridge has been made passably safe. It is well worth scrambling up the hill to get in, for although the castle is not in a wonderful state of repair, the views over Palmyra and the surrounding desert are magical. It's best to go in the late afternoon, when the sun is behind you and the shadows are long. Townspeople will happily drive you up for an exorbitant fee if you don't fancy the climb (an asphalted road winds up behind the castle to within spitting distance of the entrance).

Opening hours depend largely on whim, but are roughly from 9 am to dusk. Admission is S£200.

Museum

It's debatable whether Palmyra's modest museum is worth a visit. With no labelling to speak of and poor presentation it provides no additional context for understanding the site and adds little to your experience of Palmyra. In fact, the National Museum in Damascus, with its reconstructed hypogeum, is far more worthwhile.

Still, Palmyra's museum has some good points. In the second room is a fabulous large-scale model of the Temple of Bel that gives an excellent idea of how the complex would have looked in its original state. In the next room are some fascinating friezes depicting camel trains and cargo ships, attesting to the importance trade played in the wealth of Palmyra.

Continuing anticlockwise, the western gallery has a couple of very dynamic mosaics that were found in what are presumed to have been nobles' houses, located just east of the Temple of Bel. One mosaic represents a scene from the *Iliad* in which Ulysses discovers Achilles disguised in women's clothes and concealed among the daughters of the king of Scyros (this scene is also portrayed in a fresco in the Hypogeum of the Three Brothers); the other depicts centaurs hunting deer. Also in this hall is a large photo of Qasr al-Heir ash-Sharqi (see that section later in this chapter).

The far end of the museum, the eastern gallery, contains the most outstanding piece in the collection, a 3m-high statue of the goddess Allat, associated with the Greek Athena, and found in 1975 by a Polish team of archaeologists. Also in this room is a collection of coins, including some depicting Zenobia and her son, which were discovered as recently as 1991.

The last few rooms hold countless busts and carved portraits that formed part of the panels used to seal the loculi in Palmyra's many funerary towers and hypogea. Many of these sculpted portraits possess an uncanny animation – it's quite unnerving to think that you're gazing on the faces of people who died close to 2000 years ago.

The museum is on the edge of the new town and is open from 8 am to 1 pm and 4 to 6 pm (2 to 4 pm in winter) daily except Tuesday. The entrance fee is S£300 (S£25 for students).

Museum of Popular Culture

The whitewashed building just by the Temple of Bel houses the Museum of Popular Culture. It contains the usual scenes from Arab life, re-created using mannequins, although it is, admittedly, a little better than most others of its type. There is also a lot of interesting information written in French and posted up about the Bedouin tribal system. The museum is officially open from 8.30 am to 2.30 pm daily except Tuesday, but it may open up if you hang around outside these hours. Entry is S£150 (S£15 for students).

Efca Spring

Just past the Palmyra Cham Palace Hotel and heading into town is the Efca Spring. Tourist office tales that the spring has dried up seem unlikely. All the same it is no longer possible to visit the spring, which has been used for bathing since Roman times.

The Bedouin

Mounted on a camel, swathed in robes and carrying a rifle for security and a coffee pot for hospitality, the archetypal Arab, as portrayed by Omar Sharif in *Lawrence of Arabia*, is no more. Certainly not in Syria, anyway. Although still known as *bedu* (meaning 'nomad'), these days few of Syria's 100,000 Bedouin population could be regarded as desert wanderers. They used to make their living guiding caravans across the deserts and supplying camels and protection against bandits but the overland trade routes died with the coming of the aeroplane. Most Bedouin are now settled in towns and villages and the furthest they roam is to find new pastures for their goats and sheep. For the most part, the camels are long gone and, instead, most Bedouin drive battered pick-ups.

Many of the Bedouin continue to wear traditional dress, though, and this can include, for men, a dagger – a symbol of dignity, but these days used for precious little else. Women tend to dress in colourful garb, or sometimes black robes, and occasionally sport facial tatooing and kohl around the eyes.

Another aspect of Bedouin tradition still very much in evidence is their famed hospitality. Born of the codependency the nomads developed in order to survive in the desert, modern-day hospitality manifests itself in unmitigated generosity extended to strangers. Should you be fortunate enough to encounter the Bedouin (and in Palmyra this is quite possible as some of the hotels, such as the New Afqa, arrange trips out to Bedouin camps) you can expect to be invited into their black goat-hair tents (*beit ash-sha'ar*; literally 'house of hair'), and offered bitter coffee, then sweet tea and possibly even something to eat. Money is not expected in return so you should try to be a gracious guest and not take advantage of the hospitality.

Special Events

Since 1993, Palmyra has been the scene of an annual popular folk festival. Horse and camel races take place on the hippodrome below the Qala'at ibn Maan, and in the evenings there are music and dance performances, some of which take place in the old theatre. Aimed largely at tourists, the festival runs for three or four days, usually towards the end of April or beginning of May.

Places to Stay

Palmyra is very much affected by the swings of the seasonal tourism trade. In the peak season, from around April to September, beds can be scarce and prices are inflated. At other times, there are far more beds in Palmyra than visitors, and competition between hotels becomes fierce. At such times, you definitely shouldn't accept the first rate quoted. When we last visited out of season one hotel manager dropped his price from US$24 for a double down to S£700 (US$15) at the shake of a head. It should be pointed out, though, that the places willing to make these drastic discounts may later try to make money by reneging on the agreement or adding supplementary charges for hot water or extortionate charges for breakfasts. The better hotels rarely give much of a discount.

Places to Stay – Budget

New Tourist Hotel (☎ *910 333, Sharia al-Quwatli*) was at one time about the only hotel in town. It has failed to keep up with the times, however, and is looking a bit grotty and battered. Nevertheless, it remains a favourite with hardcore travellers. A bed in a shared room is S£150, while singles/doubles are S£200/325 with ensuites; S£175/275 without. There is, though, a mosque virtually next door, so you will be subjected to the early morning call to prayer.

New Afqa Hotel (☎ *910 386*) is possibly the best backpackers' option in town. The

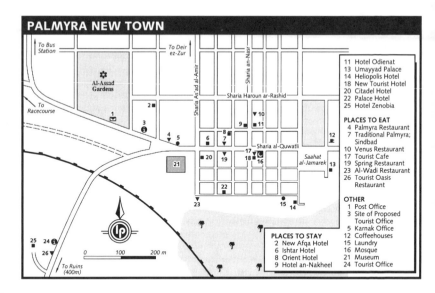

PALMYRA NEW TOWN

PLACES TO STAY
2 New Afqa Hotel
6 Ishtar Hotel
8 Orient Hotel
9 Hotel an-Nakheel
11 Hotel Odienat
13 Umayyad Palace
14 Heliopolis Hotel
18 New Tourist Hotel
20 Citadel Hotel
22 Palace Hotel
25 Hotel Zenobia

PLACES TO EAT
4 Palmyra Restaurant
7 Traditional Palmyra;
   Sindbad
10 Venus Restaurant
17 Tourist Cafe
19 Spring Restaurant
23 Al-Wadi Restaurant
26 Tourist Oasis
   Restaurant

OTHER
1 Post Office
3 Site of Proposed
   Tourist Office
5 Karnak Office
12 Coffeehouses
15 Laundry
16 Mosque
21 Museum
24 Tourist Office

friendly owner, Maher, speaks good English and can organise nights in the desert with Bedouin people; reception has a TV with CNN and you can get a beer. Rooms are spartan but clean, and cost S£250 per person with ensuite, or S£600 for a triple with shared facilities. You can also sleep on the roof for S£100. The hotel is away from the crowd, down a little side street by the Palmyra Restaurant.

Umayyad Palace (☎/fax 910 755, Saahat al-Jamarek) had only been open a few months when we visited and many rooms were still being built. It looked to have great potential with a lovely courtyard area, and we stayed in a fine ensuite double for a 'discount price' of S£400. However, there have been complaints about some sleazy behaviour by staff here, so female travellers should be wary.

Citadel Hotel (☎ 910 537, Sharia As'ad al-Amir), which is located opposite the east side of the museum, is a fairly nondescript place. It only has a small number of very simple rooms with shared facilities costing S£200 per bed, as well as a couple of en-

suite doubles that are severely overpriced at S£700.

Ishtar Hotel (see Places to Stay – Mid-Range & Top End) has some cheaper, basement doubles with shared facilities for S£500.

Places to Stay – Mid-Range & Top End
There are several mid-range hotels on Sharia al-Quwatli, the main hotel drag, but most are overpriced. If you have time it might be worth trawling through them to see if you can bargain for a more reasonable rate.

Hotel an-Nakheel (☎ 913 844, fax 910 744, Sharia an-Nasr) and *Hotel Odienat* (☎/fax 912 058, Sharia an-Nasr) are similarly gloomy two star establishments with dreary, run-down rooms priced nominally at US$17/24 for singles/doubles, but which can probably be had for less than half that – though even with a discount we'd still hesitate.

Palace Hotel (☎ 913 941, fax 911 707) is not bad at all, quiet and well looked after, and some of the rooms have good views of the ruins. The hotel is used frequently by French groups. Ensuite singles/doubles are listed at US$17/24 but, again, we were offered a generous discount.

Ishtar Hotel (☎ *913 073, fax 913 260, Sharia al-Quwatli*) is about the first place you come to, on the left, as you enter the town. It's new and modern and the rooms, if a little on the small side, are immaculately kept with clean sheets and fresh towels. Ensuite air-con singles/doubles are US$17/24. Discounts are most unlikely here as the place is good enough not to require such measures.

Heliopolis Hotel (☎ *913 921, fax 913 923*), which opened in 1998, is a five storey, three star place and probably marks the start of a trend to overload the small town with oversized accommodation. However, it has beautiful, large rooms with all modern facilities and unsurpassable views over the oasis to the ruins. Singles/doubles go for US$40/50.

Hotel Zenobia (☎ *910 107, fax 912 407*) is a really classic old establishment originally dating from the French Mandate, although little evidence of that bygone era remains. Unfortunately, these days it's also badly run (by the Damascus-based tourism company Orient Tours); we've received unverified complaints concerning, among other things, surly service, smelly plumbing and coaches consistently blocking the much-vaunted views of the ruins. Singles/doubles cost US$58/79 including breakfast. Visa, MasterCard and American Express are all accepted. For S£250, you can pitch a tent out the back, and hot showers are available.

Palmyra Cham Palace Hotel (☎ *912 231, fax 912 245*), by the Efca Spring some 2km south-west of the new part of town, is not one of the better hotels in this chain – the nearby funerary towers have more life and warmth in them. Singles/doubles cost US$150/180. Access to the swimming pool costs S£200 a day for nonguests.

Places to Eat

You don't come to Palmyra for the food. In fact, as far as dining goes, this may be among the worst places in Syria, alongside Tartus and Homs. Menus are almost without exception strictly limited to kofta, kebabs, spaghetti and chips, and despite the simple nature of the dishes, they're invariably badly prepared. Maybe you should bring sandwiches.

Most travellers seem to end up at one of the trio of restaurants on the main drag, Sharia al-Quwatli: ***Traditional Palmyra, Sindbad Restaurant*** next door, or ***Spring Restaurant*** across the street. There's little to choose between them. The food is no better than acceptable at each although the spicy soups are good. The *mensaf* (see Bedouin Cuisine in the Facts for the Visitor chapter) at Traditional Palmyra is also worth ordering (S£250 for two). All three have a pleasantly laid-back atmosphere and greatly benefit from the fact that there's little to do at night in Palmyra except take a street-side table and linger over a meal and several teas (none of the three serves beer).

Venus Restaurant on Sharia an-Nasr, just north of the main drag, is a relatively new place that's trying hard (friendly, enthusiastic staff) but serves very bland fare. It is, however, cheap and does serve beer.

Palmyra Restaurant on the main square, opposite the museum, does fairly awful food but the garden setting with fountains and plenty of leafy shade is extremely pleasant. Beer is served (S£75). ***Al-Wadi Restaurant*** at the southern end of Sharia As'ad al-Amir, past the Citadel Hotel and behind the museum, is similar – an open-air place with seating among the date palms. While we didn't get the chance to eat there, travellers' reports have been favourable.

Moving upmarket is not, unfortunately, any guarantee of a decent meal. The restaurant at ***Heliopolis Hotel*** does seriously lousy package-tour buffet food at S£250 a head – bland and boring *mezze* (starters), main courses from packets and tins, although with a couple of nice desserts. We didn't have the opportunity to dine at ***Hotel Zenobia*** but reports indicate that while you'll be paying around S£300 per person the food is nothing special.

Entertainment

Once the sun goes down and you can't look at the old stones any more, there's very little to do in Palmyra. But before the sun completely slips away, it's worth taking a seat at Hotel Zenobia's *outdoor terrace*, where the tables are Roman column capitals, and over a chilled beer (S£100) watch the ruins turn a flaming pink. The pity is the sun drops so very quickly and once it has gone the site is in complete darkness with only the monumental arch illuminated. However, back in the town a few of the restaurants do serve beer, most notably the open-air Palmyra Restaurant.

Plenty of travellers choose to hang out at the restaurants on Sharia al-Quwatli or at the *Tourist Cafe*, next to the mosque.

Getting There & Away

Bus/Minibus There is no luxury bus station in Palmyra; however, the Karnak bus company has its office on the main square opposite the museum. From here there are three buses a day on Tuesday, Friday and Sunday directly to Damascus (S£130, four hours), while Monday, Wednesday, Thursday and Saturday there is just one Damascus service, which goes via Homs (S£65, two hours) and takes 4½ hours to reach Damascus. North-east from Palmyra, there are five buses a day to Deir ez-Zur (S£75, three hours) and one to Qamishle (S£160, six hours), which goes via Hassake (S£135, five hours).

Otherwise, you can try to jump on any of the buses that regularly pass through enroute between Damascus and Deir ez-Zur (and beyond). For Deir ez-Zur, try waiting at one of the restaurants on the Deir ez-Zur highway (head north about 1.5km up Sharia As'ad al-Amir, to where the highway forms into a T-junction about 200m past the last tree). The Damas Tour company is ensconced in the Sahara Restaurant out here, and offers regular runs to Damascus, Deir ez-Zur, Hassake and Qamishle and fares are about 30% more expensive than Karnak's.

There is also a bus station north of the centre with frequent departures to Damascus, Deir ez-Zur and Homs but the vehicles are old and many are minibuses rather than large, air-con buses. The fares are about half to two-thirds those of Karnak. To get to the station, walk west out of town past the Al-Assad Gardens and north to a T-junction; at this junction, bear right, then take the first left. In all it's about a 1km walk from the museum.

QASR AL-HEIR ASH-SHARQI

If you have some spare cash, a worthwhile excursion is to head 120km north-east of Palmyra into the desert to see one of the most isolated and startling monuments to Umayyad Muslim rule in the 8th century AD. The palace here held a strategic position, commanding desert routes into Mesopotamia. As support from the nomadic Arab tribes (of which they themselves were a part) was one of the main Umayyad strengths, it is no coincidence that they made their presence felt in the desert steppes.

The palace complex and rich gardens, once supplied by an underground spring about 30km away, covered a rough square with 16km sides. Built by Hisham around 730 AD, the palace long outlived its Umayyad creators. Haroun ar-Rashid, perhaps the best known of the Abbasid rulers, made it one of his residences, and evidence suggests that it was only finally abandoned in the 14th century.

The partly restored walls of one of the main enclosures, with their mighty defensive towers, are the most impressive remaining sign of what was once a sumptuous anomaly in the harsh desert. The ruins to the west belong to what may well have been a *khan* (merchants' inn). In the south-eastern corner are remnants of a mosque – the column with stairs inside between the two areas was a minaret. The remains of baths are just to the north of the main walls. Traces of the old perimeter wall can just be made out to the south, and in fact border the best track leading here from the highway.

This castle has a counterpart south-west of Palmyra, Qasr al-Heir al-Gharbi, but little of interest remains at that site (its impressive facade has been superimposed over that of the National Museum in Damascus).

Getting There & Away

The only way to get to Qasr al-Heir ash-Sharqi is by private transport. A planned asphalted road will, if it's ever laid, considerably facilitate the trip, but until then a 4WD is probably the best way to cover the last part of the ride. This leg is about 35km north from the town of As-Sukhna, which is just off the Palmyra-Deir ez-Zur highway. You could probably manage the trip in a Renault 4 or something similar (the higher the chassis the better). A local driver or guide, at least from As-Sukhna, is indispensable. In the unlikely event that it has rained in the previous days (it does happen), it is best not to attempt the drive – getting bogged in the desert is hardly fun.

You can arrange with a local to go from Palmyra – your hotel or hostel can usually arrange this, or try the people at the New Afqa or Citadel hotels. Prices start at S£2000 (roughly US$40) for the car and you'll be doing well to get them below S£1500. Take plenty of water and some food with you. Unless you end up in one of the few Bedouin houses scattered around the desert (none is very close to the site) for a cup of tea, it can be a thirsty trip, especially if your driver or guide gets lost in the labyrinth of tracks left in the desert by Bedouin pick-ups.

The Euphrates River

The Euphrates River ('Al-Furat' in Arabic) starts out high in the mountains of eastern Anatolia in Turkey and winds through the north-east of Syria into Iraq, finally emptying into the Shatt al-Arab waterway and the Persian Gulf – a total distance of more than 2400km. Like a cool green ribbon, it makes a change to see some water and fertile land after all the steppes and desert of the interior.

One of the few tributaries of the Euphrates, the Kabur, flows down through north-eastern Syria to join it below Deir ez-Zur. These two rivers make it possible to irrigate and work the land, and the cotton produced in this area has become an important source of income for the country.

The Jezira (literally 'island'), bounded loosely by the Kabur and, further east, the Tigris (which just touches Syria on its way from Turkey into Iraq), constitutes some of the richest land in the country. Locals say the best of it is to be found in the strip just south of the Turkish border, an area that is mostly populated by Kurds. Cotton and wheat are the two big crops.

Oilfields at Qaratchok in the far north-eastern corner of the country produced oil for nearly three decades, but it was only low-grade stuff that had to be mixed with better imported oil for refining.

Big high-grade oil finds around Deir ez-Zur in the 1980s changed all that. Production from the area, which had until then stood at zero, has plateaued at nearly 400,000 barrels a day, two-thirds of the country's total. National and foreign companies are searching for more reserves, but there are fears this small-scale oil bonanza may already have peaked.

LAKE AL-ASSAD

By the time the Euphrates enters Syria at Jarablos (once the capital of the Neo-Hittite empire) it is already a very mighty river. To harness that power for irrigation and hydro-electricity production, one of the Assad

Highlights

- **Rasafa** – striking ruins of a remote walled city half-buried in the desert sands (see page 274)
- **Dura Europos** – little to see at the ancient site itself but the setting overlooking the Euphrates River is wonderful (see page 279)

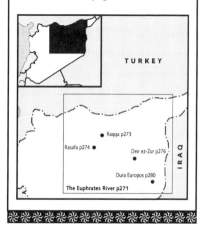

TURKEY

Raqqa p273

Rasafa p274

Deir ez-Zur p276

Dura Europos p280

The Euphrates River p271

IRAQ

regime's most ambitious plans, to dam the Euphrates, went into effect in the 1960s.

Work began at Tabaqah in 1963 and the reservoir started to fill in 1973. Now that it's full, it stretches for some 60km. The dam is Syria's pride and joy and the electricity produced was supposed to make the country self-sufficient.

The flow of the Euphrates, however, has been reduced by the construction of the Ataturk dam in Turkey, and Syria and Iraq are concerned that the Turks may at any time decide to regulate the flow for political reasons. The decision by Istanbul in late 1995 to proceed with construction of a further dam, the Birecik, has only served to

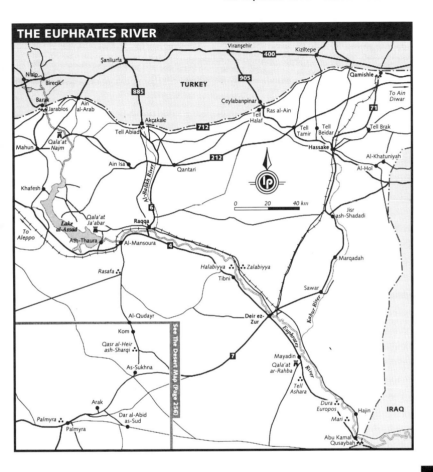

THE EUPHRATES RIVER

heighten the two Arab countries' worst fears. The Turks deny all claims of having thus far used their position to reduce the flow of the river, attributing any slowing down to natural causes.

While the lack of water in the river has been a disappointment, the regular power cuts that were once a daily reality across the country have been all but eliminated.

The dormitory town of Ath-Thaura (the Revolution) was built at Tabaqah to accommodate the dam workers and peasants who had to be relocated because of the rising water levels. Not only were the villages inundated but also some sites of both historical and archaeological importance. With aid from UNESCO and other foreign missions, these were investigated, documented and, whenever possible, moved to higher ground. The 27m-high minaret of the Maskana Mosque and the 18m-high minaret from Abu Harayra were both segmented and then transported, the latter to the centre of Ath-Thaura.

QALA'AT NAJM

Qala'at Najm, the northernmost castle of its kind along the Euphrates in Syria, has been partly restored. Originally built under Nur ad-Din (Nureddin) in the 12th century, it was later reconstructed under Salah ad-Din (Saladin). It commands a natural defence position over the Euphrates plain, and the views out across what was once a strategic crossing point are alone worth some effort.

Watch out for the warden – he or his son will soon get wind of your presence and invite you in for a friendly cup of tea in their house at the foot of the castle. The hand will then be out for a friendly bit of baksheesh.

To get here, take a bus for Ain al-Arab from the east bus station in Aleppo (S£30, two hours) and get off at the village of Haya Kebir (tell people on board where you want to go). You may be able to get an Ain al-Arab bus from the station behind Aleppo's Amir Palace hotel, too. From Haya Kebir it's 15km to the castle, and hitching is the only way.

The earlier you get going the better, as there is not a lot of traffic on this dead-end trail. The road passes through rolling wheat fields that form a cool green carpet in spring. It appears there are no buses at all to Ain al-Arab on Fridays.

QALA'AT JA'ABAR & ATH-THAURA

Impressive from a distance, Qala'at Ja'abar, a citadel built entirely of bricks in classic Mesopotamian style, does not add up to all that much once you're inside. It is situated on a spit of land connected to the bank of Lake al-Assad, about 15km north of Ath-Thaura. Before the lake was built, the original castle had rested on a rocky perch since before the arrival of Islam, and had then been rebuilt by Nur ad-Din and altered by the Mamluks.

The castle makes a great backdrop for a day by the lake, and on Friday this is an extremely popular spot with Syrians. It's a great place for a picnic. It is also an ideal place for a swim, unless you happen to be a woman, in which case it could be decidedly uncomfortable.

You will have to pass through Ath-Thaura to get to the citadel, and it may be worth a quick visit anyway to have a look at the dam. The town itself, however, has nothing at all to recommend it and is a confusing place to get around when searching for the right road to the citadel or anywhere else. Even the buses don't seem to terminate in the same place. Ask about and you will, eventually, work it out.

Getting There & Away

Without your own car, Qala'at Ja'abar can be a pain to get to. You'll have to go via Ath-Thaura, either coming from Raqqa (S£25 by microbus) or Aleppo (S£50 by bus). Raqqa is the much closer base; from Aleppo it can be a long and hassle-filled day. From the centre of Ath-Thaura, you have to head out towards the north of town and try to hitch across the dam (as-sidd). The turn-off for the citadel is a few kilometres further on to the left. From here it is about 10km.

Friday is a good day to hitch across the dam, as the place is truly crowded with day-trippers. If you want peace and quiet on the other days, be prepared for longer waits, or negotiate with a local driver to take you out (expect to pay about S£200).

Note that there are few, if any, buses or microbuses from Ath-Thaura to anywhere after about 4 pm.

RAQQA

These days it's a small dusty town with little to detain a traveller, but from 796 to 808 AD, the city of Raqqa (then Ar-Rafika) was a glorious place that served as a summer residence of the legendary Abbasid caliph Haroun ar-Rashid, of *The Thousand and One Nights* fame. The area around the city had been the site of numerous cities that had come and gone in the preceding millennia, including Nikephorion, founded by the Seleucids (sometimes attributed by legend to Alexander the Great). After the Mongol invasion in 1260, Ar-Rafika virtually ceased to exist. It is only since the end of WWII that it has again come to life and become an important Euphrates basin commercial centre.

PAUL DOYLE

CHRISTOPHER WOOD

Palmyra, an astonishing ruined city in the middle of the Syrian desert, is now the country's prime tourist attraction. Restoration has seen the number of standing columns increase from 150 in the 1950s to more than 300 today.

Palmyra's funerary towers held up to five levels of coffins and were decorated with friezes.

Entrance to funerary tower

The 17th century Arab castle, Qala'at ibn Maan

Carved stone from the Camp of Diocletian

RAQQA

1 Al-Rashid Restaurant
2 Ammar Hotel
3 Al-Waha Restaurant
4 Clock Tower
5 Hotel Tourism
6 Aladdin
7 Museum
8 Bank
9 Post Office
10 Assad Statue
11 Bus Station
12 Microbus Station

Things to See & Do

Only a few scant, badly worn remnants that barely hint of the city's old glory remain. The partly restored **Bab Baghdad**, Raqqa's only remaining city gate, lies about a 10 minute walk to the east of the clock tower, a central landmark when you arrive in the city. The old **Abbasid city wall**, restored at some points to a height of 5m, runs north from the gate past the **Qasr al-Banaat** (Maidens' Palace), which served as a residence under the Ayyubids.

To the north-east are the remains of the old **Great Mosque**, built during the reign of the Abbasid caliph Al-Mansur in the 8th century and reconstructed in 1165 by Nur ad-Din. It is slowly being replaced in importance by an Iranian-financed monstrosity behind the Bab Baghdad, although given the lack of progress in building, it is tempting to think someone has run out of money.

A small **museum**, halfway between the Bab Baghdad and the clock tower, has some interesting artefacts from excavation sites in the area that have been worked on since the 1920s. The museum is open from 9 am to 6 pm daily except Tuesday, and entry costs S£200 (students S£25).

Every day but Friday, an impressively sized livestock market is held early in the morning about 2km north of Bab Baghdad. Follow the city wall to the end and ask for the *souq ad-dawab*.

Places to Stay

There are a few hotels around the clock tower, all of them amazingly expensive considering that none is particularly appealing.

Ammar Hotel (☎ 222 612, Sharia al-Quneitra), just north of the clock tower, has very basic, grotty rooms with shared shower and toilet facilities for S£400 a double. Don't accept the kind offers of coffee or tea – they'll only be added to the bill at double the normal price.

Hotel Tourism (☎ 220 725, Sharia al-Quwatli), one block east of the clock tower, is gloomy but the rooms are reasonably clean and have their own cold showers (though toilet facilities are shared). It charges S£300/500 for singles/doubles.

Places to Eat

Aladdin, just across from the museum, is about the best there is. The food is nothing special (chicken or kebabs) but at least the interior is fan-cooled and airy and the place is reasonably clean.

Other options include ***Al-Rashid Restaurant (Sharia al-Malek Faisal)***, which is very run down, or ***Al-Waha Restaurant (Sharia ath-Thaura)*** which does a set meal known as *wajabeh*, including soup, rice and stew, for S£100.

Getting There & Away

Bus There's a new bus station about 200m south of the clock tower. Several different bus companies have their offices here and between them there are quite regular bus services to Aleppo (S£85, 2½ hours), Damascus (S£225, seven hours) and Deir ez-Zur (S£60, two hours).

Microbus From the microbus station, about 200m south of the clock tower (on the road leading out of town), there are regular microbuses west to Al-Mansoura (S£15), Ath-Thaura (S£25) and Aleppo (S£90, three hours).

Train The train station in Raqqa does not inspire confidence. Its windows are smashed, doors are boarded up, and there was an awful stink coming from what we presume must have been the toilet block. But a guy we found sleeping on a bare mattress in a back room assured us that a train for Aleppo came through at 4 am each day and there was one for Deir ez-Zur and on to Qamishle at 2 am. To get to the station walk north up Sharia al-Quneitra and its continuation At-Tahrir for about 2km.

RASAFA

This startling walled city lies in the middle of nowhere, rising up out of the featureless desert. Possibly inhabited in Assyrian times, Diocletian established a fort here as part of a defensive line against the Sassanian Persians (or Sassanids) late in the 3rd century AD. A desert road led through Rasafa from the Euphrates south to Palmyra, a trail that can be followed today with a 4WD and guide or adequate orienteering skills. About this time a cult to the local martyr St Sergius began to take hold, so that by the 5th century the place had been expanded and an impressive basilica had been raised.

A century later, Emperor Justinian further expanded the centre's defences against Persian assault, but in the end the real threat emerged from another quarter – the Muslim Arab invasion of the 630s. The city was eventually taken over by the Umayyad caliph, Hisham, who built a palatial summer residence here. The Abbasids completely destroyed the residence some years after Hisham's death in 743 and thereafter the city fell into ruin. The Mongols finished the job when they swept across northern Syria in the 13th century.

The walls, enclosing a quadrangle measuring 550m by 400m, are virtually all complete. As you enter by the northern gate, you are confronted by the immensity of the place, mostly bare now save for the churches inside. Little excavation has yet been done here. You can walk along the complex defensive perimeter before exploring the site.

Three churches remain standing. The grandest is the partially restored **St Sergius basilica**. The wide central nave is flanked by two aisles, from which it is separated by a series of sweeping arches each resting on pillars and a pair of less ambitious arch and column combinations. This and the two other churches date from the 6th century. In the south-western corner of the complex lie huge underground **cisterns** (watch your step) that could keep a large garrison supplied with water through long sieges.

Speaking of water, there is nobody at the site selling the stuff, or anything else for that matter, so bring food and water with you – it gets stinking hot in summer.

Admission to the site costs S£300.

Getting There & Away

It requires quite a bit of patience to get to Rasafa as transport is infrequent. Catch a microbus from Raqqa to Al-Mansoura (S£15,

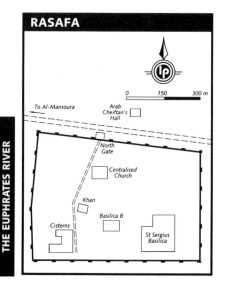

RASAFA

0   150   300 m

To Al-Mansoura

Arab Cheiftan's Hall

North Gate

Centralised Church

Khan

Cisterns

Basilica B

St Sergius Basilica

20 minutes) – that's the easy bit. Now it's just a matter of waiting at the signposted turn-off for a pick-up to take you the 35km to the ruins for about S£20. Wait a while and one *will* turn up eventually. If you're impatient, you can ask one of the pick-up drivers lounging around here to take you there and back for some extraordinary sums – S£200 would not be unusual. Or you could always try hitching.

HALABIYYA & ZALABIYYA

Halabiyya was founded by Zenobia, the rebellious Palmyrene leader, in the years immediately preceding her fall in 272 AD. It was later refortified under Emperor Justinian, and it is mainly the result of his work that survives today.

The fortress town was part of the Byzantine empire's eastern defensive line against the Persians, who took it in 610 AD. The walls are largely intact, and there are remnants of the citadel, basilicas, baths, a forum and the north and south gates. The present road follows the course of the old colonnaded street.

Across the river and further south is the much less intact forward stronghold of the main fort, Zalabiyya. In summer, the Euphrates is sometimes passable between the town and the fort, which is what made Zalabiyya necessary.

Getting There & Away

Neither Halabiyya or Zalabiyya is easy to get to. Halabiyya is the more interesting of the two, and at least the first stage of this hike is straightforward enough. Get a Deir ez-Zur bus from Raqqa and get out at the Halabiyya turn-off. From here you'll have to hitch or, if you feel up to it, do the two hour walk. Alternatively, negotiate with a local to take you out there – this could cost you up to S£500 for the round trip.

For Zalabiyya, the hardest bit is getting back. There aren't many buses plying the right bank of the Euphrates, and that's what makes the return trip a pain. If you're here in the afternoon, you'll just have to sit it out and hope for a passing truck.

The train line passes by Zalabiyya, and you could follow it north a couple of kilometres to a small station and wait for a train – locals swear they actually stop here.

DEIR EZ-ZUR

Deir ez-Zur ('Deir' to the locals) is a busy little market town by the Euphrates. On weekdays its streets are filled with colourfully dressed peasants from the surrounding countryside, in town to buy and sell produce at the small but thriving *souq* (market) around the main square. While it did become something of a boom town in the early 1990s with the discovery of high-grade oil in the surrounding area, this does not seem to have affected the essential character of the place in any way.

That character is heavily influenced by Deir's distance from Damascus and proximity to Iraq. The dialect spoken here is much rougher than the Syrian Arabic spoken elsewhere in the country and some of the vocabulary even differs – for instance, the standard Syrian greeting of *kifak*, in Deir becomes *shlonak*.

Deiri culture is also heavily influenced by the Bedouin, something that comes through very clearly in the music produced locally which is very raw and simple. If you want to listen, look out for a tape called *Warda* by Housen al-Hasan, which you should be able to find in the cassette shops around town – it has one excellent track called 'Fatouma' which seemed to be playing in every microbus and taxi around here at the time of our last visit.

Many travellers find themselves stopping over in Deir enroute to Qamishle or the ancient sites of Mari and Dura Europos. Although there really isn't that much to see in town, it does benefit from a pleasant riverside setting and it's interesting enough for a night or two.

Orientation

The centre of town is the main square, Saahat 8 Azar, a scruffy, dusty place that catches the overspill from the busy souq on its east side. The main north-south road,

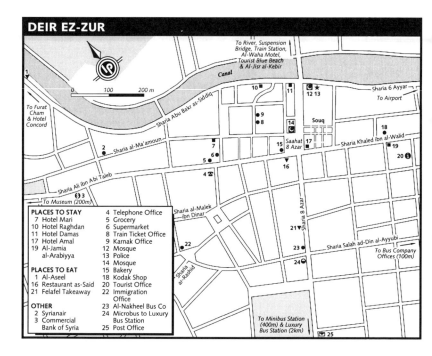

DEIR EZ-ZUR

To River, Suspension
Bridge, Train Station,
Al-Waha Motel,
Tourist Blue Beach
& Al-Jisr al-Kebir

Canal

To Furat
Cham
& Hotel
Concord

To Airport

Sharia 6 Ayyar

Sharia Abu Bakr as-Siddiq

Sharia al-Ma'amoun

Souq

Sharia Khaled ibn al-Walid

Saahat
8 Azar

Sharia Ali ibn Abi Taleb

To Museum (200m)

Sharia 8 Azar

Sharia al-Malek
ibn Dinar

Sharia
ar-Rashid

Sharia Salah ad-Din al-Ayyubi

To Bus Company
Offices (100m)

To Minibus Station
(400m) & Luxury
Bus Station (2km)

PLACES TO STAY		
7	Hotel Mari	
10	Hotel Raghdan	
11	Hotel Damas	
17	Hotel Amal	
19	Al-Jamia	
	al-Arabiyya	

PLACES TO EAT	
1	Al-Aseel
16	Restaurant as-Said
21	Felafel Takeaway

OTHER	
2	Syrianair
3	Commercial
	Bank of Syria

4	Telephone Office
5	Grocery
6	Supermarket
8	Train Ticket Office
9	Karnak Office
12	Mosque
13	Police
14	Mosque
15	Bakery
18	Kodak Shop
20	Tourist Office
22	Immigration
	Office
23	Al-Nakheel Bus Co
24	Microbus to Luxury
	Bus Station
25	Post Office

which runs from the river through the square and down on past the new post office to the microbus station is called Sharia 8 Azar. This is bisected by the main east-west axis, which also runs through the square and is called Sharia Khaled ibn al-Walid to the east, and Sharia Ali ibn Abi Taleb to the west.

The body of water flowing just north of the square is not the Euphrates/Al-Furat but a tributary canal; the river itself is 500m north, straight up Sharia 7 Nissan, the continuation of Sharia 8 Azar.

Information

Tourist Offices The tourist office (☎ 226 150) is in a side street off Sharia Khaled ibn al-Walid, about a 10 minute walk east of the main square. It's not particularly helpful but the staff are friendly and they do have a very good free map that also covers the Raqqa and Hassake areas. The office is open from 9 am to 2 pm daily except Friday.

Visa Extensions Deir ez-Zur is a good place to extend your visa; the process takes only about half an hour and we got an extension of two months with no questions asked. You need two photos and it costs S£25. To find the office, walk south from the telephone office, then diagonally across the square turning right onto Sharia ar-Rashid; the immigration office is a low concrete building on your right. It's open from 8 am to 1.30 pm daily except Friday.

Money The Commercial Bank of Syria is about a 10 minute walk west of the main square along Sharia Ali ibn Abi Taleb. It takes travellers cheques, for which there's a commission of S£25. The bank is open from 8.30 am to 12.30 pm daily except Friday.

You can also change money at the Furat Cham hotel.

Post & Communications The big new post office, halfway between the main square and the minibus station on Sharia 8 Azar, opens daily from 8 am to 8 pm (to 1 pm on Friday). For phone calls, there's an office on Sharia Ali ibn Abi Taleb, 250m west of the main square; it's open from 8 am to 10 pm daily except Friday.

Museum

Opened in 1996, Deir ez-Zur's museum is a fair bit better than most other museums in Syria, outside of Damascus. While the pieces in the collection may not individually be as valuable or striking as those in the big national museums, for once the presentation of the exhibits is excellent and there are detailed explanations provided in a number of languages including English. The focus of the collection is on prehistoric and ancient Syria, and some of the most important finds from digs in the Euphrates and Jezira region are on show. Very laudably, the artefacts are backed up by text, drawings, diagrams and models that provide the historical context sorely missing from all Syria's other museums. There are also smaller sections devoted to Classical Syria and the Arab Islamic period.

The museum is about 1km west of the centre on Saahat ar-Reis (President Square), out along Sharia Ali ibn Abi Taleb. It's open from 8 am to 6 pm daily except Tuesday and admission is S£300 (students S£25).

River

To get to the main body of the Euphrates you need to cross the canal and head north up Sharia 7 Nissan (the continuation of Sharia 8 Azar) for 500m. You hit the river at a point where it's crossed by a narrow 400m-long **suspension bridge** that is for pedestrians and bicycles only. This is a favourite place with the locals for an evening promenade. On the other side of the bridge is a small recreation ground where the local boys swim.

Places to Stay – Budget

The budget options in Deir ez-Zur are really bad. In the past most backpackers used to stay at *Hotel Damas (☎ 221 481)* on the corner of Sharia 8 Azar overlooking the canal, but we no longer recommend this place – it's filthy and battered to the point of being uninhabitable. More objectionable is that we've received several letters from female travellers warning about being spied on and hassled while staying there.

The alternatives are hardly better from a hygienic point of view. *Hotel Amal (☎ 222 245)* on the corner of the main square is a dump where singles/doubles cost S£200/250 (some quite remarkable odours waft out of the loos), while the clutch of crummy places along Sharia Khaled ibn al-Walid are definite no-go zones. The exception may be *Al-Jamia al-Arabiyya (☎ 221 371)* down near the tourist office, which actually had clean sheets, hot showers and a friendly manager. It charged S£200 per person.

Places to Stay – Mid-Range & Top End

Many budget travellers wisely opt to spend a little more in Deir ez-Zur and find a room in a mid-range hotel. The pity is these too are all way overpriced for what they offer – they're actually budget-style places but with dollar room rates.

Hotel Raghdan (☎ 222 053, fax 221 169, Sharia Abu Bakr as-Siddiq) overlooking the canal has grotty air-con singles/doubles for US$17/23 with bathroom, or US$14/20 without.

Hotel Mari (☎ 224 340, fax 221 657) is even worse value than the Raghdan; rooms are very badly looked after but cost US$24/33, while the staff were thoroughly unpleasant.

For those who can afford to spend more, the place to stay would be *Al-Waha Motel* which we only heard about after leaving Deir and so didn't visit; however, we were told that the place is new, very smart and reasonably priced. It's beside the train station on the north bank of the river, 500m east of the suspension bridge.

Otherwise you can rub shoulders with foreign oil-company employees at *Furat Cham* (☎ *225 418, fax 225 950),* 5km out of town along the river where rooms go for US$160/190. Nonguests can use the pool for S£200 a day. A little closer to town and inland from the river, there's also *Hotel Concord* (☎ *225 411, fax 224 272)* with rooms for US$130/160 plus 10% taxes.

Places to Eat

Just as accommodation options are severely limited in Deir, there isn't a lot of choice when it comes to eating, either. One good fall back is an excellent felafel takeaway on Sharia 8 Azar about 200m south of the square. A filling sandwich will cost S£15. You can recognise the place by its red and white tiling.

Otherwise, there are numerous shwarma, chicken and kebab places along Sharia Khaled ibn al-Walid but none of them appear particularly appealing. One exception is *Restaurant as-Said* on the south-west side of the main square, a very basic kebab and grilled chicken place but one that stands out from the competition by virtue of having some notion of hygiene. The meat comes with salad and fries and the full meal will cost around S£100.

Al-Aseel (Sharia Abu Bakr as-Siddiq) is a small place beside the canal, about 800m west of the centre. It has outside seating in summer and an indoor restaurant for the colder months but, most importantly, according to one longtime expat resident it does the best kebabs in all Syria. We never got there, so we can't confirm this but given the generally dire food situation in Deir, it's got to be worth a visit. For the same sort of fare, *Cairo Restaurant*, across the road from the canal and the Al-Aseel, also isn't too bad.

There are also a couple of restaurants on the south bank of the Euphrates – *Tourist Blue Beach* just to the north of the suspension bridge and *Al-Jisr al-Kebir* ('Big Canal') just to the south. Both are little more than open-air terraces but with excellent riverside settings that go some way to compensate for indifferent, overpriced food. Beer is also served, although that too is extremely pricey at S£75 for a bottle of the local stuff.

Hotel Mari has a rooftop restaurant that also does pretty lousy food but is an OK place to sit and sink a few beers (S£45) accompanied by *mezze*.

Self-Catering There is an excellent little hole-in-the-wall *bakery* on the south-east corner of the main square where huge flat disks of hot bread (S£5) are pulled out of the clay ovens continually between 5 am and 11 pm daily except Friday. For condiments to add to your bread there's a decent *supermarket* just around the corner from Hotel Mari and a *grocery* round the corner from that, opposite the telephone office.

Getting There & Away

Air The airport is about 7km east of town and the twice-weekly flight between Deir ez-Zur and Damascus costs S£600. A shuttle bus runs from the Syrianair office (☎ 221 801), a block east of the bank, which is open from 8.30 am to 12.30 pm daily closed Friday.

Luxury Bus The new luxury bus station is 2km south of town, at the end of Sharia 8 Azar. There's a local microbus service (S£5) from a stop about a five minute walk south of the main square, on the right-hand side, otherwise a taxi (ask for 'al-karaj') will cost you S£25. Several companies have their offices here and between them they offer regular services to Damascus (S£175, seven hours) via Palmyra (S£100, three hours) and to Aleppo (S£135, five hours) via Raqqa (S£60, two hours).

There's little need to book in advance – just show up and get a ticket. However, if you want to be certain of getting a particular bus, then Qadmous, Al-Furat and Raja all have town centre offices on Sharia Salah ad-Din al-Ayyubi, about 400m east of Sharia 8 Azar – none of the companies have signs in English but they are all in the block past the mosque.

Services to Hassake (S£75, two hours) and Qamishle (S£110, three hours) are less frequent, and in fact to the latter there's only one service a day, operated by Qadmous and departing at 3.30 pm. The Al-Nakheel bus company, whose town centre office is on Sharia 8 Azar, has regular Hassake-only services but it's still advisable to book a day in advance.

Karnak Karnak has its office in a horrible concrete mall-type building off the north-west corner of the main square. Its services to/from Deir ez-Zur are very limited – at the time of research they went to Aleppo and Palmyra only.

Minibus The minibus station is on Sharia 8 Azar about 1km south of the main square. From here there's an hourly minibus to Raqqa (S£60, two hours) and plenty to Hassake in the north-east (S£75) and on to Qamishle on the Turkish border (S£125). There are also frequent departures to Abu Kamal (often pronounced 'bukaMEL') by minibus (S£30) and by microbus (S£50).

Train The train station is across the river to the north of town, about 3km from the centre. If you feel like a half-hour walk, cross the suspension bridge, continue to the T-junction and turn right. The alternative is to catch one of the yellow shuttle buses that run from the train ticket office to the train station for S£5. These only run when a train is due to leave. The train ticket office is in town in the concrete mall north-east of the main square, open from 9 am to 1 pm and 4 to 8 pm daily.

The train to Aleppo leaves at 1.30 am daily (S£90/60 in 1st/2nd class, S£225 for a sleeper), while the Damascus service departs at 8.30 pm daily (S£155/105 in 1st/2nd class, S£455 for a sleeper). Several trains run to Hassake and on to Qamishle (S£60/40, three hours), although, typically, all but the 12.30 pm service are in the early hours of the morning. Anyway, the bus trip is much more interesting as it follows the heavily cultivated region alongside the Kabur River, passing through a series of mud-brick villages.

SOUTH-EAST OF DEIR EZ-ZUR

The route south-east of Deir ez-Zur follows the Euphrates River down to the closed Iraqi border, and is dotted with sites of archaeological and historical interest. The impatient traveller with a car could visit the lot and be back in Deir ez-Zur for dinner on the same day. With a very early start, it might just be possible to do the same with a combination of microbuses and hitching.

Qala'at ar-Rahba

The 13th century defensive citadel of Qala'at ar-Rahba, which was finally abandoned after the battles between Mongol invaders and the Mamluks subsided, is a few kilometres south of the town of Mayadin. You can see it in the distance (it's about 4km west of the main road) shortly after leaving Mayadin.

Like many castles it is more impressive from the outside than in, but the views of the desert to the west, and the Euphrates and occasional oilfield to the east, are really quite breathtaking. Take the Abu Kamal minibus/microbus, ask the driver where to get off, and walk out (about an hour).

Tell Ashara

Just 17km south of Mayadin is the sleepy village of Ashara. Three sites that date back to the early centuries AD are being excavated by Italian teams, but there is not a lot of real interest here. An old mud-brick mosque, with only a fragile eight storey minaret surviving, is the main item of note. Most of the area under excavation overlooks or lies near the Euphrates. From Deir ez-Zur you need to catch the Abu Kamal minibus/microbus and ask where to be let off.

Dura Europos

For the uninitiated, the extensive, largely Hellenistic/Roman fortress city of Dura Europos is by far the most intriguing site to visit on the road from Deir ez-Zur to Abu Kamal.

Based on earlier settlements, the Seleucids founded Europos here in around 280 BC. The town also retained the ancient Assyrian name of Dura (wall or fort), and is

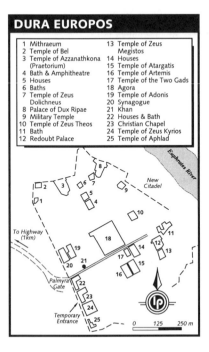

DURA EUROPOS

1 Mithraeum	13 Temple of Zeus
2 Temple of Bel	Megistos
3 Temple of Azzanathkona	14 Houses
(Praetorium)	15 Temple of Atargatis
4 Bath & Amphitheatre	16 Temple of Artemis
5 Houses	17 Temple of the Two Gads
6 Baths	18 Agora
7 Temple of Zeus	19 Temple of Adonis
Dolichneus	20 Synagogue
8 Palace of Dux Ripae	21 Khan
9 Military Temple	22 Houses & Bath
10 Temple of Zeus Theos	23 Christian Chapel
11 Bath	24 Temple of Zeus Kyrios
12 Redoubt Palace	25 Temple of Aphlad

now known to locals as Tell Salhiye. The desert plateau abruptly ends in a wall of cliffs dropping 90m into the Euphrates here, making this the ideal location for a defensive installation.

In 128 BC the city fell to the Parthians and remained in their hands (although under the growing influence of Palmyra) until the Romans succeeded in integrating it into their defensive system in 165 AD. As the Persian threat to Roman pre-eminence grew, so did the importance of Dura Europos. It is famous for its reputed religious tolerance, seemingly confirmed by the presence of a church, synagogue (now in the National Museum in Damascus) and other Greek, Roman and Mesopotamian temples side by side.

The Sassanian Persians seized control of the site in 256 AD, and from then on its fortunes declined. French and Syrian archaeologists continue to work on the site.

Ruins The western wall stands out in the stony desert 1km east of the main road; its most imposing element is the **Palmyra Gate**. You will have to deal with a gun-toting guardian here, to whom you must pay your S£150 (students S£10) admission.

Just inside the Palmyra Gate and past some houses and a bath was a Christian chapel to the right, and a synagogue to the left. The road leading towards the river from the gate passed Roman **baths** on the right, a **khan** on the left and then the site of the Greek **agora**.

Opposite the agora are the sites (little remains) of three temples dedicated to Artemis, Atargatis and the Two Gads. The original Greek temple to Artemis was replaced by the Parthians with a building along more oriental lines, characterised by an internal courtyard surrounded by an assortment of irregular rooms. These were added to over the years, and even included what appears to have been a small theatre for religious gatherings. In the block next door, the temple dedicated to Atargatis was built along similar lines. Precious little remains of the temple of the Two Gads, where a variety of gods were worshipped.

At the north-western end of the city the Romans installed themselves, building barracks, baths, a small amphitheatre and a couple of small temples, one to Zeus Dolichenus. West of the **new citadel**, which commands really extraordinary views over the Euphrates Valley, the Romans placed their **Palace of Dux Ripae**, built around a colonnaded courtyard of which nothing much is left.

Getting There & Away Any microbus between Abu Kamal and Deir ez-Zur will drop you on the highway (it takes an hour to get here from Deir). Ask to be dropped off at Tell Salihye and the site is clearly visible from the road about 1km distant.

Mari

The ruins of Mari (Tell Hariri), an important Mesopotamian city dating back some 5000 years, are about 10km north of Abu Kamal.

THE EUPHRATES RIVER

The mud-brick ruins are the single greatest key serving to unlock the door on the very ancient past of Mesopotamia, but while they are fascinating for their age, they do not grab the neophyte's imagination as much as you might hope.

The most famous of Mari's ancient Syrian leaders, and about the last of its independent ones, was Zimri-Lim, who reigned in the 18th century BC and controlled the most important of the trade routes across Syria into Mesopotamia, making his city-state the object of several attacks. The **Royal Palace of Zimri-Lim** was enormous, measuring 200m by 120m with more than 300 rooms. Today sheltered from the elements by a modern protective roof, the palace remains the main point of interest of the whole site. The city was finally destroyed in 1758 BC by the Babylonians under Hammurabi. Before this, Mari had not only been a major commercial centre but also an artistic hothouse, as the many fragments of ceramics and wall paintings discovered since 1933 amply attest.

Large chunks of pottery lie scattered all over the place, but most of the good stuff is on display in the museums in Aleppo, Damascus and the Louvre. Excavations begun in 1933, financed largely by the French, revealed two palaces (including Zimri-Lim's), five temples and the remains of a **ziggurat**, a kind of pyramidal tower peculiar to Mesopotamia and usually surmounted by a temple. Perhaps more importantly, a great many archives in Akkadian – some 25,000 clay tablets – were also discovered, providing valuable insights into the history and workings of this ancient city-state. French teams continue to work at the site.

Although attributed to Zimri-Lim, the Royal Palace had been around for hundreds of years by the time he came to the throne. Comprising a maze of almost 300 rooms disposed around two great courtyards, it was protected by earthen ramparts. Interpretations of what each room was used for vary. For instance, some say the room directly south of the central courtyard is a throne room, others say it is a sacred hall dedicated to a water goddess. It appears that the area to the north-west of the central courtyard served as the royal living quarters, the baths located immediately to the right (directly north of the central courtyard).

Just to the south-east of the palace complex are the ziggurat and several temples. A temple to Ishtar stood to the west of the palace. Admission is S£300 (students S£25).

Getting There & Away There is a microbus from Abu Kamal that goes right by Mari. It leaves from a side street east of the square and takes about half an hour by a circuitous route (S£10). Alternatively if you are coming from Deir ez-Zur, buses will drop you at the turn-off from the highway (ask for Tell Hariri). From this same spot it is normally possible to hitch a ride or pick up a passing microbus for the return trip to Deir ez-Zur.

Abu Kamal

Abu Kamal (also known as Albu Kamal) is a frontier town 140km south-east of Deir ez-Zur, close to the Iraqi border. This border has been closed for some years because of

One of the finds at Mari includes this statue of a water goddess, dating from around 1800 BC.

Syria's support for Iran in the first Gulf War, and its subsequent participation in the anti-Iraq coalition after Baghdad's invasion of Kuwait in 1990. The frontier is about 10km out of town.

Places to Stay & Eat There only appears to be one cheap hotel in the centre – the *Jumhuriyya* (there is no sign in English), on Sharia Alrifi (off Sharia Baghdad) two blocks south of the main square. Ask around for directions. It has pretty awful doubles for S£300 and cold water only. There are a few cafes and cheap eateries around the square.

Getting There & Away Most buses and microbuses leave from the main square or nearby. The microbuses to Deir ez-Zur follow a set timetable and cost S£50. They are a better deal than the older, slower minibuses that leave only when full and charge S£30.

The microbus for Mari leaves from a side-street east of the square (S£10, 30 minutes).

Some bus companies have their offices on Sharia Baghdad, the main drag through town that passes by the square. Al-Furat is one of them, and it has three buses a day to Damascus (S£185), two to Aleppo (S£150) and one to Homs (S£160). The Al-Halab company runs cheaper, older buses from the square.

The North-East

Bordered by Turkey and Iraq, there are no major monuments or must-see sites in the north-eastern corner of the country, but this does not mean it is empty of attractions. Perhaps the greatest is the chance to meet the Kurds, a people without a state, who have yet to give up their struggle. Only about one million of a total of some 20 million Kurds live in Syria. The rest are spread across south-eastern Turkey, northern Iraq and north-western Iran.

The area between the Kabur and Tigris rivers, also known as the Jezira, is an increasingly rich agricultural zone, helped along by underground aquifers and the irrigation schemes born of the Lake al-Assad project on the Euphrates to the west. The heavy crude oilfields right up in the northeast corner have paled into insignificance beside the fields around Deir ez-Zur.

The numerous *tells* (artificial hills) dotted around the place are a sign that this area has been inhabited since the 3rd millennium BC, its mainstay being the wheat and cotton crops that still predominate. They are increasingly attracting archaeological teams, and although there is generally precious little for the uninitiated to see, you can visit the sites so long as you respect the teams' work. They are generally present in spring and summer. **Tell Brak**, 45km north of Hassake, was excavated under the direction of one Max Mallowan, Agatha Christie's husband (see the boxed text 'Agatha Christie & Sir Max').

Since 1992 a Franco-Syrian team has been digging at **Tell Beidar**, 35km northwest of Hassake. Some of the tablets found there are on display in the museum at Deir ez-Zur.

HASSAKE

The capital of the *muhafaza* (governorate) of the same name, Hassake doesn't offer the visitor an awful lot to do, but it's not a bad base from which to explore the area, unless you're planning on entering Turkey, in which case you may as well push on to Qamishle.

Orientation & Information

The main drag is Sharia Fares al-Khouri, which ends at the statue of Assad. From the statue, Sharia Jamel Abdel Nasser leads to the central square and clock tower. There is a Commercial Bank of Syria on this road and it opens daily except Friday from 8.30 am to 12.30 pm. You can change cash and travellers cheques.

Places to Stay & Eat

There are two basic hotels near the clock tower. *Heliopolis* has simple singles/doubles for S£175/275, much better than those at *Hotel Ramsis*, for the same price. Close

Agatha Christie & Sir Max

Agatha Christie's husband was Sir Max Mallowan, a noted archaeologist who in the late 1930s excavated in north-east Syria.

Between 1934 and 1939, accompanied by his already famous crime-writing wife, he spent summer seasons at Chagar Bazar, 35km north of Hassake, where they had built a mud-brick house with a beehive dome. While at Chagar Bazar, Mallowan was also digging at Tell Brak, 30km to the east, where he unearthed the remains of the so-called 'Eye Temple', the finds from which are displayed in Aleppo's national museum. During this time, Agatha wrote.

Surprisingly, given all the time spent in the country, Syria did not find its way into any of her mysteries. During this time she instead dreamed up *Appointment With Death*, set around Petra, which she and Max had visited on one of their journeys home, and *Murder on the Orient Express*, set aboard the train on which she frequently travelled between Europe and Aleppo.

Her time on site did result, however, in a charming autobiographical work called *Come, Tell Me How You Live* (now out of print). This is the tale of an archaeologist's wife, a lively account of hiring mouse-killing cats, disinterring corpses and constipation. Solving murders seems a breeze by comparison.

---

to the Heliopolis, *Hotel Ugarit* has pretty unenticing dens for S£200/325. Some 50m further on, *Cassr al-Hamra* (☎ *226 307*) may have grand pretensions, but at US$18/22 plus US$2 for a shower, it offers barely more than the Heliopolis.

Near the sports ground in the east end of the town is the best deal in town, *Stars Hotel* (☎ *313 250*) with doubles for US$22 and singles at whatever price you can negotiate. *Hotel Sanabel* (☎ *224 283*) has singles starting at US$12 and doubles ending at US$30. It's OK, but avoid the windowless rooms.

There are a few of the usual places to eat around the centre, mostly run by Iraqi Christians from the nearby refugee camp at Al-Hol. *Karnak Restaurant, (Sharia Hafez al-Assad)* offers copious quantities of felafel, homous, shwarma, fuul and the like for around S£200 per person, and it has a garden too.

Getting There & Away

Bus The more expensive luxury buses to Damascus cost S£250 and take about seven hours. Companies like Hatab operate such services from Sharia Jamel Abdel Nasser. The trip to Deir ez-Zur takes just over two hours and costs S£75. Al Salam buses serve Aleppo (S£150, four hours) and Homs (S£250).

Microbus The station to head to for destinations like Qamishle, Deir ez-Zur and Ras al-Ain is about 2km north of the town centre. You can catch a shuttle there from a sidestreet just east of the clock tower for S£5.

If you want to inspect Tell Beidar, take a Derbassieh microbus (S£20). For Tell Brak, pick up a Qamishle bus and get out at the turn-off for the village. From the village it's about 2km.

Train To get to the train station, walk about 50m north along Sharia Fares al-Khouri and turn left. The train station is at the end of the street – about a 10 minute walk. There are at least two departures a day for Qamishle (S£30/24 in 1st/2nd class). There are up to three departures a day for Deir ez-Zur, Raqqa and Aleppo, but only one continues (direct) to Damascus.

Service Taxi The service-taxi station is just south of the bridge on the left-hand side. Hiring a taxi to yourself to visit Tell Beidar would cost S£700, round trip.

RAS AL-AIN

There's not a lot to this largely Kurdish town on the Turkish border (you cannot cross here), but there's a chance you'll be invited to eat with the locals. Don't be surprised if the subject of conversation turns to politics. The Kurds are not much more pleased with their position in Syria than elsewhere, and discretion may be the better part of valour when chatting. In summer, the attraction is the restaurant in the main park (near the road to Hassake), where they set the tables in the shin-deep water from nearby sulphur springs. You cool your heels as you eat.

Three kilometres away is **Tell Halaf**, the site of an ancient northern Mesopotamian settlement discovered in 1899 by Baron Max von Oppenheim, a Prussian engineer overseeing the construction of the much trumpeted Berlin-Baghdad railway. Although plenty more artefacts are said by locals to be buried here, you'll see nothing other than a bald artificial hill. The bulk of what was found went to Berlin and was destroyed in WWII. Some artefacts had replicas made and can be seen at Aleppo's national museum, including the giant basalt statues at its entrance.

Getting There & Away

The microbus from Hassake, about 75km away, takes about 1½ hours and costs S£45. No public transport returns in the afternoon, especially on Friday and holidays; other than this you should be OK until 4 pm.

QAMISHLE

Situated at a crossing point on the Turkish border in the north-east, Qamishle is full of Kurds and Turks and the cheaper hotels will sometimes quote prices in Turkish lire rather than Syrian pounds.

There is nothing to see in Qamishle, but the mix of people makes it an intriguing spot. Because of its proximity to the border, be prepared for passport checks at the hotels (even during the night), and when getting on or off buses or trains. The Turkish border is only about 1km from the town centre.

Note, you cannot drive across the border here but must walk. The crossing is open (in theory) only from 9 am to 7 pm.

Places to Stay & Eat

About 100m south of the microbus station is the town's top establishment, the two star *Hotel Semiramis* (☎ 421 185), which costs foreigners US$15/22/24 for clean singles/doubles/triples with fan. Expatriate workers in the oilfields often stay here.

Just around the corner is *Chahba Hotel*, which is certainly nothing to write home about and asks S£100 a bed (women must take a double). The upstairs terrace is OK, though.

Mamar, a block south, is better value, although a tad more expensive at S£300/400 for singles/doubles. The rooms featuring balconies are quite good, and there is hot water.

The cheapest and lousiest is *Umayyad Hotel*, in a sidestreet across from the Semiramis. A bed here costs S£100, although you may find yourself being charged for a double.

In Sharia al-Wahida, which crosses the northern end of the main drag, *Hadaya Hotel* (☎ 420 141) is not exactly the friendliest place on earth, and the rooms are certainly nothing special either. They cost US$15/22.

Across from the Chahba is a pleasant *restaurant* with an outdoor section. A good meal of kebabs and the usual side orders of humous, fuul and other mezze will cost about S£200.

Getting There & Away

Air The airport is 2km south of town. Take a taxi or any Hassake-bound bus. The Syrianair office is just off the main street, two blocks south of the Semiramis. There are three flights a week to Damascus (S£900).

Bus Several Pullman and more expensive private companies operate buses from Qamishle to most major destinations. The better buses run from a station opposite the Gabriel Restaurant, south-east along Sharia Zaki al-Arsuzi, the street that runs beside the river. The trip to Damascus takes up to 10 hours and costs around S£340. For Aleppo, reckon on at least six to eight hours and S£175. More rickety buses do the same trips from another station and cost as little as S£150 and S£90 respectively.

Microbus The microbus station is on the main street, 100m north of the Semiramis. There are departures for Hassake, Ras al-Ain and Al-Malkyer in the east.

Train The train station is a long way from the centre, and you'll have to catch a taxi. There is, however, a booking office in the centre, virtually opposite Chahba Hotel. It's open from 8.30 am to 3 pm and 4.30 to 6 pm daily. Up to three trains go as far as Aleppo (S£132/87 in 1st/2nd class, S£350 for a sleeper), and one or two proceed all the way to Damascus (S£200/135 and S£560 respectively). The Damascus train, calling at all stops along the line, can take from 16 to 19 hours.

AIN DIWAR

In the extreme north-east corner of the country is an impressive medieval bridge over the Tigris. Unfortunately, relations between Turkey and Syria are not brilliant, and a Syrian border garrison may stop you from getting out to it – they say because the Turkish border troops tend to shoot first and ask questions later. You may have guessed that there is no crossing here.

There are great views from the plateau (which may be as far as you can safely get) which overlooks the Tigris, north-east to the snowcapped mountains of southern Turkey, and east to Jebel Zakho in Iraq (some locals call it Jebel Barzani, after one of the rebel Kurdish leaders there). On a clear day, you might just make out mountains in Iran through the gap between Jebel Zakho and the Turkish ranges.

If you want to try your luck, take a microbus from Qamishle to Al-Malkyer (S£45, two hours). From there, negotiate with one of the kids to take you out on a motorbike, or just hitch. Bear in mind that there is not much traffic on this last stretch of road.

Language

Arabic is the official language of Syria. Though French is also spoken – and English is rapidly gaining ground – any effort to communicate with the locals in Arabic will be well rewarded. No matter how far off the mark your pronunciation or grammar might be, you'll often get the response (usually with a big smile): 'Ah, you speak Arabic very well!'. Greeting Syrian officials, who are often less than helpful, with *salām alaykum* (peace be upon you), will often work wonders.

Learning a few basics for day-to-day travelling doesn't take long at all, but to master the complexities of Arabic would take years of consistent study. The whole issue is complicated by the differences between Classical Arabic (Fus-ha), its modern descendant MSA (Modern Standard Arabic) and regional dialects. The classical tongue is the language of the Quran and Arabic poetry of centuries past. For long it remained static, but in order to survive it had to adapt to change, and the result is more or less MSA, the common language of the press, radio and educated discourse. It is as close to a *lingua franca* (common language) as the Arab world comes, and is generally understood – if not always well spoken – across the Arab world.

As it happens, the spoken dialects of Syria are not too distant from MSA. For most outsiders trying to learn Arabic, the most frustrating element remains understanding the spoken language (wherever you are), there is virtually no written material to refer to for back up. Acquisition of MSA is a long-term investment: an esoteric argument flows back and forward about the relative merits of learning MSA first (and so perhaps having to wait some time before being able to communicate adequately with people in the street) or a dialect. All this will give you an inkling of why so few non-Arabs, or non-Muslims, embark on a study of the language.

Pronunciation

Pronunciation of Arabic can be tongue-tying for someone unfamiliar with the intonation and combination of sounds. Pronounce the transliterated words slowly and clearly.

This language guide should help, but bear in mind that the myriad rules governing pronunciation and vowel use are too extensive to be covered here.

Vowels

Technically, there are three long and three short vowels in Arabic. The reality is a little different, with local dialect and varying consonant combinations affecting their pronunciation. This is the case throughout the Arabic-speaking world. More like five short and five long vowels can be identified:

a	as the 'a' in 'had'
e	as the 'e' in 'bet'
i	as the 'i' in 'hit'
o	as the 'o' in 'hot'
u	as the 'oo' in 'book'

A macron over a vowel indicates that the vowel has a long sound:

ā	as the 'a' in 'father'
ī	as the 'e' in 'ear', only softer
ū	as the 'oo' in 'food'

Consonants

Pronunciation for all Arabic consonants is covered in the alphabet table on the following page. Note that when double consonants occur in transliterations, both are pronounced. For example, *el-hammam* (toilet), is pronounced 'el-ham-mam'.

Other sounds

Arabic has two sounds that are very tricky for non-Arabs to produce, the 'ayn and the glottal stop. The letter 'ayn represents a sound with no English equivalent that

The Arabic Alphabet

Final	Medial	Initial	Alone	Transliteration	Pronunciation
ـا			ا	ā	as the 'a' in 'father'
ـب	ـبـ	بـ	ب	b	as in 'bet'
ـت	ـتـ	تـ	ت	t	as in 'ten'
ـث	ـثـ	ثـ	ث	th	as in 'thin'
ـج	ـجـ	جـ	ج	g	as in 'go'
ـح	ـحـ	حـ	ح	H	a strongly whispered 'h', almost like a sigh of relief
ـخ	ـخـ	خـ	خ	kh	as the 'ch' in Scottish *loch*
ـد			د	d	as in 'dim'
ـذ			ذ	dh	as the 'th' in 'this'
ـر			ر	r	a rolled 'r', as in the Spanish word *caro*
ـز			ز	z	as in 'zip'
ـس	ـسـ	سـ	س	s	as in 'so', never as in 'wisdom'
ـش	ـشـ	شـ	ش	sh	as in 'ship'
ـص	ـصـ	صـ	ص	ş	emphatic 's'
ـض	ـضـ	ضـ	ض	ḍ	emphatic 'd'
ـط	ـطـ	طـ	ط	ţ	emphatic 't'
ـظ	ـظـ	ظـ	ظ	ẓ	emphatic 'z'
ـع	ـعـ	عـ	ع	'	the Arabic letter 'ayn; pronounce as a glottal stop – like the closing of the throat before saying 'Oh oh!' (see Other Sounds on p.286)
ـغ	ـغـ	غـ	غ	gh	a guttural sound like Parisian 'r'
ـف	ـفـ	فـ	ف	f	as in 'far'
ـق	ـقـ	قـ	ق	q	a strongly guttural 'k' sound; in Egyptian Arabic often pronounced as a glottal stop
ـك	ـكـ	كـ	ك	k	as in 'king'
ـل	ـلـ	لـ	ل	l	as in 'lamb'
ـم	ـمـ	مـ	م	m	as in 'me'
ـن	ـنـ	نـ	ن	n	as in 'name'
ـه	ـهـ	هـ	ه	h	as in 'ham'
ـو			و	w	as in 'wet'; or
				ū	long, as the 'oo' on 'food'; or
				aw	as the 'ow' in 'how'
ـي	ـيـ	يـ	ي	y	as in 'yes'; or
				ī	as the 'e' in 'ear', only softer; or
				ay	as the 'y' in 'by' or as the 'ay' in 'way'

Vowels Not all Arabic vowel sounds are represented in the alphabet. See Pronunciation on p. 286.

Emphatic Consonants Emphatic consonants are similar to their nonemphatic counterparts but are pronounced with greater tension in the tongue and throat.

comes even close. It is similar to the glottal stop (which is not actually represented in the alphabet) but the muscles at the back of the throat are gagged more forcefully – it has been described as the sound of someone being strangled. In many transliteration systems 'ayn is represented by an opening quotation mark, and the glottal stop by a closing quotation mark. To make the transliterations in this language guide (and throughout the rest of the book) easier to use, we have not distinguished between the glottal stop and the 'ayn, using the closing quotation mark to represent both sounds. You should find that Arabic speakers will still understand you.

Transliteration

It's worth noting here that transliteration from the Arabic script into English – or any other language for that matter – is at best an approximate science.

The presence of sounds unknown in European languages and the fact that the script is 'defective' (most vowels are not written) combine to make it nearly impossible to settle on one universally accepted method of transliteration. A wide variety of spellings is therefore possible for words when they appear in Latin script – and that goes for places and people's names as well.

The whole thing is further complicated by the wide variety of dialects and the imaginative ideas Arabs themselves often

---

The Transliteration Dilemma

TE Lawrence, when asked by his publishers to clarify 'inconsistencies in the spelling of proper names' in *Seven Pillars of Wisdom* – his account of the Arab Revolt in WWI – wrote back:

'Arabic names won't go into English. There are some "scientific systems" of transliteration, helpful to people who know enough Arabic not to need helping, but a washout for the world. I spell my names anyhow, to show what rot the systems are.'

---

have on appropriate spelling in, say, English (and words spelt one way in Jordan may look very different again in Syria, heavily influenced by French); not even the most venerable of western Arabists have been able to come up with a satisfactory solution.

While striving to reflect the language as closely as possible and aiming at consistency, this book generally spells place, street and hotel names and the like as the locals have done. Don't be surprised if you come across several versions of the same thing.

Pronouns

I	*ana*
you	*inta* (m)/*inti* (f)
he	*huwa*
she	*hiyya*
we	*naHnu/eHna*
you	*ento*
they	*humma*

Greetings & Civilities

Arabs place great importance on civility and it's rare to see any interaction between people that doesn't begin with profuse greetings, enquiries into the other's health and other niceties.

Arabic greetings are more formal than in English and there is a reciprocal response to each. These sometimes vary slightly, depending on whether you're addressing a man or a woman. A simple encounter can become a drawn-out affair, with neither side wanting to be the one to put a halt to the stream of greetings and well-wishing. As an *ajnabi* (foreigner), you're not expected to know all the ins and outs, but if you come up with the right expression at the appropriate moment they'll love it.

The most common greeting is *salām alaykum* (peace be upon you), to which the correct reply is *wa alaykum as-salām* (and upon you be peace). If you get invited to a birthday celebration or are around for any of the big holidays, the common greeting is *kul sana wa intum bi-khīr* (I wish you well for the coming year).

After having a bath or shower, you will often hear people say to you *na'iman*, which roughly means 'heavenly' and boils down to an observation along the lines of 'nice and clean now, huh'.

Arrival in one piece is always something to be grateful for. Passengers will often be greeted with *al-Hamdu lillah al as-salāma* – 'thank God for your safe arrival'.

Hi.	*marHaba*
Hello.	*ahlan wa sahlan* or just *ahlan* (Welcome)
Hello. (response)	*ahlan bēk*
Goodbye.	*ma'a salāma/ Allah ma'ak*
Good morning.	*sabaH al-khayr*
Good morning. (response)	*sabaH 'an-nūr*
Good evening.	*masa' al-khayr*
Good evening. (response)	*masa 'an-nūr*
Good night.	*tisbaH 'ala khayr*
Good night. (response)	*wa inta min ahalu*

Basics

Yes.	*aiwa/na'am*
Yeah.	*ay*
No.	*la*
Please. (request)	*min fadlak* (m)/ *min fadlik* (f)
Please. (formal)	*law samaHt* (m)/ *law samaHti* (f)
Please. (come in)	*tafaddal* (m)/ *tafaddali*(f)/ *tafaddalū* (pl)
Thank you.	*shukran*
Thank you very much.	*shukran jazīlan*
You're welcome.	*'afwan/ahlan*
Pardon/Excuse me.	*'afwan*
Sorry!	*āsif!*
No problem.	*mish mushkila/ mū mushkila*
Never mind.	*maalesh*
Just a moment.	*laHza*
Congratulations!	*mabrouk!*

Small Talk

Questions like 'Is the bus coming?' or 'Will the bank be open later?' generally elicit the inevitable response: *in sha' Allah* – 'God

willing' – an expression you'll hear over and over again. Another common one is *ma sha' Allah* – 'God's will be done' – sometimes a useful answer to probing questions about why you're not married yet.

How are you?	*kayf Hālak?* (m)/ *kayf Hālik?* (f)
How are you?	*shlonak?* (m)/ *shlonik?* (f)
Fine.	*al-Hamdu lillah* (lit: Thanks be to God)
What's your name?	*shu-ismak?* (m)/ *shu-ismik?* (f)
My name is ...	*ismi ...*
Pleased to meet you. (departing)	*furṣa sa'ida*
Nice to meet you.	*tasharrafna* (lit: you honour us)
Where are you from?	*min wayn inta?*

I'm from ...	*ana men ...*
Algeria	*al-jazīr*
Australia	*ustrālya*
Canada	*kanada*
Egypt	*masir*
Europe	*oropa*
Japan	*yaban*
Libya	*libya*
Morocco	*maghreb*
New Zealand	*nyu zīlanda*
South Africa	*afrika el janubiya*
Tunisia	*tūnes*
the USA	*amerka*

Are you married?	*inta mutajawwiz?* (m)/ *inti mutajawwiza?* (f)
Not yet.	*mesh Halla*
How old are you?	*ay 'amrak?* (m)/ *kam sana 'andak?* (f)
I'm 20 years old.	*'andī 'ashrīn sana*
I'm a student.	*ana tālib* (m)/ *ana tāliba* (f)
I'm a tourist.	*ana sa'iH* (m)/ *ana sa'iHa* (f)
Do you like ...?	*inta batHib?*
I like ...	*ana baHib ...* (m)/ *ana uHib...* (f)
I don't like ...	*ana ma baHib ...* (m)/ *ana lā uHib ...* (f)

Language Difficulties

Do you speak English?	*bitiHki inglīzi?*
	Hal tatakallam(i) inglīzi?
I understand.	*afham*
I don't understand.	*ma bifham la afham*
I speak ...	*ana baHki .../*
	ana atakallam ...
English	*inglīzi*
French	*faransi*
German	*almāni*
I speak a little Arabic.	*ana behke arabe shway*
I don't speak Arabic.	*ana ma behke arabe*
I want an interpreter.	*urīd mutarjem*
Could you write it down, please?	*mumkin tiktabhu, min fadlak?*
What does this mean?	*yānī ay?*
How do you say ... in Arabic?	*kayf taqul ... bil'arabi?*

Getting Around

Where is ...?	*wayn ...?*
airport	*al-matār*
bus station	*maHattat al-bās/ maHattat al-karaj*
railway station	*maHattat al-qitār*
ticket office	*maktab at-tazākar*
What time does ... leave/arrive?	*sa'a kam biyitla'/ biyusal...?*
aeroplane	*tīyara*
boat/ferry	*al-markib/as-safina*
bus	*al-bās*
train	*al-qitār*
I want to go to ...	*ana badeh rūh ala ...*
Which bus goes to ...?	*aya otobīs beh rūh ala ...?*
Does this bus go to ...?	*hal otobīs beh rūh ala ...?*
How many buses per day go to ...?	*kam otobīs be rūh ben wa'har ...?*
How long does the trip take?	*kam as-sa'a ar-raHla?*

Please tell me when we get to ...	*omol mārūf elleh hamma nūsal ...*
Stop here, please.	*wakef, omal mārūf*
Please wait for me.	*ntov, omal mārūf*
May I sit here?	*feneh ekād Hon?*
1st class	*daraja ūla*
2nd class	*daraja thāni*
ticket	*at-tazkarah*
to/from	*ila/min*
Where can I hire a ...?	*wayn feneh esta'jer ...?*
bicycle	*al-'ajila*
car	*as-sayyāra/ārabeye*
motorcycle	*motosaikul*
guide	*ad-dalīl*

Directions

How do I get to ...?	*kīf būsal ala ...?*
Can you show me (on the map)?	*wayn (fil kharīta)?*
How many kilometres?	*kam kilometre?*
What ... is this?	*shū ... hey?*
street/road	*ash-sharia*
village	*al-qariyya*
on the left	*'ala yasār/shimāl*
on the right	*'ala yamīn*
opposite	*muqābil*
straight ahead	*'ala tūl/sawa/dugri*
at the next corner	*tanī zarūb*
this way	*min hon*
here/there	*hon/honāk*
in front of	*amām*
near	*qarīb*
far	*ba'īd*
north	*shimāl*
south	*junub*
east	*sharq*
west	*gharb*

Around Town

I'm looking for ...	*ana abHath ...*
Where is the ...?	*wayn ...?*
bank	*al-masraf/al-bank*
beach	*ash-shāti'*
chemist/pharmacy	*as-sayidiliyya*

city/town	*al-medīna*
city centre	*markaz al-medīna*
customs	*al-jumruk*
entrance	*ad-dukhūl*
exchange office	*masref*
exit	*al-khuruj*
hotel	*al-funduq*
information	*isti'lāmāt*
market	*as-sūq*
mosque	*al-yamā'/al-masjid*
museum	*al-matHaf*
old city	*al-medīna qadīma*
passport &	*maktab al-jawazāt*
immigration	*wa al-hijra*
office	
police	*ash-shurṭa*
post office	*maktab al-barīd*
restaurant	*al-maṭa'am*
telephone office	*maktab at-telefon*
temple	*al-ma'abad*
tourist office	*maktab as-siyaHa*

I want to change ...	*baddeh sarref ...*
money	*maṣāri*
travellers cheques	*sheket msefrīn*

What time does it open/close?	*aymata bteftah/ byeftah?*
I'd like to make a telephone call.	*fene talfen omol mārūf*

Paperwork
date of birth	*tarīkha al-mūlid*
name	*ism*
nationality	*jensīya*
passport	*jawaz as-safar*
permit	*tasrīH*
place of birth	*makan al-mūlid*
visa	*sima*

Accommodation
I'd like to book a ...	*feneh ehjuz ...*
Do you have a ...?	*fī ...?*
(cheap) room	*ghurfa (rkīsa)*
single room	*ghurfa mufrada*
double room	*ghurfa bi sarīrayn*

for one night	*la leile waHde*
for two nights	*leiltēn*

Can I see it?	*mumkin atfarraj-ha?*
It's very noisy/ dirty.	*fī khēr dajeh/waṣaq*
How much is it per person?	*qad aysh li kul waHid?*
How much is it per night?	*adeh bel leil?*
Where is the bathroom?	*Wayn al-Hammam?*
We're leaving today.	*eHna musafirīn al-youm*

address	*al-'anwān*
air-conditioning	*kondishon*
blanket	*al-baṭāniyya*
camp site	*mukhaym*
electricity	*kahraba*
hotel	*funduq*
hot water	*mai Harra/sākhina*
key	*al-miftaH*
manager	*al-mudīr*
shower	*dūsh*
soap	*sabūn*
toilet	*twalet/mirhad*

Food
I'm hungry/thirsty.	*ana ju'ān/aṭshān*
What is this?	*ma hādha?/ shu hādha?*
I'd like ...	*bheb ...*
Another ... please.	*... waHid kamān, min fadlak*

breakfast	*al-fuṭūr*
dinner	*al-'ashā*
food	*al-akl*
grocery store	*al-mahal/al-baqaliyya*
hot/cold	*harr/bārid*
lunch	*al-ghada*
restaurant	*al-maṭ'am*
set menu	*tabak*

Vegetarianism is a nonconcept in the Middle East. Even if you ask for meals without meat, you can be sure that any gravies, sauces etc will have been cooked with meat or animal fat. See Food in the Facts for the Visitor chapter for more information.

Shopping

Where can I buy ...?	*wayn feneh eshtereh ...?*
What is this?	*shu hadha?*
How much?	*qad aysh/bikam?*
How many?	*kam waHid?*
How much money?	*kam fulūs?*
That's too expensive.	*mayda ghalī khēr*
Is there ...?	*fi ...?*
There isn't (any).	*ma fi*
May I look at it?	*feneh etallā 'alaya?*

chemist/pharmacy	*farmasiya*
laundry	*gaṣīl*
market	*sūq*
newsagents	*maktaba*

big	*kabīr*
bigger	*akbar*
cheap	*rakhīs*
cheaper	*arkhas*
closed	*maghlūq/musakkar*
expensive	*ghāli*
money	*al-fulūs/al-maṣāari*
open	*maftūH*
small/smaller	*ṣaghīr/as-ghar*

Time & Date

What's the time?	*as-sā'a kam?*
When?	*matā/emta?*
now	*Halla'*
after	*bādayn*
on time	*al waket*
early	*bakīr*
late	*ma'qar*
daily	*kil youm*
today	*al-youm*
tomorrow	*bukra/ghadan*
day after tomorrow	*ba'ad bukra*
yesterday	*imbārih/ams*
minute	*daqīqa*
hour	*sā'a*
day	*youm*
week	*usbū'*
month	*shahr*
year	*sana*
morning	*soubeh*
afternoon	*bād deher*

evening	*massa*
night	*leil*

Monday	*al-itnein*
Tuesday	*at-talata*
Wednesday	*al-arbi'a*
Thursday	*al-khamīs*
Friday	*al-jum'a*
Saturday	*as-sabt*
Sunday	*al-aHad*

Months

The Islamic year has 12 lunar months and is 11 days shorter than the western (Gregorian) calendar, so important Muslim dates will fall 11 days earlier each (western) year. There are two Gregorian calendars in use in the Arab world. In Egypt and westwards, the months have virtually the same names as in English (January is *yanāyir*, October is *octobir* and so on), but in Jordan, Syria and eastwards, the names are quite different. Talking about, say, June as 'month six' is the easiest solution, but for the sake of completeness, the months from January are:

January	*kanūn ath-thani*
February	*shubāt*
March	*azār*
April	*nisān*
May	*ayyār*
June	*Huzayrān*
July	*tammūz*
August	*'āb*
September	*aylūl*
October	*tishrīn al-awal*
November	*tishrīn ath-thani*
December	*kānūn al-awal*

Numbers

Arabic numerals are simple to learn and, unlike the written language, run from left to right. Pay attention to the order of the words in numbers from 21 to 99.

0	·	şifr
1	١	waHid
2	٢	itnein/tintein
3	٣	talāta
4	٤	arba'a
5	٥	khamsa
6	٦	sitta
7	٧	saba'a
8	٨	tamanya
9	٩	tis'a
10	١٠	'ashara
11	١١	Hid-'ashr
12	١٢	itn-'ashr
13	١٣	talat-'ashr
14	١٤	arba'at-'ashr
15	١٥	khamast-'ashr
16	١٦	sitt-'ashr
17	١٧	saba'at-'ashr
18	١٨	tamant-'ashr
19	١٩	tisa'at-'ashr
20	٢٠	'ashrīn
21	٢١	waHid wa 'ashrīn
22	٢٢	itnein wa ashrīn
30	٣٠	talātīn
40	٤٠	'arba'īn
50	٥٠	khamsīn
60	٦٠	sitteen
70	٧٠	saba'īn
80	٨٠	tamanīn
90	٩٠	tis'īn
100	١٠٠	mia
101	١٠١	mia wa waHid
200	٢٠٠	miatein
300	٣٠٠	talāta mia
1000	١٠٠٠	alf
2000	٢٠٠٠	alfein
3000	٣٠٠٠	talāt-alaf

Ordinal Numbers

first	awal
second	tanī
third	talet
fourth	rabeh
fifth	khames

The Hejira months, too, have their own names:

1st	MoHarram
2nd	Safar
3rd	Rabi' al-Awal
4th	Rabei ath-Thāni
5th	Jumāda al-Awal
6th	Jumāda al-Akhira
7th	Rajab
8th	Shaban
9th	Ramadan
10th	Shawwal
11th	Zuul-Qeda
12th	Zuul-Hijja

PLACE NAMES

Damascus

Al-Merjeh	المرجه
Damascus	دمشق
Jebel Qassioun	جبل قاسيون
Salihiyya	الصالحية
Sayyida Zeinab Mosque	جامع السيدة زينب
Souq al-Hamidiyya	سوق الحميدية
Souq Saroujah	سوق ساروجه

Around Damascus

Ad-Dumeir	الضمير
Ain al-Fijeh	عين الفيجه
An-Nabk	النبك
Baalbek	بعلبك
Bludan	بلودان
Maalula	معلول
Mar Musa	مار موسى
Seidnayya	صيدنايا
Sirghayya	سرقايا
Zabadani	الزبداني

The Hauran

Bosra	بصره
Der'a	درعا
Ezra'a	ازرع
Khan Arnabah	خان أرنبة
Qanawat	قناوات
Quneitra	القنيطرة
Shahba	شهبا
Suweida	السويدا

The Coast & Mountains

Al-Haffa	الحفه
Al-Hamidiyya	الحميدية
Amrit	عمريت
Arwad	أرواد
Baniyas	بانياس
Hosn Suleiman	حصن سليمان
Jabla/Baniyas	بانياس / جبلة
Krak des Chevaliers	قلعة الحصن
(Qala'at al-Hosn)	
Lattakia	أللاذقية
Qala'at Marqab	قلعة مرقب
Qala'at Salah ad-Din	قلعة صلاح الدين
Ras al-Bassit	رأس البسيط
Safita	صافيتا
St George's	دير سان جورج
Monastery	
Shaati al-Ahlam	شاطئ الاحلام
Slunfeh	صلنفه
Tartus	طرطوس
Ugarit (Ras Shamra)	رأس شمرا

Orontes Valley

Al-Anderine	العندرين
Al-Ghab	الغاب
Al-Hamra	دير صليب الحمره
Apamea	أفاميا
Deir Soleib	دير صليب
Hama	حماه
Homs	حمص
Maharde	محرده
Musyaf	مصياف
Qala'at al-Mudiq	قلعة المضيق
Qala'at ash-Shmemis	قلعة الشميس
Qala'at Burzei	قلعة برزاي
Qala'at Sheisar	قلعة شيزار
Qasr ibn Wardan	قصر إبن وردان
Salamiyya	السلمية
Sarouj	ساروج
Suqeilibiyya	سقيلبيه
Twalid Dabaghein	توالد دباقين

Aleppo

Ain Dara	عين داره
Al-Bara	البارى
Aleppo	حلب
Al-Jdeida	الجديدة
Azaz	عزاز
Babila	بابيلا
Cyrrhus (Nabi Houri)	النبي حوري
Daret Azze	ديرة عزة

Ebla (Tell Mardikh)	تل مرديخ
Harim	حارم
Jerada	جاراده
Kafr Nabl	كفر نبل
Ma'arat an-Nu'aman	مغارة النعمان
(Al-Ma'ara)	
Mahardiyya	محارديه
Nahr Afreen	نهر عفرين
Qala'at Samaan	قلعة سمعان
Qalb Lozeh	قلب لوزه
Qatura	قطوره
Ruweiha	رويحه
Serjilla	سرجيله
Shinshira	شنشيره

The Desert

Palmyra (Tadmor)	تدمر
Qala'at ibn Maan	قلعة إبن معان
Qasr al-Heir al-Gharbi	قصر الحير الغربي
Qasr al-Heir ash-	قصر الحير الشرقي
Sharqi	

The Euphrates River

Abu Kamal	البوكمال
Ain al-Arab	عين العرب
Ain Diwar	عين ديوار
Al-Malkyer	المالكية
Al-Mansur	المنصورة
Ath-Thaura	الثورة
Deir ez-Zur	دير الزور
Derbassieh	الدرباسية
Dura Europos (Tell Salhiye)	تل صالحية
Halabiyya	حلبيه
Hassake	الحسكة
Haya Kebir	حيا كبير
Lake al-Assad	بحيرة الاسد
Mari (Tell Hariri)	تل حريري
Mayadin	الميادين
Qala'at ar-Rahba	قلعة الرحبة
Qala'at Ja'abar	قلعة جعبر
Qala'at Najm	قلعة نجم
Qamishle	القامشلي
Raqqa	الرقة
Rasafa	رصافا
Ras al-Ain	رأس العين
Tell Ashara	تل عشاره
Tell Beidar	تل بيدر
Tell Brak	تل براك
Tell Halaf	تل حلف
Tibni	التبني
Zalabiyya	زلبيه

Glossary

abd – servant of
abeyya – women's gown
ablaq – alternating courses of coloured stone
abu – father, saint
acropolis – citadel of an ancient city (usually Greek)
ain – well, spring

bab (s), **abwab** (pl) – gate or door
bahr – river
baksheesh – tip
baladi – local, rural
beit – house
bey – term of respect
bir – spring, well
birket – lake
burj – tower

caliph – Islamic ruler; also spelt 'khalif'
capital – the top, decorated part of the column
caravanserai – see *khan*
cardo – the main north-south street of a Roman-era town
chai – tea

decumanus – the main east-west street of a Roman-era town
deir – monastery, convent
donjon – castle keep or great tower

eid – feast
Eid al-Adha – Feast of Sacrifice marking the pilgrimage to Mecca
Eid al-Fitr – Festival of Breaking the Fast; celebrated at the end of *Ramadan*
emir – Islamic ruler, military commander or governor

funduq – hotel

haj – pilgrimage to Mecca
hamam – pigeon
hammam – bathhouse
hara – small lane, alley

haramlik – women's quarters
hejab – headscarf
hypogeum – burial chamber

iconostasis – screen with doors and icons set in tiers, used in eastern Christian churches
imam – a man schooled in Islam and who often doubles as the *muezzin*
iwan – vaulted hall, opening into a central court, in the *madrassa* of a mosque

jalabiyya – full-length robe worn by men
jebel – mountain or mountain range
jezira – island

kalybe – open-fronted shrine
karaj/karajat – garage/garage of
khan – a merchants' inn
kineesa – church
kubri – bridge
kuttab – Quranic school

loggia – colonnaded arcade providing a sheltered extension of a hall

madrassa – school where Islamic law is taught
mahatta – station
mar – saint
maristan – hospital
mashrabiyya – ornately carved wooden panel or screen
matar – airport
mihrab – niche in the wall of a mosque that indicates the direction of Mecca
minbar – pulpit in a mosque
muezzin – mosque official who calls the faithful to prayer five times a day from the minaret
muqarnas – stalactite-type stone carving used to decorate doorways and window recesses

narjileh – water pipe
nymphaeum – monumental fountain

oud – a kind of lute

pasha – lord, but also a term used more generally to denote someone of standing
propylaeum – monumental temple gateway

qa'a – reception room
qahwa – coffee or coffeehouse
qala'at – fortress
qasr – palace

rais – waiter
Ramadan – ninth month of the lunar Islamic calendar during which Muslims fast from sunrise to sunset
ras – headland

saahat – square
sabil – public drinking fountain
sharia – road or way
Shari'a – Islamic law, the body of doctrine that regulates the lives of Muslims
souq – bazaar or market

speos – rock-cut tomb or chapel
stele (s), **stelae** (pl) – stone or wooden commemorative slab or column decorated with inscriptions or figures
Sufi – follower of any of the Islamic mystical orders which emphasise dancing, chanting and trances in order to attain unity with God

tabla – small hand-held drum
tell – artificial mound
tetrapylon – four columned structure

ulema – group of Muslim scholars or religious leaders; a member of this group
umm – mother of

wadi – desert watercourse, dry except in the rainy season
waha – oasis

zikr – long sessions of dancing, chanting and swaying carried out by *Sufis* to achieve oneness with God

LONELY PLANET

Guides by Region

onely Planet is known worldwide for publishing practical, reliable and no-nonsense travel information in our guides and on our Web site. The Lonely Planet list covers just about every accessible part of the world. Currently there are nine series: travel guides, shoestring guides, walking guides, city guides, phrasebooks, audio packs, travel atlases, diving and snorkeling guides and travel literature.

AFRICA Africa – the South • Africa on a shoestring • Arabic (Egyptian) phrasebook • Arabic (Moroccan) phrasebook • Cairo • Cape Town • Central Africa • East Africa • Egypt • Egypt travel atlas • Ethiopian (Amharic) phrasebook • The Gambia & Senegal • Kenya • Kenya travel atlas • Malawi, Mozambique & Zambia • Morocco • North Africa • South Africa, Lesotho & Swaziland • South Africa, Lesotho & Swaziland travel atlas • Swahili phrasebook • Tanzania, Zanzibar & Pemba • Trekking in East Africa • Tunisia • West Africa • Zimbabwe, Botswana & Namibia • Zimbabwe, Botswana & Namibia travel atlas
Travel Literature: The Rainbird: A Central African Journey • Songs to an African Sunset: A Zimbabwean Story • Mali Blues: Traveling to an African Beat

AUSTRALIA & THE PACIFIC Australia • Australian phrasebook • Bushwalking in Australia • Bushwalking in Papua New Guinea • Fiji • Fijian phrasebook • Islands of Australia's Great Barrier Reef • Melbourne • Micronesia • New Caledonia • New South Wales & the ACT • New Zealand • Northern Territory • Outback Australia • Papua New Guinea • Papua New Guinea (Pidgin) phrasebook • Queensland • Rarotonga & the Cook Islands • Samoa • Solomon Islands • South Australia • South Pacific Languages phrasebook • Sydney • Tahiti & French Polynesia • Tasmania • Tonga • Tramping in New Zealand • Vanuatu • Victoria • Western Australia
Travel Literature: Islands in the Clouds • Sean & David's Long Drive

CENTRAL AMERICA & THE CARIBBEAN Bahamas and Turks & Caicos • Barcelona • Bermuda • Central America on a shoestring • Costa Rica • Cuba • Dominican Republic & Haiti • Eastern Caribbean • Guatemala, Belize & Yucatán: La Ruta Maya • Jamaica • Mexico • Mexico City • Panama
Travel Literature: Green Dreams: Travels in Central America

EUROPE Amsterdam • Andalucía • Austria • Baltic States phrasebook • Barcelona • Berlin • Britain • British phrasebook • Canary Islands • Central Europe • Central Europe phrasebook • Corsica • Croatia • Czech & Slovak Republics • Denmark • Dublin • Eastern Europe • Eastern Europe phrasebook • Edinburgh • Estonia, Latvia & Lithuania • Europe • Finland • France • French phrasebook • Germany • German phrasebook • Greece • Greek phrasebook • Hungary • Iceland, Greenland & the Faroe Islands • Ireland • Italian phrasebook • Italy • Lisbon • London • Mediterranean Europe • Mediterranean Europe phrasebook • Norway • Paris • Poland • Portugal • Portugal travel atlas • Prague • Provence & the Côte d'Azur • Romania & Moldova • Rome • Russia, Ukraine & Belarus • Russian phrasebook • Scandinavian & Baltic Europe • Scandinavian Europe phrasebook • Scotland • Slovenia • Spain • Spanish phrasebook • St Petersburg • Switzerland • Trekking in Spain • Ukrainian phrasebook • Vienna • Walking in Britain • Walking in Italy • Walking in Ireland • Walking in Switzerland • Western Europe • Western Europe phrasebook
Travel Literature: The Olive Grove: Travels in Greece

INDIAN SUBCONTINENT Bangladesh • Bengali phrasebook • Bhutan • Delhi • Goa • Hindi/Urdu phrasebook • India • India & Bangladesh travel atlas • Indian Himalaya • Karakoram Highway • Nepal • Nepali phrasebook • Pakistan • Rajasthan • South India • Sri Lanka • Sri Lanka phrasebook • Trekking in the Indian Himalaya • Trekking in the Karakoram & Hindukush • Trekking in the Nepal Himalaya
Travel Literature: In Rajasthan • Shopping for Buddhas

LONELY PLANET

Mail Order

Lonely Planet products are distributed worldwide. They are also available by mail order from Lonely Planet, so if you have difficulty finding a title please write to us. North and South American residents should write to 150 Linden St, Oakland, CA 94607, USA; European and African residents should write to 10a Spring Place, London NW5 3BH, UK; and residents of other countries to PO Box 617, Hawthorn, Victoria 3122, Australia.

ISLANDS OF THE INDIAN OCEAN Madagascar & Comoros ● Maldives ● Mauritius, Réunion & Seychelles

MIDDLE EAST & CENTRAL ASIA Arab Gulf States ● Central Asia ● Central Asia phrasebook ● Iran ● Israel & the Palestinian Territories ● Israel & the Palestinian Territories travel atlas ● Istanbul ● Jerusalem ● Jordan & Syria ● Jordan, Syria & Lebanon travel atlas ● Lebanon ● Middle East on a shoestring ● Turkey ● Turkish phrasebook ● Turkey travel atlas ● Yemen
Travel Literature: The Gates of Damascus ● Kingdom of the Film Stars: Journey into Jordan

NORTH AMERICA Alaska ● Backpacking in Alaska ● Baja California ● California & Nevada ● Canada ● Chicago ● Florida ● Hawaii ● Honolulu ● Los Angeles ● Louisiana ● Miami ● New England USA ● New Orleans ● New York City ● New York, New Jersey & Pennsylvania ● Pacific Northwest USA ● Puerto Rico ● Rocky Mountain States ● San Francisco ● Seattle ● Southwest USA ● Texas ● USA ● USA phrasebook ● Vancouver ● Washington, DC & the Capital Region
Travel Literature: Drive Thru America

NORTH-EAST ASIA Beijing ● Cantonese phrasebook ● China ● Hong Kong ● Hong Kong, Macau & Guangzhou ● Japan ● Japanese phrasebook ● Japanese audio pack ● Korea ● Korean phrasebook ● Kyoto ● Mandarin phrasebook ● Mongolia ● Mongolian phrasebook ● North-East Asia on a shoestring ● Seoul ● South-West China ● Taiwan ● Tibet ● Tibetan phrasebook ● Tokyo
Travel Literature: Lost Japan

SOUTH AMERICA Argentina, Uruguay & Paraguay ● Bolivia ● Brazil ● Brazilian phrasebook ● Buenos Aires ● Chile & Easter Island ● Chile & Easter Island travel atlas ● Colombia ● Ecuador & the Galapagos Islands ● Latin American Spanish phrasebook ● Peru ● Quechua phrasebook ● Rio de Janeiro ● South America on a shoestring ● Trekking in the Patagonian Andes ● Venezuela
Travel Literature: Full Circle: A South American Journey

SOUTH-EAST ASIA Bali & Lombok ● Bangkok ● Burmese phrasebook ● Cambodia ● Hanoi ● Hill Tribes phrasebook ● Ho Chi Minh City ● Indonesia ● Indonesia's Eastern Islands ● Indonesian phrasebook ● Indonesian audio pack ● Jakarta ● Java ● Laos ● Lao phrasebook ● Laos travel atlas ● Malay phrasebook ● Malaysia, Singapore & Brunei ● Myanmar (Burma) ● Philippines ● Pilipino (Tagalog) phrasebook ● Singapore ● South-East Asia on a shoestring ● South-East Asia phrasebook ● Thailand ● Thailand's Islands & Beaches ● Thailand travel atlas ● Thai phrasebook ● Thai audio pack ● Vietnam ● Vietnamese phrasebook ● Vietnam travel atlas

ALSO AVAILABLE: Antarctica ● Brief Encounters: Stories of Love, Sex & Travel ● Chasing Rickshaws ● Not the Only Planet: Travel Stories from Science Fiction ● Travel with Children ● Traveller's Tales

FREE Lonely Planet Newsletters

We love hearing from you and think you'd like to hear from us.

Planet Talk

Our FREE quarterly printed newsletter is full of tips from travellers and anecdotes from Lonely Planet guidebook authors. Every issue is packed with up-to-date travel news and advice, and includes:

- a postcard from Lonely Planet co-founder Tony Wheeler
- a swag of mail from travellers
- a look at life on the road through the eyes of a Lonely Planet author
- topical health advice
- prizes for the best travel yarn
- news about forthcoming Lonely Planet events
- a complete list of Lonely Planet books and other titles

To join our mailing list, residents of the UK, Europe and Africa can email us at go@lonelyplanet.co.uk; residents of North and South America can email us at info@lonelyplanet.com; the rest of the world can email us at talk2us@lonelyplanet.com.au, or contact any Lonely Planet office.

Comet

Our FREE monthly email newsletter brings you all the latest travel news, features, interviews, competitions, destination ideas, travellers' tips & tales, Q&As, raging debates and related links. Find out what's new on the Lonely Planet Web site and which books are about to hit the shelves.

Subscribe from your desktop: www.lonelyplanet.com/comet

Lonely Planet On-line

Whether you've just begun planning your next trip, or you're chasing down specific info on currency regulations or visa requirements, check out Lonely Planet On-line for up-to-the minute travel information.

As well as mini guides to more than 250 destinations, you'll find maps, photos, travel news, health and visa updates, travel advisories, and discussion of the ecological and political issues you need to be aware of as you travel. You'll also find timely upgrades to popular guidebooks which you can print out and stick in the back of your book.

There's also an on-line travellers' forum where you can share your experience of life on the road, meet travel companions and ask other travellers for their recommendations and advice.

And of course we have a complete and up-to-date list of all Lonely Planet travel products including travel guides, diving and snorkeling guides, phrasebooks, atlases, travel literature and videos, and a simple on-line ordering facility if you can't find the book you want elsewhere.

Lonely Planet Diving & Snorkeling Guides

Beautifully illustrated with full-colour photos throughout, Lonely Planet's Pisces Books explore the world's best diving and snorkeling areas and prepare divers for what to expect when they get there, both topside and underwater.

Dive sites are described in detail with specifics on depths, visibility, level of difficulty, special conditions, underwater photography tips and common and unusual marine life present. You'll also find practical logistical information and coverage on topside activities and attractions, sections on diving health and safety, plus listings for diving services, live-aboards, dive resorts and tourist offices.

LONELY PLANET

Lonely Planet Journeys

Journeys is a unique collection of travel writing – published by the company that understands travel better than anyone else. It is a series for anyone who has ever experienced – or dreamed of – the magical moment when they encountered a strange culture or saw a place for the first time. They are tales to read while you're planning a trip, while you're on the road or while you're in an armchair in front of a fire.

These outstanding titles explore our planet through the eyes of a diverse group of international writers. JOURNEYS books catch the spirit of a place, illuminate a culture, recount a crazy adventure or introduce a fascinating way of life. They always entertain, and always enrich the experience of travel.

MALI BLUES
Traveling to an African Beat
Lieve Joris (translated by Sam Garrett)
Drought, rebel uprisings, ethnic conflict: these are the predominant images of West Africa. But as Lieve Joris travels in Senegal, Mauritania and Mali, she meets survivors, fascinating individuals charting new ways of living between tradition and modernity. With her remarkable gift for drawing out people's stories, Joris brilliantly captures the rhythms of a world that refuses to give in.

THE GATES OF DAMASCUS
Lieve Joris (translated by Sam Garrett)
This best-selling book is a beautifully drawn portrait of day-to-day life in modern Syria. Through her intimate contact with local people, Lieve Joris draws us into the fascinating world that lies behind the gates of Damascus. Hala's husband is a political prisoner, jailed for his opposition to the Assad regime; through the author's friendship with Hala we see how Syrian politics impacts on the lives of ordinary people.

THE OLIVE GROVE
Travels in Greece
Katherine Kizilos
Katherine Kizilos travels to fabled islands, troubled border zones and her family's village deep in the mountains. She vividly evokes breathtaking landscapes, generous people and passionate politics, capturing the complexities of a country she loves.

'beautifully captures the real tensions of Greece' – *Sunday Times*

KINGDOM OF THE FILM STARS
Journey into Jordan
Annie Caulfield
Kingdom of the Film Stars is a travel book and a love story. With honesty and humour, Annie Caulfield writes of travelling in Jordan and falling in love with a Bedouin with film-star looks.

She offers fascinating insights into the country – from the tent life of traditional women to the hustle of downtown Amman – and unpicks tight-woven western myths about the Arab world.

Lonely Planet Travel Atlases

L onely Planet has long been famous for the number and quality of its guidebook maps. Now we've gone one step further and produced a handy companion series: Lonely Planet travel atlases – maps of a country produced in book form.

Unlike other maps, which look good but lead travellers astray, our travel atlases have been researched on the road by Lonely Planet's experienced team of writers. All details are carefully checked to ensure the atlas corresponds with the equivalent Lonely Planet guidebook.

- full-colour throughout
- maps researched and checked by Lonely Planet authors
- place names correspond with Lonely Planet guidebooks
- no confusing spelling differences
- legend and travelling information in English, French, German, Japanese and Spanish
- size: 230 x 160 mm

Available now: Chile & Easter Island • Egypt • India & Bangladesh • Israel & the Palestinian Territories • Jordan, Syria & Lebanon • Kenya • Laos • Portugal • South Africa, Lesotho & Swaziland • Thailand • Turkey • Vietnam • Zimbabwe, Botswana & Namibia

---

Lonely Planet TV Series & Videos

L onely Planet travel guides have been brought to life on television screens around the world. Like our guides, the programs are based on the joy of independent travel, and look honestly at some of the most exciting, picturesque and frustrating places in the world. Each show is presented by one of three travellers from Australia, England or the USA and combines an innovative mixture of video, Super-8 film, atmospheric soundscapes and original music.

Videos of each episode – containing additional footage not shown on television – are available from good book and video shops, but the availability of individual videos varies with regional screening schedules.

Video destinations include: Alaska • American Rockies • Australia – The South-East • Baja California & the Copper Canyon • Brazil • Central Asia • Chile & Easter Island • Corsica, Sicily & Sardinia – The Mediterranean Islands • East Africa (Tanzania & Zanzibar) • Ecuador & the Galapagos Islands • Greenland & Iceland • Indonesia • Israel & the Sinai Desert • Jamaica • Japan • La Ruta Maya • Morocco • New York • North India • Pacific Islands (Fiji, Solomon Islands & Vanuatu) • South India • South West China • Turkey • Vietnam • West Africa • Zimbabwe, Botswana & Namibia

The Lonely Planet TV series is produced by: Pilot Productions
The Old Studio
18 Middle Row
London W10 5AT, UK

LONELY PLANET

Phrasebooks

Lonely Planet phrasebooks are packed with essential words and phrases to help travellers communicate with the locals. With colour tabs for quick reference, an extensive vocabulary and use of script, these handy pocket-sized language guides cover day-to-day travel situations.

- handy pocket-sized books
- easy to understand Pronunciation chapter
- clear & comprehensive Grammar chapter
- romanisation alongside script to allow ease of pronunciation
- script throughout so users can point to phrases for every situation
- full of cultural information and tips for the traveller

'...vital for a real DIY spirit and attitude in language learning'
– Backpacker

'the phrasebooks have good cultural backgrounders and offer solid advice for challenging situations in remote locations'
– San Francisco Examiner

Arabic (Egyptian) • Arabic (Moroccan) • Australian *(Australian English, Aboriginal and Torres Strait languages)* • Baltic States *(Estonian, Latvian, Lithuanian)* • Bengali • Brazilian • British • Burmese • Cantonese • Central Asia • Central Europe *(Czech, French, German, Hungarian, Italian, Slovak)* • Eastern Europe *(Bulgarian, Czech, Hungarian, Polish, Romanian, Slovak)* • Ethiopian (Amharic) • Fijian • French • German • Greek • Hill Tribes • Hindi/Urdu • Indonesian • Italian • Japanese • Korean • Lao • Latin American Spanish • Malay • Mandarin • Mediterranean Europe *(Albanian, Croatian, Greek, Italian, Macedonian, Maltese, Serbian, Slovene)* • Mongolian • Nepali • Papua New Guinea • Pilipino (Tagalog) • Quechua • Russian • Scandinavian Europe *(Danish, Finnish, Icelandic, Norwegian, Swedish)* • South-East Asia *(Burmese, Indonesian, Khmer, Lao, Malay, Tagalog Pilipino, Thai, Vietnamese)* • South Pacific Languages • Spanish (Castilian) *(also includes Catalan, Galician and Basque)* • Sri Lanka • Swahili • Thai • Tibetan • Turkish • Ukrainian • USA *(US English, Vernacular, Native American languages, Hawaiian)* • Vietnamese • Western Europe *(Basque, Catalan, Dutch, French, German, Greek, Irish)*

Index

Text

Bold indicates maps.

Bold indicates maps.

Boxed Text

MAP LEGEND

BOUNDARIES

- ▬·▬·▬·▬· .... International
- ▬··▬··▬··▬· .... State
- ▬ ▬ ▬ ▬ ...... Disputed

HYDROGRAPHY

- .... Coastline
- .... River, Creek
- .... Lake
- .... Intermittent Lake
- .... Salt Lake
- .... Canal
- ◎ ⤞ .... Spring, Rapids
- ⊣⊢ .... Waterfalls
- ⸯ ⸯ ⸯ .... Swamp

- ❂ **CAPITAL** .... National Capital
- ◉ **CAPITAL** .... State Capital
- ● **CITY** .... City
- ● **Town** .... Town
- ● Village .... Village
- ○ .... Point of Interest
- ■ .... Place to Stay
- ⚑ .... Camping Ground
- ▼ .... Place to Eat
- ▮ .... Pub or Bar
- ✈ .... Airport
- ...... Ancient or City Wall
- ∴ .... Archaeological Site
- ✪ .... Bank

ROUTES & TRANSPORT

- ════════ .... Freeway
- ════════ .... Highway
- ════════ .... Major Road
- ════════ .... Minor Road
- ══════ .... Unsealed Road
- ════════ .... City Freeway
- ════════ .... City Highway
- ════════ .... City Road
- ════════ .... City Street, Lane

- ════════ .... Pedestrian Mall
- ⟩═ ═ ═ ═ .... Tunnel
- ⊢⊢⊢⊢⊙⊢⊢ .... Train Route & Station
- ═ ═ Ⓜ ═ ....Metro & Station
- ▬ ▬ ▬ ▬ ....Tramway
- ⊩⊩⊩⊩⊩⊩ .... Cable Car or Chairlift
- ─ ─ ─ ─ ─ ... Walking Track
- · · · · · · · · · .... Walking Tour
- ─ ─ ─ ─ ─ .... Ferry Route

AREA FEATURES

- .... Building
- ✿ .... Park, Gardens
- + + × ⸯ .... Cemetery
- ....Market
- .... Beach, Desert
- .... Urban Area

MAP SYMBOLS

- ⚹⚹ .... Border Crossing
- ☕ .... Café
- ♜ .... Castle or Fort
- ⌒ .... Cave
- ⛪ .... Church
- ⌒⌒⌒ .... Cliff or Escarpment
- ✆ .... Embassy
- ⊕ .... Hammam
- ✛ .... Hospital
- ☪ .... Mosque
- ▲ .... Mountain or Hill
- ⌒⌒ .... Mountain Range
- ⚱ .... Monument
- 🏛 .... Museum

- ☏ ....National Park
- Ⓝ .... Noria
- ← .... One Way Street
- Ⓟ .... Parking
-)(........................... Pass
- ★ .... Police Station
- ✉ .... Post Office
- ▭ .... Swimming Pool
- ☎ .... Telephone
- ⚲ .... Toilet
- ▣ .... Tomb
- ❶ .... Tourist Information
- ◒ .... Transport
- 🐘 .... Zoo

Note: not all symbols displayed above appear in this book

LONELY PLANET OFFICES

Australia
PO Box 617, Hawthorn, Victoria 3122
☎ 03 9819 1877 fax 03 9819 6459
email: talk2us@lonelyplanet.com.au

USA
150 Linden St, Oakland, CA 94607
☎ 510 893 8555 TOLL FREE: 800 275 5555
fax 510 893 8572
email: info@lonelyplanet.com

UK
10a Spring Place, London NW5 3BH
☎ 020 7428 4800 fax 020 7428 4828
email: go@lonelyplanet.co.uk

France
1 rue du Dahomey, 75011 Paris
☎ 01 55 25 33 00 fax 01 55 25 33 01
email: bip@lonelyplanet.fr
minitel: 3615 lonelyplanet *(1,29 F TTC/min)*

World Wide Web: www.lonelyplanet.com *or* AOL keyword: lp
Lonely Planet Images: lpi@lonelyplanet.com.au